ACCA

Applied Skills

Performance Management

Workbook

For exams in September 2020, December 2020, March 2021 and June 2021

BPP
LEARNING
MEDIA

First Edition 2020

ISBN 9781 5097 8438 7

Internal ISBN 9781 5097 3179 4

e-ISBN 9781 5097 2924 1

British Library Cataloguing-in-Publication Data: A catalogue record for this book is available from the British Library

Published by

BPP Learning Media Ltd BPP House, Aldine Place 142–144, Uxbridge Road, London, W12 8AA

www.bpp.com/learningmedia

Printed in the United Kingdom

Your learning materials, published by BPP Learning Media Ltd, are printed on paper sourced from sustainable, managed forests.

We are grateful to the Association of Chartered Certified Accountants for permission to reproduce past examination questions and extracts from the syllabus. The suggested solutions in the practice answer bank have been prepared by BPP Learning Media Ltd, except where otherwise stated.

A note about copyright

Contents

Helping you to pass

BPP Learning Media – ACCA Approved Content Provider

As an ACCA Approved Content Provider, BPP Learning Media gives you the opportunity to use study materials reviewed by the ACCA examining team. By incorporating the examining team's comments and suggestions regarding the depth and breadth of syllabus coverage, the BPP Learning Media Workbook provides excellent, ACCA-approved support for your studies.

These materials are reviewed by the ACCA examining team. The objective of the review is to ensure that the material properly covers the syllabus and study guide outcomes, used by the examining team in setting the exams, in the appropriate breadth and depth. The review does not ensure that every eventuality, combination or application of examinable topics is addressed by the ACCA Approved Content. Nor does the review comprise a detailed technical check of the content as the Approved Content Provider has its own quality assurance processes in place in this respect.

BPP Learning Media does everything possible to ensure the material is accurate and up to date when sending to print. In the event that any errors are found after the print date, they are uploaded to the following website: www.bpp.com/learningmedia/Errata.

The PER alert

Before you can qualify as an ACCA member, you not only have to pass all your exams but also fulfil a three-year practical experience requirement (PER). To help you to recognise areas of the syllabus that you might be able to apply in the workplace to achieve different performance objectives, we have introduced the 'PER alert' feature (see the next section). You will find this feature throughout the Workbook to remind you that what you are learning to pass your ACCA exams is equally useful to the fulfilment of the PER requirement. Your achievement of the PER should be recorded in your online My Experience record.

Chapter features

Studying can be a daunting prospect, particularly when you have lots of other commitments. This Workbook is full of useful features, explained in the key below, designed to help you to get the most out of your studies and maximise your chances of exam success.

Key term

Central concepts are highlighted and clearly defined in the Key terms feature. Key terms are also listed in bold in the Index, for quick and easy reference.

Formula to learn

This boxed feature will highlight important formula which you need to learn for your exam.

PER alert

This feature identifies when something you are reading will also be useful for your PER requirement (see 'The PER alert' section above for more details).

Real world examples

These will give real examples to help demonstrate the concepts you are reading about.

Illustration

Illustrations walk through how to apply key knowledge and techniques step by step.

Activity

Activities give you essential practice of techniques covered in the chapter.

Essential reading

Links to the Essential reading are given throughout the chapter. The Essential reading is included in the free eBook, accessed via the Exam Success Site (see inside cover for details on how to access this).

At the end of each chapter you will find a Knowledge diagnostic, which is a summary of the main learning points from the chapter to allow you to check you have understood the key concepts. You will also find a Further study guidance section that contains suggestions for ways in which you can continue your learning and enhance your understanding. This can include: recommendations for question practice from the Further question practice and solutions, to test your understanding of the topics in the chapter; suggestions for further reading which can be done, such as technical articles and ideas for your own research. The chapter summary provides more detailed revision of the topics covered and is intended to assist you as you prepare for your revision phase.

Introduction to the Essential reading

The digital eBook version of the Workbook contains additional content, selected to enhance your studies. Consisting of revision materials and further explanations of complex areas (including illustrations and activities), it is designed to aid your understanding of key topics which are covered in the main printed chapters of the Workbook.

To access the digital eBook version of the BPP Workbook, follow the instructions which can be found on the inside cover; you'll be able to access your eBook, plus download the BPP eBook mobile app on multiple devices, including smartphones and tablets.

A summary of the content of the Essential reading is given below.

Chapter		Summary of Essential reading content

1	Managing information	• The role of information systems in
		  – Recording transactions
		  – Decision-making
		  – Planning
		  – Performance measurement
		• How intranets may be used within a business
		• Wireless technology and its drawbacks
		• Security and confidential information
		  – Passwords
		  – Logical access systems
		  – Database controls
		  – Firewalls
		  – Encryption
		  – Other safety measures
		  – Personal data
		  – Personal security planning
		  – Anti-virus and anti-spyware software
		• Internal sources of information
		• External sources of information
		• Information for control
		  – Internal information, eg payroll, inventory, sales
		  – External information for benchmarking

2	Information systems and data analytics	• Strategic planning, control and decision making and its external orientation • Examples of management/tactical planning activities • Examples of management control activities • Comparison of management control and strategic planning • Example showing the link between strategic plans and operational/management control decisions • Illustration on how an ERP system works • Real world example of company using big data • McKinsey's *Big data report* (McKinsey, 2011) showing benefits of big data

Chapter		Summary of Essential reading content
3	Activity based costing	• Traditional absorption costing – For inventory valuation – For pricing decisions – For establishing profitability • Revision of allocation, apportionment and overhead absorption • Choosing an appropriate absorption basis • Illustrations on choosing a basis, calculating OAR and under- and over-absorption (brought forward knowledge from Management Accounting) • Marginal costing (brought forward knowledge from Management Accounting)
4	Target costing	• No Essential reading
5	Life cycle costing	• No Essential reading
6	Throughput accounting	• No Essential reading
7	Environmental management accounting	• No Essential reading
8	Cost volume profit (CVP) analysis	• How breakeven charts can be drawn if a constant product sales mix is assumed • Multi-product PV charts
9	Limiting factor analysis	• Two potentially limiting factors • Non-financial considerations in make or buy decisions • Shadow prices and limiting factors • Slack example
10	Pricing decisions	• Influences on price
11	Short-term decisions	• Examples of non-quantifiable factors
12	Risk and uncertainty	• The role of market research • The use of focus groups • Example of simulation and spreadsheets • Standard deviation and coefficient of variation
13	Budgetary systems	• Objectives of budgeting systems • The planning and control cycle • Other aspects of budget preparation such as budget manuals, functional budgets, master budgets
14	Quantitative analysis in budgeting	• How to derive the learning rate • The relevance of learning curve effects in management accounting • Limitations of learning curve theory
15	Budgeting and standard costing	• Deriving standards • Flexible budgets and performance management

Chapter		Summary of Essential reading content
16	Variance analysis	• Basic variances and illustration • Reasons for variances • Operating statements
17	Planning and operational variance analysis	• Variances and the learning curve
18	Performance analysis and behavioural aspects	• Analysing past performance with variance analysis and who is responsible • Using variance analysis to improve future performance
19	Performance measurement	• Which non-financial performance indicators should be measured? • Methods to encourage a long-term view • Steps to improvement • The balanced scorecard – goals and measures • Building block model (Fitzgerald and Moon)
20	Divisional performance and transfer pricing	• ROI and new investments • RI versus ROI: marginally profitable investments • Problems with transfer pricing
21	Further aspects of performance management	• Problems with performance measurement of not for profit organisations • The 3Es • External factors – stakeholders, economic environment, competition

Introduction to Performance Management (PM)

Overall aim of the syllabus

The aim of the syllabus is to develop knowledge and skills in the application of management accounting techniques to quantitative and qualitative information for planning, decision-making, performance evaluation and control. PM is the middle exam in the management accounting section of the qualification structure. Management Accounting (MA) concerns just techniques and Advanced Performance Management (APM) thinks strategically and considers environmental factors. PM requires you to be able to apply techniques and think about their impact on the organisation.

Brought forward knowledge

The Performance Management syllabus includes a number of topics which were covered in Management Accounting but develops them further, requiring you to apply them to more complex scenarios in the exam. For example, CVP analysis in PM covers multiple-product situations and variance analysis covers mix and yield variances and planning and operational variances. You therefore need a good understanding of the basic CVP and variance analysis that you covered in MA. Absorption costing and marginal costing are also key brought-forward knowledge.

The syllabus

The broad syllabus headings are:

A	Information, technologies and systems for organisational performance
B	Specialist cost and management accounting techniques
C	Decision-making techniques
D	Budgeting and control
E	Performance measurement and control

Main capabilities

On successful completion of this exam, you should be able to:

A	Deal with the objective test questions demonstrating understanding of the subject across the entire syllabus.
B	Carry out calculations for longer questions, with **clear workings** and a logical structure.
C	**Interpret** data.
D	**Explain** management accounting techniques and **discuss** whether they are appropriate for a particular organisation.
E	**Apply** your skills in a practical context.

Links with other exams

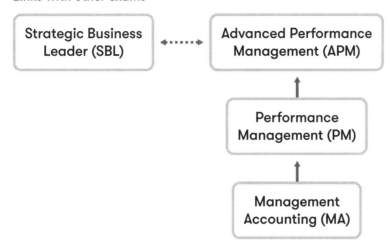

The diagram shows where direct (solid line arrows) and indirect (dashed line arrows) links exist between this exam and other exams preceding or following it. The Performance Management (PM) syllabus assumes knowledge acquired in Management Accounting (MA) and develops and applies this further and in greater depth.

Achieving ACCA's Study Guide Learning Outcomes

This BPP Workbook covers all the PM syllabus learning outcomes. The tables below show in which chapter(s) each area of the syllabus is covered.

A	Information, technologies and systems for organisational performance	

A1	Managing information	Chapter 1
A2	Sources of information	Chapter 1
A3	Information systems and data analytics	Chapter 2

B	Specialist cost and management accounting techniques	

B1	Activity-based costing	Chapter 3
B2	Target costing	Chapter 4
B3	Life-cycle costing	Chapter 5
B4	Throughput accounting	Chapters 6 & 9
B5	Environmental accounting	Chapter 7

C	Decision-making techniques	

C1	Relevant cost analysis	Chapter 11
C2	Cost volume profit analysis (CVP)	Chapter 8
C3	Limiting factors	Chapter 9
C4	Pricing decisions	Chapter 10

C5	Make or buy and other short-term decisions	Chapter 11
C6	Dealing with risk and uncertainty in decision-making	Chapter 12

D	Budgeting and control	

D1	Budgeting systems and types of budget	Chapters 13 & 18
D2	Quantitative analysis in budgeting	Chapter 14
D3	Standard costing	Chapter 15
D4	Material mix and yield variances	Chapter 16
D5	Sales mix and quantity variances	Chapter 16
D6	Planning and operational variances	Chapter 17
D7	Performance analysis	Chapter 18

E	Performance and measurement and control	

E1	Performance analysis in private sector organisations	Chapters 19
E2	Divisional performance and transfer pricing	Chapter 20
E3	Performance analysis in not for profit organisations and the public sector	Chapters 19 & 21
E4	External considerations and the impact on performance	Chapter 21

The complete syllabus and study guide can be found by visiting the exam resource finder on the ACCA website: www.accaglobal.com/gb/en.html.

The exam

Computer-based exams

Applied Skills exams are all computer-based exams.

Approach to examining

- There is no choice in this exam; all questions have to be answered. You must therefore study the **entire syllabus,** there are no short-cuts.
- You should then practise extensively on examination-style questions. Practice will improve your ability to answer questions well, and should enable you to answer them more quickly. BPP's Practice & Revision Kit contains questions on all areas of the syllabus.
- Keep an eye out for **articles,** as the **examining team** will use Student Accountant to communicate with students.
- Read journals etc to pick up on ways in which real organisations apply management accounting and think about your own organisation if that is relevant.

Essential skills areas to be successful in Performance Management (PM)

We think there are three areas you should develop in order to achieve exam success in PM:

(a) Knowledge application

(b) Specific PM skills

(c) Exam success skills

These are shown in the diagram below.

Specific PM skills

These are the skills specific to PM that we think you need to develop in order to pass the exam.

In this Workbook, there are five **Skills Checkpoints** which define each skill and show how it is applied in answering a question. A brief summary of each skill is given below.

Exam success skills

Passing the PM exam requires more than applying syllabus knowledge and demonstrating the specific PM skills; it also requires the development of excellent exam technique through question practice.

We consider the following six skills to be vital for exam success. The skills checkpoints show how each of these skills can be applied in the exam.

Exam skill 1: Managing information

Questions in the exam will present you with a lot of information. The skill is how you handle this information to make the best use of your time. The key is determining how you will approach the exam and then actively reading the questions.

Advice on developing managing information

Approach

The exam is three hours long. There is no designated 'reading' time at the start of the exam. However, one approach that can work well is to start the exam by spending 10–15 minutes carefully reading through all of the questions to familiarise yourself with the exam. Once you feel familiar with the exam consider the order in which you will attempt the questions; always attempt them in your order of preference. For example, you may want to leave to last the question you consider to be the most difficult. If you do take this approach, remember to adjust the time available for each question appropriately – see Exam success skill 6: Good time management.

If you find that this approach doesn't work for you, don't worry – you can develop your own technique.

Active reading

You must take an active approach to reading each question. In Section C questions in particular, focus on the requirement first, making a note of key verbs such as 'explain' and 'discuss', to ensure you answer the question properly. Then read the rest of the question, making notes on important and relevant information you think you will need.

Exam skill 2: Correct interpretation of the requirements

The active verb used often dictates the approach that written answers should take (eg 'explain', 'discuss'). It is important you identify and use the verb to define your approach. The **correct interpretation of the requirements** skill means correctly producing only what is being asked for by a requirement. Anything not required will not earn marks.

Advice on developing the correct interpretation of the requirements

This skill can be developed by analysing question requirements and applying this process:

Step 1	**Read the requirement**
	Firstly, read the requirement a couple of times slowly and carefully and note the active verbs. Use the active verbs to define what you plan to do. Make sure you identify any sub-requirements.
Step 2	**Read the rest of the question**
	By reading the requirement first, you will have an idea of what you are looking out for as you read through the scenario. This is a great time saver and means you do not end up having to read the whole question in full twice. You should do this in an active way – see Exam success skill 1: Managing information.
Step 3	**Read the requirement again**
	Read the requirement again to remind yourself of the exact wording before starting your written answer. This will capture any misinterpretation of the requirements or any missed requirements entirely. This should become a habit in your approach and, with repeated practice, you will find the focus, relevance and depth of your answer plan will improve.

Exam skill 3: Answer planning: Priorities, structure and logic

This skill requires the planning of the key aspects of an answer which accurately and completely responds to the requirement.

Advice on developing answer planning priorities, structure and logic

Everyone will have a preferred style for an answer plan. For example, it may be a mind map, bullet pointed lists or simply making some notes. Choose the approach that you feel most comfortable with, or, if you are not sure, try out different approaches for different questions until you have found your preferred style.

Exam skill 4: Efficient numerical analysis

This skill aims to maximise the marks awarded by making clear to the marker the process of arriving at your answer. This is achieved by laying out an answer such that, even if you make a few errors, you can still score subsequent marks for follow-on calculations. It is vital that you do not lose marks purely because the marker cannot follow what you have done.

Advice on developing efficient numerical analysis

This skill can be developed by applying the following process:

Step 1	**Use a standard proforma working where relevant**
	If answers can be laid out in a standard proforma then always plan to do so. This will help the marker to understand your working and allocate the marks easily. It will also help you to work through the figures in a methodical and time-efficient way.
Step 2	**Show your workings**
	Keep your workings as clear and simple as possible and ensure they are cross-referenced to the main part of your answer. Where it helps, provide brief narrative explanations to help the marker understand the steps in the calculation. This means that if a mistake is made you do not lose any subsequent marks for follow-on calculations.
Step 3	**Keep moving!**
	It is important to remember that, in an exam situation, it can sometimes be difficult to get every number 100% correct. The key is therefore ensuring you do not spend too long on any single calculation. If you are struggling with a solution then make a sensible assumption, state it and move on.

Exam skill 5: Effective writing and presentation

Written answers should be presented so that the marker can clearly see the points you are making, presented in the format specified in the question. The skill is to provide efficient written answers with sufficient breadth of points that answer the question, in the right depth, in the time available.

Advice on developing effective writing and presentation

Step 1	**Use headings**
	Using the headings and sub-headings from your answer plan will give your answer structure, order and logic. This will ensure your answer links back to the requirement and is clearly signposted, making it easier for the marker to understand the different points you are making. Making your headings bold will also help the marker.
Step 2	**Write your answer in short, but full, sentences**
	Use short, punchy sentences with the aim that every sentence should say something different and generate marks. Write in full sentences, ensuring your style is professional.
Step 3	**Do your calculations first and explanation second**
	Questions sometimes ask for a discussion or explanation with suitable calculations. The best approach is to prepare the calculation first then add the explanation. Performing the calculation first should enable you to explain what you have done.

Exam skill 6: Good time management

Good time management

This skill means planning your time across all the requirements so that all tasks have been attempted at the end of the three hours available and actively checking on time during your exam. This is so that you can flex your approach and prioritise requirements which, in your judgement, will generate the maximum marks in the available time remaining.

Advice on developing good time management

The exam is 3 hours long, which translates to 1.8 minutes per mark. Therefore a 10-mark requirement should be allocated a maximum of 18 minutes to complete your answer before you move on to the next task. At the beginning of a question, work out the amount of time you should be spending on each requirement. If you take the approach of spending 10–15 minutes reading and planning at the start of the exam, adjust the time allocated to each question accordingly.

Keep an eye on the clock

Aim to attempt all requirements but be ready to be ruthless and move on if your answer is not going as planned. The challenge for many is sticking to planned timings. Be aware this is difficult to achieve in the early stages of your studies and be ready to let this skill develop over time. If you find yourself running short on time and know that a full answer is not possible in the time you have, consider recreating your plan in overview form and then add key terms and details as time allows. Remember, some marks may be available, for example, simply stating a conclusion which you don't have time to justify in full.

1

Managing information

Learning objectives

On completion of this chapter, you should be able to:

	Syllabus reference no.
Explain the role of information systems in organisations	A1 (a)
Discuss the costs and benefits of information systems	A1 (b)
Explain the uses of the internet, intranet, wireless technology and networks	A1 (c)
Discuss the principal controls required in generating and distributing internal information	A1 (d)
Discuss the procedures that may be necessary to ensure security of highly confidential information that is not for external consumption	A1 (e)
Identify the principal internal and external sources of management accounting information	A2 (a)
Demonstrate how these principal sources of management information might be used for control purposes	A2 (b)
Identify and discuss the direct data capture and process costs of management accounting information	A2 (c)
Identify and discuss the indirect costs of producing information	A2 (d)

Exam context

Accountants are surrounded by data and information and the volume of information is only getting bigger. In this chapter, we look at **information systems**, their role within organisations and their costs and benefits. We also look at how the internet, intranet, wireless technology and networks are used.

We then move on to the principal controls and procedures involved in generating and distributing information and information security. We also look at internal and external sources of management information, including financial accounting records, government agencies and consumer panels.

The topics covered in this chapter could form part of a scenario question in the exam or could feature as an objective test question in Section A or B. Ensure that you are able to **discuss** these topics as well as being able to answer objective test (OT) questions.

Chapter overview

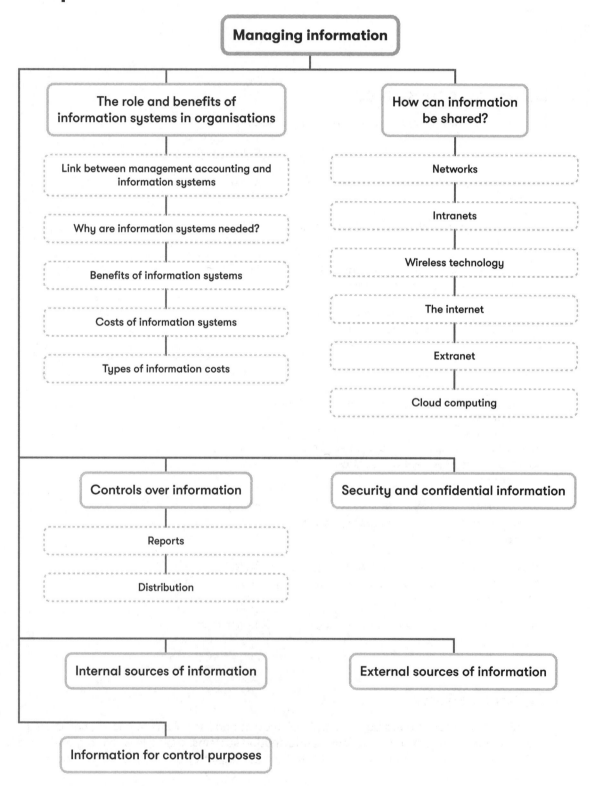

BPP
LEARNING
MEDIA

1 The role and benefits of information systems in organisations

1.1 Link between management accounting and information systems

Information systems: An information system is a combination of hardware, software and communications capability, where information is collected, processed and stored.

The title of this exam is **Performance Management. Management accounting** and **information systems** play a **vital role** in performance management because they **provide the information** that managers use as a basis for **planning, control, decision-making and measuring performance**.

1.2 Why are information systems needed?

Most organisations **rely heavily** on their information systems and some businesses **cannot function without** their **information system** (eg banks).

Organisations require information systems for a range of purposes.

Supporting operations:

- Processing and recording transactions (eg as legal requirement/information about profitability)

Supporting managerial activities:

- Planning (eg available resources/timescales)
- Control
- Decision making
- Performance measurement

Planning: Planning means formulating ways of proceeding.

Decision-making: Decision-making means choosing between various alternatives. This and planning are virtually inseparable: you decide to plan in the first place and the plan you make is a collection of decisions.

Control: Control is used in the sense of monitoring something to keep it on course (like the 'controls' of a car) not merely in the sense of imposing restraints or exercising power over something.

As well as facilitating **communication**, information systems can be used **for sales and marketing, HR management, inventory control** and **process efficiency**.

Activity 1: Use of information systems in hotels

1 Required

For each of the following activities, suggest how an information system in a hotel may be used.

- Processing and recording transactions
- Planning
- Control
- Decision-making

Essential reading

See Chapter 1 Section 1 of the Essential reading for more detail on information systems.

The Essential reading is available as an Appendix of the digital edition of the Workbook.

1.3 Benefits of information systems

Information is now recognised as a valuable resource, and a **key tool in the quest for a competitive advantage**.	For example, information on customers' preferences can help inform businesses on what to produce, how to sell it (eg online) and so on.
Easy **access** to information, the **quality** of that information and **speedy methods of exchanging** the information have become essential elements of business success.	For example, a business that has timely information on how well a product is being received by customers, can react quickly to ensure that inventory is sufficient and demand is met.
Organisations that make **good use of information** in decision-making, and which use new technologies to access, process and exchange information are likely to be **best placed to survive** in increasingly competitive world markets.	For example, many taxi firms now take bookings via a mobile phone app which can report real time locations and calculate prices in advance based on current traffic conditions.

Real life example

The use of technology and the resulting information for business decisions are, at times, almost unbelievable. Chocolate manufacturer, Cadbury, has state of the art machinery capable of measuring taste. When tasting-staff chew the chocolate, they breathe through their nose into the machine and it records the way the chocolate is perceived in the mouth. Cadbury used this technology to develop their new bar containing 30% less sugar. The machine showed that the new chocolate bar created the same profile and therefore the same signature flavour that customers would expect from a Cadbury bar.

1.4 Costs of information systems

Set-up costs for a new system include **hardware and software costs, implementation costs** associated with development and installation (especially labour costs) and **day-to-day costs**, such as salaries and accommodation.

Many organisations invest large amounts of money in information systems, but not always wisely. The unmanaged proliferation of IT is likely to lead to expensive mistakes. Two key benefits of information systems, the ability to **share** information and the **avoidance of duplication**, are likely to be lost.

All IT expenditure should therefore require approval to ensure that it enhances rather than detracts from the overall information strategy.

Effective budgeting may be required to keep costs under control, particularly the purchase of new equipment. An activity-based approach may be appropriate.

1.5 Types of information costs

The costs to an organisation of the collection, processing and production of internal information can be divided into three types:

- Direct data capture costs (ie using technology to capture data)
- Process costs
- Indirect costs of internal information

Cost	Examples
Direct data capture	• Use of bar coding and scanners (eg in retailing and manufacturing) • Use of OCR (optical character recognition) to capture data from printed documents • Use of ICR (intelligent character recognition) to capture data from hand written documents • Use of RFID (radio frequency identification) tags to identify, locate and track (eg tracking vehicles, staff, inventory)
Process	• Payroll department time spent processing and analysing personnel costs • Time for personnel to input data (eg in relation to production) on to the management information system
Indirect costs of producing information	• Information collected but not needed • Information stored long after it is needed • Information disseminated more widely than necessary • Collection of same information by more than one method • Duplication of information

Exam focus point

The syllabus states that you need to be able to identify the indirect costs of producing information. You need to remember that a direct cost can be completely attributed to obtaining the information. An indirect cost cannot be completely attributed to it.

2 How can information be shared?

Communicating information is much easier when computers are connected to form a network. Various forms of networks can be formed – global in the form of the internet and local in the form of the intranet. Wireless technology (covered below) facilitates mobile networking.

2.1 Networks

Computers which are connected and can send information together are networked. This boosts **efficiency** and **productivity** with some computers within the network dedicated to file storage, known as **file servers**, or other dedicated services such as printing. Others could be charged with performing major number crunching tasks. These server computers are usually stored in a dedicated room in a secure location.

The main benefits are:

(a) **Resource sharing** – eg file sharing or sharing hardware such as a printer

(b) **Storage requirement reduction** – eg storing shared files on a central server

(c) **Software cost reduction** – eg single licence on central server

2.2 Intranets

A cluster of computers can be networked together to form an organisation-wide network. This is known as an intranet and used to share information internally. Intranets are effectively private networks.

Potential applications include company newspapers, induction material, online procedure and policy manuals, employee web pages where individuals post details of their activities and progress, and internal databases of the corporate information store.

Essential reading

See Chapter 1 Section 2 of the Essential reading for more detail on the uses of intranets.

The Essential reading is available as an Appendix of the digital edition of the Workbook.

2.3 Wireless technology

Historically, networks would have been physically connected via cables (eg ethernet). However, the development of portable computers and radio technologies has led to wireless networks (WiFi).

Wireless technology allows easier communication as WiFi converts an internet signal into radio waves which can then be picked up by devices (eg laptops and tablets) containing a wireless adaptor.

The main benefits of wireless technology include:

(a) Remote working and increased mobility

(b) Increased productivity (because employees can work together wherever they need to)

(c) Reduced costs as the business expands (because it is easier to add new users to a wireless network than to install new cabling)

2.4 The internet

The internet is a global network connecting millions of computers.

The internet is essentially a public network and hence allows communication with external stakeholders such as other businesses. Computers across the world communicate via telecommunications links and information can be exchanged through email or through accessing and entering data via a website. Over 10% of sales in the second quarter of 2019 in the US were via e-commerce.

2.5 Extranet

An extranet is a form of intranet that authorised parties outside of the organisation can access using a username and password. They are a useful means for business partners to share information.

2.6 Cloud computing

This is the provision of computing services, generally applications and data centres, over a network (usually the internet). Google is one of the most prominent companies offering software as a free online service. Software and storage for your account will exist on the service's computer cloud rather than on your computer. A cloud can be public or private.

The main benefits of a cloud computing contract include:

(a) Reduced IT costs – software and hardware upgrades may be included in the contract, which means that there is no need for expert staff

(b) Safe storage – eg back-ups stored in the cloud helping to support business continuity plans

(c) Improved access – eg file sharing of records with accountants or access for staff working from home

3 Controls over information

Controls need to be in place over the generation of internal information in routine and ad hoc reports.

3.1 Reports

Before any report is created the following controls should be adopted:

(a) Cost/benefit analysis

(b) Prototype

(c) Check that the report is not duplicated

3.2 Distribution

To ensure efficiency and security of data, the following controls should be created:

(a) Procedures manual

(b) Format controls

(c) Distribution list

(d) Disposal controls (especially if confidential)

3.3 Controls over generating internal information in routine reports

(a) Carry out a **cost-benefit analysis**. How **easy** is the report to prepare **compared** with the **usefulness** of the decisions that can be taken as a result of its production? The cost of preparing the report will in part be determined by **who** is preparing it. The cost can be reduced if its preparation can be **delegated** by a director to a junior member of staff.

(b) A **trial** preparation process should be carried out and a **prototype** prepared. Users should be asked to confirm that their requirements will be met.

(c) A **consistent** format and consistent definitions should be used to ensure that reporting is **accurate** and the chance of misinterpretation is minimised. Standard **house styles** will ensure that time is not wasted by managers, staff and report writers on designing alternative layouts.

(d) The **originator** of the report should be clearly identified so that user queries can be dealt with quickly.

(e) The report should clearly set out limits to the action that users can take as a result of the information in the report. This will ensure that the organisation's system of responsibilities is maintained.

(f) The **usefulness** of the report should be **assessed** on a periodic basis to ensure that its production is necessary.

3.4 Controls over generating internal information in ad hoc reports

(a) Carry out a **cost-benefit** analysis as above.

(b) Ensure that the required information **does not already exist** in another format.

(c) Brief the report writer so that **onlytherelevant information** is provided.

(d) Ensure that the **originator** is clearly identified.

(e) Ensure that report writers have access to the **most up-to-date information**.

3.5 Controls over distributing internal information

(a) **Procedures manual** (for standard reports)

   (i) Indicates what standard reports should be issued and when (eg budgetary control report for department X on a monthly basis)

   (ii) Sets out the format of standard reports

   (iii) Makes clear who should receive particular standard reports

   (iv) Indicates whether reports should be shredded (if confidential) or just put in the recycle bin

   (v) Makes clear what information should be regarded as highly confidential

(b) **Other controls**

   (i) **Payroll and personnel information** should be kept in a **locked** cabinet or be protected by **password** access on a computer system.

   (ii) All employees should be **contractually required not to divulge confidential information**.

   (iii) The internal mail system should make use of **'private and confidential' stamps**.

   (iv) An appropriate **email policy** should be set up.

     (1) Email is best suited for short messages rather than detailed operational problems.

     (2) Email provides a relatively permanent means of communication, which may be undesirable for confidential/'off-the-record' exchanges.

     (3) Staff may suffer from information overload.

     (4) It is uncomfortable to read more than a full screen of information. Longer messages will either not be read properly or will be printed out (in which case they may just as well have been circulated in hard-copy form).

   (v) **Physical computer security**

     (1) **Internal security.** Management can regulate which staff members have access to different types of data. For instance, access to HR records may be restricted to members of the HR team by keeping these records on a separate server or database. In this way, only certain terminals may access servers with sensitive or confidential data stored on them.

     (2) **External security.** The organisation can also protect its data from external access by using **firewalls**. A firewall is designed **to restrict access** to a network by selectively allowing or blocking inbound traffic to parts of an organisation's system. It examines messages entering and exiting the system and blocks any that do not conform to specified criteria, for example, blocking incoming traffic from non-specific IP addresses. In this way, firewalls can be used to protect data and databases from being accessed by unauthorised people or terminals. For example, access to key servers can be restricted to a small number of terminals only.

3.6 If information is held on a server

If information is held on a server, then the following are required:

(a) Controls over viruses and hacking

(b) Clearly understood policy on the use of emails and corporate IT

(c) Password system to restrict access to particular files

4 Security and confidential information

IT systems are particularly vulnerable to unauthorised access, or use, from both internal and external parties unless they are protected.

Ways of protecting information:

- Passwords – where logon access requires the entry of a string of characters
- Logical access systems – restricted access depending on user authority
- Database controls – limiting view of database content
- Firewalls – prevent unauthorised access to company systems
- Encryption – scrambling information in case of interception
- Anti-virus and anti-spyware software
- Personnel policies

Essential reading

See Chapter 1 Section 3 of the Essential reading for more detail on the protection measures.

The Essential reading is available as an Appendix of the digital edition of the Workbook.

Activity 2: IT systems

The following statements have been made about IT systems:

(a) Employees should be able to change customer records if they notice an error or omission.

(b) Transmitted data should usually be encrypted to prevent hackers gaining access to it.

Required

Which of the above statements is/are true?

- ○ (a) only
- ○ (b) only
- ○ Neither (a) nor (b)
- ○ Both (a) and (b)

Solution

5 Internal sources of information

Internal sources of **information** include the financial accounting records and other systems closely tied to the accounting system. Internal information is usually operational in nature, but can include information on customers and suppliers.

Capturing data/information from inside the organisation involves the following:

(a) A **system for collecting or measuring transactions data** (eg sales, purchases, inventory and revenue) which sets out procedures for **what** data is collected, **how frequently, by whom** and by **what methods**, and how it is **processed** and **filed** or **communicated**

(b) **Informal communication** of information between managers and staff (eg by word of mouth or at meetings)

(c) **Communication between managers**

Essential reading

See Chapter 1 Section 4 of the Essential reading for more detail on internal sources of information.

The Essential reading is available as an Appendix of the digital edition of the Workbook.

6 External sources of information

External information is more relevant than internal information to **strategic decisions**.

Capturing external information is potentially expensive as it has so many sources. Information technology is helping to reduce the cost of data collection.

Sources of external information include:

(a) Directories

(b) Associations

(c) Government agencies

(d) Customers/consumer panels

(e) Suppliers

(f) Internet

(g) Databases/data warehouses

External information can be out of date by the time it has been collated.

Extremely large amounts of data are known as big data. We will look at this in detail in Chapter 2.

Essential reading

See Chapter 1 Section 5 of the Essential reading for more detail on external sources of information.

The Essential reading is available as an Appendix of the digital edition of the Workbook.

7 Information for control purposes

Management information can be used for control purposes.

Control is dependent on the **receipt and processing of information**, both to plan in the first place and to compare actual results against the plan, so as to judge what control measures are needed.

Plans will be based on an **awareness of the environment** (from externally sourced information) and on the **current performance of the organisation** (based on internal information such as, for example, sales volumes and costs).

Control is achieved through **feedback** – information about actual results produced from within the organisation (that is, internal information) such as variance control reports for the purpose of helping management with control decisions.

Essential reading

See Chapter 1 Section 6 of the Essential reading for more detail on using management information for control.

The Essential reading is available as an Appendix of the digital edition of the Workbook.

Chapter summary

Managing information

The role and benefits of information systems in organisations

Link between management accounting and information systems

IS provide information for planning, control, decision making and managing performance

Why are information systems needed?

- Process efficiency (transactions, planning, control, decisions)
- Facilitating communication
- Inventory control
- Sales and marketing
- HR management

Benefits of information systems

- Tool used for competitive advantage
- Access to quality information quickly
- Better decisions

Costs of information systems

Hardware/software/implementation costs

Types of information costs

- Direct data capture
- Process costs
- Indirect costs of producing internal information

How can information be shared?

Networks

- Resource sharing
- Storage requirement reduction
- Software cost reduction

Intranets

- Organisation-wide network
- Sharing information internally

Wireless technology

- Remote working and increased mobility
- Increase productivity
- Reduced costs as the business expands

The internet

Public network

Extranet

An intranet that authorised parties outside organisation can access

Cloud computing

- Reduced IT costs
- Safe storage
- Improved access

Controls over information

Reports

- Cost/benefit analysis first
- Prototype
- Check for duplications

Distribution

Ensure security (eg secure disposal if confidential)

Security and confidential information

Use passwords/logical access systems/ encryption etc

Internal sources of information

Eg accounting records and other systems

External sources of information

- More relevant than internal information to strategic decisions
- Eg consumer panels/suppliers/internet/ associations

Information for control purposes

Control is achieved through feedback

Knowledge diagnostic

1. Role and benefits of information systems in organisations

Information is required for a wide range of reasons, including supporting operations and managerial activities; it is now seen as a key tool.

2. Communication of information

Communication is improved when computers are joined together. Information can be shared using:

- Networks
- Intranets
- Wireless technology
- Internet
- Extranet
- Cloud computing

3. Controls over information

Controls are required over **access to**, and **use of**, information hardware and software. This is important both when information is available to **external parties** and when it is only available internally.

4. Security of highly confidential information not for external consumption

- Passwords
- Logical access systems
- Database controls
- Firewalls
- Personnel security planning
- Anti-virus and anti-spyware software

5. Internal and external sources of information

Information can be **internal** to organisations or available in the **external** environment.

Data can be:

- Out of date
- Expensive
- Biased

6. Control and feedback

Much control is achieved through the feedback of internal information.

Further study guidance

Question practice

Now try the following from the Further question practice bank [available in the digital edition of the Workbook]:

Number	Level	Marks	Approximate time
Section A Q1	Examination	2	4 mins
Section A Q2	Examination	2	4 mins

Further reading

There is a technical article available on ACCA's website, called *Information Systems*, which covers topics included in this chapter and the next chapter.

You are strongly advised to read this article in full as part of your preparation for the PM exam.

Activity answers

Activity 1: Use of information systems in hotels

1 The correct answer is:

Activity	Use of information system
Processing and recording transactions	Taking online bookings Card payment devices Guests' details Printing customer receipts Occupancy rates Number of repeat bookings Employee management/staff details in human resource systems All transactions used to produce financial statements • Sales receipts • Payments received/outstanding • Costs, eg rates, electricity, labour, consumables • Capital expenditure on beds/furniture Cloud based software and storage costs
Planning	**Based on internal information (local level)** Budget production/resources needed: • Number of employees • Food and drink inventory levels based on average food and drink spend per customer • Cleaning products/toiletries • New bedding/other items • Forecasting costs/sales Provide communication between managers/different hotels/head office **Based on externally accessed information (global level)** • Trends/customer preferences (eg ages of visitors to region) • Sales forecasting (relates to big data in the next chapter)
Control	Weekly/monthly variance reports on occupancy/food and drink spend Customer feedback reports (eg TripAdvisor)
Decision-making	Pricing based on occupancy demand at weekends vs weekdays Profitability/expansion plans Staffing levels based on occupancy/staff cost forecasts Making changes based on customer feedback

Activity 2: IT systems

The correct answer is:

(b) only

It is not appropriate for all employees to have the ability to alter, or even view, all customer records. Instead, access controls should be in place to ensure that only information required to carry out their duties is made available to employees. Information sent outside of the organisation is especially vulnerable and so should be protected via encryption or use of firewalls, or both.

2 Information systems and data analytics

Learning objectives

On completion of this chapter, you should be able to:

	Syllabus reference no.
Identify the accounting information requirements and describe the different types of information systems used for strategic planning, management control and operational control and decision-making.	A3 (a)
Define and discuss the main characteristics of transaction processing systems; management information systems; executive information systems; enterprise resource planning systems and customer relationship management systems.	A3 (b)
Describe the characteristics (volume, velocity, variety) of big data.	A3 (c)
Explain the uses and benefits of big data and data analytics for planning, costing, decision-making and performance management.	A3 (d)
Discuss the challenges and risks of implementing and using big data and data analytics in an organisation.	A3 (e)

Exam context

This chapter covers issues relating to **performance management information systems** and their design.

We begin with a look at the **accounting information needs** at all levels of the organisation. Next, we consider the characteristics of a range of management information systems, **including transaction processing systems** and **executive information systems**.

The last section of this chapter looks at the concept of big data.

As mentioned in Chapter 1, performance management information systems provide the information which enables performance measurement to take place.

The topics covered in this chapter could form part of a Section C constructed response question in the exam or could feature as an objective test question in Section A or B. Ensure that you are able to **discuss** these topics as well as being able to answer objective test (OT) questions.

Chapter overview

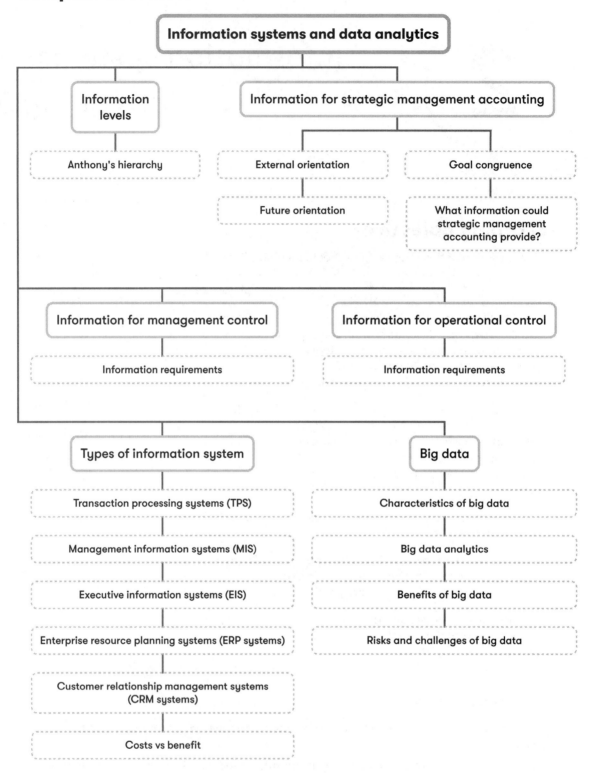

1 Information levels

Within and at all levels of the organisation, **information** is continually flowing back and forth, being used by people to formulate **plans** and take **decisions**, and to draw attention to the need for **control** action, when the plans and decisions don't work as intended. We defined planning, control and decision making in Chapter 1.

> **PER alert**
>
> One of the competencies needed for performance objective 12 of the PER is the ability to contribute to development and improvements of management accounting systems and internal reporting. You can apply the knowledge you obtain from this section of the text to help demonstrate this competence.

1.1 Anthony's hierarchy

Robert **Anthony**, a leading writer on organisational control, suggested what has become a widely used hierarchy, classifying the information used at different management levels for planning, control and decision-making into three tiers: **strategic planning**, **management control** and **operational control** (*Anthony, 1965*).

> **Strategic planning:** The process of deciding on objectives of the organisation changes the resources used to attain these objectives, and the policies that are to govern the acquisition, use and disposition of these resources.
>
> **Management (or tactical) control:** Management (or tactical) control is the process by which managers assure that resources are obtained and used effectively and efficiently in the accomplishment of the organisation's objectives. It is sometimes called 'tactics' or 'tactical planning'.
>
> **Operational control (or operational planning):** Operational control (or operational planning) is the process of assuring that specific tasks are carried out effectively and efficiently.
>
> **Strategic decisions:** Strategic decisions are long-term decisions and are characterised by their wide scope, wide impact, relative uncertainty and complexity.

Activity 1: Classifying information

Hydra Co is a bicycle retailer that has a significant presence in the South of Teeland. Each retail outlet has a manager who is responsible for day to day operations and is supported by an administrative assistant. All other staff at each location are involved in retailing operations.

Required

How would information concerning the development of new services such as the provision of car parts be classified?

○ Strategic information

○ Tactical information

○ Operational information

○ None of the above

Solution

---

2 Information for strategic management accounting

KEY TERM

> **Strategic management accounting:** Strategic management is a form of management accounting in which emphasis is placed on information about factors which are external to the organisation, as well as non-financial and internally generated information.

Strategic management accounting differs from traditional management accounting because it has an **external** and **future** orientation.

2.1 External orientation

Towards:

- Customers
- Competitors
- Suppliers
- Other stakeholders

For example, while a **traditional** management accountant would report on an **organisation's own revenues**, the **strategic management** would report on market share or trends in **market size** and **growth**.

2.2 Future orientation

A criticism of traditional management accounts is that they are **backwards looking.**

(a) Decision-making is a forward- and outwards-looking process.

(b) Accounts are based on **costs** whereas decision-making is concerned with **values.**

Strategic management accountants will use **relevant costs** (ie **incremental** costs and **opportunity** costs) for decision-making. We will revisit this topic later in the Workbook.

2.3 Goal congruence

Goal congruence is achieved when individuals or groups in an organisation take actions which are in their self-interest and also in the **best interest** of the **organisation as a whole**.

Business **strategy** involves the activities of many different functions, including marketing, production and human resource management; the strategic management accounting system will require **inputs from many areas of the business.** This **helps to ensure goal congruence** by translating business activities into the common language of finance.

2.4 What information could strategic management accounting provide?

Bearing in mind the need for goal congruence, external considerations and future orientation, the following are examples of strategic management accounting information:

Item	Information provided
Competitors' costs	What are they? How do they compare with ours? Can we beat them? Are competitors vulnerable because of their cost structure?
Financial effect of competitor response	How might competitors respond to our strategy? How could their responses affect our sales or margins?
Product profitability	A firm should not only want to know the profits or losses that are being made by each of its products, but also why one product should be making good profits compared to another equally good product which might be making a loss.
Customer profitability	Some customers or groups of customers are worth more than others.
Pricing decisions	Accounting information can help to analyse how profits and cash flows will vary according to price and prospective demand.
The value of market share	A firm ought to be aware of what it is worth to increase the market share of one of its products.
Capacity expansion	Should the firm expand its capacity and, if so, by how much? Should the firm diversify into a new area of operations, or a new market?
Brand values	How much is it worth investing in a brand which customers will choose over competitors' brands?
Shareholder wealth	Future profitability determines the value of a business.

Item	Information provided
Cash flow	A loss-making company can survive if it has adequate cash resources, but a profitable company cannot survive unless it has sufficient liquidity.
Effect of **acquisitions** and **mergers**	How will the merger affect levels of competition in the industry?
Decisions to **enter** or **leave a business area**	What are the barriers to entry or exit? How much investment is required to enter the market?

Essential reading

See Chapter 2 Section 1 of the Essential reading for more detail on strategic planning.

The Essential reading is available as an Appendix of the digital edition of the Workbook.

3 Information for management control

Management control is at the level below strategic planning in Anthony's decision-making hierarchy. While strategic planning is concerned with setting objectives and strategic targets, management control is concerned with **decisions** about the **efficient and effective use** of an organisation's **resources** to **achieve these objectives** or **targets**.

3.1 Information requirements

Futures of management control information

(a) Primarily generated **internally** (but may have a limited external component)

(b) Embraces the **entire organisation**

(c) **Summarised** at a relatively low level

(d) **Routinely** collected and disseminated

(e) Relevant to the **short** and **medium terms**

(f) Often **quantitative** (labour hours, volumes of sales and production)

(g) Collected in a **standard** manner

(h) Commonly expressed in **money terms**

Types of information

(a) Productivity measurements

(b) Budgetary control or variance analysis reports

(c) Cash flow forecasts

(d) Staffing levels

(e) Profit results within a particular department of the organisation

(f) Labour revenue statistics within a department

(g) Short-term purchasing requirements

Essential reading

See Chapter 2 Section 2 of the Essential reading for more detail on management control.

The Essential reading is available as an Appendix of the digital edition of the Workbook.

4 Information for operational control

Operational control, the lowest tier in Anthony's hierarchy, is concerned with assuring that **specific tasks** are carried out **effectively and efficiently**.

4.1 Information requirements

(a) **Operational information** is information which is **needed for the conduct of day to day implementation of plans.**

(b) It will include a lot of **'transaction data'**, such as data about customer orders, purchase orders, cash receipts and payments, and is likely to have an **endogenous (internal) source.**

(c) Operating information must usually be **consolidated into totals** in management reports before it can be used to prepare management control information.

(d) The amount of **detail** provided in information is likely **to vary with the purpose for which it is needed**, and operational information is likely to go into much more detail than tactical information, which in turn will be more detailed than strategic information.

(e) Whereas tactical information for management control is often expressed in money terms, operational information, although quantitative, is more often **expressed in terms of units, hours, quantities of material, and so on**.

Essential reading

See Chapter 2 Section 3 of the Essential reading for more detail on operational control.

The Essential reading is available as an Appendix of the digital edition of the Workbook.

5 Types of information system

You should be aware of the main characteristics of the following five systems.

5.1 Transaction processing systems (TPS)

> **Transaction processing system (TPS):** A **transaction processing system (TPS)** collects, stores, modifies and retrieves the transactions of an organisation.

TPS are used by operational staff and data in a TPS is likely to be high frequency and short term.

There are two main types: batch transaction processing which collects data as a group and processes it later and real time transaction processing, which involves immediate processing of data.

Characteristics of TPS:

(a) **Controlled processing**. The processing must support an organisation's operations.

(b) **Inflexibility**. A TPS wants every transaction to be processed in the same way regardless of user or time. If it were flexible there would be too many opportunities for non-standard operations.

(c) **Rapid response**. Fast performance is critical. Input must become output in seconds so customers are not forced to wait.

(d) **Reliability**. Organisations rely heavily on transaction processing systems. Back-up and recovery procedures must be quick and accurate as failure can potentially stop business.

An example of a TPS in a hotel chain is a booking system.

5.2 Management information systems (MIS)

Management information systems (MIS): Management information systems (MIS) generate information for monitoring performance (eg productivity information) and maintaining co-ordination (eg between purchasing and accounts payable).

Information is extracted from TPS and summarised to provide periodic reports for management for structured decision making and control.

Characteristics of MIS:

- Support structured decisions at operational and management control levels
- Report on existing operations
- Little analytical capability
- Internal focus

MIS in a hotel chain might help managers to decide on staffing levels or laundry requirements based on booking levels.

5.3 Executive information systems (EIS)

Executive information systems (EIS): Executive information systems (EIS) provide a generalised computing and communication environment for senior managers to support **strategic decisions**.

EIS are designed to facilitate **senior managers'** access to information quickly and effectively in order to analyse **organisational performance**. They have:

- Menu-driven user-friendly interfaces
- Interactive graphics to help visualisation of the situation
- Communication capabilities linking the executive to external databases

An EIS summarises and tracks **strategically critical information** from the MIS and includes data from external sources, eg competitors, legislation and databases such as Reuters.

A good way to think about an EIS is to imagine the senior management team in an aircraft cockpit with the instrument panel showing them the status of all the key business activities (a 'dashboard'). EIS typically involve lots of data analysis and modelling tools, such as **what-if analysis** to help **strategic decision-making**.

EIS in a hotel chain could provide senior managers with images that show key performance indicators, eg pie charts showing booking capacity or colour spectrums showing profitability across the different hotels.

There is a different need for volume of data at each level of the organisation. For example, the CEO is not going to be concerned with the detail of every sale (which would be represented in the TPS) but is going to require strategic information, including external data (represented in the EIS), so that they can set strategy for the business. The volume of data decreases the higher you go in the organisation.

5.4 Enterprise resource planning systems (ERP systems)

Enterprise resource planning systems (ERP systems): Enterprise resource planning systems (ERP systems) are modular software packages designed to integrate the key processes in an organisation so that a single system can serve the information needs of all functional areas.

ERP systems primarily support business operations – those activities in an organisation that support the selling process, including order processing, manufacturing, distribution, planning, customer service, human resources, finance and purchasing. ERP systems help to identify and plan the resources needed to make, account for, and fulfil customer orders, by improving the flow of information between business functions within an organisation.

The real time operation of ERP systems ensures that the exact status of everything is always available.

You may have heard of the ERP system, SAP.

Essential reading

See Chapter 2 Section 4 of the Essential reading for an ERP illustration.

The Essential reading is available as an Appendix of the digital edition of the Workbook.

5.5 Customer relationship management systems (CRM systems)

> **Customer relationship management systems (CRM systems): Customer relationship management systems** (CRM systems) are software applications that specialise in providing information concerning an organisation's products, services and customers.

Usually based on a database, these systems offer companies a cost-effective way of offering a personalised service to customers, which should lead to greater levels of customer retention. CRM software captures customers' interactions with an organisation so that this can be used to **improve** the organisation's **understanding of the customer** (eg by tailoring future marketing communications more precisely to the customer's interests or requirements).

Activity 2: ERP benefits

1 Fix It Co is a chain of garages with eight branches and one warehouse that supplies spare parts to the garages. Mechanics are assigned to a particular garage but can work in different locations. As well as repairs, the company also carries out MOTs for which specialist testing equipment is required.

Fix It Co has decided to implement an ERP system.

Required
What benefits could management hope to see following the implementation of the ERP system?

Solution

1

5.6 Costs vs benefit

> ### Exam focus point
> The benefits of information systems must outweigh the costs.

Potential costs and problems:

- Hardware
- Software
- Staff resistance and morale
- Time and disruption

6 Big data

Technological advances including **increased** data **storage** and **analytical capability** have resulted in a new concept called big data. Big data is a term given to extremely large collections of data ('data sets') that are available to organisations to analyse.

The internet, smartphones, social media, sensors and other digital technologies are all helping to create big data.

6.1 Characteristics of big data

The three V's of big data are:

Volume	The quantity of data now being produced is being driven by social media and transactional-based data sets recorded by large organisations, for example data captured from in-store loyalty cards and till receipts. Data is also now being derived from the increasing use of 'sensors' in business.
Velocity	The speed at which 'real time' data is being streamed into the organisation. To make data meaningful it needs to be processed in a reasonable time frame.
Variety	Modern data takes many different forms. Structured data may take the form of numerical data whereas unstructured data may be in the format of images, video, location information, call centre recordings, email, and social media posts. Processing these sources may require significant investment in people and IT.

6.2 Data analytics

> **Data analytics:** The process of collecting and examining data in order to extract meaningful business insights, which can be used to inform decision making and improve performance.

It is difficult to grasp the significance and meaning of big data without having a basic understanding of machine learning (ML) and algorithms. However, machine learning and algorithms are not mentioned on the PM syllabus.

> **Algorithm:** A set of instructions or rules used to solve a problem (especially by a computer).
>
> **Machine learning (ML):** A subset of artificial intelligence where a system learns automatically how to predict outcomes based on data, without being explicitly programmed to do so.

ML has been around for a long time but the advances in technology, including data capture, storage and analytical capabilities, means that it can now be used with big data to make business predictions.

Machine learning example

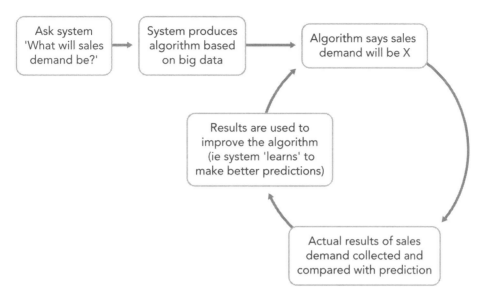

The results of the algorithm (predictions) become better and better as more data is analysed.

6.3 Benefits of big data analytics

Big data analytics could result in performance improvements in the following areas:

(a) **Better understanding of customer behaviour**

For example, identifying what customers are saying on social media about an organisation's products or its customer service could help the organisation identify how well it is meeting customers' needs.

Customers' conversations could help the organisation identify potential changes which are needed to its products, or the way they are delivered, in order to meet customers' needs more effectively – and thereby to increase sales.

(b) **Targeted marketing messages**

Big data could facilitate targeted promotions and advertising – for example, by sending a tailored recommendation to customers' mobile devices while they are in the right area to take advantage of the offers.

(c) **Decision-making**

For example, trends identified by a retailer in in-store and online sales, in real time, could be used to manage inventories and pricing.

(d) **New products and services**

More generally, big data could also provide new business opportunities in their own right.

For example, the online retailer Amazon makes recommendations for customers linked to the purchases made by other customers with similar interests.

(e) **Performance measurement**

Big data can provide more detailed and up-to-date information for performance measurement. For example, performance reports can be produced in real-time allowing management to react quickly to variances.

(f) **Costing**

Big data can be used to provide insights into costs. Big data's main use is in identifying trends and providing forecasts and this can be applied to costing. For example, it can be used to forecast events or conditions that may occur at a specific time which will have an impact on the business and its costs. A cost model can be developed.

Essential reading

See Chapter 2 Section 5 of the Essential reading for more detail about the potential value of big data.

The Essential reading is available as an Appendix of the digital edition of the Workbook.

Real world example

In 2013, Tesco used **big data analytics** to ensure its in-store refrigeration units worked at the correct temperature. On initial investigation, they were being kept much colder than the Energy and Carbon Manager expected them to be. Cooling cost savings of up to £20 million were realised by Tesco once refrigeration performance was being monitored.

Real world example

Tesco partnered with customer science company, Dunnhumby to create the Tesco Clubcard, a loyalty programme the company used to track customer behaviour through a vast database of customer data.

6.3.1 Big data and the finance professional

Five traits of a data-enabled finance professional:

- Understands the fundamental **drivers and metrics** of the business
- Has a clear sense of **what customers care about**, and how to track this
- Embraces new, **unconventional** sources of data
- Comfortable with **uncertainty**
- Looks for new visual ways to **present data with impact**

6.4 Risks and challenges of big data

Critics have argued that although data sets may be big, they are not necessarily representative of the entire data population as a whole; eg if a firm uses 'tweets' from the social networking site, Twitter to provide insight into public opinion on a certain issue, there is no guarantee the 'tweets' will be representative.

Quality of data

There can be a misconception that increasing the amount of data available automatically provides managers with better information for decision making. However, in order to be useful, data has to be relevant and reliable.

Veracity

In order to be valuable, data also needs to be reliable. A fourth V – veracity – is often added to the other 'V' characteristics of big data (volume, velocity and variety).

Using big data requires organisations to maintain strong governance on data quality. For example, the validity of any analysis of that data is likely to be compromised unless there are effective cleansing procedures to remove incomplete, obsolete or duplicated data records.

Cost

It is expensive to establish the hardware and analytical software needed, and to comply with data protection regulations which vary from country to country.

IT teams or business analysts may become burdened with increasing requests for data, ad hoc analysis and one-off reports. Equally, this will mean that the information and analysis will not be available to decision makers as quickly as the 'velocity' may initially imply.

Skills

Do organisations have staff with the necessary analytical skills to process and interpret the data? The scale and complexity of data sets may require a **data scientist's** level of analytical skills for data mining, deriving algorithms and predictive analytics.

Loss and theft of data

Companies could face legal action if data is stolen. More generally, when collecting and storing data they need to consider data protection and privacy issues, and ensure they comply with current legislation in these areas (eg having appropriate controls in place to prevent breaches of data security).

Activity 3: Big data analytics

BB Chocolat Co is a leading premium chocolate manufacturing company with a brand image built on luxury. It has both retail outlets and an online shop and uses social media for marketing purposes. It is worried about certain trends which encourage customers to avoid sugary foods due to their propensity to cause obesity and, as such, is looking to cost control.

1 **Required**
What are the benefits of big data analytics for BB Chocolat Co in its focus on customer trends and cost reduction?

Solution

1

Chapter summary

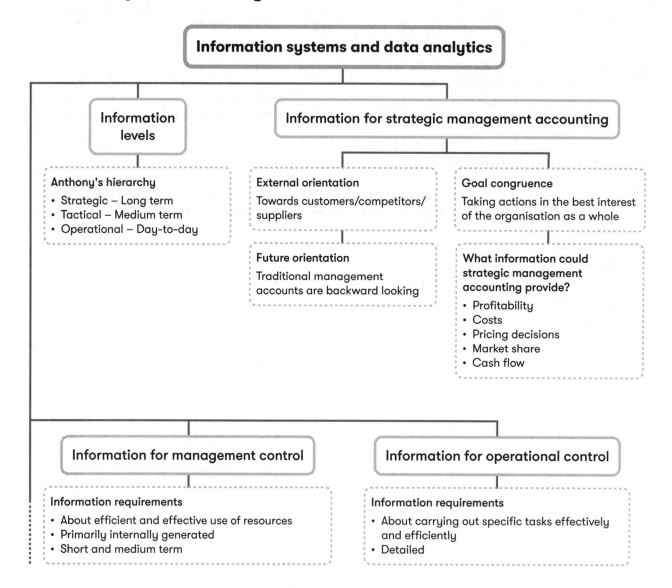

Information systems and data analytics

Information levels

Anthony's hierarchy
- Strategic – Long term
- Tactical – Medium term
- Operational – Day-to-day

Information for strategic management accounting

External orientation

Towards customers/competitors/suppliers

Future orientation

Traditional management accounts are backward looking

Goal congruence

Taking actions in the best interest of the organisation as a whole

What information could strategic management accounting provide?
- Profitability
- Costs
- Pricing decisions
- Market share
- Cash flow

Information for management control

Information requirements
- About efficient and effective use of resources
- Primarily internally generated
- Short and medium term

Information for operational control

Information requirements
- About carrying out specific tasks effectively and efficiently
- Detailed

Types of information system

Transaction processing systems (TPS)
- Used by operational staff
- High frequency/short term

Management information systems (MIS)
- Operational and management control decisions
- Internal focus

Executive information systems (EIS)
Support strategic decisions

Enterprise resource planning systems (ERP systems)
Software to integrate key processes

Customer relationship management systems (CRM systems)
Used to improve organisation's understanding of the customer

Costs vs benefit
Benefit must outweigh cost

Big data

Characteristics of big data
- Volume
- Velocity
- Variety

Big data analytics
Extracting insights and trends

Benefits of big data
- Customer behaviour insights
- Targeted marketing
- Decision making

Risks and challenges of big data
- Veracity
- Costs
- Skills
- Loss and theft of data

Knowledge diagnostic

1. Information levels

Management accounting information can be used at **strategic, tactical and operating** levels. **Managers** need **information** according to their **responsibilities**.

2. Strategic management accounting

Information aimed at long-term decisions, which will often be external to the organisation and with a future orientation.

3. Management control

Management control is concerned with **decisions about the efficient and effective use of an organisation's resources to achieve these objectives or targets.**

4. Operational control

Operational control, the lowest tier in Anthony's hierarchy, is concerned with assuring that **specific tasks** are carried out **effectively and efficiently.**

5. Information systems

Provide information at different levels and for different purposes:

- TPS
- MIS
- EIS
- ERP
- CRM

6. Big data

Refers to the mass of data created by society.

There are three V's of big data:

- Volume
- Velocity
- Variety

Further study guidance

Question practice

Now try the following from the Further question practice bank [available in the digital edition of the Workbook]:

Number	Level	Marks	Approximate time
Section A Q3	Examination	2	4 mins
Section A Q4	Examination	2	4 mins

Further reading

There is a technical article available on ACCA's website, called *Information Systems*, which covers topics included in Chapter 1 and this chapter.

You are strongly advised to read this article in full as part of your preparation for the PM exam.

Activity answers

Activity 1: Classifying information

The correct answer is:

Strategic information

Strategic information is required by the management of an organisation in order to enable management to take a longer-term view of the business and assess how the business may perform during that period. The length of this longer-term view will vary from one organisation to another, being very much dependent upon the nature of the business and the ability of those responsible for strategic direction to be able to scan the planning horizon. Strategic information tends to be holistic and summary in nature.

Activity 2: ERP benefits

1 **The correct answer is:**

Fix It Co could use an ERP system to assist with the following:

- Scheduling of repair jobs
- Scheduling of MOTs, ensuring that the testing equipment and trained MOT testing staff are available at the correct garage, reducing the need to have some at every site all day
- Invoicing customers
- Ordering parts from the central warehouse for individual garages
- Reordering inventory from suppliers to replenish the warehouse
- Planning preventative maintenance for machinery
- Producing staff rota

Activity 3: Big data analytics

1 **The correct answer is:**

The benefits of using big data analytics in its focus on cost control include:

Speed

Big data analytics allow for large quantities of data (both structured and unstructured) to be examined to identify trends and correlations. Since big data is collected by the business in real time, big data analytics will enable this data to be examined quickly, speeding up the organisation's decision making. For example, since BB Chocolat Co makes extensive use of social media for marketing purposes, it is likely that customers will also provide feedback about products through social media channels. If there is extensive negative feedback about the quality of the products then quick action could be taken to rectify the problem (for example, stopping the supply of cocoa beans from a particular supplier in the short-term). This will help to reduce external failure cost, such as refunds and damaged reputation, since the brand image is built on luxury.

Decision making

Better data analysis provided by big data analytics helps to improve organisational decision making by taking advantage of current social trends. This will help to introduce new products to the market that meet customers' needs more effectively in light of trends. For example, feedback from the market identified by our social media feed and other online sources (such as blogs) will help BB Chocolat Co to identify how quickly the trend against unhealthy foods is growing. This will help to use the design team more effectively by switching their focus from traditional flavoured chocolate to healthier alternatives, such as raw chocolate. Unnecessary development cost can therefore be avoided.

Focus on the customer

Big data analytics enables BB Chocolat Co to understand individual customers more fully so that it can apply target marketing more effectively to them. While this may be hard to achieve for customers buying chocolate in the physical shops, this could be achieved with customers purchasing chocolate online since BB Chocolat Co can link the product purchased more specifically to these customers. This will help to use the marketing resource more effectively, especially for more niche products. For example, if a customer only purchases diabetic chocolate, BB Chocolat Co can focus on advertising diabetic chocolate products to them. This may help to reduce marketing costs since a mass marketing campaign is less likely to be needed for the diabetic range.

3

Activity based costing

Learning objectives

On completion of this chapter, you should be able to:

	Syllabus reference no.
Identify appropriate cost drivers under ABC	B1 (a)
Calculate costs per driver and per unit using ABC	B1 (b)
Compare ABC and traditional methods of overhead absorption based on production units, labour hours or machine hours	B1 (c)

Exam context

In this chapter, we will be looking at a method of cost accumulation called **activity based costing (ABC)**, which is an alternative to traditional absorption costing. ABC attempts to overcome the problems of costing in a modern manufacturing environment, where a very large proportion of total production costs are overhead costs.

You can expect to see a question on ABC in the exam, either in Section A as an objective test (OT) question or in Section B as a scenario question containing five OTs.

Chapter overview

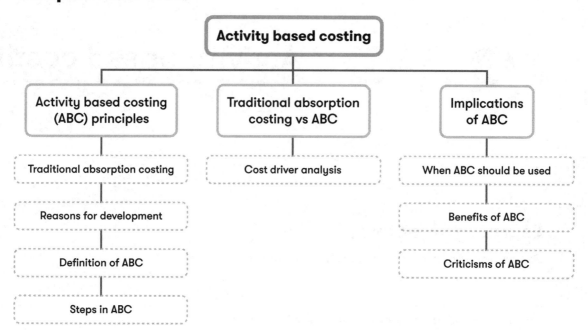

1 Activity base costing (ABC) principles

1.1 Traditional absorption costing

Traditional absorption costing uses a **single basis** for absorbing all overheads into cost units for a particular production department cost centre.

A business will choose the basis that best reflects the way in which overheads are being incurred, eg in an automated business much of the overhead cost will be related to maintenance and repair of the machinery. It is likely that this will vary to some extent with machine hours worked, so in this instance, we would have used a machine hour absorption rate.

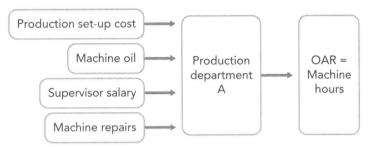

In a business where **labour is intensive**, overheads may be absorbed based on the **number of direct labour hours worked**.

Essential reading

See Chapter 3 Sections 1 and 2 of the Essential reading for more detail on traditional absorption costing, as well as marginal costing. Much of this is assumed knowledge brought forward from ACCA Management Accounting and is still examinable in Performance Management.

The Essential reading is available as an Appendix of the digital edition of the Workbook.

1.2 Reasons for the development of ABC

Traditional **absorption costing** was developed in a time when:

(a) Most manufacturers produced only a **narrow range of products**.

(b) Products underwent **similar operations** and consumed **similar proportions of overheads**.

(c) **Overhead costs were only a very small fraction of total production costs**: direct labour and direct material costs accounted for the largest proportion of the costs.

Modern businesses:

(a) Have experienced a **dramatic fall** in the costs of processing information

(b) Use advanced manufacturing technology (AMT) and therefore overhead costs have become a much larger proportion of total production costs, and direct labour has become much less important.

Therefore, it is now difficult to justify the use of direct labour hours as the basis for absorbing overheads to produce 'realistic' product costs.

Many resources are used in **non-volume related support activities**, which have increased due to AMT. Non-volume related support activities are activities that support production, but where the level of support activity (and so the level of cost) depends on something other than production volume – such as setting-up production runs, production scheduling and inspection. These support activities assist the efficient manufacture of a wide range of products and are **not, in general, affected by changes in production volume**. They tend to **vary in the long term according to the range and complexity** of the products manufactured, rather than the volume of output.

The wider the range and the more complex the products, the more support services are required.

Traditional absorption costing systems, which assume that all products consume all support resources in proportion to production volumes, tend to **allocate**:

(a) **Too great a proportion of overheads to high volume products**, which cause relatively little diversity and hence use fewer support services; and

(b) **Too small a proportion of overheads to low volume products**, which cause greater diversity and therefore use more support services.

Activity based costing (ABC) attempts to overcome this problem.

1.3 Definition of ABC

> **Activity based costing (ABC):** Activity based costing is a method of costing which involves identifying the costs of the main support activities and the factors that 'drive' the costs of each activity. Support overheads are charged to products by absorbing cost on the basis of the product's usage of the factor driving the overheads.

The major ideas behind activity based costing are as follows.

(a) **Activities cause costs.** Activities include ordering, materials handling, machining, assembly, production scheduling and despatching.

(b) **Manufacturing products creates demand for the support activities.**

(c) Costs are assigned to a product **on the basis of the product's consumption of these activities**.

ABC is an extension of absorption costing specifically considering what causes each type of overhead category to occur, ie what the cost drivers are. Each type of overhead is absorbed using a **different basis** depending on the cost driver.

> **Cost driver:** Cost driver is a factor that has most influence on the cost of an activity.

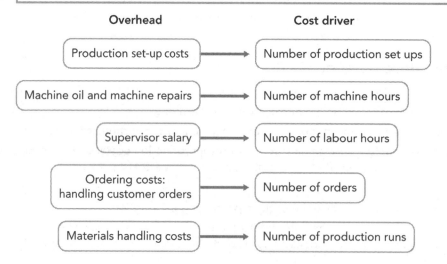

1.4 Steps in ABC

(a) Identify an organisation's major activities that support the manufacture of the organisation's products or the provision of its services.

(b) Group overheads into activities, according to how they are driven. These are known as cost pools.

(c) Identify the **cost drivers** for each activity, ie what causes the activity cost to be incurred.

(d) Calculate a **cost per unit of cost driver**.

(e) **Absorb** activity costs into production based on usage of cost drivers.

2 Traditional absorption costing vs ABC

Illustration 1: Absorption costing vs ABC

1 Suppose that Cooplan manufactures four products: W, X, Y and Z. Output and cost data for the period just ended are as follows:

	Output units	Number of production runs in the period	Material cost per unit	Direct labour hours per unit	Machine hours per unit
W	10	2	20	1	1
X	10	2	80	3	3
Y	100	5	20	1	1
Z	100	5	80	3	3
		14			

Direct labour cost per hour: $5

	$
Overhead costs	
Short-run variable costs	3,080
Set-up costs	10,920
Expediting and scheduling costs	9,100
Materials handling costs	7,700
	30,800

Required

Prepare unit costs for each product using:

(a) Conventional absorption costing

(b) ABC

Assume that, in the traditional absorption costing system, overheads are absorbed at a direct labour hour rate.

Solution

1 **The correct answer is:**

(a) Using a **conventional absorption costing approach,** the absorption rate for overheads based on direct labour hours or machine hours is:

$30,800 ÷ 440 hours = $70 per direct labour hour.

The product costs would be as follows:

	W	X	Y	Z
	$	$	$	$
Direct material	20	80	20	80
Direct labour	5	15	5	15
Overhead	70	210	70	210
Cost per unit	95	305	95	305

(b) Using activity based costing, it will be assumed that the number of production runs is the cost driver for set-up costs, expediting and scheduling costs and materials handling costs; and that machine hours are the cost driver for short-run variable costs. Product costs per unit are as follows:

	W	X	Y	Z
	$	$	$	$
Direct material (no change)	20	80	20	80
Direct labour (no change)	5	15	5	15
Overheads (W)	403	417	106	120
Cost per unit	428	512	131	215

Workings

	W	X	Y	Z
Short-run variable overheads (W1)	70	210	700	2,100
Set-up costs (W2)	1,560	1,560	3,900	3,900
Expediting, scheduling costs (W3)	1,300	1,300	3,250	3,250
Materials handling costs (W4)	1,100	1,100	2,750	2,750
	4,030	4,170	10,600	12,000
Units produced	10	10	100	100
Overhead cost per unit	403	417	106	120

Workings

1	$3,080 / 440 machine hours =	$7 per machine hour
2	$10,920 / 14 production runs =	$780 per production run
3	$9,100 / 14 production runs =	$650 per production run
4	$7,700 / 14 production runs =	$550 per production run

Summary

Product	Conventional absorption costing unit cost	ABC unit cost	Difference per unit	Difference in total
	$	$	$	$
W	95	428	+333	+3,330
X	305	512	+207	+2,070
Y	95	131	+36	+3,600
Z	305	215	-90	-9,000

These figures might suggest that the traditional volume-based absorption costing system is flawed, because the low-volume products W and X are not being charged with a 'fair share' of the costs of overhead support activities.

More specifically, **traditional absorption costing may be unsatisfactory** for two main reasons.

(a) It **under-allocates overhead costs to low-volume products** (here, W and X) and **over-allocates overheads to higher-volume products** (here Z in particular).

(b) It **under-allocates overhead costs to smaller products** (here W and Y, with just one hour of work needed per unit) and **over-allocates overheads to larger products** (here X and particularly Z).

ABC addresses these problems and arguably produces a more 'realistic' or 'satisfactory' cost.

Formula to learn

Absorption costing:
Overhead absorption rate (OAR) = budgeted production overheads / budgeted level of activity

Activity 1: Comparing absorption costing and ABC

Dodo Co manufactures three products, A, B and C. Data for the period just ended is as follows:

	A	B	C
Output (units)	20,000	25,000	2,000
Sales price $	20	20	20
Direct material cost $	5	10	10
Labour hours/unit	2	1	1
Wages paid at $5/hr			

Total production overheads for Dodo Co amount to $190,000.

1 Required
Calculate the profit per unit obtained on each product if production overheads are absorbed based on labour hours (traditional absorption costing).

2 The following data is now also available:

	$
Machining	55,000
Quality control and set up costs	90,000
Receiving	30,000
Packing	15,000
	190,000

	A	B	C
Output (units)	20,000	25,000	2,000
Cost driver data			
Labour hours/unit	2	1	1
Machine hours/unit	2	2	2
No. of production runs	10	13	2
No. of component receipts	10	10	2
No. of customer orders	20	20	20

Required
Using ABC, show the cost and gross profit per unit for each product during the period and contrast this with the profit calculated using absorption costing.

3 Required
What factors should be considered when comparing the results?

Solution

1

2

3

2.1 Cost driver analysis

Today's complex business environment means that costs are incurred because cost drivers occur at different levels.

There are four key categories for activities and their related costs.

Categories	Type of cost	Cost driver
Unit	Direct	Units produced
Batch	Set ups Inspections	Batches produced
Product	R&D Marketing	Products produced
Facility sustaining	Depreciation Rent	None

The difference between unit costs under traditional absorption costing and ABC depends upon the proportion of overheads in each category.

If most overheads are unit level or facility sustaining the costs will be similar.

If overheads are batch or product sustaining costs, the resulting unit costs will be very different.

3 Implications of ABC

3.1 When ABC should be used

(a) When **production overheads are high** relative to prime costs (eg service sector)
(b) When there is a whole **diversity of product range**
(c) When there are considerable **differences in the use of resources** by products
(d) Where consumption of **resources** is **not driven by volume**

ABC has both advantages and disadvantages and tends to be more widely used by larger organisations and the service sector.

3.2 Benefits of ABC

The use of ABC provides opportunities for:

(a) **Cost control and reduction** by the efficient management of cost drivers
(b) **Better costing information** used to assist pricing decisions
(c) Re-analysis of production and output/product mix decisions
(d) **Profitability analysis** (by customer, product line etc)
(e) A **more realistic estimate** of costs and profits which can be used in a performance appraisal

3.3 Criticisms of ABC

(a) It is **time consuming** and expensive.

(b) It will be of **limited benefit** if overhead costs are primarily **volume related.**

(c) The **benefit is reduced** if the company is producing only one product or a range of products with **similar costs.**

(d) Complex situations may have multiple cost drivers.

(e) Some **arbitrary apportionment** may still exist.

Activity 2: ABC

The following statements have been made about activity based costing.

(a) Implementation of ABC is unlikely to be cost effective when variable production costs are a low proportion of total production costs.

(b) The cost driver for materials handling and despatch costs is likely to be the number of orders.

Required

Which of the above statements is/are true?

○ (a) only

○ (b) only

○ Neither (a) nor (b)

○ Both (a) and (b)

Solution

3.4 Identifying appropriate cost drivers

Activity 3: Cost drivers

1 **Required**

Match the most appropriate cost driver to each cost.

	Cost	Cost driver
(a)	Machine set up costs	Number of production runs
(b)	Machine operating costs	Number of set-ups
(c)	Materials handling and despatch	Number of machine hours
(d)	Quality inspection	Number of orders executed

Solution

1

Chapter summary

```
                    ┌─────────────────────────┐
                    │  Activity based costing │
                    └─────────────────────────┘
```

Activity based costing (ABC) principles

Traditional absorption costing

Absorption using single basis eg labour hours

Reasons for development

- Dramatic fall in costs of processing information in modern businesses
- Overhead costs are now a much larger proportion of total production costs
- Traditional absorption costing allocates too great a proportion of overheads to high volume products

Definition of ABC

Identifying the costs of the main support activities and the factors that 'drive' the costs of each activity

Steps in ABC

- Identify major activities
- Group overheads into cost pools
- Identify cost drivers
- Calculate a cost per unit of cost driver
- Absorb activity costs into production based on usage of cost drivers

Traditional absorption costing vs ABC

Cost driver analysis

- Costs are more closely linked to the causes of overheads, making ABC more appropriate where
  - Overheads are high compared with prime costs
  - Product ranges are diverse
  - Resources are not merely driven by volume

Implications of ABC

When ABC should be used

- When production overheads are high relative to prime costs
- When there is a whole diversity of product range
- When there are considerable differences in the use of resources by products
- Where consumption of resources is not driven by volume

Benefits of ABC

- Better analysis of costs leading to
  - Cost control
  - Production decisions
  - Pricing decisions
  - Profitability analysis

Criticisms of ABC

- Time consuming
- Costly
- Still some arbitrary apportionment
- Limited benefit if products have similar cost structures

Knowledge diagnostic

1. Activity based costing

Activity based costing groups overheads into activities. These are referred to as **cost pools**.

The item that causes the costs to be incurred is the **cost driver**.

Overheads are absorbed into products using the cost drivers.

2. Absorption costing vs ABC

Overhead absorption rates under ABC should be more closely linked to the **causes of overhead** costs.

3. Implications of ABC

ABC results in a more **meaningful product cost** when overheads are high and there is a wide diversity of product range.

ABC has both advantages and disadvantages and tends to be more widely used by larger organisations and the service sector.

Further study guidance

Question practice

Now try the following from the Further question practice bank [available in the digital edition of the Workbook]:

Number	Level	Marks	Approximate time
Section A Q5	Examination	2	4 mins
Section A Q6	Examination	2	4 mins
Section B Q1-5	Examination	10	18 mins

Further reading

There is a technical article available on ACCA's website, called *Activity based costing*, which illustrates how ABC can give a more accurate estimate of costs than traditional approaches, when a business produces different types of unit. ABC may be more time consuming and costly to implement but enables managers to understand the drivers of costs.

You are strongly advised to read this article in full as part of your preparation for the PM exam.

Activity answers

Activity 1: Comparing absorption costing and ABC

1 The correct answer is:

Under traditional absorption costing

OAR = $190,000 ÷ 67,000 = $2.836/hr

	A	B	C
	$/unit	$/unit	$/unit
Revised product cost	20.67	17.84	17.84
Sales price	20.00	20.00	20.00
Profit	(0.67)	2.16	2.16

2 The correct answer is:

Under ABC

Workings: recovery rates

Machine cost

$55,000 / (40,000 + 50,000 + 4,000) = $0.585 per machine hour

QC & set up

$90,000 / (10 + 13 + 2) = $3,600 per production run

Receiving

$30,000 / (10 + 10 + 2) = $1,363.64 per component receipt

Packing

$15,000 / (20 + 20 + 20) = $250 per customer order

	A	B	C	Total
	$	$	$	$
Machining costs	23,404	29,255	2,341	55,000
Quality control & set up	36,000	46,800	7,200	90,000
Receiving	13,636	13,636	2,728	30,000
Packing	5,000	5,000	5,000	15,000
Total overhead costs	78,040	94,691	17,269	190,000
Units produced	20,000	25,000	2,000	
Overhead cost/unit	$3.90	$3.79	$8.63	

	A	B	C
	$/unit	$/unit	$/unit
Direct materials cost	5.00	10.00	10.00
Direct labour cost	10.00	5.00	5.00
Production overhead cost	3.90	3.79	8.63
	18.90	18.79	23.63
Sales price	20.00	20.00	20.00
Gross profit/unit	1.10	1.21	(3.63)

3 The correct answer is:

Items to consider are:

- How much more cost have we been able to allocate on a meaningful basis?
- Have we the right cost drivers?
- Why have the costs changed?
- Do we need to revisit selling prices?
- Do we need to alter the product mix?
- Should we cease production of C (bear in mind decisions should be based upon contribution)?

Activity 2: ABC

The correct answer is:

(b) only

Implementation of ABC is likely to be cost effective when variable costs are a low proportion of total production costs and overhead costs, meaning that Statement (a) is false.

Activity 3: Cost drivers

1 **The correct answer is:**

	Cost	Cost driver
(a)	Machine set-up costs	Number of set-ups
(b)	Machine operating costs	Number of machine hours
(c)	Materials handling and despatch	Number of orders executed
(d)	Quality inspection	Number of production runs

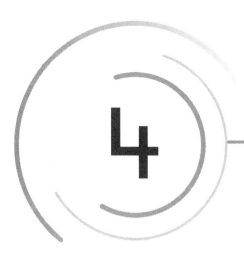

Target costing

Learning objectives

On completion of this chapter, you should be able to:

	Syllabus reference no.
Derive a target cost in manufacturing and service industries.	B2 (a)
Explain the difficulties of using target costing in service industries.	B2 (b)
Suggest how a target cost gap might be closed.	B2 (c)

Exam context

Target costing is the second specialist cost accounting technique we will consider. It is a process which involves setting a target cost for a product by subtracting a desired profit margin from a target selling price.

In a competitive market where organisations are continually redesigning older products and developing new ones, target costing can be an invaluable technique for helping them to make a satisfactory profit on the items that they sell.

Target costing may be examined in the Section A objective test questions or it may form part of a Section B mini case study question. For example, the calculation of a target cost may be required, followed by an objective test question on the theory of target costing and how a target gap might be closed.

Chapter overview

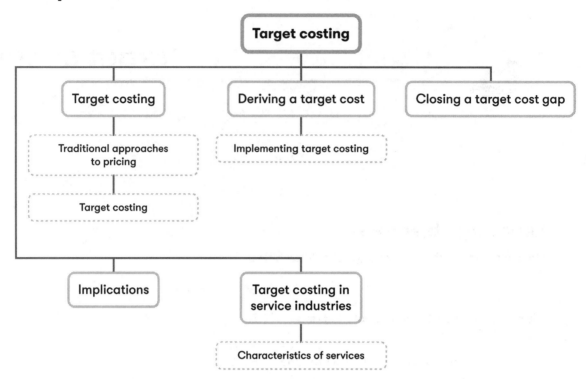

1 Target costing

1.1 Traditional approaches to pricing

Under traditional approaches to pricing, businesses calculate the **cost of manufacturing** and selling a product, and **then add mark up**, to give the profit element. These methods are known as 'cost plus pricing'.

A major criticism of cost plus pricing techniques is that they **do not consider any external factors** (eg demand for product, number of competitors). They are therefore unlikely to maximise the profits that a business will generate.

1.2 Target costing

> **Target costing:** Target costing involves setting a target cost by subtracting a desired profit margin from a target selling.
>
> **Target cost:** Target cost is the cost at which a product must be produced and sold in order to achieve the required amount of profit at the target selling price. When a product is first planned, its estimated cost will often be higher than its target cost. The aim of target costing is then to find ways of closing this target cost gap, and producing and selling the product at the target cost.

In a modern environment with **shortening product life cycles**, organisations must **redesign** their products **frequently**. As product life cycles have become much shorter, the **planning, development and design stage** of a product is **critical** to an organisation's **cost** management process. Cost reduction must be considered at this stage of a product's life cycle, rather than during the production process.

Functional analysis (ie reducing costs by amending features of a product) can be applied at the design stage of a new product and a target cost for each function can be set.

Achieving a target cost will usually require some redesigning of the product and the removal of unnecessary costs. Target costing therefore encourages a business to examine its processes and costs carefully.

2 Deriving a target cost

2.1 Implementing target costing

(a) Define product specification and estimate sales volume.

(b) Set a target selling price at which the company will be able to achieve the desired market share.

(c) Estimate required profit based on profit margins or return on investment.

(d) Calculate target cost:

	$
Target selling price	X
Less target profit	(X)
Target cost	X

(e) Prepare an estimated cost for the product based on the product specification and current cost levels.

(f) Calculate the target cost gap: Estimated product cost – target cost = cost gap

(g) Make efforts to close the cost gap. Aim to 'design out' costs before production starts.

Illustration 1: Target costing and the target cost gap

1 Great Games, a manufacturer of computer games, is in the process of introducing a new game to the market and has undertaken market research to find out about customers' views on the value of the product, as well as to obtain a comparison with competitors' products. The results of this research have been used to establish a target selling price of $60. This is the price that the company thinks it will have to sell the product at to achieve the required sales volume.

Cost estimates have been prepared based on the proposed product specification.

Manufacturing cost	$
Direct material	3.21
Direct labour	24.03
Direct machinery costs	1.12
Ordering and receiving	0.23
Quality assurance	4.60

Non-manufacturing costs	
Marketing	8.15
Distribution	3.25
After-sales service	1.30

The target profit margin for the game is 30% of the target selling price.

Required
Calculate the target cost of the new game and the target cost gap.

Solution

1 **The correct answer is:**

	$
Target selling price	60.00
Target profit margin (30% of selling price)	18.00
Target cost (60.00–18.00)	42.00
Projected cost	45.89

The projected cost exceeds the target cost by $3.89. This is the target cost gap. Great Games will therefore have to investigate ways to reduce the cost from the current estimated amount down to the target cost.

3 Closing a target cost gap

Increasing the selling price **will not** close the cost gap (because increasing the selling price will negatively affect the sales volume).

Value analysis: Value analysis involves examining the factors which affect the cost of a product or service, so as to devise ways of achieving the intended purpose most economically at the required standards of quality and reliability.

Value can be viewed from a number of different perspectives:

- **Cost value** is the cost of producing and selling an item
- **Exchange value** is the market value of the product or service
- **Use value** is what the article does; the purposes it fulfils (performance, reliability)
- **Esteem value** is the prestige the customer attaches to the product

Value analysis seeks to refine the design of the product to reduce unit cost (so cost value is the one aspect of value to be reduced) and to provide the same (or a better) use value at the lowest cost. Value analysis also attempts to maintain or enhance the esteem value of a product at the lowest cost. The aim is to reduce cost without compromising other aspects of value.

Management can set **benchmarks for improvement** towards the target cost, by improving production technologies and processes. Various techniques can be employed; for instance:

- Reducing the **number of components**
- Using **cheaper staff** (where this does not affect quality)
- Using **standard components** wherever possible
- Acquiring new, more efficient **technology**
- **Training** staff in more efficient techniques
- Cutting out **non-value added activities**
- Using **different materials** (identified using **activity analysis*** etc)

*Activity analysis is an analysis of how much is being spent on particular activities.

However, the most effective time to eliminate unnecessary cost and reduce the expected cost to the target cost level is during the product design and development phase, not after 'live' production has begun.

Exam focus point

The syllabus states that you must be able to suggest how to close a target cost gap. Make sure that you understand the list above and can apply it to a scenario in an OT question.

Activity 1: Target costing

House it Co produces rabbit hutches. It is about to launch a new top of the range hutch which it believes can be sold for $125. House it Co demands a margin of 25% on sales.

Cost information for the new hutch is as follows:

- Timber – The hutch needs 10 metres (m) of good quality planed timber. House it Co can acquire this at a cost of $48.
- Felt roofing material – 2m² are required. Roofing material costs $17.50 / m².
- Wire – 1m of wire is needed at a cost of $1.50 per metre.
- Labour – Labour is paid at a rate of $7 / hour.
- Variable overhead – These will be incurred at a rate of $1.50 per labour hour.

1 **Required**
What is the target cost of the rabbit hutch? (Give your answer to two decimal places.)

$ _____

2 **Required**
What is the expected cost to make the hutch?

○ $93.00

○ $98.50

○ $101.50

○ $125.00

3 Required

Which TWO of the following options would be the most appropriate strategies for House it Co to close the cost gap?

○ Make the hutch smaller

○ Raise the selling price

○ Make the window bigger – increasing the proportion of wire and reducing the proportion of wood

○ Use lower skilled labour for all elements of production

○ Use lower quality timber to make the hutch

Solution

1

2

4 Implications

Target costing turns the traditional cost plus approach to pricing on its head, meaning **pricing is the first consideration**. Cost control is a primary consideration of the development of the product, not merely as an activity which happens alongside production.

Performance management will therefore focus on two things; Ensuring sales targets are met as well as finding ways of improving the processes to achieve the target cost..

5 Target costing in service industries

The target costing approach is a sensible basis for estimating and reducing costs regardless of the type of business. However, due to the nature of service industries, this process is more difficult in these businesses.

5.1 Characteristics of services

Unlike manufacturing, service industries have the following characteristics which make cost and performance measurement more difficult:

- Intangibility
- Inseparability/simultaneity
- Variability/heterogeneity
- Perishability
- No transfer of ownership

5.2 Problems with target costing for services

A target cost for a product is a cost for an item whose design and make-up is specified in exact detail in a product specification. A target cost is the cost for this detailed specification.

Services are much more difficult to specify exactly. This is due to some of the characteristics of a service.

Intangibility. This refers to the lack of substance which is involved with service delivery. Unlike goods (physical products such as confectionery), there are no substantial material or physical aspects to a service: no taste, feel, visible presence, and so on.

Some of the features of a service cannot be properly specified because they are intangible. What exactly does a customer receive, for example, when they go to a cinema? When services are provided by a human, the quality of the personal service can be critically important for the customer, but this is difficult or impossible to specify.

When services do not have any material content, it is not possible to reduce costs to a target level by reducing material costs. In comparison, reducing material costs can be an effective approach to target costing for products.

Inseparability/simultaneity. Many services are created at the same time as they are consumed. (Think of dental treatment.) No service exists until it is actually being experienced or consumed by the person who has bought it.

Variability/heterogeneity. Many services face the problem of maintaining consistency in the standard of output. It may be hard to attain precise standardisation of the service offered, but customers expect it (such as with fast food). When services are delivered by humans, it is very difficult to ensure that the same service is provided in exactly the same way every time and a standard service may not exist. For example, repairing a motor car, providing an accountancy service, or driving a delivery truck from London to Paris are never exactly the same each time. When services are variable, it is possible to calculate an estimated average cost, but this is not specific and so not ideal for target costing.

Perishability. Services are innately perishable. The services of a beautician, for example, are purchased for a period of time.

No transfer of ownership. Services do not result in the transfer of property or ownership. The purchase of a service only confers on the customer access to or a right to use a facility.

Services also vary widely in nature. For example, services include banking, transport, parcel delivery, energy supply, entertainment, education, hotels and holidays, car repairs and maintenance, professional services such as law and accountancy, cleaning, security services, and so on are all examples of services.

A feature of many services, however, is that although the labour content may be high, the material content is often quite low. With products, the material content is always higher but the labour element may be lower.

Activity 2: Implementing target costing

The following statements have been made about target costing.

(a) It is more difficult to implement target costing in service industries compared to manufacturing because of the lack of a tangible product.

(b) Target costing makes the business look at what competitors are offering at an early stage in the new product development process.

Required
Which of the above statements is/are true?

O (a) only

O (b) only

O Neither (a) nor (b)

O Both (a) and (b)

Solution

Activity 3
Target cost gap

Required

Which TWO of the following methods can be used to move a currently attainable cost closer to target cost?

- ○ Using standard components wherever possible
- ○ Acquiring new, more efficient technology
- ○ Making staff redundant
- ○ Reducing the quality of the product in question

Solution

Essential reading

There is no essential reading for this chapter.

The Essential reading is available as an Appendix of the digital edition of the Workbook.

Chapter summary

Target costing

Target costing

Traditional approaches to pricing

Calculate the cost of manufacturing and selling a product, and then add mark up

Target costing

- Externally focused approach
- A selling price is set with reference to the market
- The desired profit margin is then deducted leaving a target cost

Deriving a target cost

- Cost measurement is more difficult
- Price set is based upon qualitative information

Implementing target costing

- Calculate target cost
- Calculate target cost gap
- Make efforts to close the cost gap

Closing a target cost gap

- Target cost – estimated cost = cost gap
- Any cost gap needs to be closed through product design and processing improvements

Implications

- Turns traditional pricing on its head
- Cost control is considered upfront as part of the product development
- Performance management focuses on
  - Sales targets and selling price
  - Improving processes/ development to drive down cost
- Target costing is suitable in today's environment as short product life cycles mean it is essential to consider costs upfront

Target costing in service industries

Characteristics of services
- Simultaneity
- Heterogeneity
- Intangibility
- Perishability

Knowledge diagnostic

1. Target costing

Target costing is an approach that sets the selling price of a product or service with reference to the marketplace.

2. Deriving a target cost

Selling price less desired margin = target cost.

Any cost gap should be closed via the design and development of the product.

3. Closing a target cost gap

- Reducing the number of components
- Using cheaper staff (where this does not affect quality)
- Using standard components wherever possible
- Acquiring new, more efficient technology
- Training staff in more efficient techniques
- Cutting out non-value added activities
- Using different materials

4. Implications

Cost control is considered up front during the development stage.

5. Target costing in service industries

Target costing can be applied to service industries but the measurement of cost is more difficult.

Further study guidance

Question practice

Now try the following from the Further question practice bank [available in the digital edition of the Workbook]:

Number	Level	Marks	Approximate time
Section A Q7	Examination	2	4 mins
Section A Q8	Examination	2	4 mins
Section A Q9	Examination	2	4 mins

Further reading

There is a technical article available on ACCA's website, called *Target costing and lifecycle costing*, which discusses target costing and life cycle costing (the subject of the next chapter).

You are strongly advised to read this article in full as part of your preparation for the PM exam.

BPP
LEARNING
MEDIA

Activity answers

Activity 1: Target costing

1 The correct answer is:

$93.75

	$
Selling price	125.00
Margin (25%)	31.25
Target cost	93.75

2 The correct answer is:

$101.50

	$
Expected cost	
Timber	48.00
Roofing material	35.00
Wire	1.50
Labour	14.00
Variable overhead	3.00
	101.50

3 The correct answers are:

- Make the hutch smaller
- Make the window bigger – increasing the proportion of wire and reducing the proportion of wood

Using lower quality timber and labour would be likely to reduce the quality of the finished product and so would not be suitable strategies. Again, raising the selling price is not an appropriate strategy for closing the cost gap

Activity 2: Implementing target costing

The correct answer is:

Both (a) and (b)

A lack of tangible product means that target costing cannot be easily applied to service industries, but this does not mean that it is never appropriate.

In order to identify the desirable features for a new product and set a target sales price, it is necessary to look first at what competitors are offering in the market.

Activity 3: Target cost gap

The correct answers are:

- Using standard components wherever possible
- Acquiring new, more efficient technology

To make improvements towards the target cost, technologies and processes must be improved. The use of standard components is a way of improving the production process.

Making staff redundant will not improve technologies and processes.

Reducing the quality of the product in question does not do this either.

5

Life cycle costing

Learning objectives

On completion of this chapter, you should be able to:

	Syllabus reference no.
Identify the costs involved at different stages of the life cycle.	B3 (a)
Derive a life cycle cost or profit in manufacturing and service industries.	B3 (b)
Identify the benefits of life cycle costing.	B3 (c)

Exam context

Life cycle costing is the third specialist cost accounting technique we will consider. It is an approach that accumulates costs over a product's entire life, rather than calculating them for each accounting period through the product's life. It is used to determine the total expected profitability of a product over its entire life, from its design and development stage, through its market introduction, to its eventual withdrawal from the market.

It is a costing technique used primarily for planning lifetime costs and profitability. It is not a technique for recording and reporting historical costs of production and sales.

A question on life cycle costing could appear in the exam, either in Section A as an objective test (OT) question or in Section B as a scenario question containing five OTs.

Chapter overview

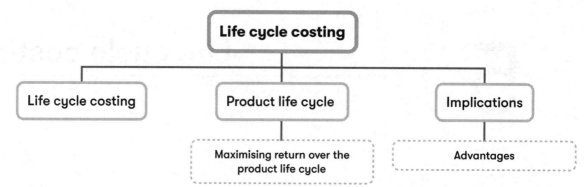

1 Life cycle costing

> **Life cycle costing: Life cycle costing** is the accumulation of costs over a product's entire life.

Life cycle costing aims to cost a product, service, customer or project over its **entire life cycle** with the aim of **maximising** the **return** over the total life while **minimising costs**.

Traditionally, the costs and revenues of a product are assessed on a financial year or period by period basis.

Product life cycle costing considers **all** the costs that will be incurred from **design** to **abandonment** of a new product and compares these to the revenues that can be generated from selling this product at different target prices throughout the product's life.

2 Product life cycle

The product life cycle (PLC) can be divided into five stages.

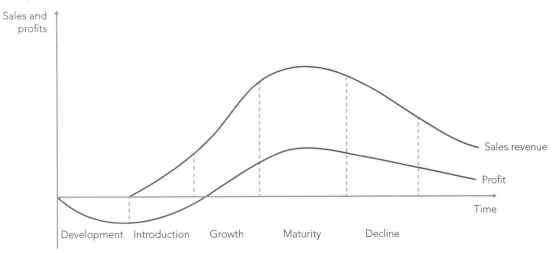

Characteristics of the product life cycle

Stage	Sales volume	Costs
Development	None	Research and development
Introduction	Very low levels	Very high fixed costs (eg non-current assets, advertising)
Growth	Rapid increase	Increase in variable costs Some fixed costs increase (eg increased number of factories)
Maturity	Stable High volume	Primarily variable costs
Decline	Falling demand	Primarily variable costs (now decreasing) Some fixed costs (eg decommissioning costs)

2.1 Costs over the product life cycle

A product's life cycle costs are incurred **from its design stage through development to market launch, production and sales, and finally to its eventual decline and withdrawal from the market.**

The component elements of a product's cost over its life cycle could therefore include the following.

- **Research and development costs**
  - Design cost
  - Cost of making a prototype
  - Testing costs
  - Production process and equipment: development and investment
- The **cost of purchasing any technical data** required (eg purchasing the right from another organisation to use a patent)
- **Training costs** (including initial operator training and skills updating)
- **Production costs**, when the product is eventually launched in the market
- **Distribution costs** (including transportation and handling costs)
- **Marketing and advertising**
  - Customer service
  - Field maintenance
  - Brand promotion
- **Inventory costs** (holding spare parts, warehousing, and so on)
- **Retirement and disposal costs,** ie costs occurring at the end of a product's life, which may include the costs of cleaning up a contaminated site

Some of these costs, such as design costs, are 'once-only costs'. Others are incurred regularly throughout the product's life but vary with production and sales volumes. Production costs, for example, will vary each year with changes in annual production volumes throughout the product's life.

Life cycle costs can also be estimated for **services**, customers and projects as well as for physical products.

Traditional cost accumulation systems are based on the financial accounting year and tend to dissect a product's life cycle into a series of 12-month periods. This means that traditional management accounting systems **do not accumulate costs over a product's entire life cycle** and **do not** therefore **assess a product's profitability over its entire life.** Instead they do it on a periodic basis.

Life cycle costing, on the other hand, **tracks and accumulates actual costs and revenues** attributable to each product **over the entire product life cycle.** Hence, the total profitability of any given product can be determined.

2.2 Maximising return over the product life cycle

There are a number of ways that return can be increased over the life cycle.

(a) Design costs out of products

Approximately 70%–90% of a product's life cycle costs are determined by decisions made early in the life cycle at the design and development stage. Therefore, design and production teams must work together to ensure costs are minimised.

(b) Minimise the time to market

This is the time from the conception of the product to its launch. If a company can get a product to the marketplace very quickly, it will give the product as long a span as possible without competitors' rival products in the marketplace. This should mean that market share is increased in the long run.

(c) **Minimise breakeven time**

Pricing strategies will affect both contribution and volumes generated. A short breakeven time is very important for liquidity purposes.

(d) **Extend the length of the life cycle itself**

For example, product development, finding other uses for a product or staggering the launch of the product in different markets.

2.2.1 Why calculate life cycle costs?

Life cycle costing has a different purpose from cost accumulation systems that measure actual costs of production and sales. Traditional costing systems are intended to measure the cost of a product in each accounting period, and the profit or loss that should be reported for the product for that period.

The purpose of life cycle costing is to assess the total costs of a product over its entire life, to assess the expected profitability from the product over its full life. Products that are not expected to be profitable after allowing for design and development costs, or clean-up costs, should not be considered for commercial development.

A feature of many competitive markets is that product life cycles are getting shorter, and organisations must continually redesign existing products and develop new ones. The planning, design and development stages of a product's cycle are therefore critical to an organisation's costs and profits. Cost reduction at this stage of a product's life cycle, rather than during the production process, is one of the most important ways of reducing product cost.

Note. The techniques of life cycle costing and target costing can be combined, to plan for achieving certain levels of cost at different stages of the product's life cycle. Both are essentially forward-looking techniques of costing.

3 Implications

Given that there will be different levels of demand for a product over its expected life, it would **not be** appropriate to set one price for the product's entire life.

An understanding of the stages a product goes through enables you to price accordingly to either manipulate demand (low price, demand will rise and the introduction stage is shortened) or to maximise profit.

All costs relating to a product including R&D are associated with the product. This enables true assessment of a product's profitability.

Looking at a product's life cycle, it is clear that the product will make a loss initially. Viewing profitability on a periodic basis can put unnecessary pressure on management because of the visibility of the loss and could lead to incorrect decisions being taken.

3.1 Advantages

There are a number of benefits associated with life cycle costing.

(a) It helps management to assess **profitability** over the **full life of a product**, which in turn helps management to decide whether to develop the product, or to continue making the product.

(b) It can be very useful for organisations that continually develop **products** with a **relatively short life**, where it may be possible to estimate sales volumes and prices with reasonable accuracy.

(c) The life cycle concept results in **earlier action**s to **generate more revenue** or to **lower costs** than otherwise might be considered.

(d) **Better decisions** should follow from a more accurate and realistic assessment of revenues and costs, at least within a particular life cycle stage.

(e) It encourages **longer-term thinking** and forward-planning and may provide **more useful information** than traditional reports of historical costs and profits in each accounting period.

Illustration 1: Life cycle costing

1 Solaris specialises in the manufacture of solar panels. It is planning to introduce a new slimline solar panel specially designed for small houses. Development of the new panel is to begin shortly, and Solaris is in the process of determining the price of the panel. It expects the new product to have the following costs:

	Year 1	Year 2	Year 3	Year 4
Units manufactured and sold	2,000	15,000	20,000	5,000
	$	$	$	$
R&D costs	1,900,000	100,000	–	–
Marketing costs	100,000	75,000	50,000	10,000
Production cost per unit	500	450	400	450
Customer service costs per unit	50	40	40	40
Disposal of specialist equipment				300,000

The Marketing Director believes that customers will be prepared to pay $500 for a solar panel but the Financial Director believes this will not cover all the costs throughout the life cycle.

Required

Calculate the cost per unit looking at the whole life cycle and comment on the suggested price.

Solution

1 The correct answer is:

	$'000
R&D (1,900 + 100)	2,000
Marketing (100 + 75 + 50 + 10)	235
Production (1,000 + 6,750 + 8,000 + 2,250)	18,000
Customer service (100 + 600 + 800 + 200)	1,700
Disposal	300
Total life cycle costs	22,235
Total production ('000 units)	42
Cost per unit	529.40

The total life cycle costs are $529.40 per solar panel, which is higher than the selling price proposed by the marketing director of $500. At this price and cost, the slimline solar panel would not be profitable. Solaris will either have to charge a higher price or look at ways to reduce costs.

It may be difficult to increase the price if customers are price sensitive and not prepared to pay more. Costs could be reduced by analysing each part of the costs throughout the life cycle and actively seeking cost savings; for example, using different materials, using cheaper staff or acquiring more efficient technology.

Activity 1: Life cycle cost per unit

X Co is in a high tech industry and is often first to market with new technological advances. It has recently spent $500,000 designing and developing a new product. The new product is expected to have a life of four years.

The anticipated performance of this product is as follows:

	Year 1	Year 2	Year 3	Year 4
Sales volume (units)	4,000	9,000	30,000	10,000
	$	$	$	$
Marketing costs	1.2m	0.4m	0.1m	0.1m
Variable production cost per unit	249	249	199	149
Customer service cost per unit	100	100	60	75
Disposal costs				0.2m

Required

What is the expected life cycle cost per unit? $ [   ]

Solution

Activity 2: When costs are determined

Required
When are the bulk of a product's life cycle costs normally determined?

O At the design/development stage

O When the product is introduced to the market

O When the product is in its growth stage

O On disposal

Solution

Activity 3: Calculating life cycle costs

Required

Which of the following items would be included in the calculation of the life cycle costs of a product?

(a)   Planning and concept design costs

(b)   Preliminary and detailed design costs

(c)   Testing costs

(d)   Production costs

(e)   Distribution and customer service costs

○   (b), (c) and (d)

○   (a), (c) and (d)

○   (d) only

○   All of them

Solution

Essential reading

There is no Essential reading for this chapter.

The Essential reading is available as an Appendix of the digital edition of the Workbook.

Chapter summary

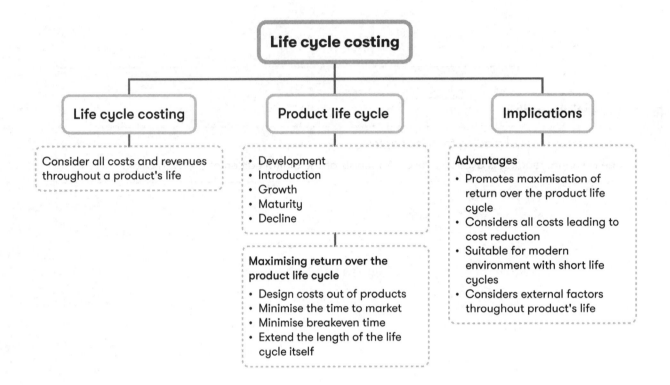

Life cycle costing

- **Life cycle costing**
  - Consider all costs and revenues throughout a product's life

- **Product life cycle**
  - Development
  - Introduction
  - Growth
  - Maturity
  - Decline

  Maximising return over the product life cycle
  - Design costs out of products
  - Minimise the time to market
  - Minimise breakeven time
  - Extend the length of the life cycle itself

- **Implications**

  Advantages
  - Promotes maximisation of return over the product life cycle
  - Considers all costs leading to cost reduction
  - Suitable for modern environment with short life cycles
  - Considers external factors throughout product's life

Knowledge diagnostic

1. Life cycle costing

Life cycle costing considers all costs and revenues of a product throughout its life rather than on a periodic basis.

2. Product life cycle

The product life cycle is divided into five stages:
- Development
- Introduction
- Growth
- Maturity
- Decline

3. Implications

Understanding the product life cycle enables you to price accordingly to either manipulate demand or maximise profit.

Further study guidance

Question practice

Now try the following from the Further question practice bank [available in the digital edition of the Workbook]:

Number	Level	Marks	Approximate time
Section A Q10	Examination	2	4 mins
Section A Q11	Examination	2	4 mins
Section A Q12	Examination	2	4 mins

Further reading

There is a technical article available on ACCA's website, called *Target costing and lifecycle costing*, which discusses target costing and life cycle costing.

You are strongly advised to read this article in full as part of your preparation for the PM exam.

Activity answers

Activity 1: Life cycle cost per unit

The correct answer is:

Required

What is the expected life cycle cost per unit? $321.64

	Year 1	Year 2	Year 3	Year 4	Total
Sales volume (units)	4,000	9,000	30,000	10,000	$m
Total variable cost per unit $	349	349	259	224	
Total variable cost $m	1.396	3.141	7.77	2.24	14.547
Marketing $m	1.2	0.4	0.1	0.1	1.8
Development cost $m	0.5	0	0	0	0.5
Disposal costs $m				0.2	0.2
					17.047
Life cycle cost per unit				53,000	$321.64

Activity 2: When costs are determined

The correct answer is:

At the design/development stage

The bulk of a product's life cycle costs will be determined at the design/development stage (being designed in at the outset during product and process design, plant installation and setting up of the distribution network).

Activity 3: Calculating life cycle costs

The correct answer is:

All of them

Life cycle costs are incurred from design stage through to withdrawal from the market

6 Throughput accounting

Learning objectives

On completion of this chapter, you should be able to:

	Syllabus reference no.
Discuss and apply the theory of constraints.	B4 (a)
Calculate and interpret a throughput accounting ratio (TPAR).	B4 (b)
Suggest how a TPAR could be improved.	B4 (c)

Exam context

Throughput accounting (TA) is the fourth management accounting technique in Section B of the syllabus. It is based on the theory of constraints and is consistent with the use of just-in-time (JIT) production methods. The basic concept in throughput accounting is that an organisation should seek to maximise 'throughput' by identifying and eliminating bottlenecks.

Questions in Section B on this topic are likely to be a mixture of (see later in this Workbook). You can also expect objective test questions on both the theory of constraints and throughput accounting calculations in Section A.

Chapter overview

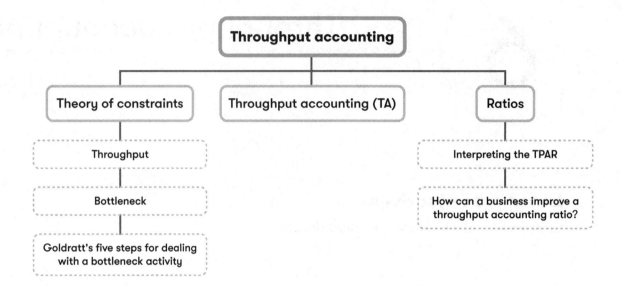

1 Theory of constraints (TOC)

1.1 Throughput

> **Theory of constraints:** The theory of constraints (TOC) is a production system where the key financial concept is the maximisation of throughput while keeping conversion and investment costs to a minimum.
>
> **Throughput contribution** (or throughput return or throughput) = sales revenue - direct material cost

TOC is an **approach to production management** and optimising production performance that was formulated by Goldratt and Cox in the US in 1986. Its key financial concept is to **turn materials into sales** as **quickly** as possible, thereby maximising the net cash generated from sales.

> **Formula to learn**
>
> Throughput = sales revenue − direct material cost

In throughput accounting, **all operational expenses except materials** are assumed to be '**fixed**' costs.

1.2 Bottlenecks

> **Bottleneck resource or binding constraint:** Bottleneck resource (or binding constraint) is a process which has a lower capacity than preceding or subsequent activities, thereby limiting throughput.

The theory of constraints also states that at all times there will be a **bottleneck resource** or factor that sets a limit on the amount of throughput that is possible. This bottleneck resource could in theory be sales demand for an organisation's output, but it is more likely to be a resource that an organisation uses.

One process will inevitably act as a bottleneck and this is known as a binding constraint. Here the bottleneck is component preparation because it can only deal with 50 units per hour whereas materials preparation and final assembly can handle 100 units per hour each.

In the exam, the bottleneck resource is likely to be a production factor, such as machine time or labour time. You may be familiar with the concept of 'limiting factor' in production. A bottleneck resource is a limiting factor. In the theory of constraints and throughput accounting, a bottleneck resource is also known as the **binding constraint**.

Activity 1: Bottleneck

A company passes its products through four production processes and is currently operating at optimal capacity. The following data is available:

Process	Loading	Washing	Drying	Labelling
Time per unit	3 mins	6 mins	1.5 mins	2 mins

Process	Loading	Washing	Drying	Labelling
Machine hours available	800	1,000	450	450

Required

Which process is the bottleneck?

O   Loading

O   Washing

O   Drying

O   Labelling

Solution

1.3   Goldratt's five steps for dealing with a bottleneck activity

The only way to **increase throughput** is to **increase** the **capacity** of the **bottleneck** constraint. All the focus of management attention should be on increasing the capacity of the bottleneck resource, or '**elevating the bottleneck**'.

Goldratt devised a **five-step approach** to summarise the key stages of **TOC**.

Step 1 – **Identify** the binding constraint/bottleneck

Step 2 – **Exploit.** The highest possible output must be achieved from the binding constraint. This output must never be delayed and as such a buffer inventory should be held immediately before the constraint.

Step 3 – **Subordinate.** Operations prior to the binding constraint should operate at the same speed as it so that work in progress (WIP) does not build up.

Step 4 – **Elevate** the system's bottleneck. Steps should be taken to increase resources or improve its efficiency.

Step 5 – **Return to Step 1.** The removal of one bottleneck will create another elsewhere in the system.

1.4   Production scheduling and the bottleneck resource

Taking the theory of constraints a stage further, since there is one bottleneck resource, it follows that all the other resources in production and elsewhere are not bottlenecks. Since production and throughput are limited by the bottleneck resource, it follows that there will be idle capacity for all the other resources.

Idle time should be accepted. Since all operational costs are fixed, idle time is not costing any money.

Resources that are not the bottleneck resource should not be used beyond the amount required for the maximum achievable throughput, given the bottleneck resource. Using non-binding constraints beyond this amount will simply result in a build-up of inventories.

(a) In traditional cost accounting, improving efficiency and creating more inventory will increase profits. Higher inventories reduce the cost of sales and increase reported profits.

(b) In the theory of constraints, using non-bottleneck resources above the amount required for maximum throughput is wasteful. It does not increase throughput; it only increases unused inventory levels.

To avoid the build-up of work in progress, **production must be limited to the capacity of the bottleneck resource** but this capacity must be **fully utilised** as the **focus** should be to **maximise throughput**.

Output through the binding constraint should never be delayed or held up, otherwise sales will be lost. To avoid this happening, a small **buffer inventory** should be built up immediately prior to the bottleneck constraint. This is the only inventory that the business should hold, with the exception of possibly a very small inventory of finished goods and raw materials, which is consistent with a JIT approach.

Operations in the production line prior to the binding constraint should operate at the same speed as the binding constraint, otherwise excess and unwanted work in progress (other than the buffer inventory) will be built up. According to TOC, inventory costs money in terms of storage space and interest costs, and so **inventory is not desirable**.

1.5 Increasing throughput: elevating the bottleneck

The theory of constraints states that the aim should be to maximise total throughput. The only way to increase throughput is to increase the capacity of the bottleneck constraint. All the focus of management attention should be on increasing the capacity of the bottleneck resource, or 'elevating the bottleneck'.

For example, time on Machine Type X may be a bottleneck resource. The only way to increase throughput is to increase the output capacity of Machine Type X. Ways in which this might be done, without buying a new Type X machine, could include:

- Moving from working five days a week to working six or seven days a week
- Moving from working a 12-hour production day to an 18-hour or 24-hour production day
- Carrying out routine maintenance work on the machine outside normal working hours, so that it does not disrupt production

If the capacity of a bottleneck resource is elevated (increased) sufficiently it will eventually cease to be a bottleneck resource. Another resource in the system will become the new bottleneck resource.

The same approach is now used for the new bottleneck resource: maximise total throughput given the restriction of this resource, and seek to increase total throughput by increasing the capacity of the bottleneck resource.

2 Throughout accounting (TA)

> **Throughout accounting: Throughput accounting** is an approach to production management which aims to maximise throughput contribution, while also reducing inventory and operational expenses.

TA is an accounting system based on the theory of constraints. It is very similar to the marginal costing technique (covered in ACCA MA) but uses a different definition of contribution (throughput contribution = sales − direct material costs). It is most appropriate to use in a just-in-time (JIT) environment because of the emphasis on throughput and inventory minimisation.

TA emphasises throughput, inventory minimisation and cost control.

(a) The **only variable cost** is **materials.** All other factory costs are fixed in the short run so this means that **labour** is treated as a **fixed cost in TA.**

(b) In a JIT environment, producing solely for inventory is a bad thing. Products should not be made unless there is a customer for them. This means **accepting some idle time** in non-bottleneck operations. **WIP should be valued at material cost only,** so that no value is added to profit until a sale is made.

(c) Profit is determined by the rate at which throughput can be generated, ie how quickly raw materials can be turned into sales to generate cash. Producing for the sole purpose of increasing inventory creates no profit and so should not be encouraged.

Traditional costing	Throughput accounting
Labour costs and variable overheads are treated as variable costs.	All costs other than materials are seen as fixed in the short term.
Inventory is valued at total production cost.	Inventory is valued at material cost only.
Value is added when an item is produced.	Value is added when an item is sold.
Product profitability can be determined by deducting a product cost from selling price.	Profitability is determined by the rate at which money is earned.

3 Ratios

By evaluating production in a throughput environment, companies can check how a product is 'performing' by comparing the returns it delivers with the costs incurred in producing it. This is done using a throughput accounting ratio (which ACCA abbreviate to **TPAR**) which is the return divided by a comparable cost.

The formulae below compare throughput return and throughput cost on a per-factory-hour basis.

The theory of constraints means that the **throughput** of the factory will be determined by the **speed** of the **bottleneck process.** This is also reflected in the following list:

Formula to learn

(a)

Total factory costs (TFC) = Fixed production costs, including labour

(b)

$$\text{Return per factory hour} = \frac{\text{Sales revenue} - \text{material purchases}}{\text{Time on bottle neck resources}}$$

(c)

$$\text{Cost per factory hour} = \frac{\text{Total factory costs}}{\text{Time on bottleneck resource}}$$

(d)

$$\text{TPAR} = \frac{\text{Rerturn per factory hour}}{\text{Cost per factory hour}}$$

Factory costs or conversion cost: These are all costs **except direct material cost** (ie all costs except totally variable costs).

Exam focus point

It's crucial that you know how to calculate and interpret the throughput accounting ratio (TPAR) for your exam.

Activity 2: TPAR

Each unit of Product B requires four machine hours. Machine time is the bottleneck resource with only 650 machine hours available per week.

Product B is sold for $120 per unit and has a direct material cost of $35 per unit. Total factory costs are $13,000 per week.

Required

What is the TPAR for Product B (to two decimal places)?

Solution

3.1 Interpreting the TPAR

Total throughput should exceed total factory costs otherwise the organisation will make a loss. This means that **the TPAR should exceed 1.0**.

A TPAR that is not much higher than 1.0 is barely profitable. The aim should be to achieve as high a TPAR as possible.

TPARs can also be used to assess the **relative earning capabilities** of different products. Products can be **ranked** in order of **priority for manufacture** and sale **in order of their TPAR**. Higher TPARs should be given priority over lower TPARs. Different divisions of a business can also be ranked based on TPAR.

3.2 How can a business improve a throughput accounting ratio?

In an exam question on throughput accounting, you may be asked about ways in which the TPAR for a product might be increased. The ratio is increased by either:

- Increasing the throughput per bottleneck hour; or

- Reducing the operating cost per bottleneck hour

The TPAR could be increased in any of the following ways:

(a) Increase the selling price for the product. This will increase the throughput per unit, and so will increase the throughput per unit of bottleneck resource.

(b) Reduce the material cost per unit. This will increase the throughput per unit, and so will increase the throughput per unit of bottleneck resource.

(c) Reduce expenditure on operating costs/factory costs. This will reduce the operating cost per unit of bottleneck resource.

(d) Improve efficiency, and increase the number of units or product that are made in each bottleneck hour. This would increase total throughput per hour. The operating costs per hour would be unaffected, therefore the TPAR ratio would increase.

(e) Elevate the bottleneck, so that there are more hours available of the bottleneck resource. Throughput per unit of bottleneck resource would be unaffected but, since operating costs are all fixed costs and there are more bottleneck hours available, the operating cost per bottleneck hour would fall, and the TPAR ratio would increase.

However, there may be adverse consequences from some of these measures.

Measures	Consequences
Increase sales price per unit	Demand for the product may fall
Reduce material costs per unit, eg change materials and/or suppliers	Quality may fall and bulk discounts may be lost
Reduce operating expenses	Quality may fall and/or errors increase

Exam focus point

Make sure you know how a TPAR could be improved as this is specifically mentioned on the syllabus.

Activity 3: Bottleneck and TPAR

MN Co manufactures automated industrial trolleys. Each trolley sells for $2,000 and the material cost per unit is $600. Labour and variable overhead are $5,500 and $8,000 per week respectively. Fixed production costs are $450,000 per year and marketing and administrative costs are $265,000 per year.

The trolleys are made on three different machines. Machine X makes the four frame panels required for each trolley. Its maximum output is 180 frame panels per week. Machine X is old and unreliable and it breaks down from time to time. It is estimated that 20 hours of production are lost per month. Machine Y can manufacture parts for 52 trolleys per week and machine Z, which is old but reasonably reliable, can process and assemble 30 trolleys per week.

The company has recently introduced a just-in-time (JIT) system and it is company policy to hold little work in progress and no finished goods inventory from week to week. The company operates a 40-hour week, 48 weeks a year.

1   **Which is the bottleneck machine?**
    O   Machine X
    O   Machine Y
    O   Machine Z
    O   All of the machines

2   **What is the throughput accounting ratio (TPAR)?**
    O   1.84
    O   3.11

○ 6.67

○ 7.03

Solution

1

2

Activity 4: Improving TPAR

Required

In the theory of constraints and throughput accounting, which THREE of the following actions may be used to improve a throughput accounting ratio?

○ Increase selling price
○ Decrease selling price
○ Buy cheaper materials
○ Reduce time spent on the bottleneck machine
○ Increase time spent on the bottleneck machine

Solution

Activity 5: Capacity and TPAR

Teeth Co is a private cosmetic dental surgery offering two types of teeth whitening procedures: A and B.

Both procedures are carried out by one of three dentists. The surgery also has two receptionists and three dental nurses.

Every patient is first seen by the receptionist, who books them in and completes the paperwork; next by the dentist, who applies the treatment; then finally a dental nurse, who rinses the treatment off. The average length of time spent with each member of staff is as follows:

	Treatment A Hours	Treatment B Hours
Receptionist	0.15	0.25
Dentist	1.25	2.4
Dental nurse	0.5	0.5

The surgery is open for eight hours each day for five days per week. It closes for two weeks each year. Staff salaries per employee are as follows:

Receptionist	$25,000
Dentist	$70,000

Dental Nurse	$30,000

The cost of the products used for procedure A is $40 and $74 for procedure B. Other surgery costs amount to $200,000 each year.

Teeth Co charges $270 for procedure A and $365 for procedure B.

The dentists' time has been correctly identified as the bottleneck activity.

1   **What is the capacity of the bottleneck activity?**

   O   Treatment A: 1,600 and Treatment B: 833

   O   Treatment A: 1,600 and Treatment B: 2,500

   O   Treatment A: 4,800 and Treatment B: 2,500

   O   Treatment A: 4,800 and Treatment B: 4,800

2   **The surgery calculated the cost per hour to be $91.67. What is the throughput accounting ratio (TPAR) for both treatments?**

   O   Treatment A: 2.01 and Treatment B 1.32

   O   Treatment A: 2.01 and Treatment B 3.98

   O   Treatment A: 2.95 and Treatment B 1.32

   O   Treatment A: 2.95 and Treatment B 3.98

3   **Which THREE of the following activities could the surgery use to improve the TPAR?**

   O   Increase the time spent by the bottleneck activity on each treatment

   O   Identify ways to reduce the material costs for the treatments

   O   Increase the level of inventory to prevent stock-outs

   O   Increase the productivity of the receptionists

   O   Improve the control of the surgery's total operating expenses

   O   Apply an increase to the selling price of the services

4   **What would be the effect on the bottleneck if the surgery employed another dentist?**

   O   The dentists' time would be the bottleneck for treatment A only.

   O   The dentists' time would be the bottleneck for treatment B only.

   O   The dentists' time will remain the bottleneck for both treatments.

   O   There will no longer be a bottleneck.

   Solution

1

2

3

4

Exam focus point

We will return to throughput accounting in the context of limiting factors in Chapter 9.

Essential reading

There is no Essential reading for this chapter.

The Essential reading is available as an Appendix of the digital edition of the Workbook.

Chapter summary

```
                    ┌─────────────────────────────┐
                    │   Throughput accounting      │
                    └─────────────────────────────┘
```

Theory of constraints

- Aim is turn materials into sales as quickly as possible
- Focuses on bottlenecks in production that stop throughput maximisation
- In the short-term, all production should be at pace of bottleneck

Throughput

Throughput = sales revenue – direct material cost

Bottleneck

Activity with lower capacity than preceding or subsequent activities, thereby limiting throughput

Goldratt's five steps for dealing with a bottleneck activity

- Identify
- Exploit
- Subordinate
- Elevate
- Return to step one

Throughput accounting (TA)

- Based on the theory of constraints
- Material is the only variable cost
- Operates in a JIT environment
- Only inventory is a small buffer inventory before bottleneck
- WIP valued at material cost only

Ratios

- Return per factory hour = (sales revenue – material purchases)/time on bottleneck resource
- Cost per factory hour = total factory costs/time on bottleneck resource
- TPAR = return per factory hour /cost per factory hour

Interpreting the TPAR

- TPAR should exceed 1
- Products or divisions can be ranked in order of their TPAR (higher = better)

How can a business improve a throughput accounting ratio?

- Increase selling price
- Buy cheaper materials
- Decrease labour/overhead
- Speed up production through the bottleneck

Knowledge diagnostic

1. Throughput accounting and the theory of constraints

Throughput accounting focuses on maximising throughput.

Throughput = sales − materials.

All labour and variable overheads are seen as fixed in the short term.

A **JIT production system** is operated, with some buffer inventory kept only when there is a **bottleneck resource**

2. Ratios

Return per factory hour = (sales revenue - material purchases) / time on the bottleneck resource

Cost per factory hour = total factory costs / time on bottleneck resources

TPAR = return per factory hour / cost per factory hour

TPAR should be as high as possible, and certainly more than 1.0.

3. Improving TPAR

Improving TPAR can be done by:
- Increasing selling price
- Buying cheaper materials
- Decreasing labour
- Decreasing overhead
- Speeding up production through the bottleneck

4. Throughput accounting and decision making

When an organisation makes more than one product, total throughput is maximised by **giving priority to those products that earn the largest throughput per unit of bottleneck resource**. Products should be ranked in order of priority according to their throughput per unit of bottleneck resource

Further study guidance

Question practice

Now try the following from the Further question practice bank [available in the digital edition of the Workbook]:

Number	Level	Marks	Approximate time
Section A Q13	Examination	2	4 mins
Section A Q14	Examination	2	4 mins
Section B Q6–10	Examination	10	18 mins

Further reading

There are two technical articles available on ACCA's website, called *Throughput accounting and the theory of constraints – parts 1 and 2*. The first article summarises the story contained in a book called *The Goal (Goldratt and Cox, 1992)* that presents the theory of constraints and throughput accounting within the context of a novel. The second article talks through a practical approach to questions on throughput accounting.

You are strongly advised to read these articles in full as part of your preparation for the PM exam.

Activity answers

Activity 1: Bottleneck

The correct answer is:

Washing

Operation	Loading Units	Washing Units	Drying Units	Labelling Units
(a) Capacity in mins	(800 × 60)	(1,000 × 60)	(450 × 60)	(450 × 60)
	48,000	60,000	27,000	27,000
(b) Time in minutes per unit	3	6	1.5	2
Capacity in units ((a)/(b))	16,000	10,000	18,000	13,500

Therefore, washing is the bottleneck as it is the process which determines the maximum number of units which can be produced.

Activity 2: TPAR

The correct answer is:

1.06

Return per factory hour = ($120 - $35)/4 = $21.25

Cost per factory hour = $13,000/650 = $20

TPAR = $21.25/$20 = 1.0625 (1.06 to two decimal places)

Activity 3: Bottleneck and TPAR

1   **The correct answer is:**

Machine Z

Machine X		
	loses 20 hours / mth = 5 hours / week	
	loss of 12.5%	
	Max output of panels is therefore 180 − 12.5%	158
	No of trolleys = panels / 4	39
Machine Y		52
Machine Z		30

The bottleneck is therefore Machine Z.

2   **The correct answer is:**

1.84

Return/hr	(2,000 − 600 hours) × 30 trolleys = 42,000	42,000 / 40 =	1,050
Cost/hr	5,500 + 8,000 + (450,000/48) = 22,875		572
TPAR	Return/hour / Cost/hour		1.84

Activity 4: Improving TPAR

The correct answers are:

- Increase selling price
- Buy cheaper materials

- Reduce time spent on the bottleneck machine

In fact, any of the following actions will improve the throughput return:

- Increase selling price
- Buy cheaper materials
- Decrease labour
- Decrease overhead
- Speed up production through the bottleneck

Activity 5: Capacity and TPAR

1 **The correct answer is:**

Treatment A: 4,800 and Treatment B: 2,500

Dentists' hours available per year: 8 hours × 5 days × 50 weeks × 3 dentists = 6,000

Treatment A: 6,000/1.25 = 4,800

Treatment B: 6,000/2.4 = 2,500

2 **The correct answer is:**

Treatment A: 2.01 and Treatment B 1.32

The correct answer is: Treatment A: 2.01 and Treatment B: 1.32

	Treatment A	Treatment B
Throughput contribution	(270 – 40) = 230	(365 – 74) = 291
Bottleneck time per treatment	1.25	2.4
Return per hour	(230/1.25) = 184	(291/2.4) = 121.25
Cost per hour	91.67	91.67
TPAR	(184/91.67) = 2.01	(121.25/91.67) = 1.32

3 **The correct answers are:**

- Identify ways to reduce the material costs for the treatments
- Improve the control of the surgery's total operating expenses
- Apply an increase to the selling price of the services

The factors which are included in the TPAR are the selling price, material costs, operating costs and bottleneck time. Increasing the selling price and reducing costs will therefore lead to an improvement in the TPAR.

Increasing the time spent on the bottleneck activity by each treatment will actually make the TPAR worse, as would increasing the productivity of the stage prior to the bottleneck as this would lead to an increase in WIP.

4 **The correct answer is:**

The dentists' time will remain the bottleneck for both treatments.

	Hours available	Treatment A capacity	Treatment B capacity
Receptionist	4,000	26,667	16,000
Dentist	6,000	4,800	2,500
Dental nurse	6,000	12,000	12,000

BPP
LEARNING
MEDIA

If another dentist was employed, this would add another 2,000 hours per year – meaning they would have the capacity to do another 1,600 treatment As or 833 treatment Bs. This would still mean that dentists' time is the bottleneck activity.

Environmental management accounting

Learning objectives

On completion of this chapter, you should be able to:

	Syllabus reference no.
Discuss the issues businesses face in the management of environmental costs.	B5 (a)
Describe the different methods a business may use to account for its environmental costs.	B5 (b)

Exam context

Environmental accounting is the fifth and final management accounting technique in Section B of the syllabus.

Environmental issues are becoming increasingly important in the business world. Businesses are responsible for the environmental impact of their operations and are becoming increasingly aware of problems such as carbon emissions.

The growth of environmental issues and regulations has also brought greater focus on how businesses **manage** and **account** for environmental costs.

The focus of this chapter is on methods of providing information to management on environmental costs. It does not deal with environmental reporting to shareholders and other stakeholders.

For your exam, you should try to understand the nature of environmental costs, and you should be able to recognise the four methods of environmental management accounting that are described in this chapter. A question on environmental costing could appear in the exam, either in Section A as an objective test (OT) question or in Section B as a scenario question containing five OTs.

Chapter overview

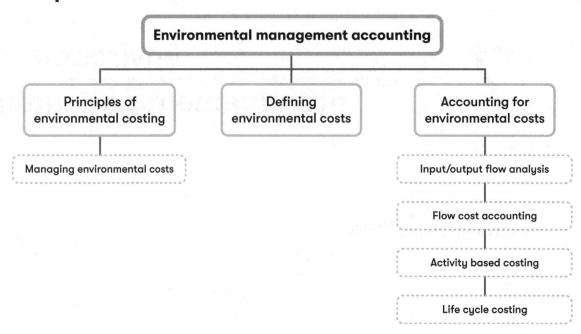

1 Principles of environmental costing

1.1 Managing environmental costs

Management accountants need to be aware of the environmental costs associated with business activities. The general **public** are becoming **more conscious** about the environment and therefore **customer habits** and **choices** are being influenced by **environmental factors** and whether businesses are perceived as being 'green'.

Businesses, however, often face difficulties with **defining, identifying** and **controlling** environmental costs.

Environmental costs such as energy costs are often **treated** as production **overheads** and therefore effectively **hidden** from management scrutiny. As well as being more difficult to identify, environmental costs may also be more difficult to **quantify**. For example, businesses may suffer a loss of **reputation** if problems arise.

Even where environmental costs are captured within accounting systems, the difficulty lies in **pinpointing** them and **allocating** them to a specific product or service. Typical environmental costs are listed below.

- Consumables and raw materials
- Transport and travel
- Waste
- Waste and effluent disposal
- Water consumption
- Energy

Once a business has **defined, identified** and **allocated** environmental costs, it can begin the task of trying to control them through **environmental management systems**.

> **Environmental management accounting (EMA): Environmental management accounting (EMA)** is the generation and analysis of both financial and non-financial information in order to support internal environmental management processes.

1.2 Benefits of understanding environmental costs

Many benefits accrue from a clear understanding and effective management of the environment-related costs of business activities.

(a) Environmental costs may be significant for some companies. Once identified, environmental **costs** can be **controlled** and **reduced**.

(b) There is increasing worldwide **regulation** and a need for regulatory reporting of environmental costs.

(c) Ethical issues – businesses should be aware of how their production methods will affect the environment (eg carbon emissions).

(d) Improved brand image – 'green' ways of doing business can be a selling point.

(e) Associating environmental costs with individual products will lead to more accurate pricing and improved profitability.

Activity 1: Environmental budget cost

Raxo plc is a multinational organisation, manufacturing chemicals for use in the agricultural industry.

Required
Which of the following environmental costs should NOT be included in an environmental cost budget?

○ Cost of disposal of unused raw materials

○ Cost of fines for environmental contamination

○ Cost of disposal of chemical packaging

○ Cost of using pollution-prevention methods and technology

Solution

2 Defining environmental costs

Definitions of environmental costs vary widely. This can make it difficult to identify the costs involved and therefore control them. They may be hidden inside 'general overheads'.

Hansen and Mendoza (1999) suggested that environmental costs could be classified as:

Classification	Definition	Examples
Environmental prevention costs	Costs of activities undertaken to **prevent** environmental **impacts** before they occur	Forming environmental policies Performing site and feasibility studies Staff training
Environmental detection costs	Costs involved with establishing whether activities **comply** with environmental **standards** and policies	Developing performance measures Monitoring, testing and inspection costs Site survey costs
Environmental internal failure costs	Costs of activities that must be undertaken when contaminants and waste have been created by a business but **not released** into the environment	Maintaining pollution equipment Recycling scrap
Environmental external failure costs	Costs that arise when a business **releases** harmful **waste** into the environment	Cleaning up oil spills Decontaminating land

To aid comparison with future periods, the environmental costs should also be expressed as a percentage of turnover or operating costs.

The US Environmental Protection Agency (1998) as cited by ACCA (2016) defined the following costs:

Classification	Definition	Examples
Conventional costs	Ordinary use of equipment, material and overhead costs where the environment would benefit from decreased use	Electricity
Potentially hidden costs	Costs hidden in overheads	Design cost of more environmentally friendly processes
Contingent costs	Costs that may be incurred at a later date	Decontaminating land
Image and relationship costs	Costs incurred to manage perception/image	Tree planting

Much business activity takes place at the cost of the environment, and some of these costs are felt by society as a whole. **Externalised costs** are those for which wider society has to 'pay' at least an element – eg global warming. Costs can also be classified as **internalised** in that the impacts are contained within the organisation.

Activity 2: Environmental costs

Required
Which of the following is an example of an environmental external failure cost?

- ○ Maintaining pollution equipment
- ○ Decontaminating land
- ○ Recycling scrap
- ○ Record keeping

Solution

3 Accounting for environmental costs

The PM syllabus is concerned with information for **internal** decision making only. It is not concerned with how environmental information is reported externally.

There are a range of management accounting techniques for the identification and allocation of environmental costs. The United Nations Division for Sustainable Development (UNDSD, 2003) as cited by ACCA (2016) identified four techniques.

3.1 Input/output flow analysis

The idea of this analysis is that what comes in, must go out. Material inflows are recorded and balanced with outflows. This forces the business to account for the difference between material input and material output and focus on environmental costs.

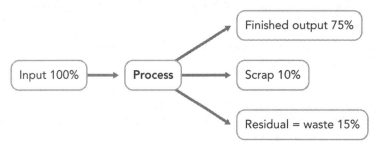

3.2 Flow cost accounting

Material flows through an organisation are divided into three categories.

* Material
* System and delivery
* Disposal

The value and cost of each material flow is then calculated. The aim is to reduce the **quantity of materials** thereby **saving costs.**

3.3 Activity based costing

In order to fully integrate environmental costs into their management accounting, organisations can apply activity based costing principles to environmental costs.

Environmental costs would be grouped together into environmental cost pools, and each pool would be associated with an environmental cost driver.

Individual products that passed through the most polluting processes would therefore absorb more environmental costs than cleaner or more 'green' products.

As for ABC in general, this will lead to:

(a) Increased awareness of how environmental costs behave

(b) Better product pricing

(c) Better production decisions

KEY TERM

Environment related costs: Environment related costs are costs that can be attributed to a cost centre such as a waste treatment centre.

Environmental driven costs: Environment driven costs are costs that are caused by events in the environment but usually hidden in general overheads, such as an increase in electricity costs.

3.4 Life cycle costing

Environmental costs are considered from the design stage of a new product right up to the end of life costs such as decommissioning and removal.

The consideration of future disposal or remediation costs at the design stage may influence the design of the product itself, saving on future costs.

Essential reading

There is no Essential reading for this chapter.

The Essential reading is available as an Appendix of the digital edition of the Workbook.

Chapter summary

Environmental management accounting

Principles of environmental costing

Managing environmental costs

Historically environmental costs were treated as production overheads and effectively hidden

Defining environmental costs

- Environmental prevention costs
- Environmental detection costs
- Environmental internal failure costs
- Environmental external failure costs

Accounting for environmental costs

Input/output flow analysis
- What comes in, must go out
- Material inflows are balanced with outflows

Flow cost accounting
- Material flows are divided into
  - Material
  - System and delivery
  - Disposal

Activity based costing

Using environmental cost pools

Life cycle costing

Environmental costs are considered from design stage to end of life

Knowledge diagnostic

1. Principles of environmental costing

Environmental costs need to be clearly understood by management, and not 'hidden' in with production overheads.

2. Defining environmental costs

Prevention, detection, internal failure, external failure.

Conventional, potentially hidden, contingent, image and relationship.

3. Accounting for environmental costs

There are four management accounting techniques for the identification and allocation of environmental costs: input/output analysis, flow cost accounting, activity based costing and life cycle costing.

Further study guidance

Question practice

Now try the following from the Further question practice bank [available in the digital edition of the Workbook]:

Number	Level	Marks	Approximate time
Section A Q15	Examination	2	4 mins
Section A Q16	Examination	2	4 mins
Section A Q17	Examination	2	4 mins
Section A Q18	Examination	2	4 mins

Further reading

There is a technical article available on ACCA's website, called *Environmental management accounting*, which covers this topic.

You are strongly advised to read this article in full as part of your preparation for the PM exam.

Activity answers

Activity 1: Environmental budget cost

The correct answer is:

Cost of fines for environmental contamination

A company may incur costs for contamination of the environment, but this cost should not be included within budgeted environmental costs as this implies that it is an acceptable cost.

Activity 2: Environmental costs

The correct answer is:

Decontaminating land

Skills checkpoint 1

Approach to objective test (OT) questions

Chapter overview

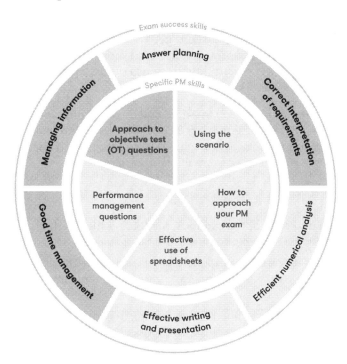

Introduction

Sections A and B of the PM exam will contain OTs worth 60 marks (ie 60% of your exam) and therefore being able to answer OT questions effectively is extremely important.

The 'specialist cost and management accounting techniques' area of the syllabus will only be examined in OT questions in Section A and B. These areas include: Activity-based costing, Target costing, Life cycle costing, Throughput accounting and Environmental accounting. You should be prepared for at least one of the Section B case questions, containing five OTs, to be on these topics.

Section A – Single OT questions

OT questions are single, short questions that are auto-marked and worth two marks each. You must answer the whole question correctly to earn their two marks. There are no partial marks.

The OT questions in Section A aim for a broad coverage of the syllabus, and so all areas of the syllabus need to be carefully studied. You need to work through as many practice objective test questions as possible, reviewing carefully to see how correct answers are derived.

The following types of OT questions commonly appear in the PM exam:

Question type	Explanation
Multiple choice (MCQ)	You need to choose one correct answer from four given response options.
Multiple response options (MRO)	These are a type of multiple-choice question where you need to select more than one answer from a number of given options. The question will specify how many answers need to be selected. It is important to read the requirement carefully.
Fill in the blank (FIB)	This question type requires you to type a numerical answer into a box. The unit of measurement (eg $) will sit outside the box, and if there are specific rounding requirements these will be displayed. You must follow any rounding requirements shown - this is very important!
Drag and drop	Drag and drop questions involve you dragging an answer and dropping it into place. Some questions could involve matching more than one answer to a response area and some questions may have more answer choices than response areas, which means not all available answer choices need to be used.
Drop down list	This question type requires you to select one answer from a drop-down list. Some of these questions may contain more than one drop down list and an answer has to be selected from each one. This requires the same skills as a multiple-choice question.

Section B – OT Case questions

As with Section A, questions can come from any area of the syllabus, reinforcing the need for candidates to study the whole syllabus. Section B will include three OT case questions.

Each OT Case contains a group of five OT questions based around a single scenario. These can be any combination of the single OT question types and they are auto-marked in the same way as the single OT questions.

OT Cases are worth ten marks (each of the five OTs contained within are worth two marks, and as with the OT questions described above, students will receive either two marks or zero marks for those individual questions).

OT cases are written so that there are no dependencies between the individual questions. So, if you did get the first question wrong, this does not affect your ability to get the other four correct. The OT Case scenario remains on-screen so you can see it while answering the questions.

Each OT case normally consists of three numerical and two discursive style questions. It is often quicker to tackle the discursive questions first leaving some additional time to tackle calculations.

You don't need to show any workings in OT answers, but you will probably have to write down some workings to help you answer calculation questions. You will be given scrap paper in the exam for this purpose and it will be collected and thrown away afterwards. Although you do not need to produce neat and tidy workings because no-one else will see them, it is worth labelling your workings with the question number so that if you have time at the end, you can go back and check them. Note that the exam software contains a 'flag' functionality, meaning that you can flag any questions that you want to return to and review, if you have spare time at the end.

Approach to OT questions

PM Skill: Approach to OT questions

A step-by-step technique for approaching OT questions is outlined below. Each step will be explained in more detail in the following sections as the OT case question, 'Triple Co' is answered in stages.

> **General guidance for approaching OT questions**
>
> **STEP 1: Answer the questions you know first.**
>
> If you're having difficulty answering a question, move on and come back to tackle it once you've answered all the questions you know.
>
> It is often quicker to answer discursive style OT questions first, leaving more time for calculations.

> **General guidance for approaching OT questions**
>
> **STEP 2: Answer all questions.**
>
> There is no penalty for an incorrect answer in ACCA exams; there is nothing to be gained by leaving an OT question unanswered. If you are stuck on a question, as a last resort, it is worth selecting the option you consider most likely to be correct and moving on. Make a note of the question, so if you have time after you have answered the rest of the questions, you can revisit it.

> **Guidance for answering specific OT questions**
>
> **STEP 3: Read the requirement first!**
>
> The requirement will be stated in bold text in the exam. Identify what you are being asked to do, any technical knowledge required and **what type of OT question** you are dealing with. Look for key words in the requirement such as "which **TWO** of the following," "which of the following is **NOT**"

> **Guidance for answering specific OT questions**
>
> **STEP 4: Apply your technical knowledge to the data presented in the question.**
>
> Take your time working through questions, and make sure to read through each answer option with care. OT questions are designed so that each answer option is plausible. Work through each response option and eliminate those you know are incorrect.

Exam success skills

The following question is a Section B OT case question from a past exam worth ten marks.

For this question, we will also focus on the following **exam success skills**:

- **Managing information.** It is easy for the amount of information contained in an OT case question in Section B to feel a little overwhelming. **Active reading** is a useful technique to avoid this. This involves focusing on each of the five requirements first on the basis that, until you have done this, the detail in the question will have little meaning and will seem more intimidating.

Focus on the requirements, noting key verbs to ensure you understand the requirement properly, and correctly identify what type of OT question you are dealing with. Then read the rest of the scenario, making a note of important and relevant information and technical information you think you will need.

Remember that Sections A and B are computer marked and so your answer will be either right or wrong. If you misread the information, you could be wasting valuable time as well as choosing the wrong answer.

- **Correct interpretation of requirements.** Identify from the requirement the different types of OT question. This is especially important with multiple response options (MRO) to ensure you select the correct number of response options.

- **Good time management.** Complete all OTs in the time available. Each OT is worth two marks and should be allocated 3.6 minutes. A whole Section B question should take 18 minutes.

Skill activity

The following scenario relates to Questions 1 to 5.

Triple Co makes three types of gold watch: the Diva (D), the Classic (C) and the Poser (P). A traditional absorption costing system is used at present, although an activity-based costing (ABC) system is being considered. Details of the product lines for a typical period are:

	Hours per unit		Materials	Production
	Labour hours	Machine hours	Cost per unit	Units
			$	
Product D	0.5	1.5	20	750
Product C	1.5	1	15	1,250
Product P	1	3	10	7,000

Direct labour costs $6 per hour and production overheads are absorbed on a machine hour basis. The overhead absorption rate for the period is $28 per machine hour.

Total production overheads are $654,500 and further analysis shows that the total production overheads can be divided as follows:

	%
Costs relating to machinery	20
Costs relating to materials handling	15

The following total activity volumes are associated with each product line for the period as a whole:

	Number of movements of materials
Product D	12
Product C	21
Product P	87
	120

(a) **What is the cost per unit for Product D using the current absorption costing system?*** Give your answer to two decimal places. **(2 marks)**

$ _____ per unit

* This is a FIB question, and so it is important you insert your answer to two decimal places (as stated). A calculation of the cost per unit under absorption costing is required. This is brought forward knowledge from ACCA Management Accounting.

(b) **What is the total amount of machining overhead that would be allocated to Product C for the period using ABC?*(2 marks)**

- $7,000
- $23,375
- $23,800
- $35,000

* This is an MCQ requiring one correct answer to be selected. A calculation of overhead cost using ABC is required. Remember that the distracters (incorrect answers) are numbers that you will obtain if you make a particular mistake. Do not look at the options until you have finished the calculation as it is possible that a "part finished calculation" is one of the incorrect distracters.

(c) **What is the overhead assigned to Product D in respect of materials handling using ABC?*** Give your answer to the nearest hundred $. **(2 marks)**

$

* This is another FIB question and you need to enter your answer to the nearest hundred $.

(d) **Triple Co is attempting to identify the correct cost driver for a cost pool called quality control. Using the drop down list below, which would be the correct cost driver to use?*(2 marks)**

Select...
Number of units produced
Number of inspections
Labour hours
Number of machine set ups

* This is drop down list question. Like an MCQ, you need to select one correct answer.

(e) **If Triple Co decides to adopt ABC, which of the following is a disadvantage that Triple Co may encounter as a result of this decision*?(2 marks)**

- ABC can only be applied to production overheads.
- The cost per unit may not be as accurate as it was under traditional absorption costing.
- The benefits obtained from ABC might not justify the costs.
- It will not provide much insight into what drives overhead costs. **(Total = 10 marks)**

* This is another MCQ and you need to correctly select one disadvantage of adopting ABC.

STEP 1 **Answer the questions you know first.**

If you are having difficulty answering a question, move on and come back to tackle it once you have answered all the questions you know. It is often quicker to answer discursive style OT questions first, leaving more time for calculations.

Questions 4 and 5 are discursive style questions. It would make sense to answer these two questions first as it is likely that you will be able to complete them comfortably within the 7.2 minutes allocated to them. Any time saved could then be spent on the more complex calculations required to answer questions 1, 2 and 3.

STEP 2 **Answer all questions.**

There is no penalty for an incorrect answer in ACCA exams so there is nothing to be gained by leaving an OT question unanswered. If you are stuck on a question, as a last resort, it is worth selecting the option you consider most likely to be correct, and moving on. Make a note of the question, so if you have time after you have answered the rest of the questions, you can revisit it.

Two of the five questions in the OT case are MCQs and one is a drop down list question. With these types of questions, you have a 25% chance of getting the question correct so do not leave any unanswered. It is obviously more difficult to get a fill in the blank question (like Questions 1 and 3) correct by guessing.

STEP 3 **Read the requirement first!**

The requirement will be stated in bold text in the exam. Identify what you are being asked to do, any technical knowledge required and **what type of OT question** you are dealing with. Look for key words in the requirement such as 'Which TWO of the following...', 'Which of the following is NOT...'

Questions 1 and 3 are FIB questions and so you need to follow the instructions carefully and insert your answer to the correct number of decimal places. Question 5 asks you to identify which statements is a disadvantage of adopting ABC. Read through each statement carefully knowing that you are looking to identify the **disadvantage**.

STEP 4 **Apply your technical knowledge to the data presented in the question.**

Take your time working through calculations, and be sure to read through each answer option with care. OT questions are designed so that each answer option is plausible. Work through each response option and eliminate those you know are incorrect.

To answer Questions 1, 2 and 3, you need to analyse the data given in the question.

Let's look at Question 1 in detail.

The question asks you to calculate the absorption cost per unit for product D. You will therefore need to find all the costs for D (materials and labour) from the data in the question, as well as the absorption rate and basis.

Triple Co makes three types of gold watch: the Diva (D), the Classic (C) and the Poser (P). A traditional absorption costing system is used at present, although an activity-based costing (ABC) system is being considered. Details of the product lines for a typical period are:

| | Hours per unit | | Materials | Production |
	Labour hours	Machine hours	Cost per unit	Units
			$	
Product D	½	1½	20	750
Product C	1½	1	15	1,250
Product P	1	3	10	7,000

Direct labour costs $6 per hour and production overheads are absorbed on a machine hour basis. The overhead absorption rate for the period is $28 per machine hour.

Total production overheads are $654,500 and further analysis shows that the total production overheads can be divided as follows:

	%
Costs relating to machinery	20
Costs relating to materials handling	15

The following total activity volumes are associated with each product line for the period as a whole:

	Number of movements of materials
Product D	12
Product C	21
Product P	87
	120

(a) **What is the cost per unit for Product D using the current absorption costing system?** Give your answer to two decimal places. **(2 marks)**

$ per unit

Using all the information, the correct answer is $65.00 per unit.

Traditional absorption cost per unit

	Product D
	$
Material	20.00
Labour @ $6 per hour	3.00
Direct costs	23.00
Production overhead @ $28 per machine hour	42.00
Total production cost per unit	65.00

Let's look briefly at Question 2.

(b) **What is the total amount of machining overhead that would be allocated to Product C for the period using ABC? (2 marks)**

- $7,000
- £23,375 ($23,375 is incorrect. 23,375 is the total number of machine hours).
- $23,800 ($23,800 is incorrect. This is the figure you will get if you forget to multiply the machine hours by the number of units of production. ($130,900 / 5.5 hours) x 1 hour = $23,800).

- $35,000 ($35,000 is incorrect. This is the figure you will get if you forget to multiply the overheads by 20%. ($654,500 / 23,375 hours) x 1,250 = $35,000)

The correct answer is: $7,000.

Product C uses 1,250 machine hours (W1) × $5.60 per hour (W2) = $7,000

Workings

(1) Total machine hours (needed as the driver for machining overhead)

Product	Hours/unit	Production units	Total hours
D	1½	750	1,125
C	1	1,250	1,250
P	3	7,000	21,000
Total machine hours			23,375

(2)

Type of overhead	Driver	%	Total overhead	Level of driver activity	Cost/driver
Machining	Machine hours	20	$130,900	23,375 (W1)	$5.60

To answer Question 5, you can start by eliminating the response options that you know are not disadvantages.

If Triple Co decides to adopt ABC, which of the following is a disadvantage that Triple Co may encounter as a result of this decision? (2 marks)

- ABC can only be applied to production overheads*.
- The cost per unit may not be as accurate as it was under traditional absorption costing because multiple OARs are calculated**.
- The benefits obtained from ABC might not justify the costs.
- It will not provide much insight into what drives overhead costs because each cost pool has its own OAR***.

* ABC can be applied to all overheads, not just production overheads.

** The cost per unit provided under ABC principles will be more accurate.

*** ABC costing will provide much better insight into what drives overhead costs.

The answers to the other questions are:

3 The correct answer is: $9,800 (to the nearest hundred $).

Type of overhead	Driver	%	Total overhead	Level of driver activity	Cost/driver
Materials handling	Material movements	15	98,175	120	818.13

Product D

Activity	Level of activity	Cost
Material handling	12	818.13 × 12 = 9,818

4 The correct answer is: Number of inspections

The number of inspections per product is likely to be the main driver of quality control costs. The number of set ups is unlikely to have an effect on the quality control costs. Some product lines may require more inspections than others, therefore 'number of units produced' is not sufficient to use as the cost driver. Labour hours will not reflect the quality control aspect of individual products.

Exam success skills diagnostic

Every time you complete a question, use the diagnostic below to assess how effectively you demonstrated the exam success skills in answering the question. The table has been completed below for the Triple Co activity to give you an idea of how to complete the diagnostic.

Exam success skills	Your reflections/observations
Managing information	Did you read each of the five requirements first? Did you actively read the scenario making a note of relevant data required such as the absorption rate and absorption basis?
Correct interpretation of requirements	Did you identify the correct technical knowledge needed to answer each requirement? For example, using the correct cost drivers to answer Questions 2 and 3. Did you identify what type of OT question you were dealing with? For example, knowing that only one correct answer is required for a multiple-choice question. Did you identify how accurate the answer should be in the FIB questions? For example, Q1 required the answer to two decimal places, whereas Q3 required the answer to the nearest $100.
Good time management	Did you manage to answer all five questions within 18 mins? Did you manage your time well by answering Questions 4 and 5 first?
Most important action points to apply to your next question	

Summary

60% of the PM exam consists of OT questions. Key skills to focus on throughout your studies will therefore include:

- Always reading the requirements first to identify what you are being asked to do and what type of OT question you are dealing with
- Actively reading the scenario, making a note of key data needed to answer each requirement
- Answering OT questions in a sensible order, dealing with any easier discursive style questions first

8

Cost volume profit (CVP) analysis

Learning objectives

On completion of this chapter, you should be able to:

	Syllabus reference no.
Explain the nature of CVP analysis.	C2 (a)
Calculate and interpret the breakeven point and margin of safety.	C2 (b)
Calculate the contribution to sales ratio, in single and multi-product situations, and demonstrate an understanding of its use.	C2 (c)
Calculate target profit or revenue in single and multi-product situations, and demonstrate an understanding of its use.	C2 (d)
Interpret breakeven charts and profit volume charts and interpret the information contained within each, including multi-product situations.	C2 (e)
Discuss the limitations of CVP analysis for planning and decision-making.	C2 (f)

Exam context

You will have already encountered cost volume profit (CVP) analysis (also known as breakeven analysis) in your earlier studies, so you should be reasonably familiar with the terminology or basic techniques that you will meet in this chapter. The PM syllabus moves on to multi-product CVP analysis.

CVP analysis could appear in any section of the PM exam.

Chapter overview

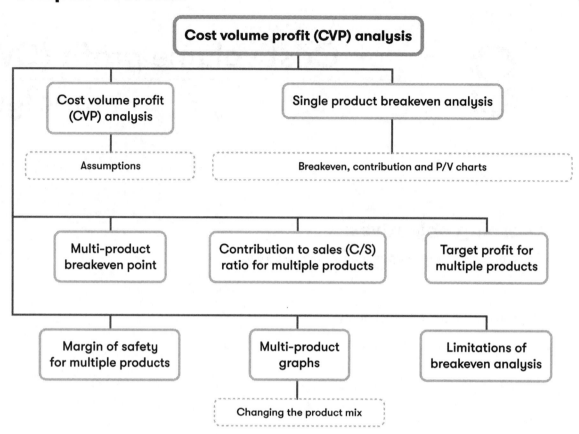

1 Cost volume profit analysis (CVP analysis)

CVP analysis looks at the effects of differing levels of activity on the financial results of a business by examining the **relationship** between **sales volume** and **profit**.

Most businesses need to at least break even when setting prices and output levels. The **breakeven point** for a company is the sales volume which will give the company a profit of $nil. If sales exceed the breakeven point the company will make a profit.

> **Breakeven point: Breakeven point** is the level of sales at which there is neither profit nor loss.

1.1 Assumptions

(a) CVP analysis can apply to one product only, or to more than one product if they are sold in a fixed sales mix (**fixed proportions**).

(b) **Fixed costs** per period are **same in total**, and **unit variable costs** are a **constant** amount at all levels of output and sales.

(c) **Sales prices** per unit are **constant** at all levels of activity.

(d) **Production** volume = **sales** volume.

These assumptions lead to linear relationships for volume and sales revenue.

2 Single product breakeven analysis

> **Formula to learn**
>
> Contribution per unit = unit selling price - unit variable costs
> Breakeven point (BEP)
>
> $$\text{Breakeven point (BEP)} = \frac{\text{Fixed costs}}{\text{Unit contribution}}$$

The **ratio of contribution to sales** is an alternative method of finding the breakeven point. It gives the amount of contribution earned per dollar of sales. It can be measured as a fraction or a percentage.

It is also known as the profit-volume (P/V) ratio and can be used to determine breakeven revenue.

> **Formula to learn**
>
> Contribution/Sales ratio
>
> $$\text{Contribution/Sales ratio} = \frac{\text{Contribution per unit}}{\text{Selling price per unit}}$$
>
> Breakeven revenue = fixed costs / C/S ratio or breakeven point × selling price per unit

The **margin of safety** is a measure of the amount by which sales must fall before we start making a loss. A loss is made if sales volume is less than the BEP.

> **Formula to learn**
>
> Margin of safety = budgeted sales - breakeven sales
>
> $$\text{Margin of safety (\%)} = \frac{\text{Budgeted sales - Breakeven sales}}{\text{Budgeted sales}}$$

The approach used to find an expression for the breakeven sales volumes can be extended to find the volume needed to attain a **required profit** level.

The required profit is like an additional fixed cost which must be covered before the company 'breaks even'.

Formula to learn

Output required for target profit

$$\text{Output required for target profit} = \frac{\text{Fixed costs} + \text{target profit}}{\text{Unit contribution}}$$

Activity 1: Revision of single product CVP analysis

A company has fixed costs of $5,700 and variable costs per unit of $6.50.

(a) If the selling price is $8.00 per unit at all levels, what is the breakeven point (in units)?

(b) What is the breakeven revenue?

(c) What is the C/S ratio?

(d) If budgeted sales are 5,000 units, what is the margin of safety in units?

(e) What is the margin of safety as a %? What does this mean?

(f) What is the sales volume (in units) required to make a profit of $10,000?

Solution

1

BPP
LEARNING
MEDIA

2.1 Breakeven, contribution and P/V charts

Breakeven chart

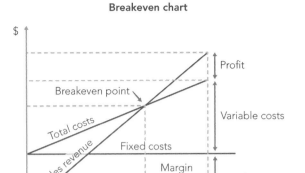

Contribution (contribution breakeven) chart

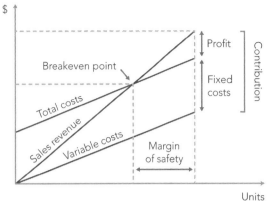

Profit/volume (P/V) chart

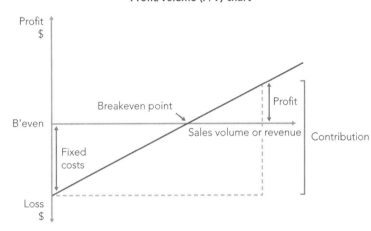

The gradient of the straight line is the contribution per unit (if the horizontal axis is measured in sales value).

2.1.1 Breakeven chart

The breakeven point can also be determined graphically using a breakeven chart.

This shows the relationship between revenue, costs and sales volume.

Activity 2: Breakeven chart

The breakeven chart for the data in Activity 1 has been sketched.

1 Required

Match the following labels to the letters on the graph

- Total cost line
- Margin of safety
- Breakeven point
- Total revenue line

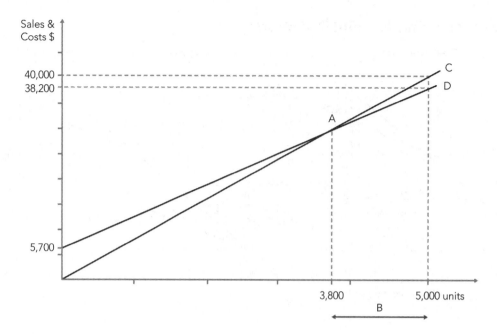

Solution

1

We can also draw a contribution graph which shows that the gap between the total revenue line and the variable cost line is the contribution:

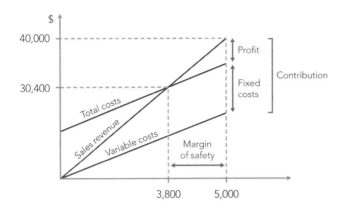

2.1.2 Profit volume chart

The profit volume chart is an alternative to the breakeven chart as it illustrates the relationship between profits and sales. It emphasises the impact of changes in volume on profit.

Activity 3: Profit volume chart

The following is a sketch of the profit volume chart for Activity 1.

Required

What does the letter Z represent?

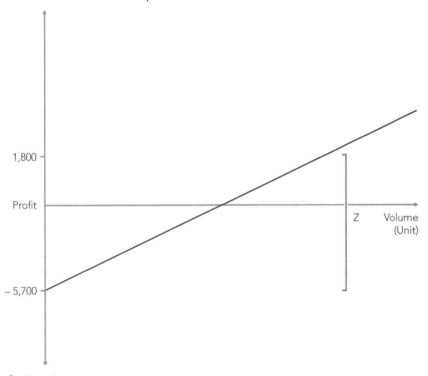

○ Breakeven point
○ Fixed costs
○ Profit
○ Contribution

Solution

3 Multi-product breakeven point

Breakeven analysis can be expanded for a 'single' mix of products using a weighted average contribution figure. A **constant product sales mix** must be assumed.

Formula to learn

$$\text{Breakeven point} = \frac{\text{Fixed costs}}{\text{Weighted average unit contribution}}$$

$$\text{Breakeven revenue} = \frac{\text{Fixed costs}}{\text{Weighted average C/S ratio}}$$

Illustration 1: Breakeven point for multiple products

Suppose that PL produces and sells two products. The M sells for $7 per unit and has a total variable cost of $2.94 per unit, while the N sells for $15 per unit and has a total variable cost of $4.50 per unit. The marketing department has estimated that for every five units of M sold, one unit of N will be sold. The organisation's fixed costs total $36,000.

Required
What is the total breakeven revenue?

$ [   ]

Solution

The correct answer is:

$58,450

We calculate the breakeven point as follows:

Step 1 Calculate contribution per unit

	M	N
	$ per unit	$ per unit
Selling price	7.00	15.00
Variable cost	2.94	4.50
Contribution	4.06	10.50

Step 2 Calculate contribution per mix

A mix in this question is 5 Ms and 1 N

= ($4.06 × 5) + ($10.50 × 1) = $30.80

Step 3 Calculate the breakeven point in terms of the number of mixes

= fixed costs/contribution per mix = $36,000/$30.80

= 1,169 mixes (rounded)

Step 4 Calculate the breakeven point in terms of the number of units of the products

= (1,169 × 5) 5,845 units of M and (1,169 × 1) 1,169 units of N (rounded)

Step 5 Calculate the breakeven point in terms of revenue

= (5,845 × $7) + (1,169 × $15)

= $40,915 of M and $17,535 of N = $58,450 in total

It is important to note that the breakeven point is not $58,450 of revenue, whatever the mix of products. The breakeven point is $58,450 provided that the sales mix remains 5:1. Likewise, the breakeven point is not at a production/sales level of (5,845 + 1,169) 7,014 units. Rather, it is when 5,845 units of M and 1,169 units of N are sold, assuming a sales mix of 5:1.

Activity 4: Multi-product breakeven point

United Trading sells three products as follows:

Product	Footballs	Baseballs	Rugby balls
	$	$	$
Selling price	7.00	6.00	9.00
Variable costs	3.00	4.50	5.00
Budgeted sales (units)	2,000	4,000	3,000

Assume that the sales mix is 'fixed' in these proportions. Fixed costs are $20,000.

1   Required

What is the breakeven sales volume? ☐ units

2   Required

What is the breakeven sales revenue? $ ☐

Solution

1

4 Contribution to sales (C/S) ratio for multiple products

The C/S ratio can be used to calculate the breakeven point in terms of sales revenue for single products and this is also the case when there are multiple products.

Illustration 2: C/S ratio for multiple products

1 We can calculate the C/S ratio and use it to calculate the breakeven point of PL (see Illustration 1).

Step 1 Calculate revenue per mix

= (5 × $7) + (1 × $15) = $50

Step 2 Calculate contribution per mix

= $30.80 (see Illustration 1)

Step 3 Calculate average C/S ratio

= ($30.80/$50.00) × 100% = 61.6%

Step 4 Calculate breakeven point (total)

= fixed costs ÷ C/S ratio

= $36,000/0.616 = $58,442 (rounded)

Step 5 Calculate revenue ratio of mix

= $35:$15, or 7:3

This shows that 7 out of every 10 products sold will be an M.

Step 6 Calculate breakeven revenue and breakeven point

Breakeven revenue M = $58,442 × 7/10 = $40,909 (rounded)

Breakeven point M = $40,090 / $7 = 5,844 units

Breakeven revenue N = $58,442 × 3/10 = $17,533 (rounded)

Breakeven point N = $17,533 / $15 = 1,169 units

Total breakeven revenue = $58,442

Solution

1 **The correct answer is:**

Total breakeven revenue = $58,442

Activity 5: Using the average C/S ratio

Alpha manufactures and sells three products: the Beta, the Gamma and the Delta. Relevant information is as follows:

	Beta	Gamma	Delta
	$ per unit	$ per unit	$ per unit
Selling price	135.00	165.00	220.00
Variable cost	73.50	58.90	146.20

Total fixed costs are $950,000.

An analysis of past trading patterns indicates that the products are sold in the ratio 3:4:5.

1 **Required**

Calculate the breakeven sales revenue of products Beta, Gamma and Delta using the approach shown above.

Beta = $

Gamma = $

Delta = $

Solution

1

5 Target profit for multiple products

The same technique that we have been applying can be used to ensure that a required profit is achieved, by adding the target profit to the fixed costs when calculating the level of sales required.

Illustration 3: Target profit for multiple products

An organisation makes and sells three products: F, G and H. The products are sold in the proportions F:G:H = 2:1:3. The organisation's fixed costs are $80,000 per month and details of the products are as follows:

Product	Selling price $ per unit	Variable cost $ per unit
F	22	16
G	15	12
H	19	13

The organisation wishes to earn a profit of $52,000 next month.

1 Required

Calculate the required sales value of each product in order to achieve this target profit.

F   =

G   =

H   =

Solution

1 The correct answer is:

Step 1 Calculate contribution per unit

	F $ per unit	G $ per unit	H $ per unit
Selling price	22	15	19
Variable cost	16	12	13
Contribution	6	3	6

Step 2 Calculate contribution per mix

= ($6 × 2) + ($3 × 1) + ($6 × 3) = $33

Step 3 Calculate the required number of mixes

= (Fixed costs + required profit)/contribution per mix

= ($80,000 + $52,000)/$33

= 4,000 mixes

Step 4 Calculate the required sales in terms of the number of units of the products and sales revenue of each product

Product	Units		Selling price	Sales revenue required
			$ per unit	$
F	4,000 × 2	8,000	22	176,000
G	4,000 × 1	4,000	15	60,000
H	4,000 × 3	12,000	19	228,000
Total				464,000

The sales revenue of $464,000 will generate a profit of $52,000 if the products are sold in the mix 2:1:3.

Alternatively, the C/S ratio could be used to determine the required sales revenue for a profit of $52,000. The method is again similar to that demonstrated earlier when calculating the breakeven point.

6 Margin of safety for multiple products

 Illustration 4: Margin of safety for multiple products

BA produces and sells two products. The W sells for $8 per unit and has a total variable cost of $3.80 per unit, while the R sells for $14 per unit and has a total variable cost of $4.20. For every five units of W sold, 6 units of R are sold. BA's fixed costs are $43,890 per period.

Budgeted sales revenue for next period is $74,400, in the standard mix.

1 Calculate the margin of safety in terms of sales revenue and also as a percentage of budgeted sales revenue.

M of S = $ sales in total

M of S =   % of budgeted sales (to one decimal place)

Solution

1 The correct answer is:

To calculate the margin of safety, we must first determine the breakeven point.

Step 1 Calculate contribution per unit

	W	R
	$ per unit	$ per unit
Selling price	8.00	14.00
Variable cost	3.80	4.20
Contribution	4.20	9.80

Step 2 Calculate contribution per mix

= ($4.20 × 5) + ($9.80 × 6) = $79.80

Step 3 Calculate the breakeven point in terms of the number of mixes

= fixed costs/contribution per mix = $43,890/$79.80

= 550 mixes

Step 4 Calculate the breakeven point in terms of the number of units of the products

= (550 × 5) 2,750 units of W and (550 × 6) 3,300 units of R

Step 5 Calculate the breakeven point in terms of revenue

= (2,750 × $8) + (3,300 × $14)

= $22,000 of W and $46,200 of R = $68,200 in total

Step 6 Calculate the margin of safety

= budgeted sales − breakeven sales

= $74,400 − $68,200

= $6,200 sales in total, in the standard mix

Or, as a percentage

= ($74,400 − $68,200)/$74,400 × 100%

= 8.3% of budgeted sales

7 Multi-product graphs

Graphs can also be used in multi-product situations to indicate the relationships between cost, revenue and volume.

Multi-product P/V charts can also be produced whereby each product is plotted individually, allowing the profitabilities to be compared. They show a profit or loss line rather than the cost and revenue lines and often two profit or loss lines are drawn. First, a straight line assuming a constant mix between the products and second, a bow shaped line where products are plotted in order of profitability, ie products are plotted in the order of their contribution/sales ratio.

Activity 6: Multi-product profit volume chart

Here is a sketch of a multi-product P/V chart for Activity 4.

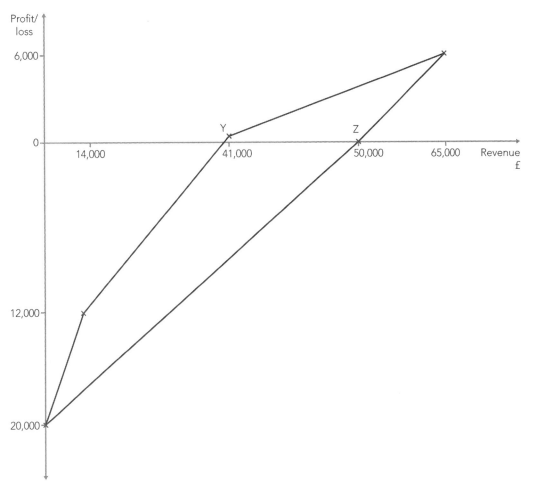

Multi-product P/V chart

You can see from the graph that when the company sells its most profitable product first, it breaks even earlier than when it sells products in a constant mix.

Required
What do the points Y and Z represent?

○ Y: Breakeven point if most profitable product made first. Z: Multi-product breakeven point

○ Y: Multi-product breakeven revenue. Z: Breakeven revenue if most profitable product made first

○ Y: Multi-product breakeven point. Z: Breakeven point if most profitable product made first

○ Y: Breakeven revenue if most profitable product made first. Z: Multi-product breakeven revenue

Solution

7.1 Changing the product mix

As the products have different C/S ratios, any changes in the product range (ie additional products offered or products discontinued) will have an impact on the breakeven point.

For example, if products are sold in a constant mix and a new product is introduced that increases the weighted C/S, then the breakeven point will fall. The breakeven point will also fall if the product with the lowest C/S ratio is discontinued.

Essential reading

See Chapter 8 Section 1 of the Essential reading for information on multi-product breakeven charts and more detail on multi-product profit-volume charts.

The Essential reading is available as an Appendix of the digital edition of the Workbook.

8 Limitations of breakeven analysis

Breakeven analysis is a useful technique for managers as it can provide simple and quick estimates. It is a form of sensitivity analysis and is therefore useful for assessing risk surrounding the estimate of sales volume.

It does, however, have a number of limitations as it assumes that:

- If there are multiple products, they are sold in a constant mix
- All costs can be split into fixed and variable elements
- Fixed costs are constant
- Variable cost per unit is constant
- Selling price is constant
- Inventory levels are constant (sales volume = production volume)

Chapter summary

Cost volume profit (CVP) analysis

Cost volume profit (CVP) analysis

Assumptions

- Fixed sales mix (fixed proportions)
- Fixed costs per period same in total and unit variable costs constant
- Sales prices per unit are constant
- Production volume = sales volume

Single product breakeven analysis

- Contribution per unit = unit selling price – unit variable costs
- Breakeven point = fixed costs/unit contribution
- Contribution/sales ratio = unit contribution/unit selling price
- Breakeven revenue = fixed costs/C/S ratio
- Margin of safety = budgeted sales – breakeven sales
- Output required for target profit = (fixed costs + target profit)/ unit contribution

Breakeven, contribution and P/V charts

- Breakeven chart

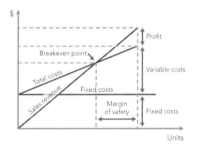

- Contribution chart

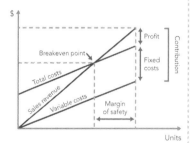

- Profit/volume (P/V) chart

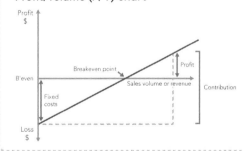

Multi-product breakeven point

- Breakeven point = Fixed costs/ weighted average unit contribution
- Breakeven revenue = Fixed costs/weighted average C/S ratio

Contribution to sales (C/S) ratio for multiple products

- **Step 1** Calculate revenue per mix
- **Step 2** Calculate contribution per mix
- **Step 3** Calculate average C/S ratio
- **Step 4** Calculate breakeven point (total)
- **Step 5** Calculate revenue ratio of mix
- **Step 6** Calculate breakeven revenue and breakeven point

Target profit for multiple products

- **Step 1** Calculate contribution per unit
- **Step 2** Calculate contribution per mix
- **Step 3** Calculate the required number of mixes
- **Step 4** Calculate the required sales in terms of the number of units of the products and sales revenue of each product

Margin of safety for multiple products

- **Step 1** Calculate contribution per unit
- **Step 2** Calculate contribution per mix
- **Step 3** Calculate the breakeven point in terms of the number of mixes
- **Step 4** Calculate breakeven point in terms of the number of units of the products
- **Step 5** Calculate the breakeven point in terms of revenue
- **Step 6** Calculate the margin of safety

Multi-product graphs

Products are plotted in the order of their C/S ratio

Changing the product mix

Any changes in the product range will have an impact on the breakeven point

Limitations of breakeven analysis

- Assumptions
  - Products are sold in a constant mix
  - All costs can be split into fixed and variable elements
  - Fixed costs are constant
  - Variable cost per unit is constant
  - Selling price is constant
  - Sales volume = production volume

Knowledge diagnostic

1. CVP analysis assumptions

Constant selling price, variable costs and fixed costs.

2. Single product breakeven analysis

Breakeven point = fixed costs / contribution per unit

3. Multi-product breakeven analysis

Multi-product breakeven analysis can only be performed if a constant product sales mix is assumed.

Breakeven point = fixed costs / weighted average contribution/per unit

On a P/V chart, products should be plotted individually in order of the size of their C/S ratio.

Further study guidance

Question practice

Now try the following from the Further question practice bank [available in the digital edition of the Workbook]:

Number	Level	Marks	Approximate time
Section A Q19	Examination	2	4 mins
Section A Q20	Examination	2	4 mins
Section A Q21	Examination	2	4 mins

Further reading

There is a technical article available on ACCA's website, called *Cost-volume-profit analysis*, which explains that profit would be maximised if management were able to make business decisions based on certainty. Profit, however, is often dependent on sales volume (an unknown) but selling price and costs are usually known with some accuracy. Breakeven analysis can therefore be used to help make business decisions. Note that if you print this article out, it refers to graphs that only appear if you click on the links within the article.

You are strongly advised to read this article in full as part of your preparation for the PM exam.

Activity answers

Activity 1: Revision of single product CVP analysis

1 **The correct answer is:**

(a) BEP = fixed costs / contribution per unit = 5,700 / (8.00 - 6.60) = 3,800 units

(b) Breakeven revenue = 3,800 × $8.00 = $30,400

(c) C/S ratio = contribution per unit / sales price = $1.50 / $8.00 = 0.1875

    Breakeven revenue = $5,700 / 0.1875 = $30,400

(d) Margin of safety = 5,000 - 3,800 = 1,200 units or 1,200 / 5,000 × 100 = 24%

    The sales volume must fall by 24% from budgeted level before a loss is made.

(e) Sales volume = (10,000 + 5,700) / $1.50 = 10,467 units

Activity 2: Breakeven chart

1 **The correct answer is:**

A – Breakeven point

B – Margin of safety

C – Total revenue line

D – Total cost line

Activity 3: Profit volume chart

The correct answer is:

The contribution is $7,500 (fixed costs 5,700 + profit 1,800).

$$\text{Gradient of line } = \frac{\text{Change in profit}}{\text{Change in volume}} = \text{contribution per unit } = \$1.50$$

Activity 4: Multi-product breakeven point

1 **The correct answer is:**

Required

What is the breakeven sales volume?   6,923 units

	Footballs	Baseballs	Rugby balls
	$	$	$
Selling price	7	6	9
Variable costs	3	4.50	5
Contribution	4	1.50	4

$$\text{Breakeven point } = \frac{\text{Fixed costs}}{\text{Average contribution (W1)}} = \frac{\$20,000}{\$2.889}$$

= 6,923 units

(W1) Average contribution =

$$\frac{(\$4 \times 2) + (\$1.50 \times 4) + (\$4 \times 3)}{2 + 4 + 3}$$

= $2.889

2 **The correct answer is:**

Required

What is the breakeven sales revenue? $50,000

The 6,923 units would be split as follows:

	Sales mix	Units	SP	Revenue
			$	$
Football	2	1,538	7	10,766
Baseball	4	3,077	6	18,462
Rugby ball	3	2,308	9	20,772
	9	6,923		50,000

Activity 5: Using the average C/S ratio

1 The correct answer is:

Calculate revenue per mix	= (3 × $135) + (4 × $165) + (5 × $220)	= $2,165
Calculate contribution per mix	= ($61.50 × 3) + ($106.10 × 4) + ($73.80 × 5)	= $977.90
Calculate average C/S ratio	= ($977.90/$2,165) × 100%	= 45.17%
Calculate breakeven point (total)	= fixed costs ÷ C/S ratio = $950,000/0.4517 =	$2,103,166 (rounded)
Calculate revenue ratio of mix	= 405:660:1,100, or 81:132:220	
Calculate breakeven sales Breakeven sales of Beta Breakeven sales of Gamma Breakeven sales of Delta	= 81/433 × $2,103,166 = $393,433 = 132/433 × $2,103,166 = $641,150 = 220/433 × $2,103,166 = $1,068,583	

Activity 6: Multi-product profit volume chart

The correct answer is:

Y: Breakeven revenue if most profitable product made first. Z: Multi-product breakeven revenue

Y is the breakeven revenue if products are plotted in order of their C/S ratio (ie the most profitable product is manufactured first). In this case, footballs would be manufactured first as they have the highest C/S ratio. (See W1 below.)

Z is the breakeven point based on the weighted average unit contribution.

W1

	Contribution	Sales	C/S ratio
	$	$	
Footballs	8,000	14,000	57.1%
Baseballs	6,000	24,000	25.0%
Rugby balls	12,000	27,000	44.4%

9 Limiting factor analysis

Learning objectives

On completion of this chapter, you should be able to:

	Syllabus reference no.
Apply throughput accounting to a multi-product decision-making problem.	B4 (d)
Identify limiting factors in a scarce resource situation and select an appropriate technique.	C3 (a)
Determine the optimal production plan where an organisation is restricted by a single limiting factor, including within the context of 'make' or 'buy' decisions.	C3 (b)
Formulate and solve a multiple scarce resource problem both linear programming graphs and using simultaneous equations as appropriate.	C3 (c)
Explain and calculate shadow prices (dual prices) and discuss their implications on decision-making and performance management.	C3 (d)
Calculate slack and explain the implications of the existence of slack for decision-making and performance management. (Excluding simplex and sensitivity to changes in objective functions.)	C3 (e)

Exam context

All companies have a maximum capacity for producing goods or providing services because there is a limit to the amount of resources available. There is always at least one resource that is more restrictive than others: this is known as a **limiting factor**. This chapter begins with a technique used to maximise contribution when there is a single limiting factor. When there is more than one resource constraint, the technique of linear programming can be used. A multiple scarce resource problem can be solved using a graphical method and simultaneous equations.

We also look at the meaning and calculation of shadow prices and slack in this chapter.

Chapter overview

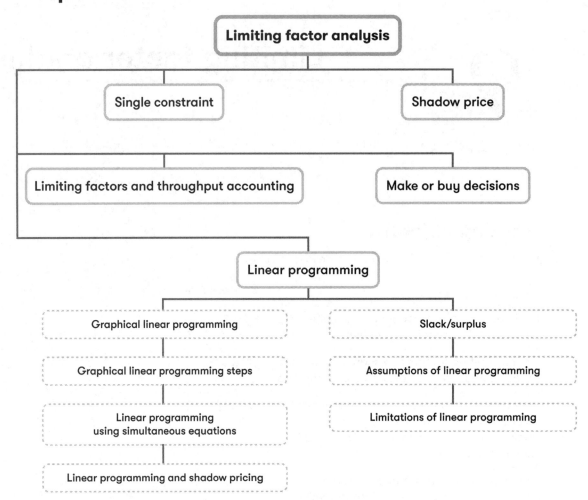

1 Single constraint

If a business is not constrained by internal factors, it will normally produce and sell as much as demand allows. However, occasionally, this may not be possible and in this situation the plans of the business must be built around this internal 'limiting' factor. This chapter looks at situations with one limiting factor as well as situations where there are multiple limiting factors.

The production and sales plans of a business may be limited by a limiting factor/scarce resource (the 'principal budget factor').

This could be:

- Market demand
- Materials
- Manpower (labour)
- Machine hours
- Money

The plans of the business must be built around this factor.

If a business makes more than one product, it will want to find the product mix that will maximise profit given the limiting factor. This is done by maximising contribution as follows:

(a) **Determine limiting factor** by producing to maximum demand.

(b) **Rank** products by **contribution per unit of limiting factor.**

(c) Prepare a **production plan.**

Illustration 1: Limiting factors

1 AB Co makes two products: Ay and Be. Unit variable costs are as follows:

	Ay $	Be $
Direct materials	1	3
Direct labour ($3 per hour)	6	3
Variable overhead	1	1
	8	7

The sales price per unit is $14 per Ay and $11 per Be. During July 20X2, the available direct labour is limited to 8,000 hours. Sales demand in July is expected to be 3,000 units for Ays and 5,000 units for Bes.

Determine the profit-maximising production mix, assuming that monthly fixed costs are $20,000 and that opening inventories of finished goods and work in progress are nil.

Optimal number of units of Ay = ☐

Optimal number of units of Be = ☐

Solution

1 **The correct answer is:**

Optimal number of units of Ay = 1,500. Optimal number of units of Be = 5,000.

Step 1 Confirm that the limiting factor is something other than sales demand.

	Ays	Bes	Total
Labour hours per unit	2 hours	1 hour	
Sales demand	3,000 units	5,000 units	
Labour hours needed	6,000 units	5,000 units	11,000 hours
Labour hours available			<u>8,000 hours</u>
Shortfall			3,000 hours

Labour is the limiting factor on production.

Step 2 Identify the contribution earned by each product per unit of limiting factor, that is, per labour hour worked.

	Ay $	Be $
Sales price	14	11
Variable cost	<u>8</u>	<u>7</u>
Unit production	<u>6</u>	<u>4</u>
Labour hours per unit	2 hours	1 hours
Contribution per labour hour (= unit of limiting factor)	$3	$4

Although Ays have a higher unit contribution than Bes, two Bes can be made in the time it takes to make one Ay. Because labour is in short supply, it is more profitable to make Bes than Ays.

Step 3 Determine the **optimal production plan**. Sufficient Bes will be made to meet the full sales demand, and the remaining labour hours available will then be used to make Ays.

(a)

Product	Demand	Hours required	Hours available	Priority of manufacture
Bes	5,000	5,000	5,000	1st
Ays	3,000	<u>6,000</u>	<u>3,000</u> (bal)	2nd
		<u>11,000</u>	<u>8,000</u>	

(b)

Product	Units	Hours required	Contribution per hour $	Total $
Bes	5,000	5,000	4	20,000
Ays	1,500	3,000	3	9,000
		8,000		29,000
Less fixed costs				20,000
Profit				9,000

Conclusion

(a) Unit contribution is **not** the correct way to decide priorities.

(b) Labour hours are the scarce resource, and therefore contribution **per labour hour** is the correct way to decide priorities.

(c) Be earns $4 contribution per labour hour, and the Ay earns $3 contribution per labour hour. Bes therefore make more profitable use of the scarce resource, and should be manufactured first.

Activity 1: Optimal production mix

Gorgo Co is preparing its production plan for the next week and has estimated maximum demand from its customers as follows:

	Units
A	50
B	50
C	50

The products have the following cost cards

	A $	B $	C $
Sales price	150	120	100
Variable cost:			
Materials ($5/kg)	50	30	15
Labour	50	50	40
Fixed cost	50	20	10
Profit	0	20	35

These demand figures do not include a long-term contract for the delivery of five units of each product to an important customer. If this contract is not satisfied, then Gorgo will have to pay a substantial penalty.

The production director is concerned as the materials used in production are likely to be in short supply. Gorgo does not hold any inventory of raw materials and the availability of materials is expected to be restricted to 845kg.

1 **Required**

Complete the following working schedules to determine the production mix that will maximise Gorgo's profit next week. Assume that labour will be paid a 10% premium.

	A	B	C
Contribution per unit			
Kg per unit			
Contribution per kg			
Rank			

Production

	A	B	C
Contract units			
Demand units			
Total units			
Contribution			

Solution

1

Essential reading

See Chapter 9 Section 1 of the Essential reading for more detail on how to deal with a situation where two factors are potentially the limiting factor (and there are also sales demand limitations). The approach is to find out which factor (if any) prevents the business from fulfilling maximum sales demand.

The Essential reading is available as an Appendix of the digital edition of the Workbook.

---

2 Shadow price

Shadow price: This is the 'increase in value which would be created by having available one additional unit of a limiting resource at the original cost'. (*CIMA Official Terminology*)

A shadow price is:

(a) The additional contribution generated from one additional unit of limiting factor.

(b) The opportunity cost of not having the use of one extra unit of limiting factor.

(c) The maximum extra amount that should be paid for one additional unit of scarce resource.

Illustration 2: Shadow price

Required

Determine the shadow price for labour in Illustration 1.

$ [   ] per hour

Solution

The correct answer is:

$3 per hour

If one extra labour hour was available this would be used to manufacture Ayes, which earn a contribution of $3 per labour hour.

Therefore, the shadow price is $3 per hour, and the maximum AB Co would be prepared to pay to obtain additional labour hours would be $6 ($3 cost per labour hour + $3 shadow price).

Activity 2: Shadow price

Required

Using the information from Gorgo in Activity 1, determine the shadow price of material.

$ [   ]

Solution

3 Limiting factors and throughput accounting

In a throughput environment, the approach is similar to the approach shown above in Section 1, except we rank products by **throughput contribution per unit of limiting factor (bottleneck resource)** instead of **contribution per unit of limiting factor**.

Note that ranking products in order of priority according to their **TPAR** will always give the **same ranking** as putting them in order of **throughput per unit of bottleneck resource**.

Illustration 3: Maximising throughput and multiple products

1   WR Co manufactures three products: A, B and C. Product details are as follows:

	Product A	Product B	Product C
	$	$	$
Sales price	2.80	1.60	2.40
Materials cost	1.20	0.60	1.20
Direct labour cost	1.00	0.80	0.80
Weekly sales demand	4,000 units	4,000 units	5,000 units
Machine hours per unit	0.5 hours	0.2 hours	0.3 hours

Machine time is a bottleneck resource and maximum capacity is 4,000 machine hours per week. Operating costs including direct labour costs are $10,880 per week. Direct labour workers are not paid overtime and work a standard 38-hour week.

Required
Determine the optimum production plan for WR Co and calculate the weekly profit that would arise from the plan.

Solution

1   **The correct answer is:**

Step 1 Determine the bottleneck resource

The bottleneck resource is machine time (4,000 machine hours available each week).

Step 2 Calculate the throughput per unit for each product

	Product A	**Product B**	**Product C**
	$	**$**	**$**
Sales price	2.80	1.60	2.40
Materials cost	1.20	0.60	1.20
Throughput/unit	1.60	1.00	1.20

Step 3 Calculate throughput per unit of limiting factor (machine hours)

	Product A	**Product B**	**Product C**
Machine hours per unit	0.5 hours	0.2 hours	0.3 hours

	Product A	Product B	Product C
Throughput per machine hour	$3.20*	$5.00	$4.00

* $1.60 / 0.5 hours = $3.20

Step 4 Rank products

Ranking	3rd	1st	2nd

Step 5 Allocate resources to arrive at optimum production plan

The profit-maximising weekly output and sales volumes are as follows:

Product	Units	Bottleneck resource hours/unit	Total hours	Throughput per hour	Total throughput
				$	$
B	4,000	0.2 hours	800	5.00	4,000
C	5,000	0.3 hours	1,500	4.00	6,000
			2,300		
A (balance)	3,400	0.5 hours	1,700	3.20	5,440
			4,000		15,440
				Less: operating expenses	(10,880)
				Profit per week	4,560

Activity 3: Optimum production plan

Tasty Bread Co makes three types of bread: rolls, baguettes and loaves. The breads pass through three processes and baking is the bottleneck process. Only 80 hours of baking time are available per day. Tasty Bread Co uses throughput accounting and the following information is available:

	Rolls	Baguettes	Loaves
	$	$	$
Selling price per unit	1.20	1.00	1.50
Ingredients cost per unit	0.25	0.10	0.35
Labour cost per unit	0.50	0.40	0.30
Overhead cost per unit	0.25	0.25	0.60
Maximum demand (units) per day	15	10	20
Baking time per unit (hours)	2.00	1.80	2.00

Required

Assuming the Tasty Bread Co wants to maximise profit, what is the optimal production plan?

○ Rolls 15, Baguettes 5, Loaves 20

○ Rolls 11, Baguettes 10, Loaves 16

○ Rolls 15, Baguettes 10, Loaves 16

○ Rolls 11, Baguettes 10, Loaves 20

Solution

4 Make or buy decisions

In a limiting factor situation, a company could make up a shortfall in its own in-house production capabilities by subcontracting work to an external supplier. To decide which products to make in-house and which to buy from the subcontractor, they would need to look at the difference between the variable cost of making it and the cost of buying it in relation to the scarce resource that would be saved by using the subcontractor.

Illustration 4: Make or buy decisions with scarce resources

1 MM manufactures three components, S, A and T, using the same machines for each. The budget for the next year calls for the production and assembly of 4,000 of each component. The variable production cost per unit of the final product is as follows:

	Machine hours	Variable costs
		$
1 unit of S	3	20
1 unit of A	2	36
1 unit of T	4	24
Assembly		20
		100

Only 24,000 hours of machine time will be available during the year, and a subcontractor has quoted the following unit prices for supplying components: S $29; A $40; T $34.

Required
Advise MM.

Solution

1 The correct answer is:

The organisation's budget calls for 36,000 hours of machine time ((3 × 4,000) + (2 × 4,000) +(4 × 4,000)), if all the components are to be produced in-house. Only 24,000 hours are available, and so there is a shortfall of 12,000 hours of machine time, which is therefore a limiting factor. The shortage can be overcome by subcontracting the equivalent of 12,000 machine hours of output to the subcontractor.

The assembly costs are not relevant costs because they are unaffected by the decision.

The decision rule is to **minimise the extra variable costs of subcontracting per unit of scarce resource saved** (that is, per machine hour saved).

	S $	A $	T $
Variable cost of making	20	36	24
Variable cost of buying	29	40	34
Extra variable cost of buying	9	4	10
Machine hours saved by buying	3 hrs	2 hrs	4 hrs
Extra variable cost of buying per hour saved	$3	$2	$2.50

This analysis shows that it is **cheaper to buy A than T** and it is **most expensive to buy S**. The **priority for making** the components in-house will be in the **reverse order**: S, then T, then A. There are enough machine hours to make all 4,000 units of S (12,000 hours) and to produce 3,000 units of T (another 12,000 hours). 12,000 hours' production of T and A must be subcontracted. The cost-minimising and so profit-maximising make and buy schedule is as follows:

Component	Machine hours used/saved	Number of units	Units variable cost $	Total variable cost $
Make: S	12,000	4,000	20	80,000
T	12,000	3,000	24	72,000
	24,000			152,000
Buy: T	4,000	1,000	34	34,000
A	8,000	4,000	40	160,000
	12,000			346,000

Total variable cost of components, excluding assembly costs = $346,000

Activity 4: Make or buy and limiting factors

TW manufactures two products, the D and the E, using the same material for each. Annual demand for the D is 9,000 units, while demand for the E is 12,000 units. The variable production cost per unit of the D is $10, that of the E $15. The D requires 3.5 kg of raw material per unit, the E requires 8 kg of raw material per unit. Supply of raw material will be limited to 87,500 kg during the year.

A subcontractor has quoted prices of $17 per unit for the D and $25 per unit for the E to supply the product. How many of each product should TW manufacture in order to maximise profits?

TW should manufacture _____ units of D and _____ units of E to maximise profits.

Solution

---

5 Linear programming

5.1 Graphical linear programming

Contribution per unit of limiting factor cannot be used when:

(a) More than one limiting factor exists

(b) Products rank differently for these resources

Under these conditions, linear programming is used and can be solved using either of:

(a) Graphs

(b) Simultaneous equations

5.1.1 Graphical linear programming steps

Follow these steps when you are trying to solve a problem using the graphical method:

(a) Define variables

(b) Formulate objective function

(c) Formulate constraints – generally in the form: amount of resource used ≤ amount available

(d) Plot constraints on a graph

(e) Identify the feasible space, ie those combinations of variables that are possible within the resource constraints

(f) Plot the slope of the objective function and slide to optimal point (away from the origin for a maximum, towards the origin for a minimum)

(g) Calculate the value of the objective function at the optimal point

> **Objective function:** This is a quantified statement of the aim of a resource allocation decision.
>
> **Constraint:** This is an "activity, resource or policy that limits the ability to achieve objectives" (*CIMA Official Terminology*).
>
> **Feasible region:** This is "The area contained within all of the constraint lines shown on a graphical depiction of a linear programming problem. All feasible combinations of output are contained within or located on the boundaries of the feasible region" (*CIMA Official Terminology*).

Illustration 5: Graphical linear programming

WX Co manufactures two products: A and B. Both products pass through two production departments, mixing and shaping. The organisation's objective is to maximise contribution to fixed costs.

Product A is sold for $1.50 whereas Product B is priced at $2.00. There is unlimited demand for Product A but demand for B is limited to 13,000 units per annum.

The machine hours available in each department are restricted to 2,400 per annum. Other relevant data is as follows:

Machine hours required	Mixing hours	Shaping hours
Product A	0.06	0.04
Product B	0.08	0.12

Variable cost per unit	$
Product A	1.30
Product B	1.70

1 **Required**

What is the optimum production plan?

Number of units of A = _____

Number of units of B = _____

Solution

1 **The correct answer is:**

Step 1 Define variables

What are the **quantities that WX Co can vary**? Obviously not the number of machine hours or the demand for Product B. The only things that it can vary are the **number of units of each type of product produced**. It is those numbers that the company has to determine in such a way as to obtain the maximum possible profit. Our variables (which are usually products being produced) will therefore be as follows:

Let x = number of units of Product A produced.

Let y = number of units of Product B produced.

Step 2 Establish objective function

We now need to introduce the question of contribution or profit. We know that the **contribution on each type of product** is as follows:

	$ per unit
Product A	($1.50 - $1.30) =	0.20
Product B	($2.00 - $1.70) =	0.20

The **objective of the company is to maximise contribution** and so the **objective function to be maximised** is as follows:

Contribution (C) = 0.2x + 0.3y

Step 3 Establish constraints

The **value of the objective function** (the maximum contribution achievable from producing Products A and B) is **limited by the constraints** facing WX Co. To incorporate this into the problem, we need to **translate the constraints into inequalities involving the variables** defined in Step 1. An inequality is an equation taking the form 'greater than or equal to' or 'less than or equal to'.

(a) Consider the **mixing department machine hours** constraint.

  (i) **Each unit of Product A** requires 0.06 hours of machine time. Producing five units therefore requires 5 × 0.06 hours of machine time and, more generally, **producing x units will require 0.06x hours.**

  (ii) Likewise, producing y units of **Product B will require 0.08y hours.**

  (iii) The total machine hours needed in the mixing department to make x units of Product A and y units of Product B is 0.06x + 0.08y.

  (iv) We know that this **cannot be greater than 2,400 hours** and so we arrive at the following inequality: **0.06x + 0.08y ≤ 2,400**

(b) The final inequality is easier to obtain. The **number of units of Product B produced and sold is y** but this has to be **less than or equal to 13,000.** Our inequality is therefore as follows: y ≤ 13,000

(c) We also need to add **non-negativity constraints** (x ≥ 0, y ≥ 0) since negative numbers of products cannot be produced. (Linear programming is simply a mathematical tool and so there is nothing in this method that guarantees that the answer will 'make sense'. An unprofitable product may produce an answer that is negative. This is mathematically correct but nonsense in operational terms.)

The **problem** has now been reduced to the following **four inequalities** and **one equation:**

Maximise contribution (C) = 0.2x + 0.3y, subject to the following constraints:

0.06x + 0.08y ≤ 2,400

0.04x + 0.12y ≤ 2,400

0 ≤ y ≤ 13,000

0 ≤ x

Steps 4 and 5 Graph the problem and define the feasible region

When there are **several constraints,** the **feasible area** of combinations of values of x and y must be an area **where all the inequalities are satisfied.**

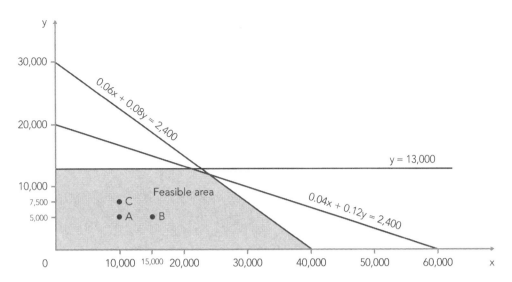

Step 6 Determine the optimal solution

The optimal solution can be found by 'sliding the iso-contribution (or profit) line out'.

The **'best' solution** is going to be at a **point on the edge of the feasible area** rather than in the middle of it.

This still leaves us with quite a few points to look at but there is a way in which we can **narrow down still further the likely points at which the best solution will be found**. Suppose that WX Co wishes to earn

contribution of $3,000. The company could sell the following combinations of the two products:

(a)   15,000 units of A, no B

(b)   No A, 10,000 units of B

(c)   A suitable mix of the two, such as 7,500 A and 5,000 B

The **possible combinations required to earn contribution of $3,000** could be **shown by the straight line 0.2x + 0.3y = 3,000**

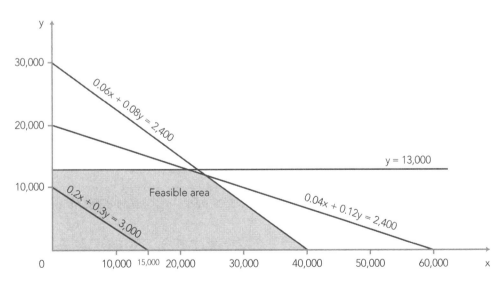

Likewise, for profits of $6,000 and $1,500, lines of 0.2x + 0.3y = 6,000 and 0.2x + 0.3y = 1,500 could be drawn **showing the combination of the two products** which would **achieve contribution of $6,000 or $1,500.**

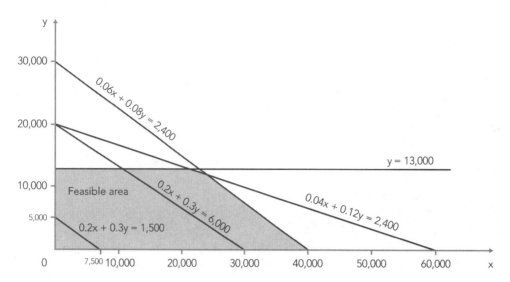

The **contribution lines are all parallel.** (They are called **iso-contribution lines,** 'iso' meaning equal.) A similar line drawn for any other total contribution would also be parallel to the three lines shown here. Bigger contribution is shown by lines further from the origin ($0.2x + 0.3y = 6,000$), smaller contribution by lines closer to the origin ($0.2x + 0.3y = 1,500$). As WX Co tries to increase possible contribution, we need to 'slide' any contribution line outwards from the origin, while always keeping it parallel to the other contribution lines.

As we do this there will come a point at which, if we were to **move the contribution line out any further**, it would cease to lie in the feasible region. Greater contribution could not be achieved, because of the constraints. In our example concerning WX Co this will happen, as you should test for yourself, where the contribution line just passes through the intersection of $0.06x + 0.08y = 2,400$ and $0.04x + 0.12y = 2,400$ (at co-ordinates (24,000, 12,000)).

The point (24,000, 12,000) will therefore give us the optimal allocation of resources (to produce 24,000 units of A and 12,000 units of B).

Assessment focus point

The syllabus states that you must be able to identify limiting factors and **select an appropriate technique** to maximise contribution.

Single limiting factor. You must read the question carefully to establish whether to use the throughput contribution per unit of limiting factor (see Chapter 6) or contribution per unit of limiting factor to rank products.

Multiple limiting factors. Reading the question will determine whether linear programming or simultaneous equations should be used.

Activity 5: Optimal contribution

KG Co makes two products, the purse and the handbag. Each purse earns $5 contribution and each handbag earns $6. Inputs are as follows:

	Purse	Handbag
Leather	1.5m²	2m²
Skilled labour	45 mins	30 mins

There are six skilled labourers each working a 35-hour week, and delivery contracts limit the amount of leather available to 600m² each week.

The maximum demand for handbags is 250 per week.

Leather costs $8 per m² and wages are paid at $4.20 per hour.

1   **Required**
Define the variables

Let [   ] = the number of purses to manufacture

Let [   ] = the number of handbags to manufacture

2   **Required**
Formulate the objective function

Maximise 5 [   ] + 6 [   ]

3   **Required**
Formulate the constraints

Leather: [   ] p + [   ] h ≤ [   ]

Skilled labour: [   ] p + [   ] h ≤ [   ]

Demand: [   ] ≤ [   ]

Non-negativity: p,h ≥ [   ]

4   **Required**
Identify the lines on the graph

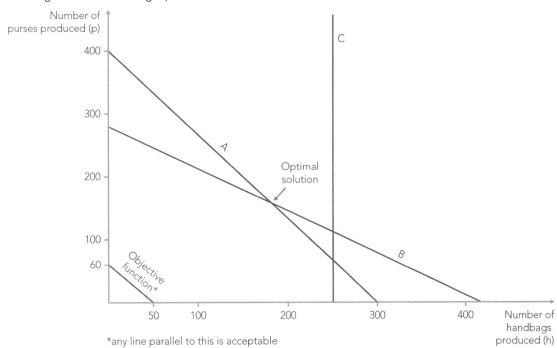

*any line parallel to this is acceptable

Line A = [   ]

Line B = [   ]

Line C = [   ]

5   **Required**
What is the optimal production plan?

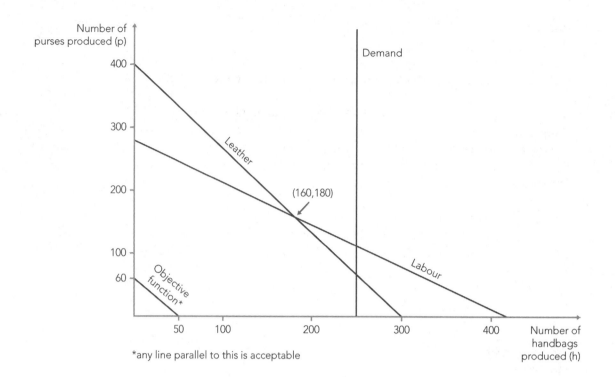

*any line parallel to this is acceptable

	Purses
	Handbags

6   **Calculate value of objective function at optimal point.**

$ [   ] per week

Solution

1

2

3

4

5

6

5.2 Linear programming using simultaneous equations

If the two binding constraints are known, we can use simultaneous equations to find the optimum number of each product to manufacture as the optimum solution is the point at which the constraint lines intersect. Using simultaneous equations will give a more accurate result than reading from the graph.

Illustration 6: Solving simultaneous equations

1 **Required**

Solve the simultaneous equations for Activity 5.

h =

p =

Solution

1 **The correct answer is:**

Equation 1:			$1.5p + 2h = 600$
Equation 2:	$0.75p + 0.5h = 210$	× 2 = Equation 2a	$1.5p + h = 420$
Equation 1 - Equation 2a			$h = 180$

When h = 180, substitute value into Equation 1:

$1.5p + 2h = 600$

$1.5p + (2 \times 180) = 600$

$1.5p = 600 - 360$

$p = 240/1.5$

$p = 160$

Assessment focus point

You need to know all of the linear programming steps, but a single objective test (OT) question is likely to focus on one step. A Section C constructed response question could ask you to interpret a graph or explain graphical linear programming.

Activity 6: Binding constraints

A company produces two products and has used linear programming to help determine the optimal number of each product to manufacture.

a = the number of units of product A to manufacture

b = the number of units of product B to manufacture

Objective function: Maximise contribution = 3a + 5b

Objective function: Maximise contribution = 3a + 5b

Constraints:

Labour	$0.5a + b\ 10,000$	(1)
Material 1	$5a + 8b\ 8,000$	(2)
Material 2	$2a + 4b\ 3,600$	(3)

Demand product A	a0	(4)
Demand product B	b5,000	(5)

The optimal production point has been determined to be at the point where constraint lines (2) and (3) intersect.

Required
Which TWO of the following are binding constraints?

O Labour
O Material 1
O Material 2
O Product A
O Product B

Solution

Activity 7: Contribution

A company produces two products and has used linear programming to help determine the optimal number of each product to manufacture.

g = the number of units of Product G to manufacture

k = the number of units of Product K to manufacture

Objective function: Maximise contribution = 6g + 9k

Constraints:

Labour	5g + 8k 8,000	(1)
Material	2g + 4k 3,600	(2)
Demand product G	g 2,000	(3)

The optimal production point has been determined to be at the intersection of constraints (1) and (2).

1 Required

What is the value of the objective function at the optimal point?

Solution

1

Activity 8: Objective function

A company produces two products: M and N, and is currently drawing up its production plan for the forthcoming month. Information is available as follows:

	M	N
Selling price per unit	$40	$50
Material P @ $4 per kg	4kg/unit	3kg/unit
Material Q @ $5 per kg	2kg/unit	3kg/unit
Labour @ $8 per hour	0.5 hours/unit	1 hour/unit
Fixed overheads per unit	$2	$3

Next month only 2,000 units of Material P will be available. Labour is also limited, at 500 hours per month. The company holds no inventory and aims to maximise profits.

Required

If m is the number of units of Product M sold per month and n is the number of units of Product N sold per month, which of the following is the correct objective function?

- ○ Maximise 40m + 50n
- ○ Maximise 4m + 3n
- ○ Maximise 8m + 19n
- ○ Maximise 10m + 15n

Solution

5.3 Linear programming and shadow pricing

Shadow prices can be calculated from the graphical method, by relaxing or constraining one of the limiting factors at a time by a small amount (usually one unit) and recalculating the optimal solution and associated contribution.

 Illustration 7: Linear programming and shadow pricing

Required

Using the information in Activity 4, what is the maximum price KG Co would be prepared to pay to obtain one further hour of labour?

- ○ $0
- ○ $1.33
- ○ $4.20
- ○ $5.53

Solution

The correct answer is:

Labour is a limiting factor so KG Co would be prepared to pay to obtain more of this resource.

Shadow price = contribution forgone due to limiting factor

= extra contribution if one more unit of limiting factor obtained at original cost

If $1.5p + 2h = 600$ (leather)

        $0.75p + 0.5h = 211$ (labour)

Optimal solution

$h = 178$

$p = 162.67$

Contribution = $5p + 6h = \$1,881.33$

Original contribution = $\underline{\$1,880.00}$

Shadow price $\$1.33$

Maximum price = shadow price + usual price = \$1.33 + \$4.20 = \$5.53

Essential reading

See Chapter 9 Section 3 of the Essential reading, for more detail on the implications of shadow prices.

The Essential reading is available as an Appendix of the digital edition of the Workbook.

5.4 Slack/surplus

KEY TERM

> **Slack: Slack** occurs when maximum availability of a resource or other constraining factor is not used.
>
> **Surplus: Surplus** occurs when more than a minimum requirement is used: surplus is the excess over the minimum amount of constraint, where the constraint is a 'more than or equal to' constraint.

If, at the optimal solution, the amount of the resource used equals the amount of the resource available, there is **no spare capacity** of a resource and so there is **no slack**.

If, at the optimal solution, the amount of the resource used is less than the amount of the resource available, there is **spare capacity** for the resource and so there is **slack**.

5.4.1 Implications of slack

(a) **High** slack indicates **inefficient** use of a particular resource. If possible, the resource should be **reallocated** to **another part** of the **business** or if it is **labour**, it could be **subcontracted out** to **another company**.

(b) **Low** slack indicates that this resource **could become** a **binding constraint**. If the resource is a particular material, management should investigate whether additional suppliers can be identified. If the resource is labour time, the human resources department should be readied for a recruitment drive, should it be needed. This way, if the availability of scarce resources increases, the company is in a better position to maximise profitability.

Activity 9: Slack

This question is based on an ACCA question in the June 2014 exam.

A company had the following limiting factors for Period 3:

Test time: 12,000 hours

Program time: 28,000 hours

The following information was established:

	Product X	Product Y
Test per unit	18	4
Program minutes per unite	36	14
Optimum production plan (unit)	20,000	66,000

What were the slack resources for test time and program time?

Test time:

☐ hours

Programme time:

┌─────────────────┐
│   │ hours
└─────────────────┘

Solution

Essential reading

See Chapter 9 Section 4 of the Essential reading for more detail on the implications of slack.

The Essential reading is available as an Appendix of the digital edition of the Workbook.

5.5 Assumptions of linear programming

Assumptions made in linear programming techniques include the following:

(a) Fixed costs are unchanged by decision.

(b) Unit variable cost is constant.

(c) Estimates of demand and resource requirements are known with certainty.

(d) Units of output are divisible.

(e) Total amount of each scarce resource is known with certainty.

(f) There is no interdependence of demand between products.

5.6 Limitations of linear programming

(a) It may be difficult to identify which resources are likely to be in short supply and what the amount of their availability will be.

(b) Management may not make product mix decisions that are profit maximising. They may have different objectives when setting the production/sales plan.

(c) Linear relationship may not exist, apart from over very small ranges.

(d) The linear programming model is essentially static and is therefore not really suitable for analysing in detail the effects of changes in the various parameters, for example over time.

(e) In some circumstances, a practical solution derived from a linear programming model may be of limited use as, for example, where the variables may only take on integer values. A solution must then be found by a combination of rounding up and trial and error.

Chapter summary

```
┌─────────────────────────────────────────┐
│          Limiting factor analysis        │
└─────────────────────────────────────────┘
```

Single constraint

Prioritise production based on contribution/
limiting factor

Shadow price

- The extra contribution from one more unit of
  scarce resource
- It is the maximum extra amount you would
  pay more one more unit

Limiting factors and throughput accounting

- Limiting factor ranking based on throughput
  per unit of bottleneck resource
- **Step 1** Determine the bottleneck resource
- **Step 2** Calculate the throughput per unit for
  each product
- **Step 3** Calculate throughput per unit of
  limiting factor
- **Step 4** Rank products

Make or buy decisions

- Total costs will be minimised if those units
  bought from the subcontractor have the
  'lowest extra variable cost per unit of scarce
  resource saved by buying'
  – Extra variable cost of buying = variable cost
    of making – variable cost of buying
  – Extra variable cost of buying per resource
    saved = extra variable cost of buying/
    resource saved by buying

Linear programming

Formulate the model:
- Define variables
- Establish constraints
- Formulate objective function

Graphical linear programming

Used when more than one limiting factor exists

Graphical linear programming steps
- Plot constraints
- Identify feasible region
- Find optimal point (using iso-contribution line)
- Calculate objective function at optimal point

Linear programming using simultaneous equations
- Plot constraints
- Identify feasible region
- Find optimal point (using simultaneous equations)
- Calculate objective function at optimal point

Linear programming and shadow pricing

Relax one of the limiting factors at a time and recalculate associated contribution

Slack/surplus
- Slack is when the maximum amount of a resource has not been used
- Surplus is when more output than the minimum requirement is made

Assumptions of linear programming
- Fixed costs are unchanged by decision
- Unit variable cost is constant
- Estimates of demand and resource requirements are known with certainty
- Units of output are divisible
- Total amount of each scarce resource is known with certainty
- There is no interdependence of demand between products

Limitations of linear programming
- May be difficult to identify which resources will be in short supply and their availability
- Management may not make product mix decisions that are profit maximising
- Linear relationship may not exist
- Model is essentially static, therefore not really suitable for analysing changes in various parameters

Knowledge diagnostic

1. Single constraint

Plans of the business are built around the limiting factor. Single limiting factor problems can be solved by **maximising contribution/limiting factor** or **return per limiting factor** if with throughput accounting.

2. Make or buy decisions

Where a company is able to **subcontract work to make up a shortfall in its own in-house production capabilities,** its total costs will be minimised if those units bought from the subcontractor have the lowest extra variable cost per unit of scarce resource saved by buying. Extra variable cost is the difference between the variable cost of in-house production and the cost of buying from the subcontractor.

3. Linear programming

The graphical method of linear programming can be used when there are just two products (or services). The steps involved are as follows.

(a) Define the problem:
   (i) Define variables
   (ii) Establish constraints
   (iii) Construct objective function
(b) Draw the constraints on a graph.
(c) Establish the feasible region for the optimal solution.
(d) Determine the optimal solution.

The optimum solution to a linear programming problem can be found by 'sliding the iso-contribution line out'.

4. Simultaneous equations

The optimal solution to a linear programming problem can also be found using simultaneous equations.

5. Slack

Slack occurs when maximum availability of a resource is not used: slack is the amount of the unused resource or other constraint where the constraint is a 'less than or equal to' constraint

Further study guidance

Question practice

Now try the following from the Further question practice bank [available in the digital edition of the Workbook]:

Number	Level	Marks	Approximate time
Section A Q22	Examination	2	4 mins
Section A Q23	Examination	2	4 mins
Section A Q24	Examination	2	4 mins

Further reading

There is a technical article available on ACCA's website, called *Linear programming*.

You are strongly advised to read this article in full as part of your preparation for the PM exam.

Activity answers

Activity 1: Optimal production mix

1 The correct answer is:

	A	B	C
Contribution per unit (W)	$45	$35	$41
Kg per unit	10	6	3
Contribution per kg (to two decimal places)	$4.50	$5.83	$13.67
Rank	3	2	1

Production plan

	A	B	C
Contract units	5	5	5
Demand units	30	50	50
Total units	35	55	55
Contribution	$1,575	$1,925	$2,255

Workings

Contribution

	A $	B $	C $
Sales	150	120	100
Materials	50	30	15
Labour (10% premium)	55	55	44
Contribution	45	35	41

	A	B	C	Total
Contract units	5	5	5	
Materials (kg)	50	30	15	95
Demand units	30 (bal)	50	50	
Materials (kg)	300	300	150	750
				845
Total units	35	55	55	
Contribution	$1,575	$1,925	$2,255	

Activity 2: Shadow price

The correct answer is:

$4.50

If 1 more kg of material were available, it would be used towards production of A. Contribution/kg for A is $4.50.

The shadow price of material is therefore $4.50

Activity 3: Optimum production plan

The correct answer is:

Rolls 11, Baguettes 10, Loaves 20

Step 1 Determine the bottleneck resource.

The question says that baking is the bottleneck.

Step 2 Calculate the throughput per unit for each product.

	Rolls	Baguettes	Loaves
	$	$	$
Sales price	1.20	1.00	1.50
Materials cost (ingredients)	0.25	0.10	0.35
Throughput/unit	0.95	0.90	1.15

Step 3 Calculate throughput per unit of limiting factor (machine hours).

	Rolls	Baguettes	Loaves
Throughput/unit	$0.95	$0.90	$1.15
Baking hours per unit	2 hours	1.8 hours	2 hours
Throughput per baking hour	$0.475	$0.50	$0.575

Step 4 Rank products.

	Rolls	**Baguettes**	**Loaves**
	3rd	2nd	1st

Step 5 Allocate resources to arrive at optimum production plan.

Product	Units	Bottleneck resource hours/unit	Total hours
Loaves	20	2 hours	40
Baguettes	10	1.8 hours	18
			58
Rolls (balance)	11	2 hours	22
			80

Activity 4: Make or buy and limiting factors

The correct answer is:

TW should manufacture 9000 units of D and 7000 units of E to maximise profits.

BPP
LEARNING
MEDIA

	D	E
	$ per unit	$ per unit
Variable cost of making	10	15
Variable cost of buying	<u>17</u>	<u>25</u>
Extra variable cost of buying	7	10
Raw material saved by buying	3.5kg	8kg
Extra variable cost of buying per kg saved	$2	$1.25
Priority for internal manufacture	1st	2nd

Production plan	Material used
	kg
∴ Make D (9,000 × 3.5kg)	31,500
E (7,000 × 8kg)	<u>56,000</u>
Total materials consumed (maximum available)	<u>87,500</u>

The remaining 5,000 units of E should be purchased from the subcontractor.

Activity 5: Optimal contribution

1 The correct answer is:

Let p= the number of purses to manufacture

Let h = the number of handbags to manufacture

2 The correct answer is:

Maximise 5p + 6h

3 The correct answer is:

Leather: 1.5p +2h ≤ 600

Skilled labour: 0.75p + 0.5h ≤ 210

Demand: h ≤ 250

Non-negativity: p,h ≥ 0

4 The correct answer is:

Line A = Leather

Line B = Labour

Line C = Demand

5 The correct answer is:

160 Purses

180 Handbags

The optimal point solution is the point where the labour and leather lines intersect.

6 The correct answer is:

$1,880 per week

Contribution = 5p + 6h = (5×160) + (6×180) = $1,880 per week

Activity 6: Binding constraints

The correct answers are:

- Material 1
- Material 2

Materials 1 and 2 are binding constraints as the optimal solution is found at the point at which these constraints intersect. The other three constraints will not actually be binding constraints, meaning that not all of the labour will be used and that there will be unsatisfied sales demand for both Products A and B.

Activity 7: Contribution

1 The correct answer is:

$9,300

Equation 1: Labour	5g + 8k 8,000		5g + 8k 8,000
Equation 2: Material	2g + 4k 3,600	×2	4g + 8k 7,200
			g = 800

Substitute g = 800 into equation 1:

5g + 8k = 8,000

(5 × 800) + 8k = 8,000

4,000 + 8k = 8,000

8k = 4,000

K = 4,000/8 = 500

Value of the objective function:

(6 × 800) + (9 × 500) = 9,300

Activity 8: Objective function

The correct answer is:

Maximise 10m + 15n

To derive the objective function, it is necessary to calculate the contribution per unit. This is the selling price less all variable costs.

	M $	N $
Selling price per unit	40	50
Less:		
Material P @ $4 per kg	(16)	(12)
Material Q @$5 per kg	(10)	(15)
Labour @ $8 per hour	(4)	(8)
Contribution per unit	10	15

Activity 9: Slack

The correct answer is:

1,600 hours

600 hours

Test time used: (20,000 x 18)/60 + (66,000 x 4)/60 = 10,400 hours

Therefore, slack hours = 12,000 – 10,400 = 1,600 hours

Program time used: (20,000 x 36)/60 + (66,000 x 14)/60 = 27,400 hours

Therefore, slack hours = 28,000 – 27,400 = 600 hours

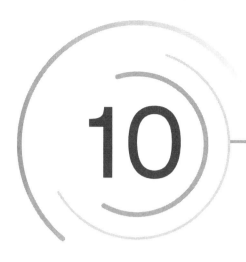

10

Pricing decisions

Learning objectives

On completion of this chapter, you should be able to:

	Syllabus reference no.
Explain the factors that influence the pricing of a product or service.	C4 (a)
Calculate and explain the price elasticity of demand.	C4 (b)
Derive and manipulate a straight line demand equation. Derive an equation for the total cost function (including volume-based discounts).	C4 (c)
Calculate the optimum selling price and quantity for an organisation, equating marginal cost and marginal revenue.	C4 (d)
Evaluate a decision to increase production and sales levels, considering incremental costs, incremental revenues and other factors.	C4 (e)
Determine prices and output levels for profit maximisation using the demand-based approach to pricing (both tabular and algebraic methods).	C4 (f)
Explain different price strategies, including: (a) All forms of cost-plus (b) Skimming (c) Penetration (d) Complementary product (e) Product-line (f) Volume discounting (g) Discrimination (h) Relevant cost	C4 (g)
Calculate a price from a given strategy using cost-plus and relevant cost.	C4 (h)

Exam context

All profit organisations and many non-profit organisations face the task of setting a price for their products or services.

In this chapter, we will begin by looking at the **factors which influence pricing** policy. Perhaps the most important of these are the prices charged by **competitors**, and the **level of demand** for the organisation's products or services. In a market that is not so competitive, pricing should still be set at a level that customers will pay but which also provides a satisfactory profit.

This chapter also considers the profit-maximising price/output level and a range of different pricing strategies.

Exam questions on pricing in Section C are likely to be a mixture of calculation and discussion and the examining team will expect a practical application of pricing theories.

Chapter overview

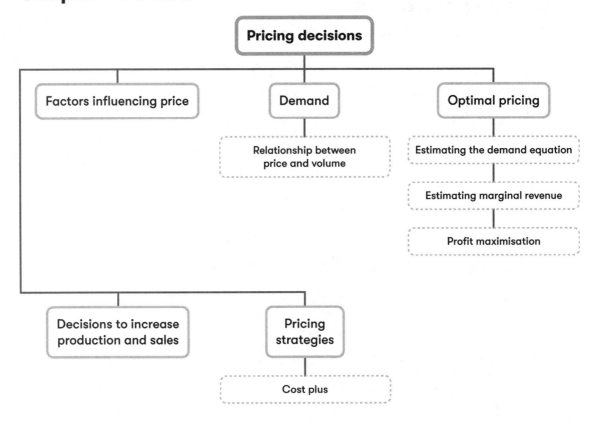

1 Factors influencing price

The price to be charged to customers for a business' products or services is an important business decision. Where there is not a prevailing market price, a business will have to select its chosen selling price using techniques and strategies that we will cover in this chapter.

Historically, the cost of a product would have had a large influence on the selling price set for that product. Today, there are many factors that will influence that price.

These factors include:

(a) Demand
(b) Quality
(c) Competitors
(d) Substitutes
(e) Inflation
(f) Age of product
(g) Disposable incomes

Essential reading

See Chapter 10 Section 1 of the Essential reading for more detail on influences on price.

The Essential reading is available as an Appendix of the digital edition of the Workbook.

2 Demand

2.1 Relationship between price and volume

Price impacts volume sold, since a higher price will normally lower the volume sold.

Despite this, organisations may consider increasing revenue if the fall in volume sold (as a percentage) is lower than the increase in the price (as a percentage).

Where this is the case, demand is said to be unresponsive to price changes or is **price-inelastic.**

> **Price elasticity of demand (PED): Price elasticity of demand (PED):** measures the extent of the change in market demand for a product or service **in response to a change in its price.**

> ## Formula to learn
>
> $$\text{PED} = \frac{\text{\% change in demand}}{\text{\% change in price}}$$

The **value of elasticity** may be anything from zero to infinity.

> **Value of elasticity:** If the result of the formula, in absolute terms, is less than one, the demand is **inelastic.** If the result of the formula in absolute terms is greater than one, the demand is **elastic.**

Demand is referred to as **inelastic** if the percentage change in demand is **lower** than the percentage change in price. This gives an absolute value of **less than one** (ignoring the negative sign, which is normal because PED is expected to be negative since demand will fall if price rises and vice versa).

Demand is referred to as **elastic** if the percentage change in demand is **higher** than the percentage change in price. This gives an absolute value of **more than one** (ignoring the negative sign).

Where demand is inelastic, prices can be raised without significantly affecting demand. If demand is elastic, a decrease in price will result in an increase in volume.

 ## Illustration 1: Price elasticity of demand

The price of a good is $1.20 per unit and annual demand is 800,000 units. Market research indicates that an increase in price of 10 cents per unit will result in a fall in annual demand of 75,000 units.

1 Required

What is the price elasticity of demand? (Ignore the negative sign and work to three decimal places.)

Annual demand at $1.20 per unit is 800,000 units.

Annual demand at $1.30 per unit is 725,000 units.

% change in demand = (75,000/800,000) × 100% = 9.375%

% change in price = ($0.10/ $1.20) × 100% = 8.333%

Price elasticity of demand = (−9.375/8.333) = −1.125 or 1.125 ignoring the negative sign

Since the demand goes up when the price falls, and goes down when the price rises, the elasticity has a negative value, but it is usual to ignore the minus sign.

Ignoring the minus sign, price elasticity is 1.125.

The demand for this good, at a price of $1.20 per unit, would be referred to as **elastic** because the **price elasticity of demand is greater than one**.

Solution

1 The correct answer is:

A price rise will therefore cause a **fall in revenue**.

Revenue before the price rise = $1.20 × 800,000 = $960,000

Revenue after the price rise = $1.30 × 725,000 = $942,500

2.1.1 Factors determining price elasticity of demand

Factor	How it might act to reduce elasticity
Income	If a good takes up a low percentage of customer income, customers will be less sensitive to price rises.
Degree of necessity	An essential item (eg medicine) will still have to be bought even if the price rises.
Availability of alternative products	If there are few alternative substitute goods or services, there will be a smaller fall in demand if price rises.

 ## Activity 1: PED

1 A football club charges $12 per ticket for home games. Average attendance at these regular games is 16,000.

When prices were increased by $1 per ticket, attendance fell by 2,500.

Required

Determine the PED if ticket price increases from $12 to $13.

Solution

1

3 Optimal pricing

It is possible to try to estimate the 'optimal' selling price by combining an analysis of both costs and demand factors. This selling price is designed to maximise short-term profitability.

3.1 Estimating the demand equation

The demand equation shows the relationship between the price charged for a product and the subsequent demand for that product.

An examination question may indicate that the demand curve for a product can be stated as a **straight line equation**: $P = a - bQ$.

In practice, a linear relationship is most unlikely to happen, but it is an assumption made in pricing theory that you need to understand.

Formula provided

When demand is linear, the **equation for demand is $P = a - bQ$**

Where P   = the selling price

Q   = the quantity demanded at that price

a   = theoretical maximum price. If price is set at 'a' or above, demand will be zero.

b   = the change in price required to change demand by unit

Illustration 2: Deriving the demand equation

1   The current price of a product is $12. At this price, the company sells 60 items a month. One month, the company decides to raise the price to $15, but only 45 items are sold at this price. Determine the demand equation, which is assumed to be a straight line equation.

Solution

1   **The correct answer is:**

Step 1 Calculate b

$$b = \frac{\text{change in price}}{\text{change in quantity}} = \frac{\$15 - \$12}{60 - 45} = \frac{3}{15} = 0.2$$

Step 2 Substitute the known value for 'b' into the demand function to find 'a'

P = a - (0.2Q)

12 = a - (0.2 x 60)

12 = a - 12

a = 24

The demand equation is therefore P = 24 – 0.2Q

Step 3 Check your equation

We can check this by finding Q when P is $15.

15 = 24 - (0.2Q)

0.2Q = 24 – 15

0.2Q = 9

$$Q = \frac{9}{0.2} = 45$$

Activity 2: Deriving and using a demand equation

A football club charges $12 per ticket for home games. Average attendance at these regular games is 16,000.

When prices were increased by $1 per ticket, attendance fell by 2,500.

Assume attendance to be purely price dependent.

Required

Derive the demand equation and calculate the ticket price to ensure a full house with capacity being 25,000.

O $6.40

O $8.40

O $13

O $18.40

Solution

3.2 Estimating marginal revenue

It is worthwhile for a company to sell further units when the increase in revenue gained from the sale of the next unit (marginal revenue) is greater than the cost of making it (marginal cost).

Marginal revenue (MR) is determined by the demand curve and can be expressed as an equation that is similar to the demand equation that we have seen already.

Formula provided

MR = a - 2bQ

Where MR	= the marginal revenue
Q	= the quantity demanded
a	= the price at which demand would be nil
b	= change in price / change in quantity

Economic theory suggests that in order to sell more, the selling price will need to be reduced. As a result, the marginal (extra) revenue generated by selling another unit will continually fall as output rises. Marginal revenue may not be the same as the price charged for all units up to that demand level, as to increase volumes the price may have to be reduced.

3.3 Profit maximisation

As economic theory suggests, that marginal (extra) revenue generated by selling another unit will continually fall as output rises, there will be a point at which it is not worth cutting the price any further because the revenue generated by selling another unit (MR) is below the marginal cost (MC) of producing it. Profits will continue to be maximised only up to the output level where marginal cost has risen to be exactly equal to the marginal revenue. At this point, the selling price is said to be 'optimal' because it is the price at which profits are maximised.

Formula to learn

Profit is maximised at the level of output where MR = MC

3.3.1 Determining the optimal price using equations

You could be required to use the equation for marginal revenue to determine the optimal price.

Remember, marginal cost is the extra cost of producing one extra unit; marginal revenue is the extra revenue from selling one extra unit.

The following approach should be used:

Step 1 – Determine the demand function.

Step 2 – Make the MR equation given equal to the value of MC.

Step 3 – Substitute the values for a and b in Step 1 into the MR formulae and solve to find Q.

Step 4 – Take the quantity in Step 3 and put this into the demand function to find the price to charge.

Illustration 3: MC = MR

1 AB Co has used market research to determine that if a price of $250 is charged for Product G, demand will be 12,000 units. It has also been established that demand will rise or fall by five units for every $1 fall/rise in the selling price.

The marginal cost of Product G is $80

Calculate the profit-maximising selling price for Product G (to the nearest $).

Solution

1 **The correct answer is:**

Step 1 – Determine the demand function.

P = a - bQ

$$b = \frac{1}{5} = 0.2$$

Rearrange P = a – bQ to get: a = P + bQ

Therefore, a = $250 + (12,000 × 0.2) = $2,650

So, P = 2,650 – 0.2Q

Step 2 – Make the MR equation given equal to the value of MC

MR = MC

Step 3 - Substitute the values found for a and b in Step 1 into the MR formulae and solve to find Q.

Profits are maximised when MC = MR, ie when 80 = a – 2bQ

80 = 2,650 – 0.4Q, so 0.4Q = 2,650 – 80, so Q = (2,650 – 80) / 0.4, therefore Q = 6,425

Profit-maximising demand = 6,425

Step 4 – Take the quantity found in Step 3 and put this into the demand function to find the price that should be charged.

Profit-maximising price: P = 2,650 – 0.2Q

= $2,650 – 0.2 × 1,285

= $1,365

Activity 3: Calculating the optimum selling price

A firm charges $18 per unit for its product. At this price it sells 17,000 units.

Research has shown that when prices were changed by $1 per unit sales changed by 2,000 units. The product has a constant variable cost per unit of $5.

The demand function is given by P = a – bQ. The marginal revenue will be MR = a – 2bQ.

Required
Determine the price to be charged to maximise profit.

O $8.50

O $15.75

O $21.50

O $26.50

Solution

3.3.2 Tabular approach

One approach to determining the profit maximising production plan is to calculate the extra (marginal) costs and revenues at different combinations of output and selling price.

Activity 4: Tabular approach

Output	Total cost	MC	Selling price	Total revenue	MR	Profit
(Units)	$	$		$	$	$
10	10	10	5.00	50	50	40
20	25	15	4.50	90	40	65
30	45	20	4.00	120		
40	70	25	3.50			
50	100		3.00			
60	135		2.50			

Required

Complete the table above to determine the selling price per unit that will maximise profit.

O $2.50

O $3.00

O $3.50

O $4.00

Solution

A tabular approach assumes that only discrete variables exist, ie that either 30 or 40 units can be sold, not, say, 35. The use of equations can solve this problem.

4 Decisions to increase production and sales

If you are required to evaluate a decision to increase production and sales levels, you will need to consider **incremental costs, incremental revenues** and other factors.

| **Incremental costs and revenues: Incremental costs and revenues** are the difference between costs and revenues for the corresponding items under each alternative being considered. |

Illustration 4: A decision to increase production

1 George manufactures a product which uses two types of material: A and B. Each unit of production currently sells for $10. A local trader has expressed an interest in buying 5,000 units but is only prepared to pay $9 per unit.

Current costs and revenues are as follows:

	$'000	$'000
Sales		350
Less: production costs		
Material A – 1kg per unit	25	
Material B – 1 litre per unit	50	
Labour – 1 hour per unit	75	
Fixed overhead	76	
Non-production costs	25	
Total cost		250
Budgeted profit		100

The following additional information has also been made available:

(a) There is minimal inventory of material available and prices for new material are expected to be 5% higher for Material A and 3% higher for Material B.

(b) George has been having problems with his workforce and is short of labour hours. He currently has the capacity to produce 36,000 units but would have to employ contract labour at $3.50 per hour to make any additional units.

(c) Included in the fixed production overhead is the salary of the production manager. He is stressed and exhausted and has threatened to leave unless he receives a pay rise of $5,000. George would not be able to fulfil any new orders without him.

Required
Evaluate whether George should accept the new order.

Solution

1 **The correct answer is:**

Current production = 350,000/10 = 35,000 units

Current cost per unit of Material A   = $25,000 / 35,000 = $0.71

Current cost per unit of Material B   = $50,000 / 35,000 = $1.43

Current cost of labour   = $75,000 / 35,000 = $2.14

	$	$
Incremental revenue (5,000 × $9)		45,000
Incremental costs		
Material A (1.05 × $0.71 × 5,000)	3,728	
Material B (1.03 × $1.43 × 5,000)	7,365	
Labour [(1,000 × $2.14) + (4,000 × $3.50)]	16,140	
Fixed overhead	5,000	
		32,233
Incremental profit		12,767

The new order would produce an additional $12,767 so is probably worthwhile but other factors may need to be considered; for example, the effect of a price cut on existing customer expectations and whether the workforce and production manager will be able to fulfil the new order with the same labour efficiency

4.1 Volume based discounts

> **Volume based discount:** A **volume-based discount** is a discount given for buying in bulk.

An organisation may wish to consider offering a volume-based discount to customers for purchases above a certain quantity. The intention may be that, by offering the sale price discount, customers will buy more of the product.

To decide whether a volume-based discount on selling prices is financially worthwhile, a calculation is needed.

By reducing the selling price with a volume-based discount and reducing the price from P1 to P2, sales volume may be expected to increase from Q1 to Q2. Assume that the variable cost of sale is $V per unit, and fixed costs will be unaffected by a change in sales volume.

	$
Total sales revenue at discounted price	(Q2 × P2)
Total sales revenue at non-discounted price	(Q1 × P1)
Increase in sales revenue	Difference
Increase in costs	(Q2 − Q1) × V

Change in profit = (Q2 × P2) − (Q1 × P1) − [(Q2 − Q1) × V]

For example, suppose that a company sells a product at a price of $10 per unit. The unit variable cost is $4. The sales manager believes that, by offering a customer a discount of 5% for buying at least 5,000 units a year, the customer will increase purchases from their current level of 4,000 units to a level of 5,000 units per year.

The effect on profits each year would be calculated as follows:

	$
Total sales revenue at discounted price: 5,000 × $10 × 95%	47,500
Total sales revenue at non-discounted price: 4,000 × $10	40,000

	$
Increase in sales revenue	7,500
Increase in costs (1,000 units × $4)	4,000
Increase in annual profit from volume-based price discounting	3,500

5 Pricing strategies

5.1 Cost plus

The price of the product is calculated by adding an appropriate profit mark up to the product's cost. This cost could be:

- Absorption / full cost (including ABC)
- Marginal cost
- Relevant cost (Chapter 11)
- Standard cost

Advantages

(a) Readily understood / easy to apply

(b) Readily determined

(c) Doesn't require / assume a linear and stable price/quantity relationship

Disadvantages

(a) Because it ignores the impact that the price will have on quantity demanded, it will not maximise profit.

(b) If the basis of absorbing overheads changes, the price of the product will change. Thus, absorption costing methods require accurate overhead and activity levels.

(c) Price may need to be adjusted to reflect market conditions.

Activity 5: Full cost plus method

A company budgets to make 20,000 units which have a variable cost of production of $4 per unit. Fixed production costs are $60,000 per year.

If the selling price is to be 40% higher than full cost, what is the selling price of the product using the full cost-plus method (to two decimal places)?

$ _____

Solution

5.2 Market penetration

> **Penetration pricing: Penetration pricing** is a policy of low prices when a product is first launched in order to obtain strong demand for the product as soon as it is launched on the market. Low prices should encourage bigger demand.

Useful if:

(a) The firm wants to **discourage new entrants** into the market.

(b) The firm wishes to **shorten the initial period** of the product's life cycle.

(c) There are significant **economies of scale** to be achieved.

(d) Demand is **highly elastic** and so would respond well to low prices.

5.3 Market skimming

> **Price skimming: Price skimming** involves charging high prices when a new product is first launched on the market, in order to maximise short-term profitability.

Initially there is heavy spending on advertising and sales promotion to obtain sales. As the product moves into the later stages of its life cycle (growth, maturity and decline), progressively lower prices will be charged. The aim of market skimming is to gain high unit profits early in the product's life.

Useful if:

(a) The product is **new and different**, so that early adopters are prepared to pay high prices to be seen to own the latest products.

(b) The strength of **demand** and the sensitivity of demand to price are unknown.

(c) High prices in the early stages of a product's life might generate **high initial cash outflows**. A firm with liquidity problems may prefer market skimming for this reason.

(d) The product has a short life cycle and needs to recover development costs and make a profit quickly.

> ### Exam focus point
> An exam question could ask you to explain why a particular pricing method might or might not be suitable for a specific business. Make sure you know the features and relevant situations for each pricing method.

5.4 Price discrimination

> **Price discrimination:** Price discrimination is the practice of charging different prices for the same product to different groups of buyers when these prices are not reflective of cost differences.

When a company can sell into two or more separate markets, it might be able to charge a different price in each market. To be successful, the company must prevent the transfer of goods from the cheap market to the more expensive one.

There are a number of bases on which such discriminating prices can be set.

(a) **By market segment**. Items such as cinema tickets and hairdressing services are often available at lower prices to over 60s, students or juveniles.

(b) **By product version**. For example, some car models have 'add on' extras.

(c) **By place**. Theatre seats are usually sold according to the type of seat and its location in the theatre auditorium.

(d) **By time**. This is perhaps the most popular type of price discrimination, eg off-peak travel bargains, hotel prices. Railway companies are successful price discriminators, charging more to rush hour rail commuters whose demand is inelastic at certain times of the day.

Price discrimination can only be effective if a number of conditions hold:

(a) The market must be **segmentable** in price terms, and different sectors must show different intensities of demand.

(b) There must be little or **no** chance of a **black market** developing (this would allow those in the lower priced segment to resell to those in the higher priced segment).

(c) There must be little or **no** chance that **competitors** can and will undercut the firm's prices in the higher priced (and/or most profitable) market segments.

(d) The cost of segmenting and **administering** the arrangements should not exceed the extra revenue derived from the price discrimination strategy.

5.5 Product-line pricing

> **Product line:** A **product line** is a group of products that are related to one another. A product line may be a range of branded products, and a consistent pricing policy should be applied to all the products in the range.

Most organisations sell not just one product but a range of products. For example, a company may manufacture a range of hygiene and skincare products, such as soaps, shower gels and bath oils, under the same brand name.

Focus is placed on the profit from the whole range rather than the profit on each single product.

There is a range of product line pricing strategies.

(a) Set prices **proportional to** full or marginal **cost** with the **same percentage profit margin** for all products. This means that prices are dependent on cost and ignore demand.

(b) Set prices reflecting the demand relationships between the products so that an **overall required rate of return** is achieved.

(c) Set prices that **reflect customer opinion** about the quality of the products, and how they compare with similar products of competitor organisations.

5.6 Complementary product pricing

> **Complementary products: Complementary products** are goods that tend to be bought and used together. If an organisation makes and sells complementary products, it may wish to decide the selling prices for the products in a single pricing policy decision.

One product would tend to be priced competitively which attracts demand for the complementary product, for example, an electric toothbrush and replacement toothbrush heads. The electric toothbrush may be priced competitively to attract demand but the replacement heads can be relatively expensive.

5.7 Volume discounts

> **Volume discount:** A **volume discount** is a reduction in price given for larger than average purchases.

These are given in order to increase sales volume without reducing prices permanently. They also allow differentiation between customers, ie wholesale v retail. The reduced costs of a large order will hopefully compensate for the loss of revenue from offering the discount.

5.8 Relevant cost pricing

Special orders may require a **relevant cost** approach to the calculation of the price. A relevant cost approach is to identify a price at which the organisation will **be no better off, but no worse off**, if it sells the item at that price. Any price in excess of this minimum price will add to net profit.

A special order is a **one-off** revenue-earning opportunity. These may arise in the following situations:

(a) When a business has a regular source of income but also has some **spare capacity**, allowing it to take on extra work if demanded. For example, a company might have a capacity of 500,000 units per month but only be producing and selling 300,000 units per month. It could therefore consider special orders to use up some of its spare capacity.

(b) When a business has **no regular source of income** and relies exclusively on its ability to respond to demand. A building firm is a typical example, as are many types of subcontractors. In the service sector, consultants often work on this basis.

The reason for making the distinction is that in the case of (a), a firm would normally attempt to cover its **longer-term running costs** in its prices for its **regular product**. Pricing for special orders therefore does **not need** to **consider unavoidable fixed costs**, which will be incurred anyway. This is clearly not the case for a firm in (b)'s position, where special orders are the only source of income for the foreseeable future.

Relevant costing is covered in the next chapter and so relevant cost pricing will mean more to you once you understand relevant costs.

Activity 6: Pricing strategies

1 The Q organisation is a large, worldwide respected manufacturer of consumer electrical and electronic goods. Q constantly develops new products that are in high demand as they represent the latest technology and are 'must haves' for those consumers that want to own the latest consumer gadgets. Recently, Q has developed a new handheld digital DVD recorder and seeks your advice as to the price it should charge for such a technologically advanced product.

Required
Suggest pricing policies that would be suitable for each stage of the product life cycle of the DVD recorder.

Solution

1

6 Other considerations

Bear in mind that pricing decisions should not be based on financial factors alone. Non-financial considerations should also be made.

These might include:

- Company objectives – sales, market share, long- term or short-term
- Competition and markets – competing products and reaction of competitors
- Production capacity – demand may exceed supply
- Product life cycle – introduction, growth, maturity, decline
- Superior innovation, technology or quality – may set higher prices
- Customers' buying power
- Other products in range – displacing or supplementary
- Availability of resources
- Impact on staff
- Impact on customers
- Competitors' reactions
- Opportunity costs
- Impact on other products

Chapter summary

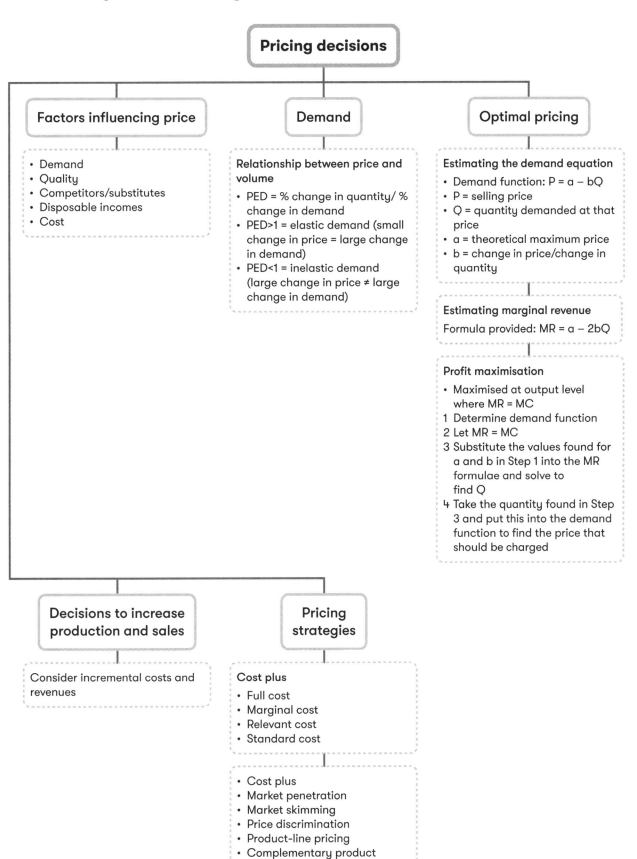

Pricing decisions

Factors influencing price

- Demand
- Quality
- Competitors/substitutes
- Disposable incomes
- Cost

Demand

Relationship between price and volume

- PED = % change in quantity/ % change in demand
- PED>1 = elastic demand (small change in price = large change in demand)
- PED<1 = inelastic demand (large change in price ≠ large change in demand)

Optimal pricing

Estimating the demand equation

- Demand function: P = a − bQ
- P = selling price
- Q = quantity demanded at that price
- a = theoretical maximum price
- b = change in price/change in quantity

Estimating marginal revenue

Formula provided: MR = a − 2bQ

Profit maximisation

- Maximised at output level where MR = MC
1 Determine demand function
2 Let MR = MC
3 Substitute the values found for a and b in Step 1 into the MR formulae and solve to find Q
4 Take the quantity found in Step 3 and put this into the demand function to find the price that should be charged

Decisions to increase production and sales

Consider incremental costs and revenues

Pricing strategies

Cost plus

- Full cost
- Marginal cost
- Relevant cost
- Standard cost

- Cost plus
- Market penetration
- Market skimming
- Price discrimination
- Product-line pricing
- Complementary product pricing
- Volume discounts
- Relevant cost pricing

Knowledge diagnostic

1. Demand

PED measures the responsiveness of demand to a change in price. PED > 1 = elastic demand. PED < 1 = inelastic demand.

Price can be determined using the demand function:

P = a – bQ.

2. Optimal pricing

The output level to maximise profit is found when MR = MC.

The output level to maximise revenue is where MR = 0.

Prices at these output levels can then be determined from the demand function.

3. Decisions to increase production and sales

Consider incremental costs and revenues

4. Pricing strategies

There are several strategies that can be applied to a product. These strategies may be changed depending upon the stage in the product life cycle.

5. Other considerations

The pricing strategy should be chosen bearing in mind both financial and non-financial factors.

Further study guidance

Question practice

Now try the following from the Further question practice bank [available in the digital edition of the Workbook]:

Number	Level	Marks	Approximate time
Section A Q25	Examination	2	4 mins
Section A Q26	Examination	2	4 mins
Section A Q27	Examination	2	4 mins
Section A Q28	Examination	2	4 mins

Activity answers

Activity 1: PED

1 **The correct answer is:**

% change in price	= $1 / $12	= 8.3% increase
% change in demand	= 2,500 / 16,000	= 15.6% decrease
PED	= -15.6% / 8.3 %	= 1.9

Demand is elastic

Activity 2: Deriving and using a demand equation

The correct answer is:

$8.40

$P = a - b Q$

$b = \$1/2,500 = 0.0004$

$12 = a - (0.0004 \times 16,000)$

$a = 18.4$

$P = 18.4 - 0.0004Q$

Therefore, to sell 25,000 tickets:

$P = 18.4 - 25,000 \times 0.0004 = \$8.40$ per ticket

Activity 3: Calculating the optimum selling price

The correct answer is:

$15.75

(a) Determine the demand function:

$P = a - bQ$

$b = \$1 / 2,000 = 0.0005$

$18 = a - (0.0005 \times 17,000)$

$a = 26.50$

$P = 26.50 - 0.0005Q$

(b) Make the MR equation given equal to the value of MC

$MR = MC$

3. Substitute the values found for a and b in Step 1 into the MR formulae and solve to find Q

$MR = a - 2bx = 26.50 - 0.001Q$

$MC = 5$

Therefore, $26.50 - 0.001Q = 5$

Therefore, $Q = 21,500$ units

4. Take the quantity found in Step 3 and put this into the demand function to find the price that should be charged

$P = 26.50 - (0.0005 \times 21,500)$

$= 15.75$ per unit

Activity 4: Tabular approach

The correct answer is:

$4.00

Output (units)	Total cost $	MC $	Selling price $	Total revenue $	MR $	Profit $
10	10	10	5.00	50	50	40
20	25	15	4.50	90	40	65
30	45	20	4.00	120	30	75
40	70	25	3.50	140	20	70
50	100	30	3.00	150	10	50
60	135	35	2.50	150	0	15

Profit is maximised at an output level of 30 units with a selling price of $4 per unit.

Activity 5: Full cost plus method

The correct answer is:

$9.80

Full cost per unit = variable cost + fixed cost

Variable cost = $4 per unit

$$\text{Fixed cost} = \frac{\$60,000}{20,000} = \$3 \text{ per unit}$$

Full cost per unit = $(4 + 3) = $7

∴ Selling price using full cost-plus pricing method = $7.00 × 140%/100 = $9.80

Activity 6: Pricing strategies

1 **The correct answer is:**

The product life cycle comprises five stages:

- Development
- Introduction
- Growth
- Maturity
- Decline

In the **introduction stage,** the company needs to price the product to achieve its market strategy using either **penetration** or **skimming** pricing policies.

A **penetration policy** is used with the objective of achieving a high level of demand very quickly by using a low price that is affordable to a large number of potential customers.

A **skimming policy** is particularly appropriate to a product that has a novelty value or that is technologically advanced such as the DVD recorder. Such a policy uses a price that is high and this restricts the volume of sales since only high worth customers can afford the product, but the high unit profitability enables the initial supplier to recover their development costs.

Competitors will be attracted to the product by its high price and will seek to compete with it by introducing their own version of the product at much lower development costs (by reverse engineering Q's product) so it is important for Q to **reduce the price** during the **growth stage** of the product's life cycle. There may be many price reductions during this phase so that the product gradually becomes more affordable to lower social economic groups.

As the product enters the **maturity stage,** the price will need to be **lowered further**, though a profitable contribution ratio would continue to be earned. Competition is often found in this stage, but contribution ratio would continue to be earned. Competition is often found in this stage but, provided Q has gained market share and survived until this stage, the opportunity to make profit and cash surpluses should exist. However, in this type of market the price will tend to be set by the market and Q will have to accept that price. Thus, Q will need to focus on the **control of its costs** to ensure that the product will remain profitable.

When the product enters the **decline phase,** a **loyal group of customers** may continue to be prepared to pay **a reasonable price** and at this price the product will continue to be profitable, especially as costs continue to reduce. Eventually, the price will be lowered to **marginal cost** or even lower in order to sell off inventories of what is now an obsolete product as it has been replaced by a more technologically advanced item.

11

Short-term decisions

Learning objectives

On completion of this chapter, you should be able to:

	Syllabus reference no.
Explain the concept of relevant costing.	C1 (a)
Identify and calculate relevant costs for specific decision situations from given data.	C1 (b)
Explain and apply the concept of opportunity costs.	C1 (c)
Explain the issues surrounding make vs buy and outsourcing decisions.	C5 (a)
Calculate and compare 'make' costs with 'buy-in' costs.	C5 (b)
Compare in-house costs and outsource costs of completing tasks and consider other issues surrounding this decision.	C5 (c)
Apply relevant costing principles in situations involving shutdown, one-off contracts and the further processing of joint products.	C5 (d)

Exam context

The concept of **relevant cost** was briefly touched on in its use in one-off contracts to identify a minimum price in the previous chapter.

In this chapter, we look in greater depth at relevant costs and at how they should be applied in **decision-making situations**.

We look at a variety of common short-run business decisions and consider how they can be dealt with using relevant costs as appropriate.

The ability to recognise relevant costs and revenues is a key skill for the Performance Management (PM) exam, and questions are likely to be based on practical scenarios.

Chapter overview

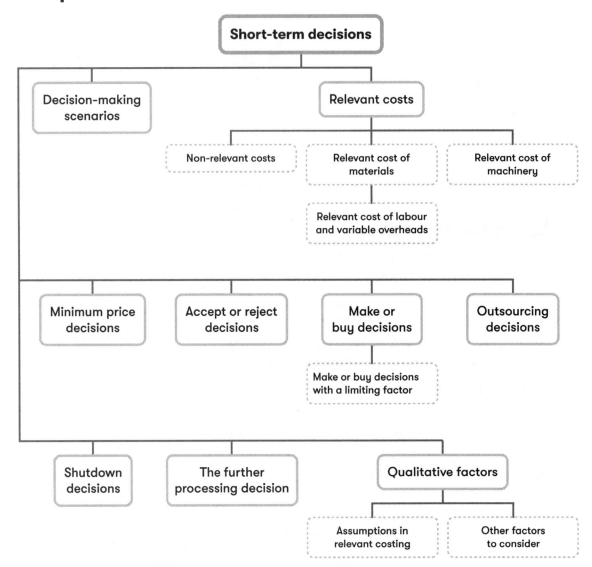

1 Decision-making scenarios

You need to be able to apply relevant costing principles to a range of short-term decisions that a business may have to make. There are lots of types of decisions including:

(a) Minimum price of an order/job/contract

(b) Accept or reject

(c) Make or buy

(d) Outsource

(e) Shutdown

(f) Further processing decisions

The calculations are important, but so too are the non-financial factors involved. For example, when deciding whether to shut down a business segment, there is more to consider than the financial implication alone.

2 Relevant costs

The costs that should be used for decision-making are referred to as relevant costs.

KEY
TERM

> **Relevant costs:** These are "Costs appropriate to specific management decisions these are represented by future cash flows whose magnitude will vary depending upon the outcome of the management decision made" *(CIMA Official Terminology)*.

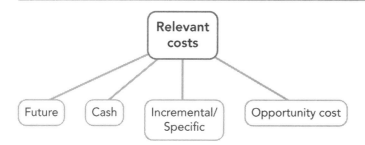

Relevant costs must be:

(a) **Future**. They must occur in the future.

(b) **Incremental**. For example, suppose a company decides to accept a contract from a customer. An existing supervisor currently earning $1,000 per month is given an extra $100 per month for taking on the extra responsibility associated with this contract. The **incremental** cost is the **additional** salary paid to the supervisor ($100) – the original salary of $1,000 was being paid anyway.

(c) **Cash flow**. This means that costs or charges which do not reflect additional **cash** spending, should be ignored for the purpose of decision-making. These are outlined in the non-relevant costs section below.

Relevant costs may also be:

Opportunity costs. The value of a benefit sacrificed when one course of action is chosen in preference to an alternative. The opportunity cost is represented by the potential benefit forgone from the best rejected course of action. Opportunity costs are relevant for decision-making and are likely to arise when there are a number of possible uses of a scarce resource.

Avoidable costs. These are the specific costs of an activity or sector of a business that would be avoided if that activity or sector did not exist. Avoidable costs are usually associated with shutdown decisions.

2.1 Non-relevant costs

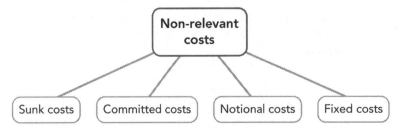

(a) **Sunk costs** are costs already incurred. They are not relevant in decision-making and are therefore ignored.

(b) **Committed costs** have already been committed to and so are not relevant to the decision. Examples might include the cost of materials under a long-term contract.

(c) **Notional costs** are non-cash items or accountancy entries.

(d) Fixed costs are allocated, and general fixed costs are not specific to a decision. Avoidable fixed costs would be relevant.

Activity 1: Relevant cost

A Co is preparing a tender for a new contract to build a bridge. The contracts manager has spent 40 hours researching the contract and preparing the tender. She is paid a fixed annual salary of $96,000 per year for working 48 weeks of 40 hours each.

1 **Required**

How much should be included in the relevant cost of building the bridge for the contracts manager's time (to the nearest whole number)?

Solution

1

BPP LEARNING MEDIA

2.2 Relevant cost of materials

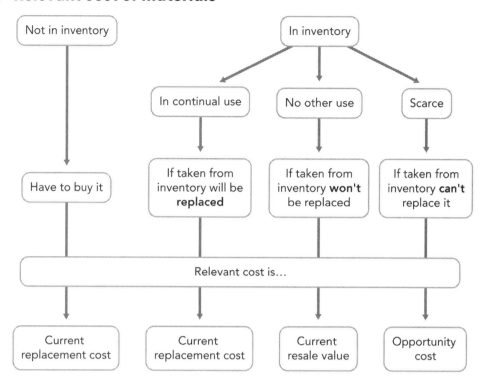

Activity 2: Relevant materials cost

X Co intends to print a catalogue for a one-off special promotion. The catalogue requires 120 boxes of a particular type of paper that is not regularly used by X Co although a limited amount remains in X Co's inventory from a similar job.

The cost when X Co bought the paper two years ago was $17 per box and there are 50 boxes in inventory. The boxes could be sold for $14 each or could be purchased in the market for $22 each.

1 Required
What is the relevant cost of the paper to be used in printing the catalogue (to the nearest whole number)?

Solution

1

2.3 Relevant cost of labour and variable overheads

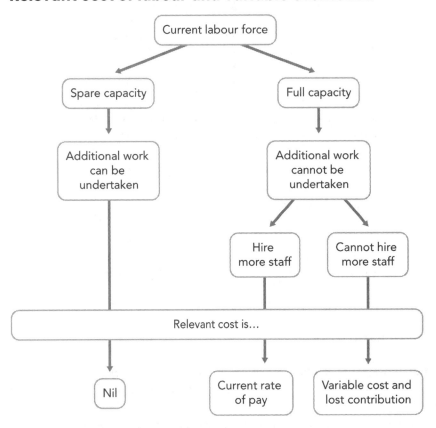

Activity 3: Relevant cost of labour

A Co is deciding whether to undertake a new contract.

15 hours of labour are required for the contract. Labour is currently at **full capacity** producing X.

Cost card for X		$ per unit
Direct materials	(10kg @ $2)	20
Direct labour	(5 hours @ $6)	30
		50
Selling price		75
Contribution		25

1 **Required**

What is the cost of using 15 hours of labour for the contract (to the nearest whole number)?

Solution

1

2.4 Relevant cost of machinery

- Repair costs arising from use
- Hire charges
- Fall in resale value arising from use

 Activity 4: Relevant cost of machinery

J Co was intending to sell one of its production machines for $10,000 as it no longer has a use for it. The machine is being depreciated at $2,000 per annum. The variable running costs for the machine are $500 per annum.

The company has been approached by a new customer and asked to manufacture one million components for a one-off order. These components can only be manufactured on this machine and production will take place over the coming year.

It has been estimated that the machine could be sold for $6,000 in one year's time.

1 **Required**
What is the relevant cost of using the machine to produce the components (to the nearest whole number)?

Solution

1

Activity 5: Relevant cost pricing

Ennerdale has been asked to quote a price for a one-off contract. The following information is available:

Materials

The contract requires 3,000kg of Material K, which is a material used regularly by the company in other production. The company has 2,000kg of Material K currently in stock which had been purchased last month for a total cost of $19,600. Since then, the price per kilogram for Material K has increased by 5%.

The contract also requires 200kg of Material L. There are 250kg of Material L in stock which are not required for normal production. This material originally cost a total of $3,125. If not used on this contract, the stock of Material L would be sold for $11 per kg.

Labour

The contract requires 800 hours of skilled labour. Skilled labour is paid $9.50 per hour. There is a shortage of skilled labour and all the available skilled labour is fully employed in the company in the manufacture of Product P. The following information relates to Product P:

	$ per unit	$ per unit
Selling price		100
Less:		
Skilled labour	38	
Other variable costs	22	
		(60)
		40

1 **Required**

Prepare, on a relevant cost basis, the lowest cost estimate that could be used as the basis for a quotation.

Solution

1

3 Minimum price decisions

The minimum price for a one-off decision is its total relevant costs. This is the price at which the business would break even.

 Illustration 1: Minimum price

LB Co has been approached by a customer to manufacture a specialised machine. This would be a one-off order which LB Co would undertake in addition to its normal budgeted production.

The assistant accountant has prepared the following quotation:

	Notes	$
Direct materials:		
Aluminium plating (20m² @ $10 per m²)	1	200
Rivets (100 @ $1 each)	2	100
Direct labour:		
Skilled (50 hours @ $16 per hour)	3	800
Semi-skilled (20 hours @ $10 per hour)	4	200
Overheads	5	100
		1,400
Administration overhead @ 10% of production cost	6	140
		1,540
Profit 20% of total cost	7	308
Selling price		1,848

Notes

1) The aluminium plating is regularly used on other work within the business. It has an inventory value of $10 per m² although the current purchase price has recently risen to $12 per m².

2) Rivets are currently held in inventory and cost $1 each although the company has no further use for them. They could be sold to a scrap merchant for $0.50 each.

3) Skilled labourers are paid $16 per hour and are currently fully utilised on other work. If the job was undertaken it would be necessary to work a maximum of 40 hours of overtime (paid at time and a half) and/or reduce the production of another product which earns contribution of $20 per hour.

4) There is currently 100 hours of idle semi-skilled labour time available.

5) Overheads represent an apportionment to cover factory fixed costs.

6) It is policy to add 10% to the production cost of each job to cover the administration cost of orders accepted.

7) Profit of 20% of total cost is added to each job as part of the standard pricing policy.

Required

Prepare, on a relevant cost basis, the minimum price which should be quoted for the job (to the nearest whole $).

$ [   ]

Solution

The correct answer is:

$1,610

Relevant costing statement

	Notes	$
Direct materials:		
Aluminium plating	1	240
Rivets	2	50
Direct labour:		
Skilled	3	1,320
Semi-skilled	4	0
Overheads	5	0
		1,610
Administration overhead	6	0
Total relevant cost		1,610
Profit 20% of total cost	7	0
Minimum price		1,610

Notes

1) Aluminium is in regular use therefore it needs to be replaced. Value at current purchase price: Relevant cost = 20 m² × $12 = $240.

2) Rivets = opportunity cost is lost scrap proceeds, 100 × $0.5 = $50.

3) Skilled labour.

Cheaper to work overtime as $24/hr is less than $36/hr (16 + 20)

	$
40 hours @ $24 =	960
10 hours @ $36 =	360
	1,320

4) Semi-skilled labour

Relevant cost = nil (spare capacity)

5) Overheads – relevant cost is nil

Incurred anyway regardless of this job

6) Administration costs will be incurred regardless of whether or not the job is accepted and are, therefore, not relevant.

7) Profit mark up is not relevant as question asks for a minimum price. A minimum price is one which just covers the total of the relevant costs.

4 Accept or reject decisions

Occasionally, a company may be given a proposal to provide a product or a service for a stated price, and they have to decide whether they should accept or reject it. Accept or reject decisions use exactly the same principles as minimum price decisions. A project with a positive return on a relevant cost basis should be accepted; a negative return should be rejected.

Activity 6: Accept or reject

Make Co makes a range of different products. It has been approached by a new customer to manufacture 12,000 units of T over 12 months at a selling price of $3 per unit. This would be in addition to normal budgeted production.

The following statement has been prepared:

	$	$
Sales revenue		36,000
Costs: Material X at historical cost	5,000	
Material Z at contract price	9,000	
Skilled manufacturing labour	10,000	
Semi-skilled manufacturing labour		
Depreciation of machine	4,000	
Variable overheads @ 30c per unit	3,600	
Fixed overheads		
(absorbed @ 60% of skilled manufacturing labour)	6,000	
		(39,600)
		(3,600)

A quotation now needs to be prepared on a relevant cost basis so that Make Co can decide whether to accept the proposal.

1 Material X cannot be used or sold for any other product. It would cost $200 to dispose of the existing inventories.

Each unit of new production uses two kilos of material Z. The company has entered into a long-term contract to buy 24,000 kilos at an average price of 37.5c per kilo. The current price is 17.5c per kilo. This material is regularly used in the manufacture of the company's other products.

Required

What is the cost of the two materials which should be included in the quotation?

O Material X: $200 and Material Z: $9,000

O Material X: $5,000 and Material Z: $4,200

O Material X: ($200) and Material Z: $9,000

O Material X: ($200) and Material Z: $4,200

2 The new product requires the use of skilled labour, which is scarce. If product T were not made this labour could be used on other activities, which would yield a contribution of $1,000. Semi-skilled labour currently has spare capacity to undertake the additional work.

Required

What cost should be included in the quotation for skilled labour and semi-skilled labour?

O Skilled Labour: $1,000 and Semi-skilled labour: $2,000

O Skilled Labour: $10,000 and Semi-skilled labour: $2,000

O Skilled Labour: $10,000 and Semi-skilled labour: $0

O Skilled Labour: $11,000 and Semi-skilled labour: $0

3 The machine which would be used to manufacture T was bought new 3 years ago for $22,000. It had an estimated life of 5 years with a scrap value of $2,000.

If the new product is not manufactured the machine could be sold immediately for $7,000. If it is used for one year it is estimated that it could then be sold for $4,000.

BPP
LEARNING
MEDIA

Required

What is the cost which should be included in the quotation for machine costs?

- ○ $4,000
- ○ $7,000
- ○ $3,000
- ○ $0

4   Required

Which statement correctly describes the treatment of the general fixed overheads when preparing the quotation?

- ○ The overheads should be included because they relate to production costs.
- ○ The overheads should be included because all expenses should be recovered.
- ○ The overheads should be excluded because they are a sunk cost.
- ○ The overheads should be excluded because they are not an incremental cost.

5   Required

Which statement correctly describes the decision Make Co should reach regarding the proposal?

- ○ Reject because the relevant costs exceed the relevant benefits
- ○ Reject because it will decrease the company's profits for the year
- ○ Accept because the relevant benefits exceed the relevant costs
- ○ Accept because it will increase the company's profits for the year

Solution

1

2

3

4

5 Make or buy decisions

Organisations may need to decide to make components or provide services, themselves in-house or alternatively, to buy them from an outside supplier. In-house production will provide greater control over the work performed but will also use capacity which will give rise to opportunity costs.

Factors to consider:

- How can spare capacity freed up by subcontracting be used most profitably?
- Could the decision to use an outside supplier cause an industrial dispute?
- Would the subcontractor be reliable with delivery times and product quality?
- Does the company wish to be flexible and maintain better control over operations by making everything itself?

Illustration 2: Make or buy

1 Shellfish Co makes four components, W, X, Y and Z, for which costs in the forthcoming year are expected to be as follows:

	W	X	Y	Z
Production (units)	1,000	2,000	4,000	3,000
Unit marginal costs	$	$	$	$
Direct materials	4	5	2	4
Direct labour	8	9	4	6
Variable production overheads	2	3	1	2
	14	17	7	12

Directly attributable fixed costs per year and committed fixed costs:

	$
Incurred as a direct consequence of making W	1,000
Incurred as a direct consequence of making X	5,000

Incurred as a direct consequence of making Y			6,000
Incurred as a direct consequence of making Z			8,000
Other fixed costs (committed)			30,000
			50,000

Directly attributable fixed costs are all items of cash expenditure that are incurred as a direct consequence of making the product in-house.

A subcontractor has offered to supply units of W, X, Y and Z for $12, $21, $10 and $14 respectively.

Required

Calculate the relevant costs of buying each component from the subcontractor.

Solution

1 **The correct answer is:**

The **relevant costs** are the differential costs between making and buying, and they consist of **differences in unit variable costs plus differences in directly attributable fixed costs**. Subcontracting will result in some **fixed cost savings.**

	W	X	Y	Z
	$	$	$	$
Unit variable cost of making	14	17	7	12
Unit variable cost of buying	12	21	10	14
	(2)	4	3	2
Annual requirements (units)	1,000	2,000	4,000	3,000
	$	$	$	$
Extra variable cost of buying (per annum)	(2,000)	8,000	12,000	6,000
Fixed costs saved by buying	(1,000)	(5,000)	(6,000)	(8,000)
Extra total cost of buying	(3,000)	3,000	6,000	(2,000)

Activity 7: Make or buy

1 Mars Co makes units Pluto and Jupiter, for which costs in the forthcoming year are expected to be as follows:

	P	J
Production (units)	1,000	1,500
	$	$
Direct materials	3	5
Direct labour	6	9
Variable production overheads	2	3
	11	17

Directly attributable fixed costs per annum and committed fixed costs:

	$
Incurred as a direct consequence of making P	1,500
Incurred as a direct consequence of making J	3,000
Other fixed costs (committed)	10,000
	14,500

Required

A sub-contractor has offered to supply units of P for $12 and J for $21.

(a) Should Mars make or buy the components?

(b)   What other factors should be considered before making a decision?

Solution

1

Remember decisions should not be purely based on financial factors.

Making the product gives the company more control whereas buying the product gives them access to an organisation with specific expertise.

They will also need to consider what the impact will be on:

(a)   The workforce

(b)   Customers

(c)   Competitors

5.1 Make or buy decisions with a limiting factor

A manufacturing organisation may want to produce items in-house but does not have sufficient capacity to produce everything that it needs, due to a limiting factor on production, such as a shortage of machine time or labour time.

In this situation, the decision is about which items to make internally and which to purchase externally. The optimal decision, based on financial considerations alone, is to arrange internal production and external purchasing in a way that minimises total costs. Total costs will be minimised if those units bought from the subcontractor have the **lowest extra variable cost per unit of scarce resource saved** by buying.

Make or buy decisions involving limiting factors were described in Chapter 8, Limiting factor analysis.

6 Outsourcing decisions

> **Outsourcing: Outsourcing** is the use of external suppliers for finished products, components or services. This is also known as **contract manufacturing** or **subcontracting**.

Outsourcing scenarios are very similar to make or buy decisions and therefore you should approach these in exactly the same way.

Consideration of non-financial factors is particularly important here.

Advantages	Disadvantages
Cost savings	Loss of control
Access to expertise	Impact on quality
Releases capital	How flexible, reliable is supplier
Frees up capacity	Potential loss of confidential information
	Loss of in-house skill
	Impact on employees' morale

7 Shutdown decisions

These decisions may involve the closure of:

(a) A **division** of a business that appears to be loss making

(b) A **product** of a business that appears to be loss making

(c) A **department** of a business that appears to be loss making

Shutdown decisions should focus on relevant costs rather than profitability under absorption costing because absorption costing fails to consider whether overheads will change as a result of the decision.

Shutdown decisions should focus on:

(a) Variable costs

(b) Avoidable costs (what constitutes an avoidable cost may be different depending upon the timing of the decision)

(c) Directly attributable costs (and revenues) if the closure is made

(d) Timing

Illustration 3: Adding or deleting products

1 A company manufactures three products: Pawns, Rooks and Bishops. The present net annual income from these is as follows:

	Pawns	Rooks	Bishops	Total
	$	$	$	$
Sales	50,000	40,000	60,000	150,000
Variable costs	30,000	25,000	35,000	90,000
Contribution	20,000	15,000	25,000	60,000
Fixed costs	17,000	18,000	20,000	55,000
Profit/loss	3,000	(3,000)	5,000	5,000

The company is concerned about its poor profit performance and is considering whether or not to cease selling Rooks. $5,000 of the fixed costs of Rooks are direct fixed costs which would be saved if production ceased (ie there are some attributable fixed costs). All other fixed costs, it is considered, would remain the same.

By **stopping production of Rooks**, the **consequences** would be a $10,000 fall in profits.

	$
Loss of contribution	(15,000)
Savings in fixed costs	5,000
Incremental loss	(10,000)

Suppose, however, it were possible to use the resources realised by stopping production of Rooks and **switch to producing a new item**, Crowners, which would sell for $50,000 and incur variable costs of $30,000 and extra direct fixed costs of $6,000. A new decision is now required.

	Rooks	Crowners
	$	$
Sales	40,000	50,000
Less: variable costs	25,000	30,000
	15,000	20,000
Less: direct fixed costs	5,000	6,000
Contribution to shared fixed costs and profit	10,000	14,000

Solution

1 **The correct answer is:**

It would be **more profitable to shut down production of Rooks and switch** resources to making Crowners, in order to boost profits by $4,000 to $9,000.

Activity 8: Shutdown decisions

Lewis Co manufactures three products: K, L and G. Forecast statements of profit or loss for next year are as follows:

	K	L	G	Total
	$'000	$'000	$'000	$'000
Sales	600	300	200	1,100
Cost of production				
Materials	200	60	30	290
Labour	95	20	10	125
Variable overhead	75	10	5	90
Fixed overhead	200	50	80	330
Gross margin	30	160	75	265
Selling costs	40	20	15	75
Net margin	(10)	140	60	190

The directors are considering the closure of the K product line, due to the losses incurred. You obtain the following information:

(a) Fixed production overheads consist of an apportionment of general factory overheads, based on 80% of direct materials cost. The remaining overheads are specific to the product concerned.

(b) Selling costs are based on commission paid to sales staff.

1 **Required**
Should the K production line be closed down?

Solution

1

8 The further processing decision

8.1 Processes and joint costs

In certain circumstances more than one product may be produced from a single process. These products may sell in their current state or may need further, separate processing before they can be sold.

The costs of the process will need to be apportioned between the products created by the process in order to:

- Value inventory
- Prepare financial accounts

These costs are **not relevant** when deciding whether to **process** any product **further** because they are:

- Sunk
- Arbitrarily apportioned

The total joint cost may be relevant for decisions regarding the viability of the process as a whole.

Joint costs can be apportioned between products based on the following:

- Physical quantity
- Relative sales value
- Net realisable value

Illustration 4: Further processing decisions

The Poison Chemical Company produces two joint products, Alash and Pottum, from the same process. Joint processing costs of $150,000 are incurred up to the split-off point, when 100,000 units of Alash and 50,000 units of Pottum are produced. The selling prices at the split-off point are $1.25 per unit for Alash and $2.00 per unit for Pottum.

The units of Alash could be processed further to produce 60,000 units of a new chemical, Alashplus, but at an extra fixed cost of $20,000 and variable cost of 30c per unit of input. The selling price of Alashplus would be $3.25 per unit.

1 Required

Should the company sell Alash or Alashplus?

- Alash
- Alashplus

Solution

1 The correct answer is:

The only relevant costs/incomes are those which compare the sale of Alash against the sale of Alashplus. Every other cost is irrelevant: they will be incurred regardless of what the decision is.

	Alash			Alashplus
Selling price per unit	$1.25			$3.25
Total sales	$125,000			$195,000
Incremental post-separation processing costs	0	Fixed	$20,000	
	0	Variable	$30,000	$50,000
Sales minus post-separation (further processing) costs	$125,000			$145,000

It is $20,000 more profitable to convert Alash into Alashplus.

Activity 9: Further processing

Product	Output	Selling price at separation	Selling price after further processing	Post-separation costs
	Units	$	$	$
X	2,500	3	5	10,000
Y	1,500	5	10	8,000
Z	2,000	8	15	12,000

Joint processing costs are £20,000.

Which products should be processed further?

- ○ X, Y and Z
- ○ X and Y
- ○ X only
- ○ Z only

Solution

9 Qualitative factors

9.1 Assumptions in relevant costing

(a) Cost behaviour patterns are known with certainty.

(b) Costs, prices and volumes are known with certainty.

(c) Objective is to maximise profit/contribution.

(d) Information is complete and reliable.

9.2 Other factors to consider

Exam questions may require a discussion of other factors, aside from the financial calculation, that should be taken into account when making any decision.

Timescale can also be relevant. Many fixed costs can be varied, but only in the long-term.

Essential reading

See Chapter 11 Section 1 of the Essential reading for more detail on other (non-financial) factors to consider.

The Essential reading is available as an Appendix of the digital edition of the Workbook.

Chapter summary

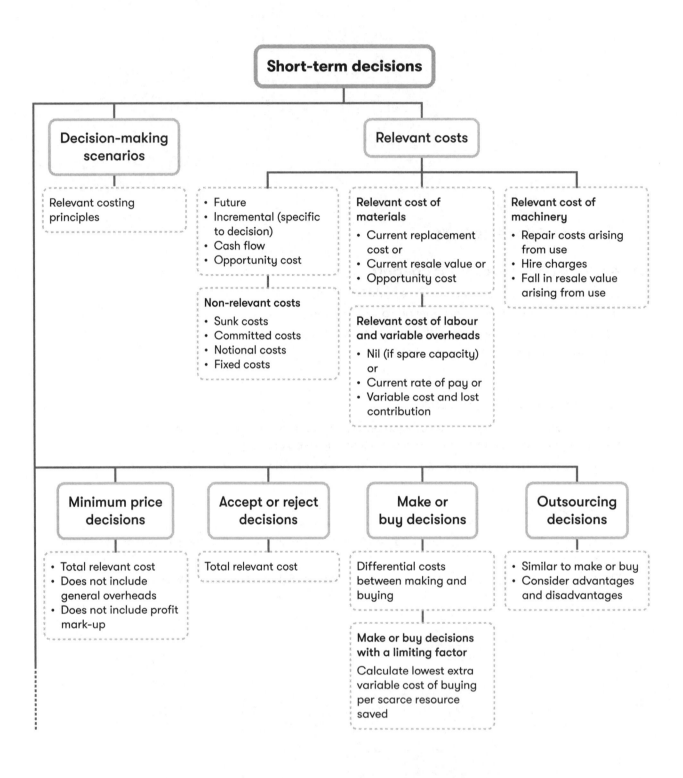

Short-term decisions

Decision-making scenarios

Relevant costing principles

Relevant costs

- Future
- Incremental (specific to decision)
- Cash flow
- Opportunity cost

Non-relevant costs

- Sunk costs
- Committed costs
- Notional costs
- Fixed costs

Relevant cost of materials

- Current replacement cost or
- Current resale value or
- Opportunity cost

Relevant cost of labour and variable overheads

- Nil (if spare capacity) or
- Current rate of pay or
- Variable cost and lost contribution

Relevant cost of machinery

- Repair costs arising from use
- Hire charges
- Fall in resale value arising from use

Minimum price decisions

- Total relevant cost
- Does not include general overheads
- Does not include profit mark-up

Accept or reject decisions

Total relevant cost

Make or buy decisions

Differential costs between making and buying

Make or buy decisions with a limiting factor

Calculate lowest extra variable cost of buying per scarce resource saved

Outsourcing decisions

- Similar to make or buy
- Consider advantages and disadvantages

```
                    ┌──────────────────────────────────────────────────────────────────────────┐
                    │                          │                                      │
            ┌───────┴───────┐          ┌───────┴────────┐                    ┌────────┴────────┐
            │   Shutdown    │          │  The further   │                    │  Qualitative    │
            │   decisions   │          │  processing    │                    │    factors      │
            └───────┬───────┘          │   decision     │                    └────────┬────────┘
                    │                  └───────┬────────┘                    ┌─────────┴─────────┐
```

Shutdown decisions

Focus on relevant costs

The further processing decision

- Joint process costs are not relevant to further processing decision
- Joint process costs may be relevant to process viability as a whole
- Joint costs can be apportioned based on:
  – Physical quantity
  – Relative sales value
  – Net realisable value

Qualitative factors

Assumptions in relevant costing

- Cost behaviour patterns are known with certainty
- Costs, prices and volumes are known with certainty
- Objective is to maximise profit/ contribution
- Information is complete and reliable

Other factors to consider

- Employees
- Customers
- Competitors
- Timing

Knowledge diagnostic

1. Relevant costs

Decisions should be made on the basis of relevant costs.

Relevant costs must be future cash flows and specific to the decision. They may also be opportunity costs.

2. Non-relevant costs

- Sunk costs
- Committed costs
- Notional costs
- Fixed costs

3. Make or buy

In a **make or buy decision**, the choice is between making items in-house or purchasing them from an external supplier. When there are no limiting factors restricting the in-house production capacity, the relevant costs are the differential costs between the two options.

4. Further processing

- A further processing decision often involves joint products from a common manufacturing process. The decision is whether to sell the products at the split-off point, as soon as they emerge from the common process, or whether they should be processed further before selling them.
- A joint product should be **processed further** past the split-off point if the additional sales revenue exceeds the relevant post-separation (further processing) costs.

5. Shutdown

Shutdown/discontinuance problems may sometimes be simplified into short-run relevant cost decisions. A shutdown decision is whether to close down an operation or stop making and selling a particular product or service.

6. Qualitative factors

Non-financial considerations should also be taken into account before making a final decision.

Further study guidance

Question practice

Now try the following from the Further question practice bank [available in the digital edition of the Workbook]:

Number	Level	Marks	Approximate time
Section A Q29	Examination	2	4 mins
Section A Q30	Examination	2	4 mins
Section A Q31	Examination	2	4 mins
Section C Q1	Examination	20	36 mins

Further reading

There is a technical article available on ACCA's website, called *Relevant costs*.

You are strongly advised to read this article in full as part of your preparation for the PM exam.

Activity answers

Activity 1: Relevant cost

1 **The correct answer is:**

$0

There are two reasons why the contracts manager's time is not a relevant cost.

(a) She is paid a fixed salary, ie not incrementally.

(b) It is a sunk cost; the time has already been spent, ie not a future cost.

Activity 2: Relevant materials cost

1 **The correct answer is:**

$2,240

		$
Scrap proceeds forgone of boxes held in inventory	(50 × $14)	700
Purchase price of remaining boxes	(70 × $22)	1,540
Total		2,240

Activity 3: Relevant cost of labour

1 **The correct answer is:**

$165

		$
Variable cost of labour	(15hrs @ $6)	90
Lost contribution from product X	(15hrs × $25/5)	75
Total		165

Activity 4: Relevant cost of machinery

1 **The correct answer is:**

$4,500

		$
Reduction in sales proceeds of machine	($10,000 - $6,000)	4,000
Variable running costs of machine		500
Total		4,500

Activity 5: Relevant cost pricing

1 **The correct answer is:**

$48,670

Relevant cost – Material K

Since the material is regularly used by the company, the relevant cost of Material K is the current price of the material.

Cost last month = $19,600 / 2,000kg

    =$9.80

Revised cost (+5%) = $9.80 x 1.05

    = $10.29

∴ Relevant cost of Material K = 3,000kg x $10.29 per kg

    = $30,870

Relevant cost – Material L

Since the material is not required for normal production, the relevant cost of this material is its net realisable value if it were sold.

∴ Relevant cost of Material L = 200kg × $11 per kg

= $2,200

Relevant cost – Skilled labour

Skilled labour is in short supply and therefore the relevant cost of this labour will include both the actual cost and the opportunity cost of the labour employed.

	$
Cost of skilled labour (800 hours × $9.50)	7,600
Opportunity cost of skilled labour (see working)	8,000
Relevant cost – skilled labour	15,600

Working

Skilled labour cost per unit of Product P = $38

Cost per skilled labour hour = $9.50

∴ Number of hours required per unit of Product P   = $38 / $9.50

                                = 4 hours

Contribution per unit of Product P   = $40

∴ Contribution per skilled labour hour   = $40 / 4hours

                                = $10 per hour

∴ Opportunity cost of skilled labour   = 800 hours × $10 per hour

                                = $8,000

The total relevant costs of this contract are therefore ($30,870 + $2,200 + $15,600) = $48,670

Activity 6: Accept or reject

1   **The correct answer is:**

Material X ($200) and Material Y $4,200

No other use for X in business, but $200 disposal costs are saved by using X to make Ts.

Z is used in the business and will have to be replaced for $0.175 × 2 × 12,000 = $4,200.

2   **The correct answer is:**

Skilled Labour: $11,000 and Semi-skilled labour: $0

Opportunity cost of using skilled labour   =   contribution foregone + cost of labour

= $1,000 + $10,000   = $11,000

The relevant cost of using semi-skilled labour is nil, since there is spare capacity.

3   **The correct answer is:**

$3,000

If the machine is used instead of scrapped, the business loses ($7,000 – $4,000) of scrap proceeds.

4   The correct answer is:

The overheads should be excluded because they are not an incremental cost.

The general fixed overheads should be excluded as they are not incremental, ie they are not arising specifically as a result of this order.

5   The correct answer is:

Accept because the relevant benefits exceed the relevant costs

Conclusion: the proposal should be accepted as it makes a positive contribution of $14,400 based on relevant costs.

		$	$
Sales revenue	(1)		36,000
Costs			
Material X	(2)	(200)	
Material Z	(3)	4,200	
Skilled labour	(4)	11,000	
Semi-skilled labour	(5)		
Variable overhead	(6)	3,600	
Depreciation	(7)	-	
Fixed overheads	(8)	-	
Lost scrap proceeds	(9)	3,000	
Non essential			(21,600)
Net relevant contributions			14,400

(1) Revenue earned as a result of producing and selling T.

(2) No other use for X in the business, but $200 disposal costs are saved by using X to make Ts.

(3) Z is used in the business and will have to be replaced for $0.175 × 2 × 12,000 = $4,200.

Assuming inventories can be bought at this price.

(4) Opportunity cost of using labour = contribution foregone + cost of labour = $1,000 + $10,000 = $11,000

(5) Semi-skilled labour the relevant cost is nil since there is spare capacity.

(6) Variable overhead is only incurred when units are made.

∴ relevant cost = 12,000 × $0.30

(7) Depreciation is not a cash flow and therefore not relevant

(8) These fixed overheads will be incurred regardless of whether or not Ts are made; therefore, cost is not relevant.

(9) If machine is used instead of scrapped, the business loses ($7,000 – $4,000) of scrap proceeds.

However, the following non-financial factors also need to be considered:

(a) The likelihood of a more profitable proposal being received

(b) Whether repeat orders would be expected at the same price in future years

(c) Whether the company's present customers can be differentiated from this special order price

Activity 7: Make or buy

1 The correct answer is:

(a)

	P	J
Production (units)	1,000	1,500
	$	$

Variable cost of making	11	17
Variable cost of buying	12	21
Extra cost of buying / unit	$\underline{1}$	$\underline{4}$
	$\$$	$\$$
Extra variable cost of buying (per annum)	1,000	6,000
Fixed costs saved by buying	(1,500)	(3,000)
Extra total cost of buying	(500)	3,000

The company would save $500 per year by sub-contracting component P but should make units of J itself.

(b) Further considerations:

   (i)   If units of P are sub-contracted, the company will have spare capacity. How should that spare capacity be profitably used? Are there hidden benefits to be obtained from sub-contracting? Would the company's workforce resent the loss of work to an outside sub-contractor, and might such a decision cause an industrial dispute?

   (ii)   Would the sub-contractor be reliable with delivery times, and would they supply components of the same quality as those manufactured internally?

   (iii)   Does the company wish to be flexible and maintain better control over operations by making everything itself?

   (iv)   Are the estimates of fixed cost savings reliable?

Activity 8: Shutdown decisions

1 The correct answer is:

(a) If K were shut down the incremental costs and revenues would be:

	$'000
Lost revenue	600
Saved	
Materials	200
Labour	95
Variable overhead	75
Fixed overhead	
$210 – (0.8 × $200)$	50
Selling costs	30
Profit forgone	150

(b) Other factors

- Losing over 54% of company's revenue – other costs likely to change
- Product interdependencies
- Possibility of changing sales commission or reducing expenses in place of closure
- Capital costs of closure not considered such as asset sales/write-offs
- Redundancy costs

Activity 9: Further processing

The correct answer is:

Z only

Product	price	Increased selling	Incremental revenue	Further costs	Inc benefit/(cost)	Process further?
X		2	5,000	10,000	(5,000)	No

Product price	Increased selling	Incremental revenue	Further costs	Inc benefit/(cost)	Process further?
Y	5	7,500	8,000	(500)	No
Z	7	14,000	12,000	2,000	Yes

Skills checkpoint 2

Using the scenario

Chapter overview

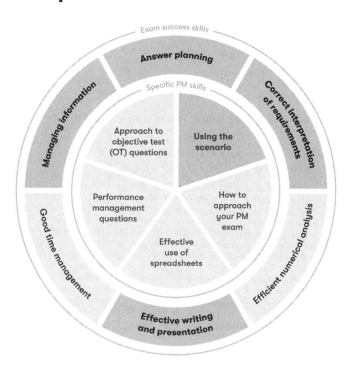

Introduction

Section C questions in the PM exam will be scenario-based. There may be several requirements, including calculations and discussion elements, and they will be based on the scenario. The scenarios are there for a reason! It is vital to spend time reading and absorbing the scenario as part of your answer planning. It is important for you to use the information in the scenario to validate that the discussion points that you are making in your answer are 'relevant'. The discussion parts of the question – applying your knowledge to the scenario – are the parts that many students fail to score well on.

As you get into the habit of practising Section C questions and reading scenarios, you will be less likely to make the mistake of including **too much general theory** in your answers. You are primarily being tested on your **ability to apply** your knowledge to the scenario in question, not your ability to simply recite it.

The skill of '**using the scenario**' is the most important skill you can learn for the discussion elements of Section C questions. Overall, the mix of calculation and discussion elements is 50/50, but it is not unreasonable to expect there to be a higher percentage of discussion marks in a Section C question. In fact, some past Section C questions have been entirely discursive.

Using the scenario

PM Skill: Using the scenario

A step-by-step technique for ensuring that your discussion points are relevant to the scenario is outlined below. Each step will be explained in more detail in the following sections, and illustrated by answering a requirement from a past exam question.

> **STEP 1:**
> Allow some of your allotted time for analysing the scenario and the requirements. Don't rush into starting to write your answer.

> **STEP 2:**
> Prepare an answer plan using key words from the requirements as headings (eg a bullet-pointed list). If you type your plan, you can then use these headings in your answer and move them around as your answer develops. The software makes it easy to change your mind.

> **STEP 3:**
> As you write your answer, explain what you mean in one (or two) sentence(s) and then in the next sentence explain why it matters (in the given scenario). This should results in a series of short punchy paragraphs containing points that address the specific content of the scenario.

Exam success skills

The following illustration is based on an extract from a past ACCA exam question about a retail store, called 'Bits and Pieces', selling spares and accessories for the car market. This extract was worth eight marks.

For this question, we will also focus on the following **exam success skills:**

- **Managing information.** It is easy for the amount of information contained in scenario-based questions to feel overwhelming. To manage this, focus on the requirement first – noting the key exam verbs to ensure you answer the question properly. Then read the rest of the question, noting important and relevant information from the scenario.
- **Correct interpretation of requirements.** Parts (b) and (c) are looking for some common (business) sense, based on the information in the scenario.
- **Answer planning.** Everyone will have a preferred style for an answer plan. For example, it may be a mind map, bullet-pointed lists, or simply making notes. Choose the approach that you feel most comfortable with or, if you are not sure, try out different approaches for different questions until you have found your preferred style.
- **Effective writing and presentation.** It is often helpful to use key words from the requirement as headings in your answer. You may also wish to use sub-headings in your answer; you could use a separate sub-heading for each paragraph from the scenario in the question that contains an issue for discussion. Underline or embolden your headings and sub-headings, and use full sentences, ensuring your style is professional.

Skill activity

STEP 1   Allow some of your allotted time for analysing the scenario and requirements; don't rush into starting to write your answer.

Start by analysing the requirements so that you know what you are looking for when you read the scenario.

(a) **Discuss whether the manager's pay deal (time off and bonus) is likely to motivate him.(4 marks)**

(b) **Briefly discuss whether offering substantial price discounts and promotions on Sunday is a good suggestion.(4 marks)**

The first key action verb is 'discuss'. This is defined by the ACCA as: 'Consider and debate/argue about the pros and cons of an issue. Examine in detail by using arguments in favour or against' and means 'write about any conflict, compare and contrast'.

These requirements are worth eight marks and at 1.8 minutes a mark, they should take 14.4 minutes.

Now move on to reading the scenario, and identifying the key pieces of information provided in it. From reading the requirements, you should know the key issues or clues you are looking for in the scenario.

Bits and pieces (8 marks)

Bits and Pieces (B&P) operates a retail store selling spares and accessories for the car market. The store has previously only opened for six days per week for the 50 working weeks in the year, but B&P is now considering also opening on Sundays.

The sales of the business on Monday through to Saturday averages at $10,000 per day with average gross profit of 70% earned.

B&P expects that the gross profit % earned on a Sunday will be 20 percentage points lower than the average earned on the other days in the week. This is because they plan to offer substantial discounts and promotions on a Sunday to attract customers. Given the price reduction, Sunday sales revenues are expected to be 60% **more than** the average daily sales revenues for the other days. These Sunday sales estimates are for new customers only, with no allowance being made for those customers that may transfer from other days.

B&P buys all its goods from one supplier. This supplier gives a 5% discount on **all** purchases if annual spend exceeds $1,000,000.

It has been agreed to pay time and a half to sales assistants who work on Sundays. The normal hourly rate is $20 per hour. In total, five sales assistants will be needed for the six hours that the store will be open on a Sunday. They will also be able to take a half-day off (four hours) during the week. Staffing levels will be allowed to reduce slightly during the week to avoid extra costs being incurred.

The staff will have to be supervised by a manager, currently employed by the company and paid an annual salary of $80,000. If they work on a Sunday, they will take the equivalent time off during the week when the assistant manager is available to cover for them at no extra cost to B&P. They will also be paid a bonus of 1% of the extra sales generated on the Sunday project.

The store will have to be lit at a cost of $30 per hour and heated at a cost of $45 per hour. The heating will come on two hours before the store opens in the 25 weeks of 'winter' to make sure it is warm enough for customers to come in at opening time. The store is not heated in the other weeks.

The rent of the store amounts to $420,000 per annum.

(a) **Discuss whether the manager's pay deal (time off and bonus) is likely to motivate them.(4 marks)**

(b) **Briefly discuss whether offering substantial price discounts and promotions on Sunday is a good suggestion.(4 marks)**

STEP 2 Now you should be ready to prepare an answer plan using key words from the requirements as headings. This could take the form of a bullet-pointed list.

Complete your answer plan by working through each paragraph of the question, identifying specific points that are relevant to the scenario and requirement to make sure you generate enough points to score a pass mark (ACCA marking guides typically allocate 1–2 marks per relevant well-explained point).

Completed answer plan

Having worked through each paragraph, an answer plan can now be completed. A possible answer plan is shown here. This uses the wording of the requirement and the initial ideas that have been noted in the margins as shown earlier.

Part (b)	Ideas
Discuss* (a) Time off (b) Bonus	As proposed: **Time off in week:** Sunday vs weekday Conclusion re-motivation **Bonus** Calc value Assumptions – estimated sales Compared to sales assistants Conclusion re motivation

* There are two elements to evaluate. Ensure you conclude on how each would/would not motivate the manager. Consider the bigger picture, eg how their reward compares to assistants. Main point of the plan is to establish the structure of the answer.

Part (c)	Ideas
Briefly discuss	**Promotion impact*:** Sunday sales rise, but Sales on other days Customer dissatisfaction Reputational impact if lower price is perceived to mean lower quality

* Think about how each could impact on the company positively or negatively.

STEP 3 As you write your answer, explain what you mean – in one (or two) sentence(s) – and then in the next sentence explain why it matters in the given scenario. This should result in a series of short, punchy paragraphs that address the specific context of the scenario.

Note, however, that addressing the specific context of the scenario does not simply mean repeating the wording in the question. You should avoid doing this; and instead try to explain why your point matters.

Be concise (don't waffle, given that any one point is normally unlikely to be worth more than two marks) and especially avoid reciting theory at length (although briefly defining your terms is often an easy way of scoring a mark).

Finally, write your answer in a time-efficient manner. If 25% of your time has been used for planning/analysis this means that when you are writing the 1.8 minutes per mark becomes 1.8 × 0.75 = 1.35 minutes per mark of writing time. Here this would equate to 3.6 minutes planning and 10.8 minutes writing.

Suggested solution

(a) **Manager's pay deal**

Time off

If[1] the manager works on a Sunday they will take the equivalent **time off**[2] during the week. They are not entitled to extra pay in the same way the sales assistants are, and this seems unfair. Weekend working is disruptive to most people's family and social life and it

[1] Firstly, make the point – using information from the scenario.

[2] Secondly explain why this is relevant to your answer.

is reasonable to expect **extra reward** for giving up time at weekends. It is unlikely that time off in lieu during the week will motivate[3] the manager.

Bonus

The bonus[4] has been calculated as $8,000 which equates to an extra $160 per day of extra work. The sales assistants will be paid $180 per day (6 × $20 × 1.5) so again the manager is not getting a fair offer.

The bonus is based on **estimated sales** so could be higher if sales are higher than predicted. However, there is a **risk** that sales and therefore the bonus could be lower. It is therefore again unlikely that this bonus will motivate the manager.

(b) Price discounts and promotions

B&P plans to offer substantial discounts and promotions on a Sunday to attract customers. This may indeed be a **good marketing strategy**[5] to attract people to shop on a Sunday, but it is not necessarily good for the business.

Customer buying pattern

B&P wants to attract **new** customers on a Sunday but customers may simply change the day they do their shopping in order to take advantage of the discounts and promotions. The effect of this would be to reduce **the margin** earned from customer purchases and not increase revenue.

Customer dissatisfaction

Customers who buy goods at full price and then see their purchases for sale at lower prices on a Sunday may be disgruntled. They could then complain or switch their custom to another shop.

The **reputation** of B&P could be damaged by this marketing policy, especially if customers associate lower prices with **lower quality**.

[3] Finally apply judgement and in this case explain why it is unlikely to motivate.

[4] Repeat the same approach (make a point, explain the point, apply the point) when discussing the bonus

[5] Try to think about the bigger picture and apply common business sense.

Exam success skills diagnostic

Every time you complete a question, use the diagnostic below to assess how effectively you demonstrated the exam success skills in answering the question. The table has been completed below for the B&P activity to give you an idea of how to complete the diagnostic.

Exam success skills	Your reflections/observations
Managing information	Did you identify the impact that the time off and bonus could have on the manager and therefore on their motivation?
Correct interpretation of requirements	Did you identify that part (b) was about **the manager's** motivation only? Did you identify that part (c) concerned the wider impact on sales?
Answer planning	Did you draw up an answer plan using your preferred approach (eg mind map, bullet-pointed list)? Did your plan help to create a structure for your answer?
Effective writing and presentation	Did you use headings (key words from requirements)? Did you use full sentences? And most importantly – **did you explain why your points related to the scenario?**
Most important action points to apply to your next question	

Summary

Section C questions in the PM exam are scenario-based. It is therefore essential that you try to create a practical answer that is relevant to the scenario, and/or addresses the issues identified in the scenario, instead of simply repeating rote-learned, technical knowledge.

As you move into practising questions as part of your final revision, you will need to practise taking in information from a scenario quickly (using active reading), accurately understanding the requirements, and creating an answer plan and a final answer that addresses the requirements in the context of the scenario.

This is not to suggest that theoretical knowledge is unimportant, because often scenario-based questions will involve applying your knowledge to the scenario. In order to pass the exam, you need to develop a sound knowledge of PM, **but equally you need to apply this knowledge to the question scenarios** (for example to address problems or issues raised in the scenario). Simply reciting your knowledge will not be sufficient to gain full marks, you must use the information given to you in the scenario.

12

Risk and uncertainty

Learning objectives

On completion of this chapter, you should be able to:

	Syllabus reference no.
Suggest research techniques to reduce uncertainty, eg focus groups, market research.	C6 (a)
Explain the use of simulation, expected values and sensitivity.	C6 (b)
Apply expected values and sensitivity to decision-making problems.	C6 (c)
Apply the techniques of maximax, maximin, and minimax regret to decision-making problems, including the production of profit tables.	C6 (d)
Interpret a decision tree and use it to solve a multi-stage decision problem.	C6 (e)
Calculate the value of perfect and imperfect information.	C6 (f)

Exam context

Management accounting exams have increasingly required a good understanding of risk and uncertainty in decision-making. In an ideal world, a decision-maker would know with certainty what the future consequences would be for each choice facing them. As this is not possible, it is useful to incorporate risk and uncertainty into the decisions made. The techniques to allow this are covered in this chapter.

Section C questions are likely to be a mixture of calculations and explanation.

Chapter overview

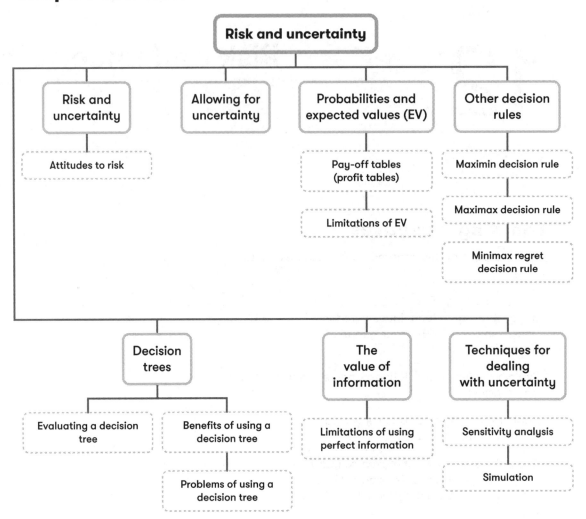

1 Risk and uncertainty

When there is a strong element of risk or uncertainty in a decision, the **decision** that is taken may be **affected** by the **extent** of the risk or uncertainty.

> **Risk: Risk** involves situations or events that may or may not occur, but whose probability of occurrence can be calculated statistically and the frequency of their occurrence predicted from past records. Thus, insurance deals with risk.
>
> **Uncertain events: Uncertain events** are those whose outcome cannot be predicted with statistical confidence.

Making decisions **now** affects **future** outcomes. This means that managers preparing and implementing budgets will need to estimate figures upon which to make decisions and set targets.

Risk exists where a decision-maker has knowledge that several different future outcomes are possible, usually due to past experience. This past experience enables a decision-maker to estimate the probability of the likely occurrence of each potential future outcome.

1.1 Attitudes to risk

Decisions should be taken with reference to the risks involved and the investor's attitude to risk. Individuals' risk attitudes have an impact on decision-making in the short-term.

> **Risk seeker:** A risk seeker is a decision maker who is interested in the best outcomes no matter how small the chance that they may occur.
>
> **Risk neutral:** A risk neutral decision-maker is concerned with what will be the most likely outcome. This involves using expected values (EV) and selecting the strategy with the highest EV.
>
> **Risk averse:** A risk averse decision maker acts on the assumption that the worst outcome might occur.

Activity 1: Attitudes to risk

Investment	A	B
Expected profit	$10,000	$10,000
Highest possible profit	$25,000	$11,000
Lowest possible profit	$(10,000)	$9,000

1 **Required**

Which investment would be chosen by a decision-maker who is:

(a) Risk seeking?

(b) Risk neutral?

(c) Risk averse?

Solution

1

2 Allowing for uncertainty

One approach to dealing with uncertainty is to **obtain more information** about the effects of the decision. Reliable information can reduce uncertainty.

Methods for obtaining more information include:

- Market research
- Focus groups

KEY TERM

> **Market research: Market research** is the systematic process of gathering, analysing and reporting data about markets to investigate, describe, measure, understand or explain a situation or problem facing a company or organisation.

A **focus group** may be used to obtain **qualitative views and opinions** from a small group of individuals. The group is asked about their opinions and attitudes towards a product or service, and members of the group are encouraged to share their views with each other as well as with the person leading the group.

Real life example

Retailers use focus groups of customers from their target market to help understand why that target market behaves in a certain way and to establish what their barriers to purchasing are.

Essential reading

See Chapter 12 Sections 1 and 2 of the Essential reading for more detail on market research and focus groups.

The Essential reading is available as an Appendix of the digital edition of the Workbook.

3 Probabilities and expected values (EV)

When the final outcome of a decision is unknown and a range of possible future outcomes have been quantified (eg best, worst and most likely) probabilities can be assigned to these outcomes and a weighted average (expected value) of those outcomes calculated.

> **Formula to learn**
>
> $$EV = \sum px$$
>
> where p is the probability of the outcome occurring and x is the value of the outcome (profit or cost).

When faced with a number of alternative decisions, the one with the **highest expected value (EV)** should be chosen.

Illustration 1: Expected values

1 Suppose a manager has to choose between options A and B. The options are mutually exclusive (meaning that only one option can be chosen) and the probable outcomes of each option are as follows:

Option A		Option B	
Probability	Profit	Probability	Profit
	$		
0.8	5,000	0.1	(2,000)
0.2	6,000	0.2	5,000
		0.6	7,000
		0.1	8,000

Solution

1 **The correct answer is:**

The EV of profit for each option would be measured as follows:

Option A					Option B				
Prob		Profit		EV of profit	Prob		Profit		EV of profit
p		x		px	p		x		px
		$		$			$		$
0.8	×	5,000	=	4,000	0.1	×	(2,000)	=	(200)
0.2	×	6,000	=	1,200	0.2	×	5,000	=	1,000
		EV	=	5,200	0.6	×	7,000	=	4,200
					0.1	×	8,000	=	800
							EV	=	5,800

In this example, since it offers a higher EV of profit, option B would be selected in preference to A, unless further risk analysis is carried out.

3.1 Pay-off tables (profit tables)

Pay-off tables **identify and record all possible outcomes (or pay-offs)** in situations where there are several decision options and the outcome from each decision depends on the eventual circumstances that arise (for example, 'worst possible', 'most likely' or 'best possible').

Illustration 2: Expected values with pay-off tables (profit tables)

1 IB Newsagents stocks a weekly lifestyle magazine. The owner buys the magazines at the beginning of each week for $0.30 each and sells them at the retail price of $0.50 each.

At the end of the week, unsold magazines are obsolete and have no value, so they are discarded as recycled waste. The estimated probability distribution for weekly demand is as follows:

Weekly demand in units	Probability
20	0.20
30	0.55
40	0.25
	1.00

The actual demand in each week does not affect the actual demand in the following week.

Required

If the owner is to order a fixed quantity of magazines per week, how many should that be?

Since the outcomes occur every week, many times over, the EV decision rule is considered appropriate here.

Assume no seasonal variations in demand.

Solution

1 The correct answer is:

Start by identifying the different decision options. These are assumed here to be the different buying decisions, with three options: buy 20 per week, buy 30 per week or buy 40 per week.

The different possible outcomes are the three possibilities for actual demand: 20 units, 30 units or 40 units.

The next step is to set up a decision matrix of possible strategies (numbers bought) and possible demand.

The 'pay-off' from each combination of action and outcome is then computed.

No sale = cost of $0.30 per magazine

Sale = profit of $0.20 per magazine ($0.50 – $0.30)

Probability	Outcome (number demanded)	Decision (number bought)		
		20	30	40
		$	$	$
0.20	20	4.00	1.00*	**(2.00)
0.55	30	4.00	6.00	*** 3.00
0.25	40	4.00	6.00	8.00

* Buying 30 and selling only 20 gives a profit of (20 × $0.5) – (30 × $0.3) = $1

** Buying 40 and selling only 20 gives a loss of (20 × $0.5) – (40 × $0.3) = $(2)

*** Buying 40 and selling 30 gives a profit of (30 × $0.5) – (40 × $0.3) = $3

We can now calculate the EV of each decision option, as the weighted average value of the different possible outcomes for each option.

Decision option		EV of weekly profit
Buy 20	($4 × 0.20) + ($4 × 0.55) + ($4 × 0.25) =	$4.00
Buy 30	($1 × 0.20) + ($6 × 0.55) + ($6 × 0.25) =	$5.00
Buy 40	($(2) × 0.20) + ($3 × 0.55) + ($8 × 0.25) =	$3.25

The strategy which gives the highest expected value of pay-off is to stock 30 magazines each week.

Note. The expected value of weekly demand in this example is (20 × 0.20) + (30 × 0.55) + (40 × 0.25) = 30.5 copies, but this does not help with the calculation of the expected value of profit, because the profit is dependent on the purchase quantity as well as the sales demand quantity.)

Activity 2: Table

Jaitinder must decide how best to use a monthly factory capacity of 1,200 units. Demand from regular customers is risky and could be either 400, 500 or 700 units per month.

Regular customers generate contribution of $5 per unit. Jaitinder has the opportunity to enter a special contract which will generate contribution of only $3 per unit. For the special contract, she must enter a binding agreement now at a level of 900, 700 or 500 units.

Required

Display all possible contributions in the table below.

	Special contract		
Demand (units)	900	700	500
400			
500			
700			

Solution

1

3.2 Limitations of EV

(a) EV is a long-term average, so will not be reached in the short term and is therefore not suitable for one off decisions.

(b) The results are dependent on the accuracy of the probability estimates.

(c) The EV itself may not represent a single possible outcome.

(d) It ignores the range of possible outcomes.

3.3 Two unknowns and joint probability

 Illustration 3: Joint probabilities

Estimates of levels of demand and unit variable costs, with associated probabilities, for Product B are shown below. Unit selling price is fixed at $100.

Levels of demand

Pessimistic	Probability of 0.4	10,000 units
Most likely	Probability of 0.5	12,500 units
Optimistic	Probability of 0.1	13,000 units

Unit variable costs

Optimistic	Probability of 0.3	$20
Most likely	Probability of 0.4	$30
Pessimistic	Probability of 0.3	$35

1 **Required**

Produce a two-way table showing levels of contribution that incorporates information about both the variables and the associated probabilities.

Solution

1 **The correct answer is:**

Table of total contributions

The bold, shaded area on this table shows the possible total contributions and the associated joint probabilities.

Demand			10,000	12,500	13,000
Probability			0.4	0.5	0.1
Unit variable cost	Probability	Unit contribution			
$20	0.3	$80	$800,000	$1,000,000	$1,040,000
			0.12*	0.15**	0.03
$30	0.4	$70	$700,000	$875,000	$910,000
			0.16	0.20	0.04
$35	0.3	$65	$650,000	$812,500	$845,000
			0.12	0.15	0.03

* Joint probability: 0.3 × 0.4 = 0.12

**Joint probability: 0.3 × 0.5 = 0.15 etc

4 Other decisions

The expected value rule is just one possible 'rule' or criterion on which to base a decision. There are other rules that a decision-maker may prefer to use.

4.1 Maximin decision rule

> **Maximin decision rule:** The **maximin decision rule** is that a decision-maker should select the alternative that offers the least unattractive worst outcome. This would mean choosing the alternative that **maximises** the **minimum** profits.

Maximin decisions:
- Maximise the minimum return of each decision.
- Apply to a risk averse decision maker.

Limitations of maximin:
- Does not consider the probability of each outcome occurring
- Is conservative (does not try to maximise profit)

Illustration 4: Maximin

Suppose that a manager is trying to decide which of three mutually exclusive projects to undertake. Each of the projects could lead to varying net profits which are classified as outcomes I, II and III. The manager has constructed the following payoff table or matrix (a conditional profit table):

Net profit if outcome turns out to be			
Project	I	II	III
A	$50,000	$65,000	$80,000
B	$70,000	$60,000	$75,000
C	$90,000	$80,000	$55,000
Probability	0.2	0.6	0.2

1 **Required**

Which project would be chosen using EV and which project would be chosen under maximin?

EV: Project

Maximin: Project

Solution

1 **The correct answer is:**

If the project with the **highest EV of profit** were chosen, this would be Project C.

Outcome	Probability	Project A EV $	Project B EV $	Project C EV $
I	0.2	10,000	14,000	18,000
II	0.6	39,000	36,000	48,000
III	0.2	16,000	15,000	11,000
		65,000	65,000	77,000

However, if the **maximin criterion** were applied, the assessment would be as follows:

Project selected	The worst outcome that could happen	Profit $
A	I	50,000
B	II	60,000
C	III	55,000

By **choosing B**, we are **'guaranteed' a profit of at least $60,000**, which is more than we would get from Projects A or C if the worst outcome were to occur for them. (We want the maximum of the minimum achievable profits.)

The decision would therefore be **to choose Project B.**

4.2 Maximax decision rule

> **Maximax criterion:** The **maximax criterion** looks at the best possible results. Maximax means 'maximise the maximum profit'. The decision with this rule is to choose the option that could provide the maximum possible profit.

Maximax decisions:

- Aim for the best possible return.
- Apply to a risk seeking decision-maker.

Limitations of maximax:

- Does not consider the probability of each outcome occurring
- Is overly optimistic

Activity 3: Maximin, maximax

Jaitinder must decide how best to use a monthly factory capacity of 1,200 units. Demand from regular customers is risky and as follows.

Monthly demand (units)	Probability
400	0.2
500	0.6
700	0.2
	1.0

Regular customers generate contribution of $5 per unit. Jaitinder has the opportunity to enter a special contract which will generate contribution of only $3 per unit. For the special contract, she must enter a binding agreement now at a level of 900, 700 or 500 units.

Profit table:

Demand (units)	P	Special contract (units) 900	700	500
400	0.2	4,200	4,100	3,500
500	0.6	4,200	4,600	4,000
700	0.2	4,200	4,600	5,000

1 **Required**

Using the profit table and expected values, what is the optimal level of special contract to commit to every month?

O 400 units

O 500 units

    ○ 700 units

    ○ 900 units

2 Required

Using the profit table and assuming a totally risk averse attitude to decision making, what is the optimal level of special contract to commit to every month?

    ○ 400 units

    ○ 500 units

    ○ 700 units

    ○ 900 units

3 Required

Using the profit table, what is the optimal level of special contract to commit to every month, assuming a risk seeking attitude to decision making?

    ○ 400 units

    ○ 500 units

    ○ 700 units

    ○ 900 units

Solution

1

2

3

4.3 Minimax regret decision rule

> **Minimax regret rule:** The **minimax regret rule** aims to minimise the regret from making the wrong decision. **Regret** is the opportunity lost through making the wrong decision.

The decision rule chooses the option which **minimises** the **maximum opportunity cost** from **making** the **wrong decision**.

  Illustration 5: Minimax regret

A manager is trying to decide which of three mutually exclusive projects to undertake. Each of the projects could lead to varying net costs which the manager calls outcomes I, II and III. The following payoff table or matrix has been constructed:

		Outcomes (not profit)		
		I (Worst)	II (Most likely)	III (Best)
Project	A	50	85	130
	B	70	75	140
	C	90	100	110

1 Required

Which project should be undertaken under minimax regret rules?

Solution

1 The correct answer is:

A table of regrets can be compiled, as follows, showing the amount of profit that might be forgone for each project, depending on whether the outcome is I, II or III:

	Outcome I	Outcome II	Outcome III	Maximum
Project A	40*	15***	10	40
Project B	20**	25	0	25
Project C	0	0	30	30

*90 – 50

**90 – 70

***100 – 85 etc

The **maximum regret** is 40 with Project A, 25 with B and 30 with C. The lowest of these three maximum regrets is 25 with B, and so Project B would be selected if the minimax regret rule is used.

Activity 4: Minimax regret

1 Required

Using the minimax regret rule, what decisions would be taken using the data table in Activity 3?

	Special contract (units)		
Demand (units)	900	700	500
400	4,200	4,100	3,500
500	4,200	4,600	4,000
700	4,200	4,600	5,000

Opportunity cost table

	Special contract (units)		
Demand (units)	900	700	500
400			

500			
700			
Maximum regret			

Solution

1

---

5 Decision trees

A decision tree is a pictorial method of showing a sequence of interrelated decisions and their expected outcomes. Decision trees can incorporate both the probabilities and value of expected outcomes and are used in decision- making.

Decision trees are most useful when there are several decisions and ranges of outcome.

5.1 Evaluating a decision tree

Once drawn, the optimal decision can be calculated using rollback analysis.

Evaluate the tree from **right to left.**

(a) Calculate expected values at outcome points. (Denoted by a circle on the tree.)

(b) Take highest benefit at decision points. (Denoted by a square on the tree.)

 Illustration 6: Decision trees

Beeth Co has a new wonder product, the vylin, of which it expects great things. At the moment, the company has two courses of action open to it, to test market the product or abandon it.

If the company test markets it, the cost will be $100,000 and the market response could be positive or negative, with probabilities of 0.60 and 0.40.

If the response is positive, the company could either abandon the product or market it full scale.

If it markets the vylin full scale, the outcome might be low, medium or high demand, and the respective net gains/(losses) would be (200), 200 or 1,000 in units of $1,000 (the result could range from a net loss of $200,000 to a gain of $1,000,000). These outcomes have probabilities of 0.20, 0.50 and 0.30, respectively.

If the result of the test marketing is negative and the company goes ahead and markets the product, estimated losses would be $600,000.

If, at any point, the company abandons the product, there would be a net gain of $50,000 from the sale of scrap. All the financial values have been discounted to the present.

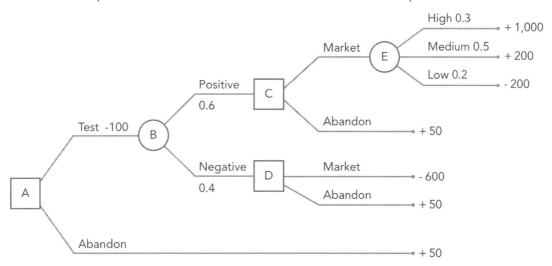

1   **Required**

Based on the decision tree, evaluate whether the company should test the product or abandon it.

The company should [▼] and should not [▼]

Pick list:

abandon

test

Solution

1   **The correct answer is:**

The company should **test** and should not **abandon**

Rollback analysis evaluates the EV of each decision option. You have to work from right to left and calculate EVs at each outcome point.

The EV of each decision option can be evaluated, using the decision tree to help with keeping the logic on track. The basic rules are as follows:

(a)   We start on the right hand side of the tree and work back towards the left hand side and the current decision under consideration. This is sometimes known as the 'rollback' technique or 'rollback analysis'.

(b)   Working from right to left, we calculate the EV of revenue, cost, contribution or profit at each outcome point on the tree.

In the above example, the right hand most outcome point is point E, and the EV is as follows:

	Profit x $'000	Probability p $'000	px $'000
High	1000	0.3	300
Medium	200	0.5	100

	Profit x $'000	Probability p $'000	px $'000
Low	(200)	0.2	(40)
		EV:	360

This is the EV of the decision to market the product if the test shows a positive response.

(a) At decision point C, the choice is as follows:

    (i) Market, EV = +360 (the EV at point E)

    (ii) Abandon, value = +50

The choice would be to market the product, and so the EV at decision point C is +360.

(b) At decision point D, the choice is as follows: .

    (i) Market, value = – 600

    (ii) Abandon, value = +50

The choice would be to abandon, and so the EV at decision point D is +50.

The second-stage decisions have therefore been made. If the original decision is to test the market, the company will market the product if the test shows a positive customer response, and will abandon the product if the test results are negative.

The evaluation of the decision tree is completed as follows:

(a) **Calculate the EV at outcome point B.**

0.6 × 360 (EV at C)

+ 0.4 × 50 (EV at D)

= 216 + 20 = 236

(b) **Compare the options at point** A, which are as follows:

    (i) Test: EV = EV at B minus test marketing cost = 236 – 100 = 136

    (ii) Abandon: value = 50

The choice would be to test market the product, because it has a **higher EV of profit.**

Activity 5: Decisions trees

Captain plc runs its business through a number of centres. One of its centres is suffering from declining sales and management has a range of options:

(a) To shut down the site and sell it for $5 million

(b) To undertake a major refurbishment

(c) To undertake a cheaper refurbishment

In the past, two-thirds of such refurbishments have achieved good results, the other one-third being less successful, achieving poor results.

The major refurbishment will cost $4,000,000 now. Estimates of the outcomes are as follows:

(a) Good results   PV = $13,500,000

(b) Poor results   PV = $6,500,000

The cheaper refurbishment, costing $2,000,000 now, would have the following outcomes:

(a) Good results PV = $8,500,000

(b) Poor results PV = $4,000,000

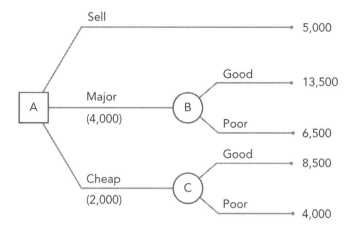

1   **Required**

Calculate the expected value at Points B and C (to the nearest whole $'000). Recommend what action should be taken.

○ Captain plc should sell the site

○ Captain plc should undertake a major refurbishment

○ Captain plc should undertake a cheaper refurbishment

Solution

1

5.2 Benefit of using a decision tree

Clearly shows all the decisions and uncertain events and how they are interrelated.

5.3 Problems of using a decision tree

- Based on EV, so suffers from same disadvantages as all EV techniques
- Heavily dependent on the probabilities used
- Oversimplification of reality

6 The value of information

Information about uncertain variables may be available, for example, from market research. If this information is guaranteed to predict the future with certainty, it is defined as perfect information. Perfect information removes risk and is therefore valuable.

Perfect information: Perfect information is information that predicts with 100% accuracy what the outcome situation will be. Having perfect information removes all doubt and uncertainty from a decision, and enables managers to make decisions with complete confidence that they have selected the best decision option.

Formula to learn

Value of perfect information (VOPI)

EV (with perfect information)	X
EV (without perfect information)	(X)
VOPI	X

Illustration 7: Perfect information

The management of Ivor Co must choose whether to go ahead with either of two mutually exclusive projects: A or B. The expected profits are as follows:

	Profit if there is strong demand	Profit/(loss) if there is weak demand
Option A	$4,000	$(1,000)
Option B	$1,500	$500
Probability of demand	0.3	0.7

1 **Required**

Ascertain what the decision would be, based on expected values, if no information about demand were available.

Project [   ]

2 **Required**

Calculate the value of perfect information about demand.

$ [   ]

Solution

1 **The correct answer is:**

Project B

Step 1 If there were no information to help with the decision, the project with the higher EV of profit would be selected.

Probability	Project A Profit $	Project A EV $	Project B Profit $	Project B EV $
0.3	4,000	1,200	1,500	450

Probability	Project A Profit $	Project A EV $	Project B Profit $	Project B EV $
0.7	(1,000)	(700)	500	350
		500		800

Project B would be selected.

This is clearly the better option if demand turns out to be weak. However, if demand were to turn out to be strong, Project A would be more profitable. There is a 30% chance that this could happen.

2 **The correct answer is:**

$750

Step 2 Perfect information will indicate for certain whether demand will be weak or strong. If demand is forecast 'weak', Project B would be selected. If demand is forecast as 'strong', Project A would be selected, and perfect information would improve the profit from $1,500, which would have been earned by selecting B, to $4,000.

Forecast demand	Probability	Project chosen	Profit $	EV if profit $
Weak	0.7	B	500	350
Strong	0.3	A	4,000	1,200
			EV of profit with Perfect information:	1,550

Step 3

	$
EV of profit without perfect information (ie if Project B is always chosen)	800
EV of profit with perfect information	1,550
Value of perfect information	750

Provided that the information does not cost more than $750 to collect, it would be worth having.

Activity 6: Perfect information

Jaitinder has been contacted by a market research company, which guarantees that the results of its survey will be 100% correct.

These results will enable Jaitinder to ascertain the demand from her regular customers every month, in advance of accepting the special order.

Without this information, Jaitinder would choose to order the special contract of 700 units which, based on the expected value calculations, will give an average profit of $4,500.

Required
What is the maximum amount that Jaitinder should pay for the survey?

Demand (units)	P	Special contract (units) 900	700	500
400	0.2	4,200	4,100	3,500
500	0.6	4,200	4,600	4,000
900	0.2	4,200	4,600	5,000

○ $0

○ $100

○ $400

○ Impossible to know

Solution

6.1 Limitations of using perfect information

In practice, useful information is never perfect, market research findings can be reasonably accurate, but could still be wrong and it is not until after the decision has been made that this would be known. This is known as **imperfect information**, which while not as valuable as perfect information, is still better than nothing.

7 Techniques for dealing with uncertainty

Sensitivity analysis is a method of analysing the uncertainty in a situation or decision. It measures the effect of changes in the estimated value of an item ('key factor') on the future outcome. It can therefore be used to assess the sensitivity of the expected outcome to variations or changes in the value of the item ('key factor').

> **Sensitivity analysis: Sensitivity analysis** is a term used to describe any technique whereby decision options are tested for their vulnerability to changes in any 'variable', such as expected sales volume, sales price per unit, material costs and labour costs.

There are two approaches to sensitivity analysis:

- Calculating the maximum percentage change in a variable before the decision would change

- Assessing if the decision would change if a variable changed by x% of estimate

Sensitivity analysis concentrates management attention on variables that are the most important for the decision under review.

Strengths of sensitivity analysis

- Easy to understand
- Highlights key variables which are crucial to the success of the project, once identified these can be closely monitored

Limitations of sensitivity analysis

- Assumes that all changes are independent; in reality, multiple variables are likely to chance simultaneously
- Only identifies the amount of change required in one variable, it does not assess the probability of that change occurring
- Does not offer a clear decision rule; appropriate management judgement is still required

Illustration 8: Sensitivity analysis

SS has estimated the following sales and profits for a new product that it may launch on to the market:

	$	$
Sales (2,000 units)		4,000
Variable costs:		
Materials	2,000	
Labour	1,000	3,000
Contribution		1,000
Less incremental fixed costs		(800)
Profit		200

1 **Required**

What are the percentages changes that would result in a loss (to the nearest whole percent)?

More than [＿＿＿＿] % increase in incremental **fixed costs**

More than [＿＿＿＿] % increase in unit cost of **materials**

More than [＿＿＿＿] % increase in **unit labour costs**

More than [＿＿＿＿] % drop in **unit selling price**

Solution

1 **The correct answer is:**

The **margin of safety** = ((budgeted sales − breakeven sales)/budgeted sales) × 100%

The breakeven point = fixed costs/contribution per unit

= $800 / ($1,000/2,000 units) = 1,600 units

Margin of safety = ((2,000 − 1,600)/2,000) × 100% = 20%

If any of the **costs increase by more than $200**, the profit will disappear and there will be a **loss**.

Changes in variables that would result in a loss

More than ((200/800) × 100%) 25% increase in incremental **fixed costs**

More than ((200/2,000) × 100%) 10% increase in unit cost of **materials**

More than ((200/1,000) × 100%) 20% increase in **unit labour costs**

More than ((200/4,000) × 100%) 5% drop in **unit selling price**

Management would now be able to judge more clearly whether the product is likely to be profitable. The **items to which profitability is most sensitive** in this example are the **selling price** (5%) and **material costs** (10%). Sensitivity analysis can help to **concentrate management attention on the most important forecasts.**

Activity 7: Margin of safety

Columbus makes and sells a single product, the Raleigh.

Financial data concerning this product is as follows:

	$/unit
Selling price	120
Direct materials	30
Direct labour	25
Fixed costs	40

Anticipated sales and production are forecast to be 750 units.

Some uncertainty has now arisen over the level of likely cost expected in the production of the Raleigh.

Required
What is the impact on the margin of safety if material costs increase by 5%?

O 4% increase

O 4% decrease

O 63% increase

O 63% decrease

Solution

8 Simulation

Sensitivity analysis can only be used to assess changes in one variable at a time. In practice, many variables may be uncertain.

Simulation models can be created using computers and random numbers. These numbers are linked to probability distributions so that the number chosen would occur with the same probability that the real-life event would occur.

Simulation can be used for estimating queues in shops, as this depends on two uncertainties; arrival of customers at the shop and service time. Two sets of probabilities and random numbers will be required.

Essential reading

See Chapter 12 Section 3 of the Essential reading for more detail on simulation. Section 4 of the Essential reading is on standard deviation which is a measure of risk. Standard deviation is not specifically mentioned in the PM syllabus but it is mentioned in the technical article on the ACCA website.

The Essential reading is available as an Appendix of the digital edition of the Workbook.

Chapter summary

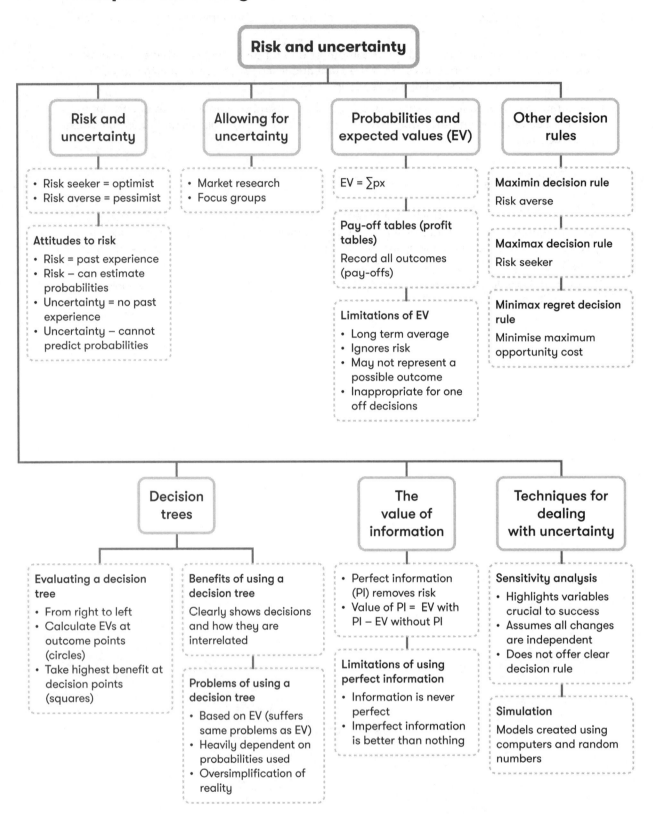

Risk and uncertainty

Risk and uncertainty
- Risk seeker = optimist
- Risk averse = pessimist

Attitudes to risk
- Risk = past experience
- Risk – can estimate probabilities
- Uncertainty = no past experience
- Uncertainty – cannot predict probabilities

Allowing for uncertainty
- Market research
- Focus groups

Probabilities and expected values (EV)

$EV = \sum px$

Pay-off tables (profit tables)

Record all outcomes (pay-offs)

Limitations of EV
- Long term average
- Ignores risk
- May not represent a possible outcome
- Inappropriate for one off decisions

Other decision rules

Maximin decision rule

Risk averse

Maximax decision rule

Risk seeker

Minimax regret decision rule

Minimise maximum opportunity cost

Decision trees

Evaluating a decision tree
- From right to left
- Calculate EVs at outcome points (circles)
- Take highest benefit at decision points (squares)

Benefits of using a decision tree

Clearly shows decisions and how they are interrelated

Problems of using a decision tree
- Based on EV (suffers same problems as EV)
- Heavily dependent on probabilities used
- Oversimplification of reality

The value of information

- Perfect information (PI) removes risk
- Value of PI = EV with PI – EV without PI

Limitations of using perfect information
- Information is never perfect
- Imperfect information is better than nothing

Techniques for dealing with uncertainty

Sensitivity analysis
- Highlights variables crucial to success
- Assumes all changes are independent
- Does not offer clear decision rule

Simulation

Models created using computers and random numbers

BPP LEARNING MEDIA

Knowledge diagnostic

1. Risk and uncertainty

Risk is where a decision maker has **past experience**. With **uncertainty,** there is **no past experience**.

2. Attitudes to risk

There are three types of risk preference:

- Risk seeker
- Risk averse
- Risk neutral

3. Probabilities and expected values

EVs are calculated as

$$\sum px$$

4. Other decision rules

Maximin - maximise the minimum return

Maximax - maximise the maximum return

Maximax regret - minimise the opportunity cost from making the wrong decision

5. Decision trees

Decision trees can be used to illustrate the **choices and possible outcomes** of a decision.

6. The value of information

Perfect information is guaranteed to predict the future with 100% accuracy. Imperfect information is valuable even though it may incorrectly predict future events.

The **value of perfect information** is calculated as:

	$
EV with perfect information	X
EV without perfect information	(X)
Value of information	X

7. Sensitivity analysis and simulation

Sensitivity analysis	An alternative way of assessing risk in which **variables are assessed in isolation.**
Simulation	A method of assessing risk where there are **several uncertain variables**

Further study guidance

Question practice

Now try the following from the Further question practice bank [available in the digital edition of the Workbook]:

Number	Level	Marks	Approximate time
Section A Q32	Examination	2	4 mins
Section A Q33	Examination	2	4 mins
Section A Q34	Examination	2	4 mins
Section C Q2	Examination	20	36 mins

Further reading

There are two technical articles available on ACCA's website, called *The risks of uncertainty* and *Decision trees*.

You are strongly advised to read these articles in full as part of your preparation for the PM exam.

Activity answers

Activity 1: Attitudes to risk

1 The correct answer is:

(a) Risk-seeker chooses A as it gives a chance of earning the best profit of $25,000.

(b) Risk-neutral decision-maker is indifferent between A and B as they give the same expected profit.

(c) Risk-averse decision-maker chooses B to avoid the chance of the loss of $(10,000) with investment

Activity 2: Table

1 The correct answer is:

Special contract			
Demand units	900	700	500
400	4,200 (W1)	4,100 (W2)	3,500 (W3)
500	4,200	4,600 (W4)	4,000 (W5)
700	4,200	4,600 (W6)	5,000 (W7)

(a) Factory capacity = 1,200 units. As such, if Jaitinder enters into the special contract for 900 units then she can only make an additional 1,200 - 900 = 300 units for regular customers. Therefore, the total contribution = (900 × $3) + (300 × $5) = $4,200.

(b) If Jaitinder enters into the special contract for 700 units then she can make an additional 1,200 - 700 = 500 units for regular customers. If demand is 400 units then:
Total contribution = (700 × $3) + (400 × $5) = $4,100

(c) If Jaitinder enters into the special contract for 500 units then she can make an additional 1,200 - 500 = 700 units for regular customers. If demand is 400 units then:
Total contribution = (500 × $3) + (400 × $5) = $3,500

(d) If Jaitinder enters into the special contract for 700 units then she can make an additional 1,200 - 700 = 500 units for regular customers.
Total contribution = (700 × $3) + (500 × $5) = $4,600

(e) Total contribution = (500 × $3) + (500 × $5) = $4,000

(f) Total contribution = (700 × $3) + (500 × $5) = $4,600

(g) Total contribution = (500 × $3) + (700 × $5) = $5,000

Activity 3: Maximin, maximax

1 The correct answer is:

700 units

EV(900) = 4,200

EV(700) = (4,100 × 0.2) + (4,600 × 0.8) = 4,500

EV(500) = (3,500× 0.2) + (4,000 × 0.6) + (5,000 × 0.2) = 4,100

∴ to maximise profits over the long-term choose 700 for special contract.

2 The correct answer is:

900 units

Maximin rule:

Maximise the possible minimum return that the decision maker could get.

BPP LEARNING MEDIA

Contract	Minimum achievable contribution
900	$4,200
700	$4,100
500	$3,500

We want the maximum of the minimum achievable contributions, therefore 900 units would be chosen.

3   The correct answer is:

500 units

Maximax rule:

Choose the option giving the highest possible return.

Maximum contribution = $5,000 under a contract of 500 units.

Activity 4: Minimax regret

1   The correct answer is:

	900	700	500
Demand			
400	0	100	700
500	400	0	600
700	800	400	0
Maximum regret	$800	$400	$700

Decision – set order level for special contract at 700 units.

Activity 5: Decisions trees

1   The correct answer is:

EV at B = $11,167

EV at C = $7,000

EV at B = (2/3 × $13,500) + (1/3 × $6,500) = $11,167

EV at C = (2/3 × $8,500) + (1/3 × $4,000) = $7,000

Captain plc should undertake a major refurbishment

The expected values of the options are:

Sell: $5,000,000

Major refurb: $7,167,000 (11,167,000 - 4,000,000)

Cheaper refurb: $5,000,000 (7,000,000 - 2,000,000)

Captain plc should undertake the major refurbishment, which will result in the highest EV of $7,167,000.

Activity 6: Perfect information

The correct answer is:

$100

EV with perfect information

Demand	Contract	Contribution	P	EV
(units)	(units)			$
400	900	$4,200	0.2	840
500	700	$4,600	0.6	2,760

700	500	$5,000	0.2	1,000
				4,600

∴ VOPI = EV with PI − EV without PI

= $4,600 − $4,500

= $100

This is the maximum Jaitinder would be willing to pay each month for the survey.

Activity 7: Margin of safety

The correct answer is:

4% decrease

Current breakeven point = $30,000 / ($120 - £30 - $25_ = 462 units

Current margin of safety = 750 - 462 = 288 units

Materials increase by 5% = $31.5

Revised breakeven point = $30,000 / ($120 - £31.5 - $25) = 473 units

Revised margin of safety = 750 - 473 = 277 units

Therefore, change in margin of safety = drop of 11 units (ie a fall of 3.8%)

13

Budgetary systems

Learning objectives

On completion of this chapter, you should be able to:

	Syllabus reference no.
Explain how budgetary systems fit within the performance hierarchy.	D1 (a)
Select and explain appropriate budgetary systems for an organisation, including top-down, bottom-up, rolling, zero base, activity base, incremental and feed-forward control.	D1 (b)
Describe the information used in budget systems and the sources of the information needed.	D1 (c)
Indicate the usefulness and problems with different budget types (including fixed, flexible, zero based, activity based, incremental, rolling, top-down, bottom up, master, functional).	D1 (d)
Prepare flexed budgets, rolling budgets and activity based budgets.	D1 (e)
Explain the beyond budgeting model, including the benefits and problems that may be faced if it is adopted in an organisation.	D1 (f)
Explain the difficulties of changing a budgetary system or type of budget used.	D1 (i)
Explain how budget systems can deal with uncertainty in the environment.	D1 (j)

Exam context

This chapter looks at the budgeting system and methods of preparing budgets. We look at how the budget is used in the **planning** and **control process**.

We then go on to look at the **traditional approach** to budget preparation – **incremental budgeting** – as well as alternative approaches to budget preparation: **zero based budgeting**, **rolling budgets** and **activity based budgeting.** You are expected to be aware of the problems of traditional budgeting systems and why organisations may be reluctant to change to more appropriate systems.

Chapter overview

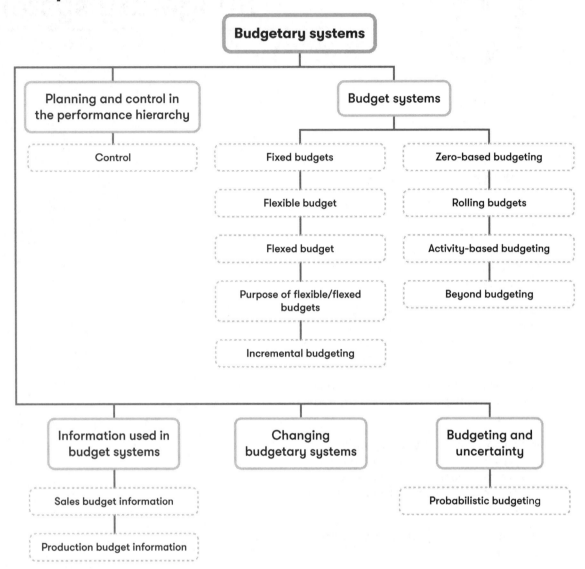

BPP
LEARNING
MEDIA

1 Planning and control in the performance hierarchy

PER alert

One of the competencies needed to fulfil performance objective 13 of the PER is the ability to contribute to setting objectives for the planning and control of business activities. You can apply the knowledge you obtain from this chapter to help demonstrate this competence.

Long-term strategic plans are broken down into short-term plans and targets. This is generally done in the form of a budget or forecast.

Budget: A **budget:** is a quantified plan of action for a forthcoming accounting period. Note that a **budget** is a plan of what the organisation is aiming to achieve and what it has set as a target, whereas a **forecast** is an estimate of what is likely to occur in the future.

Essential reading

See Chapter 13 Section 1 of the Essential reading for more detail on budgeting systems including knowledge brought forward from earlier studies.

The Essential reading is available as an Appendix of the digital edition of the Workbook.

Planning and control occurs at all levels of the performance hierarchy to different degrees. The performance hierarchy refers to the system by which performance is measured and controlled at different levels of management within the organisation.

1.1 Control

Consider how the activities of **planning** and **control** are **interrelated**.

(a) **Plans** set the targets

(b) **Control** involves two main processes

    (i) **Measure** actual results against plan

    (ii) **Take action** to adjust actual performance to achieve the plan or to change the plan altogether

Control is therefore **impossible without planning**.

The essence of control is the **measurement of results** and **comparing** them with the original **plan**. Any deviation from the plan indicates that **control action** is required to make the results conform more closely with the plan.

1.1.1 Feedback

Feedback: **Feedback** occurs when the results (outputs) of a system are used to control it, by adjusting the input or behaviour of the system. Feedback is information produced as output from operations; it is used to compare actual results with planned results for control purposes.

A business organisation uses feedback for control.

(a) **Negative feedback** indicates that results or activities must be brought back on course, as they are deviating from the plan.

(b) **Positive feedback** results in control action continuing the current course. You would normally assume that positive feedback means that results are going according to plan and that no corrective action is necessary: but it is best to be sure that the control system itself is not picking up the wrong information.

(c) **Feedforward control** is control based on **forecast** results: in other words, if the forecast is bad, control action is taken well in advance of actual results.

These are two types of feedback:

- **Single loop feedback** is control, like a thermostat, which regulates the output of a system. For example, if sales targets are not reached, control action will be taken to ensure that targets will be reached soon. The plan or target itself is not changed, even though the resources needed to achieve it might have to be reviewed.

- **Double loop feedback** is of a different order. It is information used to **change the plan itself**. For example, if sales targets are not reached, the company may need to change the plan.

1.1.2 Controls at different levels

Performance hierarchy	Features
Strategic performance reports	• Produced periodically (three, six or twelve months) • Compare strategic position vs overall business plan • Use information from outside and inside organisation
Management control (standard costing and budgetary control) performance reports	• May be monthly (eg variance report) • Compare actual performance vs planned performance in budget • Formal feedback systems for reporting • Based on feedback from within organisation
Operational level	• Control measures reported regularly (often day-to-day basis) • Compare actual performance vs standard • Sometimes non-financial, eg standard times to complete task, wastage rates etc

1.1.3 Top-down and bottom-up budgeting

'Top-down' and 'bottom-up' are two different approaches to budget preparation.

Top down budgeting: Top-down budgeting is when budget targets are set at senior management level for the organisation as a whole and for each major department or activity within the organisation.

(a) With **top-down budgeting**, the departmental budget targets are given to the departmental managers, who are required to prepare a budget that conforms to the targets that have been imposed on them from above.

(b) Similarly, when budgets have been set at departmental level, targets are then given to managers lower down the organisation hierarchy; these managers are then required to prepare budgets that meet the targets that have been imposed on them for their area of operations.

Bottom-up budgeting: Bottom-up budgeting is when the budgeting process starts at a relatively low level of management.

(c) With **bottom-up budgeting**, managers are required to draft a budget for their area of operations. These are submitted to their superior, who combines the lower-level budgets into a combined budget for the department as a whole. Departmental budgets are then submitted to senior management, where they are combined into a co-ordinated budget for the organisation as a whole.

(d) Top-down budgeting takes much less time and planning effort than bottom-up budgeting and senior management can use top-down budgets to impose their views.

(e) Bottom-up budgeting is much more time consuming, and draft budgets may have to be revised many times until they are properly co-ordinated.

However, bottom-up budgeting has two potential advantages:

- It reflects the views and expectations of managers who are closer to operations and who may therefore have a better understanding of what is and what is not achievable.
- Bottom-up budgeting is a form of participative budgeting process, which can have behavioural and motivational advantages. These are considered further in a later chapter.

2 Budget systems

PER alert

One of the competencies needed to fulfil performance objective 13 is to coordinate, prepare and use budgets, selecting suitable budgeting models. You can apply the knowledge you obtain from this chapter to help to demonstrate this competence.

2.1 Fixed budgets

Fixed budget: A **fixed budget** is a budget which remains unchanged throughout the budget period, regardless of differences between the actual and the original planned volume of output or sales.

The fixed budget is the master budget prepared before the beginning of the budget period.

It is based on budgeted volumes and costs/revenues and as such is often unrealistic as the actual level of activity will be almost certainly different from the level of activity originally planned.

The major purpose of a fixed budget is for planning. It is prepared at the planning stage, when it is used to define the objectives and targets of the organisation for the budget period (financial year).

2.2 Flexible budget

Flexible budget: A **flexible budget** is a budget which, by recognising different cost behaviour patterns, is changed as the volume of output and sales changes. It recognises cost behaviour patterns such as changes in sales revenue and variable costs as sales volumes change, and step changes in fixed costs as activity levels rise or fall by more than a certain amount.

It is useful at the **planning** stage to show different results from various possible activity levels (what-if analysis) allowing better planning for uncertainty in the future.

2.3 Flexed budgets

Used at the **control** stage, budgets need to be flexed to reflect the actual activity level achieved in a given period before the budget can meaningfully be compared with actual results and variance analysis performed.

Note that a **flexible** budget is designed at the **planning stage** to vary with activity levels, whereas a **flexed** budget is a **revised budget** that reflects the **actual activity levels** achieved in the budget period. A **flexed** budget is therefore used **retrospectively** to compare actual results achieved with what results should have been under the circumstances.

2.4 Purpose of flexible/flexed budgets

(a) Designed to cope with **different activity levels** to keep the budget meaningful and hence preserve the relevance of variances for effective control.

(b) Useful at **planning** stage to show different results from possible activity levels.

(c) Necessary as **control** device because we can meaningfully compare actual results with relevant flexible budget, ie budgetary control.

Illustration 1: Preparing a flexible budget

1 Required

Prepare a budget for 20X6 for the direct labour costs and overhead expenses of a production department flexed at the activity levels of 80%, 90% and 100%, using the information listed below.

(a) The direct labour hourly rate is expected to be $3.75.

(b) 100% activity represents 60,000 direct labour hours.

(c) *Variable costs*

Indirect labour	$0.75 per direct labour hour
Consumable supplies	$0.375 per direct labour hour
Canteen and other welfare services	6% of direct and indirect labour costs

(d) Semi variable costs are expected to relate to the direct labour hours in the same manner as for the last five years.

	Direct labour hours	Semi-variable costs
Year		$
20X1	64,000	20,800
20X2	59,000	19,800
20X3	53,000	18,600
20X4	49,000	17,800
20X5	40,000 (estimate)	16,000 (estimate)

(e) *Fixed costs*

	$
Depreciation	18,000
Maintenance	10,000
Insurance	4,000
Rates	15,000
Management salaries	25,000

(f) Inflation is to be ignored

2 Required

Calculate the budget cost allowance (ie expected expenditure) for 20X6 assuming that 57,000 direct labour hours are worked.

Solution

1 The correct answer is:

	80% level 48,000 hrs $'000	90% level 54,000 hrs $'000	100% level 60,000 hrs $'000
Direct labour	180.00	202.50	225.0
Other variable costs			
Indirect labour	36.00	40.50	45.0
Consumable supplies	18.00	20.25	22.5
Canteen etc	12.96	14.58	16.2
Total variable costs ($5.145 per hour)	246.96	277.83	308.7
Semi-variable costs (W)	17.60	18.80	20.0
Fixed costs			

Depreciation	18.00	18.00	18.0
Maintenance	10.00	10.00	10.0
Insurance	4.00	4.00	4.0
Rates	15.00	15.00	15.0
Management salaries	25.00	25.00	25.0
Budgeted costs	336.56	368.63	400.7

Using the high/low method:

	$
Total cost of 64,000 hours	20,800
Total cost of 40,000 hours	16,000
Variable cost of 24,000 hours	4,800
Variable cost per hour ($4,800/24,000)	$0.20

	$
Total cost of 64,000 hours	20,800
Variable cost of 64,000 hours (× $0.20)	12,800
Fixed costs	8,000

Semi-variable costs are calculated as follows.

			$
60,000 hours	(60,000 × $0.20) + $8,000	=	20,000
54,000 hours	(54,000 × $0.20) + $8,000	=	18,800
48,000 hours	(48,000 × $0.20) + $8,000	=	17,600

2 **The correct answer is:**

The budget cost allowance for 57,000 direct labour hours of work would be as follows:

		$
Variable costs	(57,000 × $5.145)	293,265
Semi-variable costs	($8,000 + (57,000 × $0.20))	19,400
Fixed costs		72,000
		384,665

Activity 1: Flexible budget

Chateau Larnaque has a bottling plant for its drinks and has prepared flexible budgets:

		Flexible budgets	
Bottles:	10,000	12,000	14,000
Production costs:	$	$	$
Materials	30,000	36,000	42,000
Labour	27,000	31,000	35,000
Overhead	20,000	20,000	20,000

Actual production was 12,350 bottles and the production costs incurred totalled $90,000.

Required

What is the meaningful total variance for performance evaluation purposes?

○ $0

○ $350 Adverse

○ $1,250 Adverse

○ $1,650 Adverse

Solution

2.5 Incremental budgeting

KEY
TERM

> **Incremental budgeting:** This is where the budget is based on the current year's budget (or results) plus an extra amount for estimated growth or inflation.

This method will be sufficient if current operations are as efficient, effective and economical as they can be, without any alternative courses of action available to the organisation.

Activity 2: Incremental budgeting

CP produces two products, X and Y. In the year ending 30 April 20X1, it produced 4,520 X and 11,750 Y and incurred costs of $1,217,200.

The costs incurred are such that 60% are variable. 70% of these variable costs vary with the number of X produced, with the remainder varying with the output of Y.

The budget for the three months to 31 October 20X1 is being prepared using an incremental approach based on the following:

- All costs will be 5% higher than the average paid in the year ended 30 April 20X1.
- Efficiency levels will be unchanged.
- Expected output:

X   1,210 units

Y   3,950 units

Required
What is the budgeted cost for the output of X (to the nearest $100) for the 3 months ending 31 October 20X1?

○ $100

○ $127,100

○ $136,900

○ $143,700

Solution

2.5.1 Advantages of incremental budgeting

(a) It is simple and cheap.

(b) It is relatively quick to administer.

2.5.2 Limitations of incremental budgeting

(a) It does not identify inefficient operations meaning inefficiencies will continue.

(b) Budgetary slack, (ie deliberately overestimating costs or underestimating revenues), once introduced, will be protected/carried forward into future periods.

(c) It is not suitable for changing environments, as it is based on the past and assumes that activities will continue to be the same.

(d) It encourages managers to spend up to the budget because if they do not, the budget is likely to be cut in the next period.

(e) It does not produce challenging performance targets or encourage managers to find ways of improving the business.

2.6 Zero-based budgeting (ZBB)

Zero-based budgeting: This is a method of budgeting that requires each cost element to be specifically justified, as though the activities to which the budget relates were being undertaken for the first time.

Zero based budgeting (ZBB) is a technique used to **allocate resources more efficiently,** thus reducing waste and increasing efficiency.

The process of ZBB starts from the basic premise that next year's budget is zero; every process, or item of expenditure, or intended activity (referred to as a '**decision package**') **must be justified in its entirety** before it can be included in the budget.

The incremental cost and incremental benefit of each decision package will be considered and priority given to those packages providing the most added value to the organisation's key objectives (note that ZBB is sometimes known as 'priority-based budgeting').

BPP
LEARNING
MEDIA

ZBB is not particularly suitable for direct manufacturing costs but **lends itself very well to support expenses or discretionary costs**.

ZBB is particularly useful in **public sector organisations** where funding (income) is fixed, and the best possible service for the available budget needs to be achieved.

There is a **three-step approach** to implementing a zero-based budget:

Step 1 - **Define the decision packages**	There are two types of decision packages: (a) **Mutually exclusive packages**, which contain alternative methods of getting the same job done (b) **Incremental packages**, which divide one aspect of an activity into different levels of effort (the base package being the minimum amount of work to carry out the activity)
Step 2 - **Evaluate and rank each activity** (decision package)	On the basis of its benefit to the organisation. This can be a lengthy process. Minimum work requirements and work that meets legal obligations will be given high priority.
Step 3 - **Allocate resources**	According to funds available and the evaluation in Step 2.

2.6.1 Package examples

Suppose that a cost centre manager is preparing a budget for maintenance costs. She might first consider two mutually exclusive packages. Package A might be to keep a maintenance team of two people per shift for two shifts each day at a cost of $60,000 per annum, whereas Package B might be to obtain a maintenance service from an outside contractor at a cost of $50,000. A cost-benefit analysis will be conducted because the quicker repairs provided by an in-house maintenance service might justify its extra cost. If we now suppose that Package A is preferred, the budget analysis must be completed by describing the incremental variations in this chosen alternative.

(a) The **'base' package** would describe the minimum requirement for the maintenance work. This might be to pay for one person per shift for two shifts each day at a cost of $30,000.

(b) **Incremental package 1** might be to pay for two people on the early shift and one person on the late shift, at a cost of $45,000. The extra cost of $15,000 would need to be justified, for example by savings in lost production time, or by more efficient machinery.

(c) **Incremental package 2** might be the original preference, for two people on each shift at a cost of $60,000. The cost-benefit analysis would compare its advantages, if any, over incremental package 1; and so on.

Activity 3: ZBB

Required

Which THREE of the following would be base packages for the accounting department of a listed manufacturing company, assuming that all are performed to the minimum requirements?

O Operate payroll

O Aged receivables report

O Operate payables ledger

O Publish statutory accounts

O Oversee end of year inventory count

O Enter trainee accountants for their ACCA exams

Solution

2.6.2 Advantages of ZBB

(a) It is possible to identify and **remove inefficient or obsolete operations**.

(b) It necessitates **close examination** of organisation's operations

(c) It results in a more **efficient allocation** of resources and **challenges the status quo**

(d) It responds to changes in the business environment

2.6.3 Disadvantages of ZBB

The major **disadvantage** of ZBB is the **volume of extra paperwork** created. The assumptions about costs and benefits in each package must be continually updated and new packages developed as soon as new activities emerge. The following problems might also occur:

(a) **Short-term benefits** might be **emphasised** to the detriment of long-term benefits.

(b) It may give the impression **that all decisions have to be made in the budget**. Management must be able to meet unforeseen opportunities and threats at all times, however, and must not feel restricted from carrying out new ideas simply because they were not approved by a decision package, cost-benefit analysis and the ranking process.

(c) It may **call for management skills** in both constructing decision packages and the ranking process **that the organisation does not possess**. Managers may therefore have to be trained in ZBB techniques.

(d) The organisation's information systems may not be capable of providing suitable information.

(e) **The ranking process can be difficult**. Managers face three common problems:

   (i) A large number of packages may have to be ranked.

   (ii) It can be difficult to rank packages that appear to be equally vital, for legal or operational reasons.

   (iii) It is difficult to rank activities that have qualitative rather than quantitative benefits – such as spending on staff welfare and working conditions.

One way of obtaining the benefits of ZBB while overcoming the drawbacks is to apply it selectively on a rolling basis throughout the organisation. For example, this year it could be applied to the finance department and next year, the marketing department until all departments have been appraised. In this way, all activities will be thoroughly scrutinised over a period of time.

2.6.4 Using ZBB

ZBB does not work well for direct manufacturing costs, which are usually budgeted using standard costing, work study and other management planning and control techniques.

ZBB is best applied to **support expenses**; that is, expenditure incurred in departments that exist to support the essential production function. These expenses can make up a large proportion of the total expenditure and are less easily quantifiable by conventional methods and are more **discretionary** in nature.

ZBB can also be successfully applied to **service industries** and **not-for-profit organisations** such as local and central government, educational establishments and hospitals, and in any organisation where alternative levels of provision for each activity are possible, and costs and benefits are separately identifiable.

2.7 Rolling budgets

> **Rolling budget:** This is defined as "A budget continuously updated by adding a further accounting period (month or quarter) when the earliest accounting period has expired. Its use is particularly beneficial where future costs and/or activities cannot be forecast accurately" (*CIMA Official Terminology*).

They are particularly useful when an organisation is facing a **period of uncertainty,** making it difficult to prepare accurate forecasts.

Rolling budgets are an attempt to prepare targets and plans that are more realistic and certain, particularly with regard to price levels, by **shortening the period** between preparing budgets.

Instead of preparing a **periodic budget** annually for the full budget period, budgets would be prepared, say, every 1, 2 or 3 months (4, 6, or even 12 budgets each year). Each of these budgets would plan for the next 12 months so that the current budget is extended by an extra period as the current period ends: hence the name rolling budgets. Cash budgets are usually prepared on a rolling basis.

2.7.1 Advantages of rolling budgets

(a) Uncertainty is reduced. Rolling budgets focus detailed planning and control on short-term prospects where the degree of uncertainty is much smaller, especially in times of change.

(b) Managers have to regularly **reassess the budget,** which means they should be more realistic.

(c) **Planning and control** will be based on a more recent plan.

(d) The budget is continuous and will always extend a number of months ahead, encouraging managers to think about the future. This is not the case with fixed periodic budgets.

(e) A realistic budget that takes account of recent performance and market conditions is likely to have a better motivational influence on managers.

2.7.2 Disadvantages of rolling budgets

(a) Effort and expense are required to continuously update the budget.

(b) May demotivate managers if they cannot see the benefit of regular revisions

(c) Each revised budget may require revision of standards or inventory valuations, which could put additional pressure on the accounts department each time a rolling budget is prepared.

Illustration 2: Preparing a rolling budget

A company uses a system of rolling budgets. The sales budget is displayed below.

	Jan–Mar	Apr–Jun	Jul–Sep	Oct–Dec	Total
	$	$	$	$	$
Sales	78,480	86,120	91,800	97,462	353,862

Actual sales for January–March were $74,640. The adverse variance is explained by growth being lower than anticipated and the market being more competitive than predicted.

Senior management has proposed that the revised assumption for sales growth should be 2.5% per quarter.

1 Required

Update the budget as appropriate.

Solution

1 The correct answer is:

Step 1

Using the actual sales figure for January–March, update the budget for the next four quarters (including a figure for January–March of the following year), incorporating a sales growth rate of 2.5%.

Apr–Jun = $74,640 × 1.025 = $76,506

Jul–Sept = $76,506 × 1.025 = $78,419

Oct–Dec = $78,419 × 1.025 = $80,379

Jan–Mar = $80,379 × 1.025 = $82,389

Step 2 Revised budget

	Apr–Jun	Jul–Sep	Oct–Dec	Jan–Mar	Total
	$	$	$	$	$
Sales	76,506	78,419	80,379	82,398	317,692

Activity 4: Rolling budgets

Bay Co uses a system of rolling budgets. The sales budget for the year to 31 December 20X3 is as follows:

	Q1	Q2	Q3	Q4	Total
	$	$	$	$	$
Sales	122,000	131,760	142,301	153,685	549,746

Actual sales for Q1 were 117,879. The adverse variance is explained by growth being lower than anticipated and the market being more competitive than predicted.

Senior management has proposed that the revised assumption for sales growth should be 5% per quarter.

Required

Applying the principles of rolling budgets, what would the forecast for Q4's sales be?

O $123,773

O $129,962

O $136,460

O $143,283

Solution

2.8 Activity-based budgeting (ABB)

Activity based budgeting: Uses the costs determined using activity based costing (ABC) as a basis for preparing budgets.

For example, if an organisation expects to place 500 orders and the rate per order is $100, the budgeted cost of the ordering activity will be 500 × $100 = $50,000.

Implementing ABC leads to the realisation that the **business as a whole** needs to be **managed** with far more reference to the behaviour of activities and cost drivers identified.

Activity based budgeting recognises the following:

(a) Activities drive costs

(b) The causes (drivers) of the cost should be controlled rather than the cost itself

(c) Not all activities are value-adding

(d) Demand and decisions beyond the control of a department's manager drive many departmental activities.

ABB can only be used in organisations which use ABC, therefore the advantages and disadvantages of using this budgeting technique are the same as using the ABC for costing.

2.8.1 Advantages of ABB

(a) Different activity levels will provide a foundation for the base package and incremental packages of ZBB.

(b) The organisation's overall strategy and any actual or likely changes in that strategy will be taken into account because ABB attempts to manage the business as the sum of its interrelated parts.

(c) Critical success factors (an activity in which a business must perform well if it is to succeed) will be identified and key metrics devised to monitor progress towards them.

(d) The focus is on the whole of an activity, not just its separate parts, and so there is more likelihood of getting it right first time. For example, what is the use of being able to produce goods in time for their despatch date if the budget provides insufficient resources for the distribution manager who has to deliver them?

(e) Traditional accounting tends to focus on the nature of the costs being incurred (the input side) and traditional budgeting tends to mirror this. ABB emphasises the activities that are being achieved (the outputs).

Activity 5: Activity based budget

1 The production department of EFG Co has four major activities: receiving deliveries, material handling, production runs and quality tests.

Each of these activities has an identifiable cost driver. These are provided below along with estimated volumes for the coming period:

Number of deliveries	300
Number of movements of material	400
Number of production runs	800
Number of quality tests	600

Two other activities that occur in the department are administration and supervision. While these activities are non-volume related, they are necessary functions and should not be ignored in the budgeting process.

Budgeted costs for the coming period are displayed below.

	Total $'000	Attributable to $'000
Management salary	50	Supervision $45; Administration $5
Basic wages	30	Receiving deliveries $7; Production runs $5; Administration $6; Material handling $7; Quality tests $5
Overtime	15	Receiving deliveries $6; Quality tests $1; Production runs $8
Factory overheads	12	Receiving deliveries $3; Production runs $2; Administration $1.5; Material handling $2; Quality tests $1.5; Supervision $2
Other costs	4	Receiving deliveries $1; Supervision $1; Administration $2
	111	

(a) Total cost for each activity
(b) Total cost for the production department
(c) Cost per activity unit

Solution

1

2.9 Beyond Budgeting

Beyond Budgeting is a budgeting model which proposes that traditional budgeting should be abandoned in favour of two fundamental concepts:

(a) **Use adaptive management processes rather than the more rigid annual budget.** Traditional annual plans tie managers to predetermined actions that are not responsive to current situations. Instead managers should plan on a more adaptive, rolling basis, but with the focus on cash forecasting, rather than purely on cost control. Performance is monitored against world-class benchmarks, competitors and previous periods.

(b) **Move towards devolved networks rather than centralised hierarchies.** The emphasis is on encouraging a culture of personal responsibility by delegating decision-making and performance accountability to line managers.

2.9.1 Principles of Beyond Budgeting

The Beyond Budgeting Institute has suggested that Beyond Budgeting can be distinguished from the 'traditional' management model for budgeting through 12 guiding principles.

The first six of these principles relate to the leadership model in an organisation and, in particular, the devolution of responsibility to local managers and front-line staff, enabling them to respond quickly to emerging events, and making them accountable for continuously improving performance.

The remaining principles (ie numbers 7-12) relate to the performance management systems which enable front-line teams to be more responsive to the competitive environment and to customer needs.

The 12 key guiding principles are shown in the table below.

Principle	Comment
Governance and transparency	
1. Values	Bind people to a common cause, not a central plan.
2. Governance	Govern through shared values and sound judgement, not detailed rules and regulations.
3. Transparency	Make information open and transparent, do not restrict and control it.
Accountable teams	
4. Teams	Organise around a seamless network of accountable teams, not around centralised functions.
5. Trust	Trust teams to regulate their performance, do not micro-manage them.
6. Accountability	Base accountability on holistic criteria and peer reviews, not on hierarchical relationships.
Goals and rewards	
7. Goals	Set ambitious medium-term goals, not short-term fixed targets.

Principle	Comment
8. Rewards	Base rewards on relative performance, not on meeting fixed targets.
Planning and controls	
9. Planning	Make planning a continuous and inclusive process, not a top-down annual event.
10. Co-ordination	Co-ordinate interactions dynamically, not through annual budgets.
11. Resources	Make resources available just-in-time, not just-in-case.
12. Controls	Base controls on fast, frequent feedback, not budget variances.

(Source: Beyond Budgeting Institute; www.bbrt.org)

Hope & Fraser (co-founders of the Beyond Budgeting Round Table) argue that 'traditional' budgeting processes do not meet the purposes of performance management. The table below illustrates the ways in which Hope & Fraser feel 'beyond budgeting' differs from 'traditional' budgeting, and also how 'beyond budgeting' meets the purposes of performance management better.

Purposes of performance management	Traditional budgeting processes	'Beyond budgeting' processes
Goals – to balance the need for short-term and long-term profitability	**Short-term focus:** Fixed annual targets drive short-term actions with a view to meeting annual targets.	**Longer-term focus:** KPIs and aspirational goals focus on sustained competitive success.
Rewards – to provide an effective basis for motivating and rewarding performance	Individual departments or divisions have to meet their own targets in order to gain rewards. This focus on individual incentives means departments are not willing to share expertise, skills and information with others, preferring to **defend their 'own turf'** instead.	Recognition of team-based success is important, but the organisation needs to be **viewed as one team**, thereby breaking down barriers and encouraging people to share resources and knowledge. There is an **emphasis on learning and continual innovation**.
Plans – to direct actions to maximise market opportunities	Planning is based on a premise of '**predict and control**' and is highly deterministic. This means plans are difficult to change even if the assumption on which the plans were based become unrealistic. Organisations adopt a '**company led**' rather than 'customer led' approach to strategic management.	The future is inherently unpredictable, so plans need to be **continuously updated** to adapt to events as they happen. Organisations adopt a '**customer led**' approach to strategic management.

Purposes of performance management	Traditional budgeting processes	'Beyond budgeting' processes
Resources – to ensure that resources are available to support agreed actions	Budgets are seen as a way of enabling senior managers to allocate resources to operating units. The process is **centralised**, and the 'head office' exerts control over the operating units or cost centres. But head offices are usually risk averse and prefer to allocate resources to existing products and businesses rather than to new ideas and opportunities.	Resources are available on demand, to enable a fast response to new opportunities. Resources are **allocated to strategic initiatives** rather than to departmental budgets.
Co-ordination – to harmonise actions across the business	Leaders attempt to co-ordinate plans by linking one functional budget to another. But these centrally linked budgets provide slow solutions that often fail to meet customer needs.	Co-ordination should focus around a dynamic linking of customer demands in order to provide fast, seamless solutions that **meet customer needs**.
Controls – to provide relevant information for strategic decision making and controls	Performance reports are based primarily on **financial indicators**, and usually contain lagging indicators (connected with past performance and past events). But financial indicators give little insight into the root causes of performance, and provide a poor basis for learning.	Strategic decisions are based on **multifaceted** and **multi-level information**, which gives insight into future performance as well as into past performance. Information systems need to be able to provide fast, transparent information for multi-level control.

2.9.2 Advantages of Beyond Budgeting

(a) Encourages innovation

(b) Increases motivation

(c) Allows faster responses to threats and opportunities

2.9.3 Disadvantages of Beyond Budgeting

(a) May be resistance to change from employees or management in adopting the Beyond Budgeting culture

(b) Need to plan, even if there are lots of uncertainties in the future

3 Information used in budget systems

Information used in budgeting comes from a wide variety of sources.

Past data may be used as a starting point for the preparation of budgets but other information from a wide variety of sources will also be used.

3.1 Sales budget information

For many organisations, the principal budget factor is sales volume. The sales budget is therefore often the primary budget from which the majority of the other budgets are derived. Before the sales budget can be prepared a **sales forecast** has to be made. Sales forecasting information may come from:

- Past sales patterns
- The economic environment
- Results of market research
- Anticipated advertising
- Competition
- Changing consumer taste
- Distribution
- Pricing policies and discounts offered
- Legislation
- Environmental factors

3.2 Production budget information

Sources of information for the production budget will include:

(a) Labour costs including idle time, overtime and standard output rates per hour

(b) Raw material costs including allowances for losses during production

(c) Machine hours including expected idle time and expected output rates per machine hour

This information will come from the production department and a large part of the traditional work of **cost accounting** involves attributing costs to the physical information produced.

4 Changing budgetary systems

Although the business environment may dictate that a change in budgetary system is necessary, the change will not be without its problems. The following need to be borne in mind:

(a) **Resistance by employees.** Employees will be familiar with the current system and may have built in slack so will not easily accept new targets. New control systems that threaten to alter existing power relationships may be thwarted by those affected.

(b) **Loss of control.** Senior management may take time to adapt to the new system and understand the implications of results.

(c) **Costs of implementation.** Any new system or process requires careful implementation which will have cost implications. For example, the procedures for preparing budgets will have to be rewritten in a new budget manual. Establishing a system of zero based budgeting, for example, will require the design and documentation of a large number of decision packages.

(d) **Training.** In order to prepare and implement budgets under the new system, managers will need to be fully trained. This is time consuming and expensive.

(e) **Lack of accounting information**. The organisation may not have the **systems** in place to obtain and analyse the necessary information for preparing the new style budget. For example, an organisation needs a system of activity based costing if it is to implement activity based budgeting.

5 Budgeting and uncertainty

Preparing a budget involves forecasting which is open to risk and uncertainty.

Causes of uncertainty in the budgeting process include:

(a) **Customers.** They may decide to buy less than forecast, or they may buy more.

(b) **Products/services.** In the modern business environment, organisations need to respond to customers' rapidly changing requirements.

(c) **Inflation** and movements **in interest and exchange rates**. Exchange rate fluctuations can affect the cost of imported materials, and the price that foreign customers will have to pay, which is likely to affect demand.

(d) **Materials.** The cost of raw materials may change unexpectedly.

(e) **Competitors.** They may steal some of an organisation's expected customers, or some competitors' customers may change their buying allegiance.

(f) **Employees.** They may not work as hard as was hoped, or they may work harder.

(g) **Machines.** They may break down unexpectedly.

(h) **Unrest or disaster.** There may be political unrest (eg terrorist activity), social unrest (eg public transport strikes) or minor or major natural disasters (eg storms, floods).

Some of the tools we have seen will help to deal with this. Examples include:

- Flexible budgeting
- Rolling budgets
- Probabilistic budgeting
- Sensitivity analysis

5.1 Probabilistic budgeting

You have already come across expected values when dealing with risk and uncertainty.

Budgets are subject to risk and uncertainty and, as such, expected values may be incorporated into the budget.

Activity 6: Probabilistic budgeting

Orchard has made the following predictions for the profitability of its product the Russet for the upcoming financial year:

	Profit/(loss) $'000	Probability
Best	400	0.3
Most likely	200	0.5
Worst	(150)	0.2

Required
Calculate the expected value that would be included in the budget.

O $0

O $190

O $200

O $450

Solution

Obviously, the problems discussed earlier about expected values (EVs) still hold, ie:

(a) The results are dependent on the accuracy of the probability distribution.

(b) EV takes no account of the risk associated with a decision.

(c) The EV itself may not represent a single possible outcome.

Chapter summary

Budgetary systems

Planning and control in the performance hierarchy

Control
- Feedback control involves taking action after the event
- Feedforward control involves taking action during the event
- Top down budgets are set at senior management level
- Bottom up budgets are set by low level of management

Budget systems

Fixed budgets
- Budgets set in advance
- Do not change

Flexible budget
- Budget set for several activity levels
- Good planning tool enabling 'what if' scenarios

Flexed budget
Re-state budget based on actual volumes

Purpose of flexible/flexed budgets
- Useful for control
- Like for like comparison and meaningful variances

Incremental budgeting
- Based on current year
- Builds in slack & inefficiencies

Zero-based budgeting
- Build up budgets from scratch
- Allocates resources effectively
- Suitable for discretionary spend

Rolling budgets
- Always look at 12 months of budget
- Complete 1st quarter, remove from budget and add another quarter on the end
- Useful in times of uncertainty

Activity-based budgeting
Builds up budgets by activity rather than by department

Beyond budgeting
- Use adaptive management processes
- Move towards devolved networks rather than centralised hierarchies

Information used in budget systems

Sales budget information
- Produce sales forecast first
- Sales forecast information from past patterns, competition, pricing policy etc

Production budget information
- Labour costs
- Raw material costs
- Machine hours

Changing budgetary systems

- Has various implications
  – Resistance
  – Costly
  – Training needs
  – Learning curve

Budgeting and uncertainty

- Budgets are estimates and therefore subject to risk and uncertainty. Suitable tools may be:
  – Flexible budgets
  – Rolling budgets
  – Probabilistic budgeting
  – Sensitivity analysis

Probabilistic budgeting
Expected values incorporated into budget

Knowledge diagnostic

1. Budgetary control

Budgeting is part of the planning and control process.

Control can be **feedback** or **feedforward** – comparison of past results or forecast results to plan

2. Budget systems

- **Flexible** budgets are ideal for **planning.**
- **Flexed** budgets are the best budget for **control** as they allow you to compare like for like.
- **Incremental** budgets tend to build in **slack and inefficiency.**
- **ZBB** results in efficient resource allocation and is suitable for **discretionary spend.**
- **Rolling budgets** are useful in times of **uncertainty.**
- **ABB** ensures the **causes of cost** are managed.

3. Changing budgetary systems

Changes to the budgetary system will meet with resistance due to the learning curve, loss of control, cost and training required.

4. Budgeting and uncertainty

Probabilistic budgeting incorporates expected values.

Flexible and rolling budgets can also be used.

BPP
LEARNING
MEDIA

Further study guidance

Question practice

Now try the following from the Further question practice bank [available in the digital edition of the Workbook]:

Number	Level	Marks	Approximate time
Section A Q35	Examination	2	4 mins
Section A Q36	Examination	2	4 mins
Section A Q37	Examination	2	4 mins
Section C Q3	Examination	20	36 mins

Further reading

There are two technical articles available on ACCA's website, called *Comparing budgeting techniques* and *All about budgeting*.

You are strongly advised to read these articles in full as part of your preparation for the PM exam.

Activity answers

Activity 1: Flexible budget

The correct answer is:

$1,250 Adverse

Materials:

Variable cost = $3/unit

Overhead:

Fixed cost = $20,000

Labour:	Output	Cost
	14,000	35,000
(High-low method)	10,000	27,000
	4,000	8,000

∴ VC/unit = $2

By substitution into high output:

Total VC = $28,000

∴ Total FC = $35,000 – $28,000

= $7,000

∴ Flexed budgeted cost:	$
Materials (12,350 × 3)	37,050
Labour (7,000 + 2 × 12,350)	31,700
Overhead	20,000
	88,750

Actual costs – Flexed budgeted cost   ∴ $1,250 (A)

Activity 2: Incremental budgeting

The correct answer is:

$143,700

Proportion of actual annual costs related to X = $1,217,200 × 0.6 × 0.7 = $511,224

Per unit of X $511,224/4,520 = $113.10

Cost for 1,210 units = 1,210 × $113.10 = $136,854

Inflated cost = $136,854 × 1.05 = $143,697

$100 is the budgeted cost per X. If you selected **$127,100** you forgot to adjust the quantity. If you selected **$136,900,** you forgot to inflate the cost.

Activity 3: ZBB

The correct answers are:

* Operate payroll
* Operate payables ledger
* Publish statutory accounts

All of these are essential for the operation of the business; employees will not work and suppliers will not supply goods on credit if they are not paid the correct amounts on time. Additionally, the statutory accounts must legally be prepared.

All of these are essential for the operation of the business; employees will not work and suppliers will not supply goods on credit if they are not paid the correct amounts on time. Additionally, the statutory accounts must legally be prepared.

The year-end inventory count needs to happen for inclusion in the statutory accounts, but it is not essential that it is observed by a member of the accounting team, although this may be desirable. Aged receivables reports and chasing of outstanding payments will aid credit collection and cash flow, so it is very desirable, but it is not essential.

Offering support with ACCA training and exams will improve employee motivation and enhance their skills but, again, is not essential to running an accounting department.

Activity 4: Rolling budgets

The correct answer is:

$136,460

	20X3 Q2	20X3 Q3	20X3 Q4	20X4 Q1	Total
	$	$	$	$	$
Sales	123,773	129,962	136,460	143,283	533,478

The revised budget should incorporate 5% growth, starting from Q1's actual figure.

Q2: $117,879 × 1.05 = $123,773

Q3: $123,773 × 1.05 = $129,962

Q4: $129,962 × 1.05 = $136,460

Q1: $136,460 × 1.05 = $143,283

Activity 5: Activity based budget

1 The correct answer is:

Activity based budget

	Receiving deliveries	Material handling	Production runs	Quality tests	Admin	S'vision	Total
Cost driver	No of deliveries	No of movements of material	No of production runs	Number of quality tests			
Volume	300	400	800	600			
	$'000	$'000	$'000	$'000	$'000	$'000	$'000
Management salary					5	45	50
Basic wages	7	7	5	5	6		30
Overtime	6		8	1			15
Factory overheads	3	2	2	1.5	1.5	2	12
Other	<u>1</u>				<u>2</u>	<u>1</u>	<u>4</u>
Total	17	9	15	7.5	14.5	48	111

Cost per activity unit	$56.67	$22.50	$18.75	$12.50			

Activity 6: Probabilistic budgeting

The correct answer is:

$190

Expected values are calculated as

$\sum px$

	Profit/(loss) $'000	Probability	Expected value (EV)
Best	400	0.3	120
Most likely	200	0.5	100
Worst	(150)	0.2	(30)
			190

14 Quantitative analysis in budgeting

Learning objectives

On completion of this chapter, you should be able to:

	Syllabus reference no.
Analyse fixed and variable cost elements from total cost data using the high/low method.	D2 (a)
Estimate the learning rate and learning effect.	D2 (b)
Apply the learning curve to a budgetary problem, including calculations on steady states.	D2 (c)
Discuss the reservations with the learning curve.	D2 (d)

Exam context

The success of a budget is largely dependent on the degree of accuracy in estimating the revenues and costs for the budget period.

This chapter looks at the **quantitative techniques** involved in budgeting, including the **high-low method** and the concept of the **learning curve**.

The quantitative techniques covered in this chapter could form the calculation part of a budgeting question in Section C. Techniques may also be examined regularly in short Section A objective test questions, as well as featuring in Section B questions.

Chapter overview

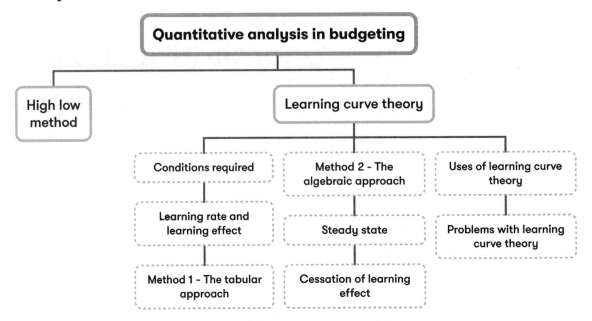

BPP
LEARNING
MEDIA

1 High-low method

In order to prepare budgets, forecasts of costs and revenues will need to be undertaken.

You will have seen in your earlier studies the use of the high-low method and linear regression to analyse total costs into their fixed and variable elements.

Illustration 1: High low method

Number of units	10,000	12,000	14,000
Overhead cost ($)	27,000	31,000	35,000

Required
Calculate the variable cost per unit and the fixed overhead cost.

Solution

1 **The correct answer is:**

Variable cost per unit = $2 and fixed costs = $7,000

Step 1 - Take the highest and lowest output levels

	Output	Cost $
Highest	14,000	35,000
Lowest	10,000	27,000
	4,000	8,000

Step 2 - Find the difference

Step 3 - Calculate the variable cost/unit

Variable cost/unit = $8,000/4,000 = $2

Step 4 - Calculate the fixed cost

Substituting the variable cost into the high output:

Fixed cost = $35,000 − (14,000 × $2) = $7,000

Activity 1: High low method

1 A department in a large organisation wishes to develop a method of predicting its total costs in a period. The following data has been recorded:

Month	Activity level (X) Units	Cost $
January	1,600	28,200
February	2,300	29,600
March	1,900	28,800

April	1,800	28,600
May	1,500	28,000
June	1,700	28,400

Required

The total cost model for a period could be represented by what equation?

Solution

1

---

2 Learning curve theory

> **Learning curve theory: Learning curve theory** applies to situations where the workforce as a whole improves in efficiency with experience. The **learning effect** or **learning curve effect** describes the speeding up of a job with repeated performance.

When new working practices or products are introduced, the theory is that as a workforce gains experience in a task, it will come to perform that task quicker.

This means that labour costs and variable overheads (if labour hour driven) will be lower in later periods of production than when the new product or production technique is introduced.

2.1 Conditions required

The theory of learning curves will only hold if the following conditions apply:

(a) There must be a significant manual element in the task being considered.

(b) The task must be repetitive.

(c) Production must be at an early stage so that there is room for improvement.

(d) There must be consistency in the workforce.

(e) There must not be extensive breaks in production, or workers will 'forget' the skill.

(f) Workforce must be motivated.

2.2 Learning rate and learning effect

Where a learning curve applies, there is a learning rate and a learning effect.

The **learning rate** is expressed as a percentage value, such as an 80% learning curve or a 70% learning curve.

The **learning effect** is that, as the workforce learns from experience how to make the new product, there is a big reduction in the time taken to make additional units.

Specifically, **every time that the cumulative output of the product doubles**, the average time to make all the units produced to date is a proportion of what it was before. This proportion is the learning rate.

There are two methods that can be used to deal with a learning curve scenario. Be prepared to use either or both in the exam.

- **Method 1.** The tabular approach
- **Method 2.** The algebraic approach

2.3 Method 1 - The tabular approach: cumulative average time and the learning rate

The rule to remember is that every time that cumulative output doubles the average production time is x% of what is was before, where x is the learning rate.

The approach is best explained with a numerical example.

Example

Tabular approach - 80% learning curve

For example, where an 80% learning effect occurs, the cumulative average time required per unit of output is reduced to 80% of the previous cumulative average time when output is doubled.

The first unit of output of a new product requires 100 hours. An 80% learning curve applies. The production times would be as follows:

Cumulative number of units	Cumulative average time per unit (hours)	Cumulative total time (hours)	Incremental number of units	Incremental total time (hours)
1	100.0	100.0	–	–
2*	80.0	160.0	1	60.0
4*	64.0	256.0	2	96.0
8*	51.2	409.6	4	153.6

*Output is being doubled each time.

The cost of the additional time can be calculated by applying the labour hour rate to the number of labour hours (and variable overhead rate, where variable overheads vary with the number of labour hours). The learning effect does not affect material costs.

Activity 2: Learning rate

A firm's workforce experiences a 75% learning rate.

The budgeted time for the first batch is 100 hours.

Required
What is the total time to produce eight batches in total?

○ 42.19 hours

○ 337.5 hours

○ 600 hours

○ 800 hours

Solution

2.4 Method 2 - The algebraic approach

The learning curve formula can be used to solve all learning curve scenarios.

Formula provided

$Y = aX^b$

where
	Y	is the cumulative average time per unit taken to produce X units
	a	is the time taken to produce the first unit
	X	is the cumulative number of units
	b	is the index of learning (log LR/log 2)
	LR	= the learning rate as a decimal

Exam focus point

This formula is provided in the exam. It refers to time rather than labour cost. The formula can also be used to calculate the labour cost per unit. The labour **times** are calculated using the curve formula and then converted to cost.

It is essential to understand how to apply the learning curve formula. You need a calculator that includes a function for calculating logarithms. Logarithms are the value of any number to the power of 10. For example, the logarithm of 3 is 0.4771213 because $10^{0.4771213} = 3$. Using a calculator, it is a simple process to obtain the log value of any number.

Illustration 2: Using the formula

1 Suppose that an 80% learning curve applies to production of a new product item ABC. To date (30 June) 30 units of ABC have been produced. Budgeted production in July is five units. The time to make the very first unit of ABC in January was 120 hours. The labour cost is $10 per hour.

(a) Calculate the time required to make the 31st unit

(b) Calculate the budgeted total labour cost for July

Solution

1 **The correct answer is:**

To solve this problem, we need to calculate the following.

(a) The cumulative total labour cost so far to produce 30 units of ABC

(b) The cumulative total labour cost to produce 31 units of ABC

(c) The cumulative total labour cost to produce 35 units of ABC; that is, adding on the extra 5 units for production in July

(d) The time taken to produce the 31st unit is the difference between (b) and (a). The cost of production of 5 units of ABC in July, as the difference between (c) and (a)

Time to produce the first 30 units

$Y = ax^b$

$b = \log 0.8/\log 2 = -0.09691/0.30103 = -0.3219281$

$Y = 120 \times (1/30^{0.3219281}) = 120 \times 0.3345594 = 40.147$ hours

Total time for first 30 units = 30 × 40.147 hours = 1,204.41 hours

Time to produce the first 31 units

$Y = 120 \times (1/31^{0.3219281}) = 120 \times 0.3310463 = 39.726$ hours

Total time for first 31 units = 31 × 39.726 hours = 1,231.51 hours

Time to produce the 31st unit = (1,231.51 – 1,204.41) = 27.1 hours

Time to produce the first 35 units

$Y = 120 \times (1/35^{0.3219281}) = 120 \times 0.3183619 = 38.203$ hours

Total time for first 35 units = 35 × 38.203 hours = 1,337.11 hours

Budgeted labour cost in July = (1,337.11 – 1,204.41) hours × $10 per hour = $1,327

Exam focus point

The examining team has stated that **you should not round 'b' to less than three decimal places.** Ideally, you should keep the long number in your calculator and use that!

Activity 3: Using the formula

1 A firm's workforce experiences a 75% learning rate.

The budgeted time for the first batch is 100 hours.

Using the formula $Y = aX^b$, calculate the time to produce:

(a) The first 10 batches in total

(b) The 10th batch only

Solution

1

See Chapter 14 Section 1 of the Essential reading for an illustration on deriving the learning rate.

Essential reading

See Chapter 14 Section 1 of the Essential reading for an illustration on deriving the learning rate.

The Essential reading is available as an Appendix of the digital edition of the Workbook.

2.5 Steady state

Eventually, the time per unit will reach a steady state where no further improvement can be made. When a steady state is reached, a standard time and standard labour cost for the product can be established.

Illustration 3: Learning curves and standard costs

1 A company needs to calculate a new standard cost for one of its products. When the product was first manufactured, the standard variable cost of the first unit was as follows.

		Cost per unit
		$
Direct material	10 kg @ $4 per kg	40
Direct labour	10 hours @ $9 per hour	90
Variable overhead	10 hours @ $1 per hour	10
Total		140

During the following year, a 90% learning curve was observed in making the product. The cumulative production at the end of the third quarter was 50 units. After producing 50 units, the learning effect ended, and all subsequent units took the same time to make.

Required
What is the standard cost per unit for the fourth quarter assuming the learning curve had reached a steady state, ie peak efficiency was reached after the 50th unit was produced?

Solution

1 **The correct answer is:**

$Y = ax^b$ where $b = \log 0.9 / \log 2$.

b = −0.0457575/0.30103 = −0.1520031

So $Y = ax^{-0.1520031}$

For **49 cumulative units** $Y = 10 \times (49^{-0.1520031}) = 10 \times 0.55346$ hours = 5.5346 hours.

Total time for first 49 units = 49 × 5.5346 hours = 271.2 hours.

For **50 cumulative units** $Y = 10 \times (50^{-0.1520031}) = 10 \times 0.55176$ hours = 5.5176 hours.

Total time for first 50 units = 50 × 5.5176 hours = 275.88 hours.

Time for 50th unit = (275.88 − 271.2) = 4.68 hours

This is the standard time for the product when the steady state has been reached.

Standard cost		Cost per unit
		$
Direct material	10 kg @ $4 per kg	40.00
Direct labour	4.68 hours @ $9 per hour	42.12
Variable overhead	4.68 hours @ $1 per hour	4.68
Total		86.80

In practice, the standard time may be rounded to a more convenient number, such as 4.5 hours or 5.0 hours.

2.6 Cessation of learning effect

Practical reasons for the learning effect to cease are:

(a) When machine efficiency restricts any further improvement.

(b) The workforce reach their physical limits.

(c) There is a 'go slow' agreement among the workforce.

Activity 4: Learning curve

Flogel Co has just produced the first full batch of a new product taking 200 hours.

Flogel has predicted a learning curve effect of 85%. b = −0.2345

1 Required

How long will it take to produce the next 15 batches?

- ○ 1,470 hours
- ○ 1,590 hours
- ○ 1,670 hours
- ○ 3,000 hours

2 Flogel expects that after the 30th batch has been produced, the learning effect will cease. From the 31st batch onwards, each batch will take the same time as the 30th batch.

Required

What is the long-run steady state time per unit?

- ○ 30 hours
- ○ 31 hours
- ○ 69 hours
- ○ 90 hours

3 The first 8 units have now been produced. The first unit took 200 hours to make and the total time for the first 8 units was 819.2.

Required

What was the actual rate of learning which occurred?

- ○ 85%
- ○ 80%
- ○ 72%

○ 50%

Solution

1

2

3

2.7 Uses of learning curve theory

The learning curve theory can be used in the business for:

- Forecasting labour hours required
- Cash forecasting
- Standard setting
- Cost calculation
- Price setting

Essential reading

See Chapter 14 Section 2 of the Essential reading for more detail on the relevance of learning curve effects in management accounting.

The Essential reading is available as an Appendix of the digital edition of the Workbook.

2.8 Problems with learning curve theory

Although it seems a useful and easy to apply technique, learning curve theory is not without problems:

- We may not be able to calculate a rate.
- We may not know when production has reached a steady state.
- The rate may not necessarily be constant.

Essential reading

See Chapter 14 Section 3 of the Essential reading for more detail on the limitations of learning curve theory.

The Essential reading is available as an Appendix of the digital edition of the Workbook.

Chapter summary

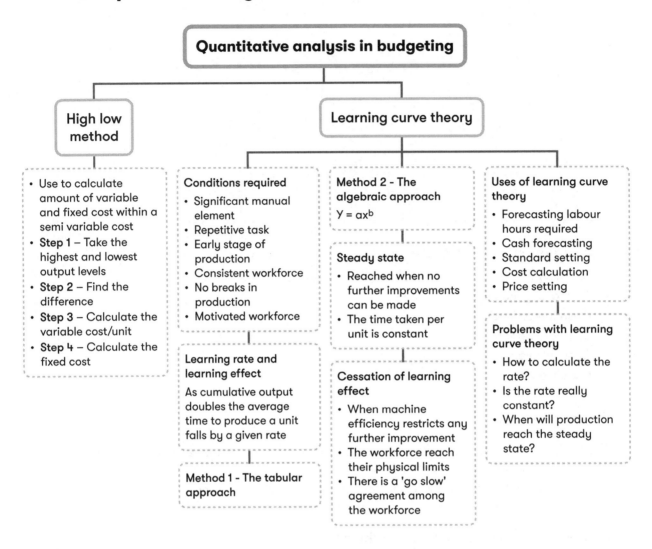

Quantitative analysis in budgeting

High low method

- Use to calculate amount of variable and fixed cost within a semi variable cost
- **Step 1** – Take the highest and lowest output levels
- **Step 2** – Find the difference
- **Step 3** – Calculate the variable cost/unit
- **Step 4** – Calculate the fixed cost

Learning curve theory

Conditions required

- Significant manual element
- Repetitive task
- Early stage of production
- Consistent workforce
- No breaks in production
- Motivated workforce

Learning rate and learning effect

As cumulative output doubles the average time to produce a unit falls by a given rate

Method 1 - The tabular approach

Method 2 - The algebraic approach

$Y = ax^b$

Steady state

- Reached when no further improvements can be made
- The time taken per unit is constant

Cessation of learning effect

- When machine efficiency restricts any further improvement
- The workforce reach their physical limits
- There is a 'go slow' agreement among the workforce

Uses of learning curve theory

- Forecasting labour hours required
- Cash forecasting
- Standard setting
- Cost calculation
- Price setting

Problems with learning curve theory

- How to calculate the rate?
- Is the rate really constant?
- When will production reach the steady state?

Knowledge diagnostic

1. High-low method

This can be used to determine the amount of fixed and variable cost which can then be used to forecast for different levels of output.

2. Learning curve theory

The amount of time needed for production may reduce when the product is **new, repetitive** and has a **significant manual element**.

Learning curve theory states that as **cumulative output doubles, the cumulative average time per unit falls to a given percentage of the previous cumulative average time per unit.**

The time/cost for production of units can be calculated if the rate of learning is known using the formula $Y = aX^b$.

Eventually a consistent time to produce a unit will be reached from which it is not possible to improve any further. This is known as steady state.

Further study guidance

Question practice

Now try the following from the Further question practice bank [available in the digital edition of the Workbook]:

Number	Level	Marks	Approximate time
Section A Q38	Examination	2	4 mins
Section A Q39	Examination	2	4 mins
Section A Q40	Examination	2	4 mins
Section B Q11–15	Examination	10	18 mins

Further reading

There is a technical article available on ACCA's website, called *The learning rate and learning effect*.

You are strongly advised to read this article in full as part of your preparation for the PM exam.

Activity answers

Activity 1: High low method

1 **The correct answer is:**

Total costs = 25,000 + 2x where x is the volume of activity in units

The highest activity level is in February and the lowest in May.

Step 1 – Take the highest and lowest output levels

	Activity level	Cost $
Highest	2,300	29,600
Lowest	<u>1,500</u>	<u>28,000</u>
	800	1,600

Step 2 - Find the difference

Step 3 - Calculate the variable cost/unit

Variable cost/unit = $1,600/800 = $2

Step 4 - Calculate the fixed cost

Substituting the variable cost into the high output:

Fixed cost = $29,600 – (2,300 × $2) = $25,000

Total costs = 25,000 + 2x where x is the volume of activity in units

Activity 2: Learning rate

The correct answer is:

337.5 hours

Output	Total time (hrs)	Cumulative average time (hrs)
1	100	100
2	150	75
4	225	56.25
8	337.5	42.1875

Activity 3: Using the formula

1 **The correct answer is:**

(a) $Y = aX^b$

a = 100

X = 10

b = log 0.75/log 2 = –0.125/0.301 = –0.415

$Y = 10 \times 10^{-0.415}$

= 38.459 hrs

Total time taken to produce 10 batches: 10 × 38.459 = 384.59 hrs

(b) $Y = aX^b$

a = 100

X = 9

b = –0.415

$Y = 100 \times 9^{-0.415}$

= 40.1781 hrs

Total time to produce 9 batches =

9 × 40.1781 = 361.60 hrs

∴ Time to produce 10th batch

= 384.59 − 361.60

= 22.99 hrs

Activity 4: Learning curve

1   **The correct answer is:**

1,470 hours

$b = \log 0.85/\log 2 = −0.2345$

To produce the next 15 batches:

find time to produce 16 and deduct time to make 1:

$y = 200 × 16^{−0.2345}$ = 104.4 hours = average time per batch, thus 16 batches will take

16 × 104.4 = 1,670.4 hours

	Hours
less time for first batch	200.0
time for the next 15 batches	1,470.4

2   **The correct answer is:**

69 hours

Time for 30 batches:

$y = 200 × 30^{−0.2345}$ = 90.08 × 30 = 2,702

Time for 29 batches:

$y = 200 × 29^{−0.2345}$ = 90.80 × 29 = 2,633

Time for 30th batch = 2,702 − 2,633 = 69 hours, so this should be the budgeted hours once the steady state has been achieved.

3   **The correct answer is:**

Let r be the rate of learning which actually occurred.

If the total time for 8 units was 819.2 hours, then the cumulative average time per unit must be 102.4.

$200 × r^3 = 102.4$

$r^3 = 102.4/200 = 0.512$

$r = 0.8$

Therefore, the rate of learning is 80%.

BPP
LEARNING
MEDIA

15

Budgeting and standard costing

Learning objectives

On completion of this chapter, you should be able to:

	Syllabus reference no.
Explain the use of standard costs.	D3 (a)
Outline the methods used to derive standard costs and discuss the different types of cost possible.	D3 (b)
Explain and illustrate the importance of flexing budgets in performance management.	D3 (c)
Explain and apply the principle of controllability in the performance management system.	D3 (d)

Exam context

In this chapter, we will be looking at **standard costs** and **standard costing**.

You will have studied standard costing before and have learned about the principles involved and how to calculate a number of cost and sales variances. We look at the topic in more depth for your studies of this syllabus.

The contents of this chapter are likely to be examined in conjunction with variance analysis, covered in the next two chapters.

Chapter overview

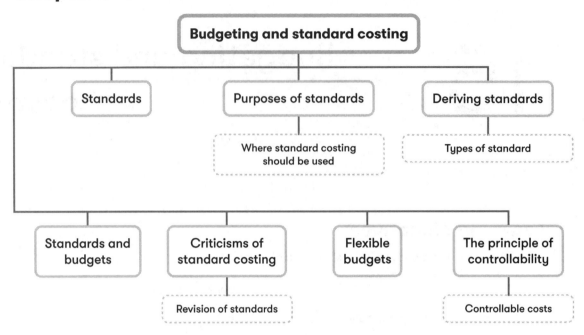

BPP
LEARNING
MEDIA

1 Standards

> **Standard cost:** A **standard cost** is an estimated unit cost.

A standard is prepared by management **in advance** and details their **expectations** of the future.

Standards are not just for items of production in manufacturing businesses. They exist in many different spheres. Standard times for repairing cars, standard punctualities for train companies and standard response times for ambulances are just some of the many examples encountered.

You will have come across standard costs before as part of costing. When trying to establish the cost of a unit, be it under absorption or marginal costing, the cost card was derived using standard costs.

As a reminder:

Example of a standard cost card for a cost unit

		$/unit
Direct costs:		
Direct materials	(5 kg @ $3/kg)	15.00
Direct labour	(3 hrs @ $6/hr)	18.00
		33.00
Indirect costs:		
Variable overheads		2.00
Fixed overheads		3.00
Full product cost		38.00

The costs in the cost card are built up using, for example, the expected amount of material at the expected price of the material.

2 Purposes of standards

> **Standard costing: Standard costing** involves the establishment of predetermined estimates of the costs of products or services, the collection of actual costs and the comparison of the actual costs with the predetermined estimates. The predetermined costs are known as standard costs and the difference between standard and actual cost is known as a **variance**. The process by which the total difference between standard and actual results is analysed is known as **variance analysis**.

The uses of standard costing are as follows:

(a) Prediction of costs and times for **decision making**, eg for allocating resources.

(b) Standard costing is used in setting **budgets** – an accurate standard will increase the accuracy of the budget.

(c) Variance analysis is a control technique which compares actual with standard costs and revenues.

(d) **Performance evaluation** systems make use of standards as motivators and as a basis for assessment.

(e) **Inventory valuation** – this is often less time consuming than alternative valuation methods such as first in, first out (FIFO) or weighted average.

(f) To enable the principle of 'management by exception' to be practised (a standard cost, when established, is an average expected unit cost and because it is only an average, actual results will vary to some extent above and below the average; only significant differences between actual and standard should be reported).

Although the other uses of standard costing should not be overlooked, we will be concentrating on variance reporting and the control aspect.

2.1 Where standard costing should be used

Although standard costing can be used in a variety of costing situations including service industries, its greatest benefit can be gained if there is a **large amount of repetition** in the production process so the average or expected usage of resources can be determined. It is therefore most suited to **mass production** and **repetitive assembly work**. It is not well suited to production systems where items are manufactured to customer demand and specifications.

3 Deriving standards

The **responsibility for deriving standard costs** should be shared between **managers who are able to provide the necessary information** about levels of expected efficiency, prices and overhead costs.

The standard cost of materials will be estimated by the purchasing department.

Activity 1: Deriving standards

(a) The forecast sales levels

(b) The amount of wastage expected

Required
Which of the above factors does the purchasing department need to consider when establishing the standard cost of materials?

O (a) only

O (b) only

O Neither (a) nor (b)

O Both (a) and (b)

Solution

Setting standards for other elements on the cost card will undergo a similar process.

Essential reading

See Chapter 15 Section 1 of the Essential reading for more detail on deriving standards.

The Essential reading is available as an Appendix of the digital edition of the Workbook.

3.1 Types of standard

KEY TERM

Ideal standard: An **ideal standard** is a standard which can be attained under perfect operating conditions: no wastage, no inefficiencies, no idle time, no breakdowns.

Attainable standard: An **attainable standard** is a standard which can be attained if production is carried out efficiently, machines are properly operated and/or materials are properly used. Some allowance is made for wastage and inefficiencies.

Current standard: A **current standard** is a standard based on current working conditions (current wastage, current inefficiencies).

Basic standard: A **basic standard** is a long-term standard which remains unchanged over the years and is used to show trends.

Activity 2: Types of standard

The following statements have been made about different types of standards in standard costing systems:

(a) Current standards provide the best basis for budgeting because they represent an achievable level of productivity.

(b) Ideal standards provide a useful short-term target for standard setting, because they lead to improvement in performance.

Required

Which of the above statements is/are true?

O   (a) only

O   (b) only

O   Neither (a) nor (b)

O   Both (a) and (b)

Solution

3.1.1 The impact on employee behaviour of the type of standard set

The type of standard set can have an impact on the behaviour of the employees trying to achieve those standards.

Type of standard	Impact on behaviour
Ideal	Some say that they provide employees with an **incentive to be more efficient** even though it is highly unlikely that the standard will be achieved. Others argue that they are likely to have an unfavourable effect on employee motivation because the differences between standards and actual results will always be adverse. The **employees may feel that the goals are unattainable** and so **they will not work so hard.**
Attainable	Might be an **incentive to work harder** as they provide a **realistic but challenging target of efficiency**
Current	**Will not motivate employees to do anything more than they are currently doing**
Basic	This may have an **unfavourable impact** on the motivation of employees. Over time, they will discover that they are easily able to achieve the standards. They may become bored and lose interest in what they are doing if they have nothing to aim for.

4 Standards and budgets

Similarities:

- Standards and budgets are very similar in terms of their impacts on employees' motivation
- Standards generally form the basis for the budget
- Both are used for control

Differences:

Standards	Budgets
By unit	In total
For areas of repetition	All areas
Financial and non-financial targets	Financial targets

5 Criticisms of standard costing

Standard costing has some disadvantages and, arguably, is less relevant in the modern environment than previously when manufacturing was mainly of standard, mass-produced products.

(a) Standard costing works best in a **stable environment**; the modern business environment is rapidly changing.

(b) **Regular revisions** to the standard are required. This process is expensive and time consuming.

(c) Meeting the standard should not necessarily be accepted as satisfactory if **further improvements** could be made.

(d) Techniques associated with standard costing (such as variance analysis) are less useful in a modern environment of **customised products**.

5.1 Revision of standards

Standards should be reviewed regularly and revised when there is a change in the basis upon which they were set. This ensures that they remain useful as a performance measure.

6 Flexible budgets

We covered flexible budgets in Chapter 13. Remember that comparison of a fixed budget with the actual results for a different level of activity is of little use for control purposes. **Flexible budgets** should be used to show what cost and revenues should have been for the actual level of activity.

Budgetary control involves drawing up budgets for the areas of responsibility for individual managers (production managers, purchasing managers, and so on) and regularly **comparing** actual results against expected results. The differences between actual results and expected results are reported as **variances** and these are used to provide a guideline for control action by individual managers.

Note that individual managers are **held responsible** for investigating differences between budgeted and actual results, and are then expected to take corrective action or amend the plan in the light of actual events.

Essential reading

See Chapter 15 Section 2 of the Essential reading for more detail on flexible budgets.

The Essential reading is available as an Appendix of the digital edition of the Workbook.

7 The principle of controllability

The **principle of controllability** means that managers of responsibility centres should only be held accountable for costs over which they have some influence.

> ### Exam focus point
> The principle of controllability is extremely important for performance management.

Budgetary control is based around a system of **budget centres**. Each budget centre will have its own budget and a manager will be responsible for managing the budget centre and ensuring that the budget is met.

Budgetary control and budget centres are therefore part of the overall system of **responsibility accounting** within an organisation.

> **Responsibility accounting: Responsibility accounting** is a system of accounting that segregates revenue and costs into areas of personal responsibility in order to monitor and assess the performance of each part of an organisation.

7.1 Controllable costs

Controllable costs are items of expenditure which can be directly influenced by a given manager within a given time span. Care must be taken to distinguish between controllable costs and uncontrollable costs in variance reporting. From a **motivation** point of view, this is important because it can be very demoralising for managers who feel that their performance is being judged on the basis of something over which they have no influence. It is also important from a **control** point of view in that control reports should ensure that information on costs is reported to the manager who is able to take action to control them.

Responsibility accounting attempts to associate costs, revenues, assets and liabilities with the managers most capable of controlling them. As a system of accounting, it therefore distinguishes between controllable and uncontrollable costs.

Most **variable costs** within a department are thought to be **controllable in the short term** because managers can influence the efficiency with which resources are used, even if they cannot do anything to raise or lower price levels.

7.1.1 The controllability of fixed costs

It is often assumed that all fixed costs are non-controllable in the short run. This is not so.

(a) **Committed fixed costs** are those costs arising from the possession of plant, equipment, buildings and an administration department **to support the long-term needs of the business**. These costs (depreciation, rent, administration salaries) are largely **non-controllable in the short term** because they have been committed to by longer-term decisions affecting longer-term needs. When a company decides to cut production drastically, the long-term committed fixed costs will be reduced, but only after redundancy terms have been settled and assets sold.

(b) **Discretionary fixed costs**, such as advertising and research and development costs, are incurred as a result of a top management decision, but could be **raised or lowered at fairly short notice** (irrespective of the actual volume of production and sales).

7.1.2 Controllability and apportioned costs

This may seem quite straightforward in theory, but it is not always so easy in practice to distinguish controllable from uncontrollable costs. **Apportioned overhead costs provide a good example**.

Suppose that a manager of a production department in a manufacturing company is made responsible for the costs of their department. These costs include **directly attributable overhead items**, such as the costs of indirect labour and indirect materials consumed in the department. The department's overhead costs also include an apportionment of costs from other cost centres, such as rent and rates for the building it shares with other departments, and a share of the costs of the maintenance department.

Should the production manager be held accountable for any of these apportioned costs?

(a) Managers should not be held accountable for costs over which they have no control. In this example, apportioned rent and rates costs would not be controllable by the production department manager.

(b) Managers should be held accountable for costs over which they have some influence. In this example, it is the responsibility of the maintenance department manager to keep maintenance costs within budget. However, their costs will be partly variable and partly fixed, and the variable cost element will depend on the volume of demand for their services. If the production department's staff treat their equipment badly we might expect higher repair costs, and the production department manager should therefore be made accountable for the repair costs that their department makes the maintenance department incur on its behalf.

(c) Charging the production department with some of the costs of the maintenance department prevents the production department from viewing the maintenance services as 'free services'. Overuse would be discouraged and the production manager is more likely to question the activities of the maintenance department, possibly resulting in a reduction in maintenance costs or the provision of more efficient maintenance services.

7.1.3 Controllability and dual responsibility

Quite often, a particular cost might be the **responsibility of two or more managers**. For example, the costs of raw materials might be the responsibility of the purchasing manager (prices) and the production manager (usage). A **reporting system must allocate responsibility appropriately**. The purchasing manager must be responsible for any increase in the prices of raw materials, whereas the production manager should be responsible for any increase in the usage of raw materials.

Chapter summary

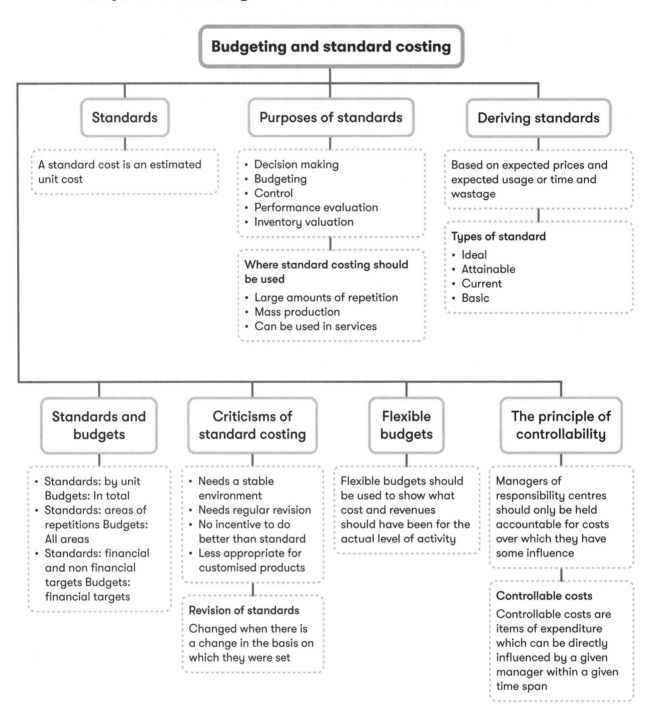

Budgeting and standard costing

Standards

A standard cost is an estimated unit cost

Purposes of standards

- Decision making
- Budgeting
- Control
- Performance evaluation
- Inventory valuation

Where standard costing should be used

- Large amounts of repetition
- Mass production
- Can be used in services

Deriving standards

Based on expected prices and expected usage or time and wastage

Types of standard

- Ideal
- Attainable
- Current
- Basic

Standards and budgets

- Standards: by unit Budgets: In total
- Standards: areas of repetitions Budgets: All areas
- Standards: financial and non financial targets Budgets: financial targets

Criticisms of standard costing

- Needs a stable environment
- Needs regular revision
- No incentive to do better than standard
- Less appropriate for customised products

Revision of standards

Changed when there is a change in the basis on which they were set

Flexible budgets

Flexible budgets should be used to show what cost and revenues should have been for the actual level of activity

The principle of controllability

Managers of responsibility centres should only be held accountable for costs over which they have some influence

Controllable costs

Controllable costs are items of expenditure which can be directly influenced by a given manager within a given time span

Knowledge diagnostic

1. Standards

A standard is prepared in advance based upon expectations of the future.

2. Purposes of standards

Standard costs have many uses in performance management. These include:

- Performance evaluation
- Control
- Decision making
- Budgeting
- Inventory valuation

3. Types of standard

The four bases are:

- Ideal
- Attainable
- Current
- Basic

Standards should be set to an attainable level to drive the best performance.

4. Deriving standards

Standards take into account future price rises, efficiencies etc, when prepared.

5. Standards and budgets

Standards are set for a unit, whereas budgets encompass the whole business.

6. Flexed budgets

Comparison of a fixed budget with the actual results for a different level of activity is of little use for control purposes. **Flexed budgets** should be used to show what cost and revenues should have been for the actual level of activity.

7. Principle of controllability

The **principle of controllability** means managers of responsibility centres should only be held accountable for costs over which they have some influence. **Controllable costs** are items of expenditure which can be directly influenced by a given manager within a given time span.

Further study guidance

Question practice

Now try the following from the Further question practice bank [available in the digital edition of the Workbook]:

Number	Level	Marks	Approximate Time
Section A Q41	Examination	2	4 mins
Section A Q42	Examination	2	4 mins
Section A Q43	Examination	2	4 mins
Section C Q4	Examination	20	36 mins

Further reading

N/A

Activity answers

Activity 1: Deriving standards

The correct answer is:

(a) only

The quantity will be relevant, as purchasing larger amounts will often mean that bulk quantity discounts are available. The expected wastage levels are not directly relevant to the purchase price per kg. Instead, they will affect the standard quantity used per unit.

Activity 2: Types of standard

The correct answer is:

Neither (a) nor (b)

Current standards are not ideal as they do not include an incentive to make improvements from the current position. Ideal standards are not achievable in the short-term, but may be useful for longer-term targets.

Skills checkpoint 3

How to approach your PM exam

Chapter overview

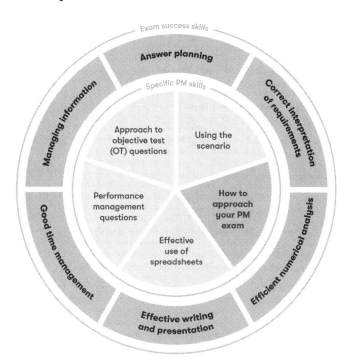

Introduction

You can answer your PM exam in whatever order you prefer. It is important that you adopt a strategy that works best for you. We would suggest that you decide on your preferred approach and practise it by doing a timed mock exam before your real exam.

Remember your PM exam will be structured as follows:

Section A – 15 **individual OT questions** worth two marks each. Questions in Section A can come from any syllabus area. There will be a mix of numerical and discursive style questions and you may find that some questions are easier than others.

Section B – Three **OT case questions** worth 10 marks each. Each case question will consist of five individual OT questions worth two marks each. There will normally be a mix of numerical and discursive questions. You do not have to answer these questions in order as the answer from one will not be required for subsequent questions. Again, questions in Section B can come from any syllabus area. Each individual case does however tend to focus on a particular syllabus area and at least one is likely to come from the syllabus area 'Specialist cost and management accounting techniques'.

Section C - Section C will contain two, 20-mark questions which will be **scenario based** and may contain both discursive and computational elements. Section C questions will mainly focus on the following syllabus areas, but a minority of marks can be drawn from any other area of the syllabus.

- Decision-making techniques (syllabus area C)
- Budgeting and control (syllabus area D)
- Performance measurement and control (syllabus area E)

This Skills Checkpoint will provide you with one suggested approach for tackling your PM exam.

Good luck!

How to approach your PM exam

We would suggest the following approach for tackling your PM exam. It is important that you adopt an approach that works best for you and practise it by completing a mock exam to time prior to your real exam.

Complete Section A first - allocated time 54 minutes

- Tackle any easier OT questions first. Often discursive style questions can be answered quickly, saving more time for calculations. Do not leave any questions unanswered. Even if you are unsure, make a reasoned guess. Skills Checkpoint 1 covers how to approach OT questions in more detail.
- If you do not feel that you need the full 54 minutes to complete Section A, you can carry this time forward to your Section C questions which tend to be more time pressured. With practice, it may be possible for you to complete Section A up to 10 minutes quicker than the allocated time of 54 minutes.

Complete Section B next - allocated time 54 minutes

- You will have 18 mins of exam time to allocate to each of the three OT case questions in Section B. Use the same approach to OT questions as discussed for Section A.
- Each individual case tends to focus on a specific syllabus area. Start with the OT case question you feel most confident with.
- There will normally be two discussion type and three numerical questions within each case. Again, it is better to tackle the discussion type questions first as they tend to be less time consuming.
- If you do not feel that you need the full 54 minutes to complete section B you can carry this time forward to your Section C questions which tend to be more time sensitive. With practice, it may be possible for you to complete Section B approximately five minutes quicker than the allocated time of 54 minutes.

Finally, complete Section C – allocated time 72 minutes

- Section C will contain two, 20-mark questions which will be scenario based and will contain both discursive and computational elements. Allocate at least 36 minutes to each question (remembering to split your time between each of the sub requirements) but you may have up to 15 minutes of extra time if you have completed Sections A and B of the exam in less than the allotted time.
- Start with the question you feel most confident with. The first sub-requirement will normally involve some detailed calculations and these tend to be very time sensitive. If possible, answer the discursive sub-requirements first. This will ensure that you don't spend too much time on the calculations and then lose out on the easier discursive marks. Make it clear to your marker which sub-requirement you are answering.
- Skills Checkpoints 2, 4 and 5 look specifically at the techniques you should use answering the scenario-based questions in Section C. It is very likely that you will get a performance management question in Section C so make sure you are confident using the techniques covered in Skills Checkpoint 5.
- You must practise written questions in full to time, as this is the only way to acquire the necessary skills to tackle discussion questions. Continuous effort in practising these skills will lead to an increased chance of success in your exam.

Set some time aside to practise this approach through the completion of a mock exam to time.

16

Variance analysis

Learning objectives

On completion of this chapter, you should be able to:

	Syllabus reference no.
Calculate, identify the cause of, and explain mixand yield variances.	D4 (a)
Explain the wider issues involved in changing material mix, eg cost, quality and performance measurement issues.	D4 (b)
Identify and explain the relationship of the material usage variance with the material mix and yield variances.	D4 (c)
Suggest and justify alternative methods of controlling production processes.	D4 (d)
Calculate, identify the cause of, and explain sales mix and quantity variances.	D5 (a)
Identify and explain the relationship of the sales volume variances with the sales mix and quantity variances.	D5 (a)

Exam context

The **actual results** achieved by an organisation will usually **differ from the expected results** (the expected results being the standard costs and revenues which we looked at in the previous chapter). These differences are **variances**. You should have learned basic variances in your previous studies but the PM exam requires some more advanced knowledge of variances including materials mix and yield variances and sales mix and quantity variances.

Chapter overview

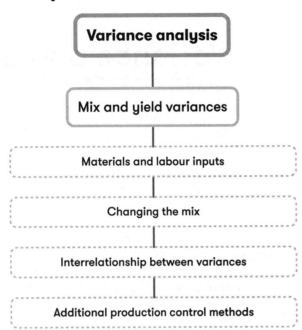

Variance analysis

Mix and yield variances

Materials and labour inputs

Changing the mix

Interrelationship between variances

Additional production control methods

1 Mix and yield variances

In order to understand more advanced variances, you need to understand the basic variances brought forward from your earlier studies.

Essential reading

See Chapter 16 Section 1 of the Essential reading for details on basic variances and operating statements.

The Essential reading is available as an Appendix of the digital edition of the Workbook.

1.1 Materials and labour inputs

Where inputs can be substituted for one another, the efficiency/usage variance can be subdivided.

For example, manufacturing processes often require that a number of different materials are combined to make a unit of finished product. When a product requires two or more raw materials in its make-up, it is often possible to **sub-analyse the materials usage variance into a materials mix and a materials yield variance**.

Adding a greater proportion of one material (therefore a smaller proportion of a different material) might make the materials mix **cheaper or more expensive**.

Similarly, if more than one type of labour is used in a product, the labour efficiency variance can be analysed further into a **labour mix (team composition) variance** and a **labour yield (team productivity or output) variance**.

Mix variance: A **mix variance** occurs when the materials are not mixed or blended in standard proportions, and is a measure of whether the actual mix is cheaper or more expensive than the standard mix.

Yield variance: A **yield variance** arises because there is a difference between what the input should have been (considering the output achieved) and the actual input.

The mix variance represents the financial impact of using a different proportion of raw materials.

The yield variance represents the financial impact of the input yielding a different level of output to the standard.

Note that calculating a mix and yield variance is only meaningful for control purposes when management is in a position to control the mix of materials used in production.

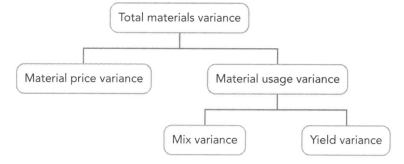

Illustration 1: Materials usage, mix and yield usage

1   A company manufactures a chemical, Dynamite, using two compounds: Flash and Bang. The standard materials usage and cost of one unit of Dynamite are as follows:

		$
Flash	5 kg at $2 per kg	10
Bang	10 kg at $3 per kg	<u>30</u>
		<u>40</u>

In a particular period, 80 units of Dynamite were produced from 600 kg of Flash and 750 kg of Bang.

Required
Calculate the materials usage, mix and yield variances.

Solution

1   **The correct answer is:**

(a)   **Usage variance**

If we do not calculate a mix and yield variance, we would calculate a usage variance separately for each material.

	Standard usage for actual output of 80 units	Actual usage	Variance	Standard cost per kg	Variance
	kg	kg	kg	$	$
Flash	400	600	200 (A)	2	400 (A)
Bang	<u>800</u>	<u>750</u>	<u>50</u> (F)	3	<u>150</u> (F)
	<u>1,200</u>	<u>1,350</u>			<u>250</u> (A)

The total usage variance of $250 (A) can be analysed into a mix variance and a yield variance and these may be reported instead of the usage variance.

(b)   **Mix variance**

To calculate the mix variance, it is first necessary to decide how the total quantity of materials used (600 kg + 750 kg) should have been divided between Flash and Bang. In other words, we need to **calculate the standard mix of the actual quantity of materials used**.

	Actual usage	Actual total usage in standard mix (5:10 or 1:2)	Mix variance
	kg	kg	kg
Flash	600	450	150 (A)
Bang	<u>750</u>	<u>900</u>	<u>150</u> (F)
	<u>1,350</u>	<u>1,350</u>	<u>0</u>

The mix variance in total quantities is always 0. This must always be the case since the expected mix is based on the total quantity actually used; hence the difference between the total expected and actual total is zero.

However, the actual mix uses:

*   More of the cheaper material, Flash (= adverse variance, because actual usage of Flash in the mix is more than the standard usage; therefore the cost for Flash is more); but
*   Less of the more expensive material, Bang (= favourable variance, because actual usage of Bang in the mix is less than the standard usage; therefore the cost for Bang is lower).

Taking both materials together, the actual mix of materials is cheaper than the standard mix, and this will produce a favourable mix variance overall.

The mix variances in quantities are converted into a monetary value at the standard price of the materials.

	Actual quantity standard mix	Actual usage/mix	Mix variance	Standard price	Mix variance
	kg	kg	kg	$ per kg	$
Flash	450	600	150 (A)	2	300 (A)
Bang	900	750	150 (F)	3	450 (F)
	1,350	1,350	0		150 (F)

The total mix variance is $150 (F).

(c) Yield variance

The yield variance can be calculated in total or for each individual material input.

Method 1

	Standard quantity standard mix	Actual quantity standard mix	Yield variance	Standard price	Yield variance
	kg	kg	kg	$ per kg	$
Flash	400	450	50 (A)	2	100 (A)
Bang	800	900	100 (A)	3	300 (A)
	1,200	1,350	150		400 (A)

Method 2

The weighted average cost per kilogram of materials = $40/15 kg = $2.67 per kg.

	kg
80 units of product should use in total (× 15 kg)	1,200
They did use (600 + 750)	1,350
Yield variance in kg	150 (A)
Weighted average price per kg	$2.67
Yield variance in $	$400 (A)

Method 3

	Units
1,350 kg of material should produce (÷ 15)	90
They did produce	80
Yield variance in units of output	10 (A)
Standard material cost per unit	$40
Yield variance in $	$400 (A)

The mix variance $150 (F) plus the yield variance $400 (A) add up to the usage variance $250 (A).

Exam focus point

In the exam, use whichever method you prefer.

Activity 1: Materials mix and yield variances

Brenda and Eddie are analysing the main ingredients to their basic pasta sauce.

The standard ingredients for one batch of tomato pasta sauce are:

			$
Onions	5 kg	@ $2/kg	10
Tomatoes	5 kg	@ $4/kg	<u>20</u>
			<u>30</u>

During June, 100 batches of sauce were prepared, using the following ingredients:

Onions	600 kg
Tomatoes	900 kg

1   Required

Calculate the materials mix variance and determine whether it is adverse or favourable.

[▼]

O   Adverse

O   Favourable

2   Required

Calculate the materials yield variance and determine whether it is adverse or favourable.

[▼]

O   Adverse

O   Favourable

Solution

1

2

1.2 Changing the mix

> ### Exam focus point
> Always consider the impact on quality and the related impact on sales of a change in the mix.

The materials mix variance indicates the **cost** of a change in the mix of materials, while the yield variance indicates the **productivity** of the manufacturing process. A change in the mix can have wider implications. For example, rising raw material prices may cause pressure to change the mix of materials. Even if the yield is not affected by the change in the mix, the **quality** of the final product may change. This can have an adverse effect on sales if customers do not accept the change in quality.

The production manager's performance may be measured by mix and yield variances, however these **performance measures** may fail to indicate problems with falling quality and the impact on other areas of the business. **Quality targets** may also be needed.

1.3 Interrelationship between variances

A **favourable mix** variance occurs when the **actual mix** of materials is **cheaper** than the standard mix.

Using a cheaper mix of materials may result in an output/yield that is less than the standard output. In other words, a **favourable mix** variance may result in an **adverse yield** variance.

For similar reasons, when there is an **adverse mix** variance because the actual mix of materials is more **expensive** than the standard mix, there may possibly be an **interrelated favourable yield** variance.

Activity 2: Implications of changing the mix

The following statements have been made about the implications of changing the mix of materials used in the production of soup:

(a) Using proportionally more of the cheaper ingredients will always lead to lower yields.

(b) Altering the mix could affect the taste and therefore the number of units sold.

Required
Which of the above statements is/are true?

O (a) only
O (b) only
O Neither (a) nor (b)
O Both (a) and (b)

Solution

Activity 3: Material yield

A company manufactures a fruit flavoured drink by mixing two liquids: A & J. The standard cost for ten litres of the drink is shown below:

	$
5 litres of liquid A at $16 per litre	80
6 litres of liquid J at $25 per litre	150
	230

During August the company produced 4,800 litres of the drink. This was 200 litres below budgeted production. The company purchased and used 2,200 litres of A for $18 per litre and 2,750 litres of J for $21 per litre.

Required

What is the material yield for August?

O $450 A

O $450 F

O $6,900 F

O $6,900 A

Solution

1.4 Additional production control methods

In a modern manufacturing environment with an emphasis on quality management, using mix and yield variances for control purposes may not be possible or may be inadequate. Other control methods could be more useful, such as:

- Rates of wastage
- Average cost of input calculations
- Percentage of deliveries on time
- Customer satisfaction ratings
- Yield percentage calculations or output to input conversion rates

2 Sales mix and quantity variances

The sales volume profit variance can be analysed further into a sales mix variance and a sales quantity variance.

Sales mix variance: The **sales mix variance** occurs when the proportions of the various products sold are different from those in the budget.

Sales quantity variance: The **sales quantity variance** shows the difference in contribution/profit because of a change in sales volume from the budgeted volume of sales.

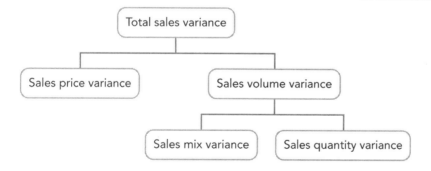

 Illustration 2: Sales volume, mix and quantity variance

1 Just Desserts Co makes and sells two products, Chocolate Crunch and Strawberry Sundae. The budgeted sales and profit are as follows:

	Sales Units	Revenue $	Costs $	Profit $	Profit per unit $
Chocolate Crunch (CC)	400	8,000	6,000	2,000	5

	$	$	$	$	$
Strawberry Sundae (SS)	300	12,000	11,100	<u>900</u>	3
				2,900	

Actual sales were 280 units of Chocolate Crunch and 630 units of Strawberry Sundae. The company management is able to control the relative sales of each product through the allocation of sales effort, advertising and sales promotion expenses.

Calculate the sales volume variance, the sales mix variance and the sales quantity variance.

Solution

1 The correct answer is:

(a) **Sales volume variance**

	CC		SS
Budgeted sales	400 units		300 units
Actual sales	<u>280</u> units		<u>630</u> units
Sales volume variance in units	120 units (A)		330 units (F)
× standard profit per unit	<u>× $5</u>		<u>× $3</u>
Sales volume variance in $	<u>$600</u> (A)		<u>$990</u> (F)
Total sales volume variance		**<u>$390</u> (F)**	

The favourable sales volume variance indicates that profit was better than budget because on balance more units were sold than budgeted. However, the favourable variance may be due to selling a larger proportion of the more profitable product (sales mix variance) or selling more units in total (sales quantity variance).

Now we will see how to analyse this favourable volume variance into its mix and quantity elements.

(b) **Sales mix variance**

This is calculated in a similar way to the materials mix variance. Start with the total quantity of products sold and calculate what sales of each product would have been if they had been sold in the budgeted proportions.

	Actual sales in standard mix (4:3)	Actual sales in actual mix	Sales mix variance	Standard profit	Sales mix variance
	Units	Units	Units	$ per unit	$
CC	520	280	240 (A)	5	1,200 (A)
SS	390	630	<u>240</u> (F)	<u>3</u>	<u>720</u> (F)
	910	910	<u>0</u>		<u>480</u> (A)

The total sales mix variance is $480 (A)

(c) **Sales quantity variance**

Method 1

	Standard sales in standard mix	Actual sales in standard mix	Sales mix variance	Standard profit	Sales mix variance
	Units	Units	Units	$ per unit	$
CC	400	520	120 (F)	5	600 (F)
SS	300	390	90 (F)	3	270 (F)
	700	910	30		870 (F)

Method 2

The standard weighted average profit per unit of sale, taken from the budget, is $2,900/700 = $29/7

	Units
Budgeted sales in total	700
Actual sales in total	910
Sales quantity variance in units	210 (F)
Standard weighted average profit per unit	$29/7
Sales quantity variance in $	**$870** (F)

Sales mix variance $480 (A) + Sales quantity variance $870 (F) = Sales volume variance $390 (F).

The overall favourable sales volume variance was achieved by selling products in a cheaper sales mix, but achieving a higher total quantity of sales units than budgeted.

Activity 4: Sales variances

Puddingsrus makes and sells two products: Sticky Toffee and Chocolate Goo. The budgeted sales and profit are as follows:

	Sales	Revenue	Costs	Profit	Profit per unit
	Units	$	$	$	$
Sticky Toffee	800	5,600	2,400	3,200	4
Chocolate Goo	900	4,500	2,700	1,800	2

Actual sales in November were 600 units of Sticky Toffee and 1,200 units of Chocolate Goo. The company management is able to control the relative sales of each product through the allocation of sales effort, advertising and sales promotion expenses.

1 **Required**
What is the sales volume profit variance for Puddingsrus?

O $800 Adverse

O $800 Favourable

O $200 Adverse

O $200 Favourable

2 **Required**
What is the sales mix variance for Puddingsrus?

O $494 Adverse

○ $494 Favourable

○ $247 Adverse

○ $247 Favourable

3 Required

What is the sales quantity variance for Puddingsrus?

○ $294 Adverse

○ $294 Favourable

○ $200 Adverse

○ $800 Favourable

Solution

1

2

3

Chapter summary

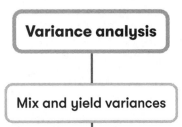

Variance analysis

Mix and yield variances

Materials and labour inputs
- Materials usage variance = materials mix variance + materials yield variance
- Mix = financial impact of using different proportions from standard
- Yield = financial impact of input yielding different output level from standard

Changing the mix
- Quality and its impact on sales
- How managers' performance is measured (eg saving money at expense of quality)

Interrelationship between variances
Favourable mix may lead to adverse yield variance

Additional production control methods
- Quality control measures
- Customer satisfaction scores
- Wastage rates
- Number of late deliveries

Knowledge diagnostic

1. Material mix and yield variations

A **mix** variance is the result of a different mix of materials to the standard being used.

A **yield** variance occurs when a different quantity from standard is input in order to achieve the desired output.

However, calculating a mix and yield variance is only meaningful for control purposes when management is in a position to control the mix of materials used in production.

2. Sales mix and quantity variance

A sales mix variance is the result of selling a different proportion of products to the standard.

A sales quantity variance occurs when a different volume of units is sold.

This may be useful for control purposes where management is in a position to control the sales mix; for example, through the allocation of spending on advertising and sales promotion

Further study guidance

Question practice

Now try the following from the Further question practice bank [available in the digital edition of the Workbook]:

Number	Level	Marks	Approximate time
Section A Q44	Examination	2	4 mins
Section A Q45	Examination	2	4 mins
Section A Q46	Examination	2	4 mins
Section A Q47	Examination	2	4 mins
Section A Q48	Examination	2	4 mins

Further reading

There is a technical article available on ACCA's website, called *Material mix and yield variances*. You are strongly advised to read this article in full as part of your preparation for the PM exam.

Activity answers

Activity 1: Materials mix and yield variances

1 The correct answer is:

Adverse

$300 Adverse

Total mix variance

	Std mix	Actual mix	Difference	× Std cost	Variance
Onions	750	600	150 (F)	$2	300 (F)
Tomatoes	750	900	150 (A)	$4	600 (A)
	1,500	1,500			300 (A)

2 The correct answer is:

Adverse

$1,500 Adverse

Total yield variance

	Std in std mix	Actual in std mix	Difference	× Std cost	Variance
Onions	500	750	250 (A)	$2	500 (A)
Tomatoes	500	750	250 (A)	$4	1,000 (A)
	1,000	1,500			1,500 (A)

OR

	Batches
1,500 kg of input should yield	150
1,500 / (5 + 5)	
1,500 kg of input did yield	100
	A 50
Value at std cost per batch ($30)	A $1,500

Activity 2: Implications of changing the mix

The correct answer is:

(b) only

Using cheaper ingredients in the mix could lead to lower yields, but this will not always be the case. However, changing the recipe could have an impact on the taste and quality. For example, increasing the water content in soup would increase the yield, but it may not taste as good.

Activity 3: Material yield

The correct answer is:

$6,900 F

Yield

	Litres
4,950 litres should yield @ 10/11	4,500
Did yield	4,800
Valued at standard cost $230/10	F 6,900

Alternative yield calculations

	Proportion	Should use for actual production	Should use in std mix	Difference	Value $	Variance $
A	5/11	2,400	2,250	150	16	2,400 F
J	6/11	2,880	2,700	180	25	4,500 F
Total		5,280 (W1)	4,950			6,900 F

(W1) 4,800 adjusted for losses 4,800/0.909 = 5,280 litres.

Or

The weighted average cost per litre of ingredients is $230 / 11 litres = $20.91

4,800 litres of drink should use (× 11/10)	5,280 litres
But did use	4,950 litres
Yield variance in litres	330 litres(F)
Weighted average price per litre	× $20.91
Yield variance in $	$6,900(F)

Activity 4: Sales variances

1 **The correct answer is:**

$200 Adverse

Sales volume profit variance

	Sticky Toffee		Chocolate Goo
Budgeted sales	800 units		900 units
Actual sales	600 units		1,200 units
Sales volume variance in units	200 units (A)		300 units (F)
× standard margin per unit	× $4		× $2
Sales volume variance in $	$800 (A)		$600 (F)
Total **sales volume variance**		$200 (A)	

Profit is lower as a result of a lower sales volume compared with budget.

2 **The correct answer is:**

$494 Adverse

Sales mix variance

	Units
Total quantity sold (600 + 1,200)	1,800
Budgeted mix for actual sales: 8/17 Sticky Toffee	847
9/17 Chocolate Goo	953
	1,800

	'Should' mix Actual sales Standard mix	'Did' mix Actual sales Actual mix	Difference	× Standard margin $	Variance $
Sticky Toffee	847 units	600 units	247 (A)	× 4	988 (A)

Chocolate Goo	<u>953 units</u>	1,200 units	<u>247</u> (F)	× 2	<u>494</u> (F)
	<u>1,800 units</u>	<u>1,800 units</u>	–		<u>494</u> (A)

The profit would have been $494 higher if the 1,800 units had been sold in the budgeted mix of 8:9.

3 **The correct answer is:**

Sales quantity variance

	Standard sales Standard mix	Actual sales Standard mix	Difference in units	× Standard profit $	Variance $
Sticky Toffee	800 units	847 units	47 units (F)	× 4	188 (F)
Chocolate Goo	<u>900 units</u>	<u>953 units</u>	<u>53 units</u> (F)	× 2	<u>106</u> (F)
	<u>1,700 units</u>	<u>1,800 units</u>	<u>100 units</u>		<u>294</u> (F)

Summary

	$
Sales mix variance	494 (A)
Sales quantity variance	<u>294</u> (F)
Sales volume profit variance	<u>200</u> (A)

17

Planning and operational variance analysis

Learning objectives

On completion of this chapter, you should be able to:

	Syllabus reference no.
Calculate a revised budget.	D6 (a)
Identify and explain those factors that could and could not be allowed to revise an original budget.	D6 (b)
Calculate, identify the cause of and explain planning and operational variances for: (a) Sales, including market size and market share (b) Materials (c) Labour, including the effect of the learning curve.	D6 (c)
Explain and discuss the manipulation issues in revising budgets.	D6 (d)

Exam context

In this chapter, we discuss the circumstances in which management may consider it appropriate to revise the budget or the standard cost.

When a budget or standard cost is revised after the budget period has begun, the reporting of variances should allow for this revision. One way of doing this is to present variances in the form of planning variances and operational variances.

Chapter overview

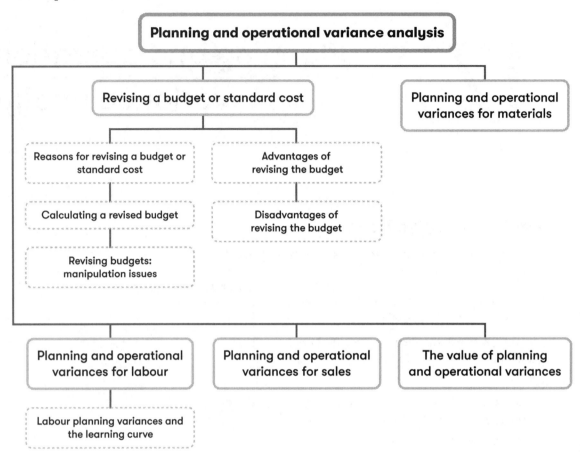

BPP
LEARNING
MEDIA

1 Revising a budget or standard cost

> ### PER alert
>
> One of the competencies needed to fulfil performance objective 13 of the PER is to monitor business activities. You can apply the knowledge you obtain from this section of the text to help demonstrate this competence.

Occasionally, it may be appropriate to **revise a budget or standard cost**. When this happens, variances should be reported in a way that distinguishes between variances caused by the revision to the budget and variances that are the responsibility of operational management.

1.1 Reasons for revising a budget or standard cost

Assumption	Changes
Sales budget may be **based** on expectations of the **total size of the market** for the organisation's product	But market size may be much larger or much smaller than first assumed due to: • Unexpected change in economic conditions • Unexpected technological change • Radical change in customer attitudes • Unexpected new regulations
Standard cost of materials may be based on an **assumption** about what the **market price** for the materials should be	Due to a major change in the market, the available **market price** for the materials may become **much higher** or **much lower** than originally expected
Standard quantity of materials made may be based on product specification	Standard quantity of materials may be significantly altered due to an unexpected change in specification, requiring much more or much less of the material in the product content
Standard labour cost may be based on expected labour rates	Standard labour rate may become unrealistic due to an unexpected increase in pay rates for employees
Standard time to produce a unit of product is estimated	The standard time could be affected by a change in the labour grade or upgraded machinery

If the budget or standard cost is not revised in these circumstances, variances reported to operational managers will be unrealistic. A large part of the **variances will be due to changes that are outside the control of the operational managers.**

A budget revision should be allowed if something has happened which is **beyond the control** of the organisation or individual manager and which makes the original budget unsuitable for use in performance management.

1.2 Calculating a revised budget

Illustration 1: Calculating a revised budget

1 A company produces Widgets and Splodgets which are fairly standardised products. The following information relates to Period 1.

The standard selling price of Widgets is $50 each and Splodgets $100 each. In Period 1, there was a special promotion on Splodgets with a 5% discount being offered. All units produced are sold and no inventory is held.

To produce a Widget they use 5kg of X and in Period 1, their plans were based on a cost of X of $3 per kg. Due to market movements, the actual price changed; if they had purchased efficiently, the cost would have been $4.50 per kg. Production of Widgets was 2,000 units.

A Splodget uses raw material Z, but again the price of this can change rapidly. It was thought that Z would cost $30 per tonne but in fact they only paid $25 per tonne and if they had purchased correctly the cost would have been less, as it was freely available at only $23 per tonne. It usually takes 1.5 tonnes of Z to produce one Splodget and 500 Splodgets are usually produced.

Each Widget takes three hours to produce and each Splodget two hours. Labour is paid $5 per hour. At the start of Period 1, management negotiated a job security package with the workforce in exchange for a promised 5% increase in efficiency – that is, that the workers would make the Widgets and Splodgets in 95% of the time stated in the original budget.

Fixed overheads are usually $12,000 every period and variable overheads are $3 per labour hour.

Required
Produce the original budget and a revised budget allowing for controllable factors in a suitable format.

Solution

1 The correct answer is:

Original budget for Period 1

	$
Sales revenue ((2,000 × $50) + (500 × $100))	150,000
Material costs X (2,000 × 5 kg × $3)	30,000
Material costs Z (500 × $30 × 1.5)	22,500
Labour costs ((2,000 × 3 × $5) + (500 × 2 × $5))	35,000
Variable overheads ((2,000 × 3 × $3) + (500 × 2 × $3))	21,000
Fixed overheads	12,000
Profit	29,500

Revised budget for Period 1

	$
Sales revenue ((2,000 × $50) + (500 × $100))	150,000
Material costs X (2,000 × 5 kg × $4.5)	45,000
Material costs Z (500 × $23 × 1.5)	17,250
Labour costs ((2,000 × 3 × $5) + (500 × 2 × $5)) × 0.95	33,250
Variable overheads ((2,000 × 3 × $3) + (500 × 2 × $3)) × 0.95	19,950
Fixed overheads	12,000
Profit	22,550

1.3 Revising budgets: manipulation issues

Revisions to the budget or standard cost may be manipulated in such a way as to make operating results seem much better than is really the case.

To prevent manipulation, there should be **strict rules** about revising a budget or standard cost. In particular, the revision to the budget or standard cost should ideally be based on **independent evidence** (and verifiable evidence) that operational managers are not in a position to manipulate.

Change	Evidence
Total size of the market for the company's product	There should ideally be independent evidence from an external source (such as a market research firm) about the revised expectations of the market size
Market price for materials	There should ideally be an official price index or price benchmark for the material item
Standard material usage for a product	This should ideally be evidenced by a documented change in the product specification

1.4 Advantages of revising the budget

(a) Highlights those variances which are controllable and those which are not

(b) Ensures that operational performance is appraised by reference to realistic targets

(c) Should ensure that future budgets are more realistic

1.5 Disadvantages of revising the budget

(a) Determination of revised budget

- May be biased
- May need external information

(b) Use of revised budget may undermine original budget as a target and as a motivator.

(c) Employees may use this system to their advantage by excusing operating problems as poor planning if this method is used.

A budget should **only be revised** for items that are **beyond the control** of the organisation. Such changes would **render the original budget inappropriate** as a performance management tool.

Budgets **should not be revised for operational issues**.

2 Planning and operational variances for materials

The traditional variances we have seen so far can be investigated further to look at the elements driven by a wrong standard (**planning variances**) and the elements that were within the manager's control (**operational variances**).

Illustration 2: Material planning price and usage variances

1 The standard materials cost of a product is 5kg × $7.50 per kg = $37.50. Actual production of 10,000 units used 54,400kg at a cost of $410,000.

In retrospect, it was realised that the standard materials cost should have been 5.3kg per unit at a cost of $8 per kg. The standard cost was revised to this amount.

Required
Calculate the materials planning and operational variances in as much detail as possible.

Solution

1 **The correct answer is:**

Original standard cost: 5kg × $7.50 per kg = $37.50 per unit of product

Revised standard cost: 5.3kg × $8 per kg = $42.40 per unit of product

In this example, both the material price and the material usage per unit have been revised. There are planning variances for both material price and material usage.

Material price planning variance

This is the difference between the original standard price for Material M and the revised standard price multiplied by the **actual quantity of materials used.**

Original standard price per kg	$7.50
Revised standard price per kg	$8.00
Material price planning variance	$0.50 (A)
× actual quantity of materials used	× 54,400 kg
Material price planning variance	$27,200 (A)

The planning variance is adverse because the change in the standard price increases the material cost and this will result in lower profit.

Material usage planning variance

	kg
10,000 units of product X should use: original standard	50,000
10,000 units of product X should use: revised standard	53,000
Material usage planning variance in kg of material	3,000 (A)
Original standard price per kg of material	$7.50
Material usage planning variance in $	$22,500 (A)

The planning variance is adverse because the revised standard is for a higher usage quantity (so higher cost and lower profit).

Material price operational variance

This compares the actual price per kg of material with the revised standard price. It is calculated using the actual quantity of materials used.

	$
54,400kg of material should cost (revised standard $8)	435,200
They did cost	410,000
Material price operational variance	25,200 (F)

Material usage operational variance

This variance is calculated by comparing the actual material usage with the standard usage in the revised standard, but it is then **converted into a monetary value by applying the original standard price for the materials, not the revised standard price**. This is an important rule.

	kg
10,000 units of product X should use (× 5.3kg)	53,000
They did use	54,400
Material usage (operational) variance in kg of material	1,400 (A)
Original standard price per kg of Material M	$7.50
Material usage (operational) variance in $	$10,500 (A)

The variances may be summarised as follows:

	$	$
10,000 units of product at original std cost ($37.50)		375,000
Actual material cost		410,000
Total material cost variance		35,000 (A)
Material price planning variance	27,200 (A)	
Material usage planning variance	22,500 (A)	
Material price operational variance	25,200 (F)	
Material usage operational variance	10,500 (A)	
Total of variances		35,000 (A)

Activity 1: Material planning and operational variances

Mason Co makes plastic patio furniture for sale to garden centres. One of its most popular products is the recliner chair. The standard amount of plastic per chair is 4kg and the standard cost per kg is $9. Budgeted production in June was 15,000 units. Actual production in June was only 14,000 units, which used 54,000kg of plastic at a cost of $9.50 per kg.

At the end of May, it was agreed that in order to boost sales the quality of the chairs needed to be improved. This meant purchasing better quality plastic at a standard cost of $9.30 per kg, whilst reducing the standard kg per chair to 3.8kg due to less waste.

1 Required

Calculate the following variances for Mason Co.

(a) Material price planning variance

(b) Material price operational variance

(c) Material usage planning variance

(d) Material usage operational variance

2 Required

Assess the performance of the production manager for the month of June.

Solution

1

2

---

3 Planning and operational variances for labour

 Illustration 3: Labour planning and operational variances

1 A company makes a single product. At the beginning of the budget year, the standard labour cost was established as $8 per unit, and the standard time to make each unit was 0.5 hours.

However, during the year, the standard labour cost was revised. A new quality control procedure was introduced to the production process, adding 20% to the expected time to complete a unit. In addition, due to severe financial difficulties facing the company, the workforce reluctantly agreed to reduce the rate of pay to $15 per hour.

In the first month after revision of the standard cost, budgeted production was 15,000 units but only 14,000 units were actually produced. These took 8,700 hours of labour time, which cost $130,500.

Required

Calculate the labour planning and operational variances in as much detail as possible.

Solution

1 The correct answer is:

Original standard cost = 0.5 hours × $16 per hour = $8 per unit

Revised standard = 0.6 hours × $15 per hour = $9 per unit

Planning and operational variances for labour are calculated in a similar way to planning and operational variances for materials. We need to look at planning and operational variances for labour rate and labour efficiency.

Labour rate planning variance

The following is the difference between the original standard rate per hour and the revised standard rate per hour:

	$ per hour
Original standard rate	16
Revised standard rate	<u>15</u>
Labour rate planning variance	<u>**1**</u> (A)

The planning variance for labour rate is favourable, because the revised hourly rate is lower than in the original standard. The variance is converted into a total monetary amount by multiplying the planning variance per hour by the **actual number of hours worked**.

Labour rate planning variance = 8,700 hours × $1 (F) = **$8,700 (F)**.

Labour efficiency planning variance

This is the difference between the original standard time per unit and the revised standard time, for the quantity of units produced. **The efficiency planning variance is converted into a total monetary value by applying the original standard rate per hour, not the revised standard rate.**

	Hours
14,000 units of product should take: original standard (× 0.5)	7,000
14,000 units of product should take: revised standard (× 0.6)	<u>8,400</u>
Labour efficiency planning variance in hours	<u>1,400</u>
Original standard rate per hour	<u>**$16**</u>
Labour efficiency planning variance in $	**$22,400** (A)

The planning variance is adverse because the revised standard is for a longer time per unit (so higher cost and lower profit).

Labour rate operational variance

This is calculated using the actual number of hours worked and paid for.

	$
8,700 hours should cost (revised standard $15)	130,500
They did cost	<u>130,500</u>
Labour rate operational variance	<u>0</u>

In this example, the workforce was paid exactly the revised rate of pay per hour.

Labour efficiency operational variance

This variance is calculated by comparing the actual time to make the output units with the standard time in the revised standard. It is then **converted into a monetary value by applying the original standard rate per hour.**

	Hours
14,000 units of product should take (× 0.6 hours)	8,400

They did take	8,700
Labour efficiency (operational variance in hours)	300 (A)
Original standard rate per hour	**$16**
Labour efficiency (operational variance in $)	**$4,800** (A)

The variances may be summarised as follows:

	$	$
14,000 units of product at original standard cost ($8)		112,000
Actual material cost		130,500
Total material cost variance		18,500 (A)
Labour rate planning variance	8,700 (F)	
Labour efficiency planning variance	22,400 (A)	
Labour rate operational variance	0	
Labour efficiency operational variance	4,800 (A)	
Total of variances		18,500 (A)

3.1 Labour planning variances and the learning curve

We looked at the learning curve in Chapter 14 and we said that a standard labour cost can only be established when a 'steady state' is reached, ie production of each additional unit should take the same amount of time. In principle, however, it would be possible to combine standard costing with the learning curve, as follows.

(a) Establish an original standard labour cost per unit, even though a learning effect will apply to production.

(b) At the end of the budget period, revise the standard time per unit. The revised standard time could be calculated using the learning curve formula and applying this to the number of units produced in the period.

(c) With the original standard cost and the revised standard cost, planning and operational variances for labour can be calculated. Because of the learning effect, the labour efficiency planning variance will always be favourable.

Essential reading

See Chapter 17 Section 1 of the Essential reading for an illustration on variances and the learning curve.

The Essential reading is available as an Appendix of the digital edition of the Workbook.

4 Planning and operational variances for sales

The sales volume variance can be reported as:

(a) A **sales volume planning variance**, or **market size variance**, which is caused by the difference between the sales volume in the original budget and the sales volume in the revised budget.

(b) A **sales volume operational variance**, or **market share variance**, which is caused by the difference between actual sales volume and the sales volume in the revised budget.

Illustration 4: Market size and market share variance

1   Dimsek budgeted to make and sell 400 units of its product, the Role, in the four-week Period 8, as follows:

	$
Budgeted sales (100 units per week)	40,000
Variable costs (400 units × $60)	24,000
Contribution	16,000
Fixed costs	10,000
Profit	6,000

At the beginning of the second week, production came to a halt because inventories of raw materials ran out, and a new supply was not received until the beginning of Week 3. As a consequence, the company lost one week's production and sales. Actual results in Period 8 were as follows:

	$
Sales (320 units)	32,000
Variable costs (320 units × $60)	19,200
Contribution	12,800
Fixed costs	10,000
Actual profit	2,800

In retrospect, it is decided that the optimum budget, given the loss of production facilities in the third week, would have been to sell only 300 units in the period.

Required

Calculate appropriate planning and operational variances for sales volume.

Solution

1   **The correct answer is:**

The **sales volume planning** variance **compares the revised budget** with the **original budget**. It may be called a market size variance.

Revised sales volume, given materials shortage	300 units
Original budgeted sales volume	400 units
Sales volume planning variance in units of sales	100 units (A)
× standard contribution per unit	× $40
Sales volume planning variance in $	$4,000 (A)

Arguably, **running out of raw materials is an operational error** and so the loss of sales volume and contribution from the shortage of materials is an opportunity cost that could have been avoided with better purchasing arrangements. Despite this, we are treating this as a planning variance. The operational variances are variances calculated in the usual way, except that actual results are compared with the revised standard or budget. There is a sales volume variance which is an **operational variance**, as follows.

Actual sales volume	320 units
Revised sales volume	300 units
Operational sales volume variance in units	20 units (F)
(possibly due to production efficiency or marketing efficiency)	
× standard contribution per unit	× $40
Operational sales volume variance in $ contribution	$800 (F)

The operational variance for sales volume may be called a market share variance. These planning and operational variances for sales volume can be used as **control information** to reconcile budgeted and actual profit.

	$	$
Operating statement, Period 8		
Budgeted profit		6,000
Planning variance: sales volume	4,000 (A)	
Operational variance: sales volume	800 (F)	
		3,200 (A)
Actual profit in Period 8		2,800

You may have noticed that, in this example, sales volume variances were **valued at contribution forgone**. This is because it is assumed that a marginal costing system applies.

Activity 2: Market size and market share variances

A sales volume variance can be analysed into a market size variance and a market share variance.

The following statements have been made about these variances:

(a) In a competitive market, the market share variance is controllable by the sales management.

(b) In a competitive market, a market size variance is controllable by sales management.

Required
Which of the above statements is/are true?

O (a) only
O (b) only
O Neither (a) nor (b)
O Both (a) and (b)

Solution

Activity 3: Sales planning and operational variances

Chianti Co manufactures and sells a single product, the Chil. The company uses a standard costing system, and the standard cost per unit is $7.40 and the budgeted selling price is $16.00 per unit.

Budgeted production and sales for 20X8 were 5,000 units. The budgeted fixed overhead was $20,000.

Actual production in 20X8 was 5,200 units, and 5,100 units were sold for $81,000.

You have discovered that industry sales of Chils were 10% lower than forecast.

Required

For the sales volume planning variance and the sales volume operational variance was there a favourable or adverse result in 20X8?

O   The sales volume planning variance was adverse and the sales volume operational variance was favourable

O   The sales volume planning variance was favourable and the sales volume operational variance was adverse

O   Both variances were adverse

O   Both variances were favourable

Solution

There may be a situation where a revision is made to the budgeted or standard selling price for a product. When this happens, a sales price planning variance and a sales price operational variance can be calculated.

The planning variance is generally outside the control of sales management, but the operational sales price variance is a sales management responsibility.

Illustration 5: Planning and operational variances for sales price

1   KSO budgeted to sell 10,000 units of a new product during 20X0. The budgeted sales price was $10 per unit, and the variable cost $3 per unit.

Actual sales in 20X0 were 12,000 units and variable costs of sales were $30,000, but sales revenue was only $5 per unit. With the benefit of hindsight, it is realised that the budgeted sales price of $10 was hopelessly optimistic, and a price of $4.50 per unit would have been much more realistic.

Required

Calculate planning and operational variances for sales price.

Solution

1 **The correct answer is:**

The only variances are selling price variances.

Planning (selling price) variance

	$ per unit
Original budgeted sales price	10.00
Revised budgeted sales price	4.50
Sales price planning variance	5.50 (A)
× the actual number of units sold	× 12,000
Sales price planning variance	**$66,000 (A)**

The planning variance is adverse because the revised sales price is lower than the sales price in the original budget. As a result, actual profit will not achieve the budgeted profit level.

Operational (selling price) variance

The **sales price operational variance** is calculated in the same way as a 'normal' sales price variance, except that the sales price in the revised budget is used, not the original budget.

	$
12,000 units sold for (12,000 × $5)	60,000
They should have sold for (× $4.50)	54,000
Sales price operational variance	**6,000 (F)**

5 The value of planning and operational variances

Advantages of a system of planning and operational variances

- The analysis highlights those variances which are **controllable** (operational variances) and those which are non-controllable (planning variances).
- **Managers' acceptance** of the use of variances for performance measurement, and their **motivation**, is likely to increase if they know they will not be held responsible for poor planning and faulty standard setting.
- The **planning and standard-setting processes** should improve; standards should be more accurate, relevant and appropriate.
- Operational variances will provide a more realistic and **'fair' reflection of actual performance**.

Limitations of planning and operational variances, which must be overcome if they are to be applied in practice

- It is difficult to **decide in hindsight** what the **realistic standard** should have been.
- It may become **too easy to justify all the variances as being due to bad planning**, so no operational variances will be highlighted.
- Establishing realistic revised standards and analysing the total variance into planning and operational variances can be a **time-consuming** task, even if a spreadsheet package is devised.
- Even though the intention is to provide more meaningful information, **managers may be resistant** to the very idea of variances and refuse to see the virtues of the approach. Careful presentation and explanation will be required until managers are used to the concepts.

Exam focus point

If you get a variance question in Section C of the exam, you should use the spreadsheet to do your calculations. By all means check your answers on your calculator but try to avoid just typing in your calculator answers into the spreadsheet. The spreadsheet has the functionality to perform the calculations and using this makes it much easier for the marker to see what you have done.

Chapter summary

Planning and operational variance analysis

Revising a budget or standard cost

Reasons for revising a budget or standard cost
- Changes to market size
- Change in market price
- Changes in quantities of materials
- Change in labour rates
- Changes in production times

Calculating a revised budget
Original budget and revised budget to allow for controllable factors

Revising budgets: manipulation issues
- Rules should be applied
- Independent evidence should be obtained

Advantages of revising the budget
- Highlights variances that are controllable
- Ensures operational performance is appraised by reference to realistic targets
- Should ensure future budgets are more realistic

Disadvantages of revising the budget
- May be subjective
- May undermine use of original budget as a target/motivator
- May be manipulated

Planning and operational variances for materials
- Incorrect standards (planning variances)
- Within the manager's control (operational variances)
- Price planning
- Usage planning
- Price operational
- Usage operational

Planning and operational variances for labour
- Rate planning
- Efficiency planning
- Rate operational
- Efficiency operational

Labour planning variances and the learning curve
Because of the learning effect, the labour efficiency planning variance will always be favourable

Planning and operational variances for sales
- Sales volume planning (market size)
- Sales volume operational (market share)
- Sales price planning
- Sales price operational

The value of planning and operational variances
- Highlights those variances which are controllable
- May increase manager motivation
- Standard setting processes should improve
- Can be difficult to decide with hindsight
- Can be time consuming

Knowledge diagnostic

1. Planning variances

Planning variances represent the difference between the original and revised budget.

2. Operational variances

Operational variances are those items which were **within a manager's control**. They are the difference between the revised budget and the actual.

3. Market size variance

When the sales budget is revised, a **sales volume planning variance** may be reported. This is the difference in profit caused by the difference between the original sales budget and the revised sales budget. This planning variance is called a **market size variance.**

4. Market share variance

When the sales budget is revised, a **sales volume operational variance** may be reported, for which operational sales managers should be held responsible. This is the difference in profit caused by the difference between actual sales volume and the sales volume in the revised sales budget. This operational variance is called a **market share variance.**

Further study guidance

Question practice

Now try the following from the Further question practice bank [available in the digital edition of the Workbook]:

Number	Level	Marks	Approximate time
Section A Q49	Examination	2	4 mins
Section A Q50	Examination	2	4 mins
Section A Q51	Examination	2	4 mins
Section C Q5	Examination	20	36 mins

Further reading

N/A

Activity answers

Activity 1: Material planning and operational variances

1 The correct answer is:

(a) Material price planning variance

Original standard price per kg	$9.00
Revised standard price per kg	$9.30
Material price planning variance	$0.30 (A)
× actual quantity of materials used	× 54,000 kg
	$16,200 (A)

(b) **Material usage planning variance**

	$
(2) 54,000 kg should now cost @ $9.30	502,200
(3) 54,000 kg did cost @ $9.50	(513,000)
	10,800 (A)

(c) **Material usage operational variance**

	Kg
(1) 14,000 units should use @ 4kg	56,000
(2) 14,000 units should now use @ 3.8kg	(53,200)
	2,800
Valued at original standard cost $9	$25,200 (F)

(d) **Material usage operational variance**

	Kg
(2) 14,000 units should now use @ 3.8kg	53,200
(3) 14,000 units did use	(54,000)
	(800)
@ original standard cost $9	($7,200) (A)

2 The correct answer is:

Only the material usage variances are relevant for consideration of the performance of the production manager. There is a total favourable usage variance of $18,000 during the period. If we only consider the total variance it would appear that the production manager had performed well in managing to produce the recliners using less materials. However, we need to strip out the impact of the decision to purchase better quality materials in order to appraise their true performance.

The better quality materials accounted for the favourable variance; however, the material usage operational variance was adverse. This means that the production manager was not able to stick to the revised standard quantity of 3.8kg per chair. This could be because the standard was too challenging or because of a lack of effort controlling efficiency. More information would be needed to establish which was the case but, overall, the production manager has not been able to achieve the efficiency savings anticipated.

Activity 2: Market size and market share variances

The correct answer is:

(a) only

In a competitive market, the sales team are in a position to influence the market share, for example through advertising, sales promotion and pricing policy. As it is controllable a change in market share forms the operating variance. However, the size of the overall market is not going to be controllable by one company and so this is part of the planning variance.

Activity 3: Sales planning and operational variances

The correct answer is:

The sales volume planning variance was adverse

The sales volume operational variance was favourable

Sales volume variances

Revised sales volume	4,500 units
Original budgeted sales volume	5,000 units
Sales volume planning variance in units of sales	500 units (A)
× standard contribution per unit	× $8.60
Sales volume planning variance in $	$4,300 (A)

Operational   Units
(2) Should now   Revised budget sales   4,500
(3) Did   Actual sales   5,100
                                                                                      600 (F)
@ original standard contribution / unit $8.60   5,160 (F)

Skills checkpoint 4

Effective use of spreadsheets

Chapter overview

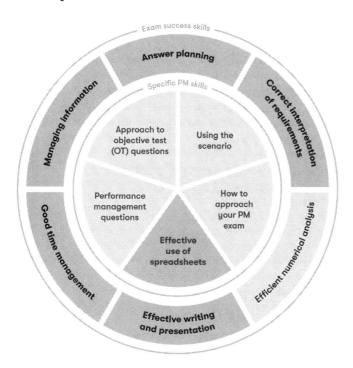

Introduction

The spreadsheet is one of the response options available in the constructed workspace for Section C questions. The PM syllabus area 'Budgetary control' is commonly assessed through variance calculations and you are likely to be provided with a spreadsheet for these questions. It is imperative that you know how to use the spreadsheet functions to prepare accurate and easy to follow variance calculations. Efficient use of the spreadsheets will save valuable time, which you can then use to address the discursive elements. In the case of variance questions, there will usually be marks for both calculation and discussion within a Section C question and both must be answered within the allotted 36 minutes.

Effective use of spreadsheets

The key steps in applying this skill are outlined below and will be explained in more detail in the following sections as the past exam question, 'Kappa' is answered.

STEP 1:

Use standard variance calculation proformas. These will help the marker to understand your workings and allocate the marks easily. It will also help you to work through the figures in a methodical and time-efficient way, for example by calculating total figures.

STEP 2:

Input easy numbers from the question directly onto your proformas. This will make sure that you pick up as many easy marks as possible before dealing with more complex figures. It will also enable you to score method marks if you make a minor mistake.

STEP 3:

Always use formulae to perform calculations. Do not waste time doing calculations manually when the spreadsheet can do them for you.

STEP 4:

Show clear workings for any complex calculations.

More complex calculations such as standard mix of actual sales will require a separate working. Keep your workings as clear and simple as possible and ensure they are cross-referenced to your proforma.

Exam success skills

The following question is an extract from a past exam question worth 11 marks.

For this question, we will also focus on the following **exam success skills**:

- **Managing information.** It is easy for the amount of information contained in a Section C question to feel over-whelming. **Active reading** is a useful technique to use to avoid this. This involves focusing on the requirement first, on the basis that until you have done this, the detail in the question will have little meaning.

This is especially important in variance questions where you need to clearly identify the 'should' and the 'did' amounts and in the case of planning and operational variances the 'should now' too.

- **Correct interpretation of requirements.** At first glance, it looks like part (i) of the following question is just asking for the usage variance of each ingredient, but it also requires the total usage variance.

- **Efficient numerical analysis.** The key to success here is applying a sensible proforma for typical variance calculations, backed up by clear, referenced, workings wherever needed. Learning a standard proforma layout will save time and reduce the amount of planning and thinking required in the exam.

- **Utilise the spreadsheet functionality.** Do not waste time doing calculations manually when the spreadsheet can do them for you.

Skill activity

Kappa Co produces Omega, an animal feed made by mixing and heating three ingredients: Alpha, Beta and Gamma.

The company uses a standard costing system to monitor its costs.

The standard material cost for 100kg of Omega is as follows:

Input	Kg	Cost per kg	Cost per 100kg of Omega
		$	$
Alpha	40	2.00	80.00
Beta	60	5.00	300.00
Gamma	20	1.00	20.00
Total	120		400.00

Notes

(a) The mixing and heating process is subject to a standard evaporation loss.

(b) Alpha, Beta and Gamma are agricultural products and their quality and price vary significantly from year to year. Standard prices are set at the average market price over the last five years. Kappa Co has a purchasing manager who is responsible for pricing and supplier contracts.

(c) The standard mix is set by the finance department. The last time this was done was at the product launch, which was five years ago. It has not changed since.

Last month 4,600kg of Omega was produced, using the following inputs:

Input	Kg	Cost per kg	Total cost
		$	$
Alpha	2,200	1.80	3,960
Beta	2,500	6.00	15,000
Gamma	920	1.00	920
	5,620		19,880

At the end of each month, the production manager receives a standard cost operating statement from Kappa Co's performance manager. The statement contains material price and usage variances, labour rate and efficiency variances, and overhead expenditure and efficiency variances for the previous month. No commentary on the variances is given and the production manager receives no other feedback on the efficiency of the Omega process.

Required

Calculate the following variances for the last month:

(a) **The material usage variance for each ingredient and in total (4 marks)**

(b) **The total material mix variance(4 marks)**

(c) **The total material yield variance(3 marks)**

STEP 1 Use standard variance calculation proformas. These will help the marker to understand your workings and allocate the marks easily. It will also help you to work through the figures in a methodical and time-efficient way, for example by calculating total figures.

This is an 11-mark question and, at 1.8 minutes a mark, should take approximately 20 minutes. Using a standard variance proforma will help you to work through the information in the question in a methodical, time efficient way. Your proforma should look like this:

STEP 2 Input easy numbers from the question directly onto your proformas. This will make sure that you pick up as many easy marks as possible before dealing with more complex figures. It will also enable you to score method marks if you make a minor mistake.

There are some easy numbers from the question that you can put straight onto your proforma such as the actual quantity of materials used and the standard cost per unit. Using the proforma will ensure that you can quickly and efficiently organise your thoughts in the exam and extract the right information from the scenario.

	A	B	C	D	E	F	G
1	**i) Material usage variance**						
2			4,600kg	But	Variance	Std	$
3			should	did		cost/kg	
4			use	use			
5			Kg		Kg		
6		Alpha					
7		Beta					
8		Gamma					
9		Total					
10							
11							
12	**ii) Material mix variance**						
13			Actual	Actual	Variance	Std	$
14			usage	usage in		cost/kg	
15				std mix			
16			Kg	Kg	Kg		
17		Alpha					
18		Beta					
19		Gamma					
20							
21							
22							
23	**iii) Material yield variance**						
24							
25			4,600kg	Actual	Variance	Std	$
26			should	usage in		cost/kg	
27			use	std mix			
28			Kg	Kg	Kg		
29		Alpha					
30		Beta					
31		Gamma					
32							
33							

STEP 3 Always use formulae to perform basic calculations. Do not waste time doing calculations manually when the spreadsheet can do them for you.

For example, you can use the sum formula to give the total usage variance once you have calculated the individual usage variances.

This will be quicker than adding the figures with a calculator.

Examples of the formulae you would use are shown below:

	A	B	C	D	E	F	G	H
1	**i) Material usage variance**							
2			4,600kg	But	Variance	Std	$	
3			should	did		cost/kg		
4			use	use				
5			Kg		Kg			
6		Alpha	=4600*(40/100)	2200	=C6-D6	2	=E6*F6	Adverse
7		Beta	=4600*(60/100)	2500	=C7-D7	5	=E7*F7	Favourable
8		Gamma	=4600*(20/100)	920	=C8-D8	1	=E8*F8	-
9			=SUM(C6:C8)	=SUM(D6:D8)			=SUM(G6:G8)	Favourable
10								

STEP 4 Show clear workings for any **complex calculations.**

More complex calculations such as standard mix of actual usage will require a separate working. Keep your workings as clear and simple as possible and ensure they are cross-referenced to your proforma.

For example, you could prepare a working to show the actual usage in the standard mix. This could look like the following:

▲	A	B	C	D	E	F	G	H
10								
11								
12	**ii) Material mix variance**							
13			Actual	Actual	Variance	Std	$	
14			usage	usage in		cost/kg		
15				std mix				
16			Kg	Kg	Kg			
17		Alpha	2200	1,873.33	326.67	2	653.33	Adverse
18		Beta	2500	2,810.00	- 310.00	5	- 1,550.00	Favourable
19		Gamma	920	936.67	- 16.67	1	- 16.67	Favourable
20			5620	5620			- 913.33	Favourable
21								

▲	A	B
22	Working - actual usage in std mix:	
23		
24	Alpha	=(40/120)*C20
25	Beta	=(60/120)*C20
26	Gamma	=(20/120)*C20
27		=SUM(B24:B26)
28		

Exam success skills diagnostic

Every time you complete a question, use the diagnostic below to assess how effectively you demonstrated the exam success skills in answering the question. The table has been completed below for the 'Kappa' activity to give you an idea of how to complete the diagnostic.

Exam success skills	Your reflections/observations
Managing information	Did you identify the correct standard cost per unit?
Correct interpretation of requirements	You need to calculate six variances. Did you remember to calculate the total usage variance?
Efficient numerical analysis	Did your answer present a neat set of variances in a proforma that would have been easy for a marker to follow?
Good time management	Did you manage your time to ensure you completed the variance calculations in the time available, leaving yourself enough time to attempt the discursive elements?
Most important action points to apply to your next question	

We have shown you an example of a variance question which uses a spreadsheet but there are other types of question that may require you to use a spreadsheet too. Here are some general tips on using the spreadsheet.

(a) **Label your numbers so that the examiner can see what you mean.**

This is particularly important for variance questions. The examiner needs to know what you are calculating!

A list of labels in a column with the numbers in the next column is generally better than a column for each label and one row of numbers.

	A	B	C
1			
2	Number of rooms		120
3	Number of nights		31
4	Total room nights		3720
5	Occupancy rate		50%
6	Total nights occupied		1860
7	Rate per night		70
8	Total room revenue		130200

	A	B	C	D	E	F	G	H
1	Number of	Number of	Total room	Occupancy	Total night	Rate per n	Total room revenue	
2	120	31	3720	50%	1860	70	130200	
3								

(b) **Ensure the numbers are in a separate cell from the label.**

This makes the numbers easier to mark for the examiner as well as making it possible to use spreadsheet formulae for any necessary calculations.

	A	B	C
1			
2	Total nights occupied		1,860
3	Rate per night		70
4	Total room revenue		130200

	A	B	C
1			
2	Total nights occupied 1,860		
3	Rate per night 70		
4	Total room revenue 130200		

(c) **Always use formulae to perform calculations.**

It is generally better to use a column to do this. Do not write out your working (eg 800-700+400=600) in a single cell because it wastes time and you may make a mistake. Use the spreadsheet functions instead! You can always double check your answer on your calculator.

	A	B	C
1			
2	Total nights occupied		1860
3	Rate per night		70
4	Total room revenue		=C2*C3

	A	B	C
1			
2	Total nights occupied 1,860		
3	Rate per night 70		
4	Total room revenue = 1860*70=1302000		

✓	✗
The total room revenue is showing as 130200 and when the examiner clicks on the cell C4, they can see the formula as shown above.	The student here has not used the spreadsheet formula and has wasted time typing 1860*70. They have then made a mistake writing down the answer and have added an extra zero.

(d) **Make efficient use of the SUM function**

If some of the numbers in a list need to be deducted, enter a minus sign for these and then use the 'SUM' formula to add all of the numbers together. Type '=sum(' then select the cells you want to add together with your mouse and press return. This is quicker than entering = A1-A2+A3 and so on, and you are less likely to make a mistake.

	A	B
1	**Incremental running**	$
2	Staff costs	120000
3	Less manager's salary	-2500
4	Less chef's salary	-200
5		=SUM(B2:B4)

	A	C
1	**Incremental running**	
2	Staff costs	120000
3	Less manager's salary	2500
4	Less chef's salary	2000
5		=B2-B3+B4

✓	✗
	Here, the student has wasted time trying to add and deduct each cell instead of using the SUM function. They have also made a mistake and added B4 instead of deducting it.

(e) **Cross reference any workings using '=' rather than re-typing the numbers**

	A	B	C	D	E	F
1	**Material mix variance**					
2						
3		Std usage for	Actual	Variance	Std cost	Variance
4		actual output	usage	kg	per kg	$
5		(W1)			$	
6	Alpha	=D14	2200	=B6-C6	2	=D6*E6
7	Beta	=D15	2500	=B7-C7	5	=D7*E7
8	Gamma	=D16	920	=B8-C8	1	=D8*E8
9		=SUM(B6:B8)	=SUM(C6:C8)			=SUM(F6:F8)
10						
11						
12	Workings					
13	1					
14	Alpha	=40/100	4600	=B14*C14		
15	Beta	=60/100	4600	=B15*C15		
16	Gamma	=20/100	4600	=B16*C16		

Here, the student has worked out the standard usage for actual output in cells D14 to D16. Then, instead of typing the standard usage into cells B6 to B8, they have used the spreadsheet function '=' to pick up the numbers. This ensures that the examiner can see exactly where the numbers have come from, and also reduces the chances of making a mistake.

	A	B	C	D	E	F	G
1	**Material mix variance**						
2							
3		Std usage for	Actual	Variance	Std cost	Variance	
4		actual output	usage	kg	per kg	$	
5		(W1)			$		
6	Alpha	1840	2200	-360	2	-720	A
7	Beta	2760	2500	260	5	1300	F
8	Gamma	9200	920	8280	1	8280	
9		13800	5620			8860	F
10							
11							
12	Workings						
13	1						
14	Alpha	0.4	4600	1840			
15	Beta	0.6	4600	2760			
16	Gamma	0.2	4600	920			

Here, the student has typed the standard usage into cells B6 to B8 and has made a mistake.

(f) Does your answer look reasonable?

Have you used some numbers in thousands and some in hundreds? Take a moment to look at your answers and see whether any of the numbers look odd. If they do, re-check your calculations. If your calculations are correct, then it is likely that these 'odd' numbers need to be discussed. For example, in a performance management question, you may calculate a very high receivables days ratio for one of the divisions. This implies that the division is not collecting its debts efficiently.

Summary

Section C of the PM exam could contain a question that focuses on variance analysis and asks you to perform mix and yield variance calculations or planning and operational variance calculations.

This is a commonly examined type of calculation question and it is important that you know the proformas so that you can quickly and accurately populate them so that you have sufficient time to complete the discussion elements of the question too. You will get credit for discussion based on your own numbers, even if they are incorrect, but it is obviously better if your numbers are accurate.

You therefore need to ensure that you:

- Use clear, standard proformas to performance variance calculations.
- Use spreadsheet formulae to perform basic calculations.
- Score well on the easier parts of the question.
- Allow sufficient time for discussion elements.

Note that there is detailed commentary on the use of spreadsheets for the Mar/Jun 19 sample question 'Belton Park', found on the ACCA website. You should read this to build on the skills discussed in this Checkpoint.

18

Performance analysis and behavioural aspects

Learning objectives

On completion of this chapter, you should be able to:

	Syllabus reference no.
Discuss the issues surrounding setting the difficulty level for a budget.	D1 (g)
Explain the benefits and difficulties of the participation of employees in the negotiations of targets.	D1 (h)
Analyse and evaluate past performance using the results of variance analysis.	D7 (a)
Use variance analysis to assess how future performance of an organisation or business can be improved.	D7 (b)
Identify the factors which influence behaviour.	D7 (c)
Discuss the effect that variances have on staff motivation and action.	D7 (d)
Describe the dysfunctional nature of some variances in the modern environment of just-in-time (JIT) and total quality management (TQM).	D7 (e)
Discuss the behavioural problems resulting from using standard costs in rapidly changing environments	D7 (f)

Exam context

In this chapter we discuss the effects of standard costing and variance reporting on management and employee behaviour.

We also discuss the problems of using standard costing in the modern, rapidly changing business environment.

The behavioural aspects of performance analysis and variances may form the discussion part of a Section C question, but you should also be prepared for a Section A question, or Section B case questions, on any of the topics in this chapter.

Chapter overview

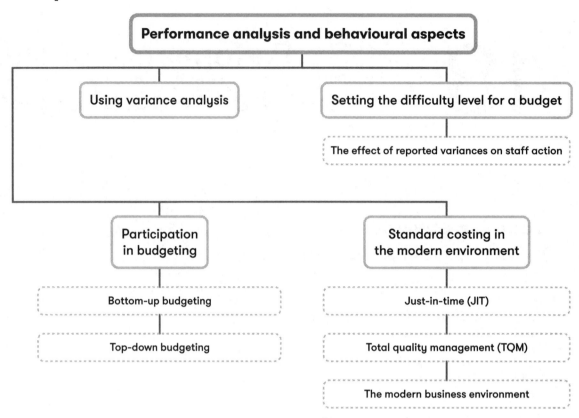

1 Using variance analysis

Variance analysis is used to analyse and **evaluate past performance**.

It is also used for control purposes: significant variances may indicate that an aspect of performance is out of control and that measures should be taken to improve performance in the future.

The appropriate use of control information depends not only on the content of the information itself but also the behaviour of its recipients. Problems can arise because of the following:

(a) The **managers who set the budget** or standards are **often not the managers** who are then made **responsible for achieving budget targets**.

(b) The **goals of the organisation as a whole**, as expressed in a budget, **may not coincide with the personal aspirations of individual managers**.

(c) **Control is applied at different stages by different people.** A supervisor may receive weekly control reports, and act on them; their superior may receive monthly control reports, and decide to take different control action. Different managers can get in each other's way and resent the interference from others.

Essential reading

See Chapter 15 Section 1 of the Essential reading for more detail on using variance analysis.

The Essential reading is available as an Appendix of the digital edition of the Workbook.

2 Setting the difficulty level for a budget

Budgets can **motivate** managers to achieve a **high** level of **performance** or they can **demotivate** managers depending on the **difficulty level**.

(a) A **demotivating** effect is likely where an **ideal standard** of performance is set (all efficiency variances will be adverse).

(b) A **low standard** of efficiency is also **demotivating** (no sense of achievement and no incentive to try harder).

(c) A budgeted level of attainment could be the **same** as the level that has been achieved in the past (but might encourage **budgetary slack**).

Individual aspirations might be much higher or much lower than the organisation's aspirations. The solution might be to have **two budgets**.

- A budget for **planning and decision-making** based on **reasonable expectations**
- A budget for **motivational purposes**, with more **difficult targets of performance**

These two budgets might be called an '**expectations budget**' and an '**aspirations budget**' respectively.

Similarly, the level of difficulty in a standard cost may vary.

Type of standard	
Ideal	This is a standard of performance that assumes the **highest possible** level of achievement. This can be **demotivating** for the managers responsible for performance.

Type of standard	
Target	This is a **standard cost** that sets performance targets at a **higher** level than is **currently being achieved** yet is **realistic.** Improvements in performance will be needed to turn adverse variances into favourable variances. An incentive scheme may be needed to persuade managers to 'buy in' to the target standard.
Currently attainable	This standard is based on levels of performance that are **currently being achieved.** They provide **no incentive** to **improve** performance but may **prevent deterioration** in performance.
Basic standard	This is an **original standard** that is unchanged over a long period of time. It is used to **measure trends** and changes in performance standards over time. It is **not useful** for **control** purposes.

2.1 The effect of reported variances on staff action

Reported variances, if significant and adverse, should prompt managers into taking control action to improve performance. The success of a variance reporting system in achieving this objective will depend on several factors.

(a) The **manager** who is considered responsible for the variance should **agree** and **accept** that the cause of the variance is their **responsibility.** Variances should be reported to the appropriate manager. The manager must believe that the cause of the variance is something that they are in a **position to control.**

(b) The manager should consider the reported variance to be **'fair'.** Variances should be a realistic measure. This is why separating planning variances from operational variances is useful.

(c) The manager should want to do something to deal with the causes of the variance. **Incentives** and motivation are **important** factors.

(d) **Variances** should be reported in a **timely** manner. If a reported variance relates to events that occurred a long time ago, managers will be reluctant to investigate them 'now' because the variance will seem out of date.

The **control culture** within the organisation may also **affect the response** of managers to variances. If there is a **'blame culture',** managers will be blamed for adverse variances and accused of poor performance. This is likely to provoke **a defensive reaction,** with the manager trying to justify what has gone wrong.

In contrast, if there is an **'improvement culture', variances** are considered as **useful indicators** for control action and improving performance. Managers are not blamed for adverse variances, but encouraged to look for suitable control measures whenever significant adverse variances occur.

3 Participation in budgeting

In Chapter 13 we briefly explained top-down budgeting (an imposed style of budgeting) and bottom-up budgeting (a participative style of budgeting). You need to understand the benefits and difficulties of participative budgeting.

3.1 Bottom-up budgeting

Participative budgets may be effective in the following circumstances:

- In **well-established organisations**

- In **very large businesses**
- During periods of **economic affluence**
- When operational managers have **strong budgeting skills**
- When an organisation's different units act **autonomously**

The **advantages** of participative budgets are as follows:

- They are based on **information from employees** most familiar with the department.
- **Knowledge spread** among several levels of management is pulled **together**.
- **Morale** and **motivation** are improved: employees feel more involved and that their opinions matter to senior management.
- They **increase operational managers' commitment** to organisational objectives.
- In general, they are **more realistic**.
- **Co-ordination** between units is **improved**.
- **Specific resource requirements** are **included**.
- **Senior managers' overview** is mixed with operational level details.

There are, on the other hand, a number of **disadvantages** of participative budgets.

- They **consume more time.**
- When individuals are involved in negotiating their budget targets, they may want to set targets that are easily attainable rather than targets that are challenging. In other words, an ability to negotiate targets may tempt managers to introduce **budgetary slack** into their targets.
- Individuals may not properly understand the strategic and budgetary objectives of the organisation, and they may argue for targets that are not in the best interests of the organisation as a whole.
- **Changes implemented** by senior management may **cause dissatisfaction** if they seem to ignore the opinions of employees who have been involved in negotiating targets.
- Budgets may be **unachievable** if managers are not sufficiently experienced or knowledgeable to contribute usefully.
- They can support **'empire building'** by subordinates.
- An **earlier start** to the budgeting process will be required, compared with top-down budgeting and target setting.

3.2 Top down budgeting

The times when imposed budgets are effective are as follows.
- In newly formed organisations
- In very small businesses
- During periods of economic hardship
- When operational managers lack budgeting skills
- When an organisation's different units require precise co-ordination

There are, of course, advantages and disadvantages to this style of setting budgets.

Advantages
- **Strategic plans** are likely to be incorporated into planned activities.
- They **enhance** the **co-ordination** between the plans and objectives of divisions.
- They use **senior management's awareness** of total resource availability.
- They **decrease the input from inexperienced or uninformed lower-level employees.**
- They **decrease the period of time taken** to draw up the budgets.

Disadvantages
- **There may be dissatisfaction, defensiveness** and **low morale** among employees.
- The **feeling of team spirit** may disappear.
- The **acceptance of organisational goals** and **objectives** could be limited.
- The feeling of the budget as a **punitive device** could arise.

- **Unachievable budgets** for overseas divisions could result if consideration is not given to local operating and political environments.
- **Lower-level management initiative** may be **stifled**.

4 Standard costing in the modern environment

Standard costing and variance analysis may sometimes be inappropriate in a production environment based on just-in-time (JIT) methods or a total quality management (TQM) approach.

4.1 JIT

In a JIT manufacturing environment, production is managed on the principle that items should **not be produced until** they are **required** to meet **sales** orders. There should be no accumulation of inventories of work in progress (WIP) and finished goods.

A JIT approach implies that if there are **no sales orders, production** resources should be **kept idle.** In addition, as explained in the earlier chapter on the **theory of constraints**, the volume of production should be restricted to the output capacity of the bottleneck resource, meaning that there will **inevitably be idle capacity** for all resources that are not the bottleneck resource.

(a) In **JIT manufacturing, idle time** should therefore be **expected**.

(b) In a system of **standard costing**, idle time is an adverse labour efficiency variance, and is **undesirable**.

If idle time variances are reported for a manufacturing operation that is based on JIT methods, the variances will encourage managers to use idle capacity in a productive way, by producing more and building up inventories. With increases in inventory, there will be a higher reported profit.

4.2 Total quality management (TQM)

Total quality management (TQM) is a business philosophy aimed at improving quality.

4.2.1 Get it right, first time

The cost of preventing mistakes is less than the cost of correcting them if they occur.

4.2.2 Continuous improvement

Never be satisfied with current achievement. It is always possible to improve performance.

4.2.3 Goals of TQM

(a) To gain competitive advantage via continuously improved quality

(b) To continuously reduce the cost of providing enhanced quality

(c) Innovation

(d) Provide first class customer service

(e) To involve all employees

4.2.4 Design for quality

Design quality into an organisation's products and operations from the outset.

(a) Reduce the number of parts in a product.

(b) Use components common to other products in the organisation.

(c) Improve physical characteristics to meet customers' needs.

4.2.5 TQM and standard costing

(a) The philosophy in TQM of **'right first time'** may be **inconsistent** with a standard cost that includes an **allowance for wastage**. TQM is more consistent with environmental cost accounting (material flow cost accounting) than a costing system that allows for normal loss in the standard cost.

(b) The principle of 'kaizen' or continuous improvement is that a steady state of production will never be achieved, because further improvements will always be possible. A **standard cost** is based on an assumption of a **desirable steady state**; this view is **inconsistent** with the principle of **continuous improvement.**

4.3 The modern business environment

Traditional manufacturing	Modern environment	Impacts of standard costing
High labour cost, low overhead	Low labour cost, high overhead	Overhead variances do not have enough detail to aid performance measurement.
Stable environment/ products	Rapidly changing environment/products	Regular revision of standards can be demotivating for employees as the goal posts keep moving.
Standard product	Customised product	Differences between products make developing a standard difficult. Resulting variances may not be meaningful and certain employees may be unfairly penalised.
Focus on cost	Focus on quality	Variance analysis encourages cost control. Desired quality may drive adverse price variances.
Raw material and finished goods inventories are important	JIT philosophy	Inventory may be built up in an effort to improve efficiency variances.

Despite the criticisms and impacts, many businesses still operate with standard costing as it does aid planning and control. Other non-financial measures should be used alongside it such as punctual deliveries, customer satisfaction measures and so on.

Activity 1: TQM

The following statements have been made about the use of a TQM approach.

(a)   Standard costing systems are not compatible with a TQM approach to operations.

(b)   TQM can only be used in industries which operate in a rapidly changing environment.

Required
Which of the above statements is/are true?

O   (a) only

O   (b) only

O   Neither (a) nor (b)

O   Both (a) and (b)

Solution

Chapter summary

Performance analysis and behavioural aspects

Using variance analysis

- Used to evaluate past performance
- Used to improve performance in the future

Setting the difficulty level for a budget

- Too difficult - demotivating
- Too easy - also demotivating and offers no incentive

The effect of reported variances on staff action

- Managers need to accept and agree responsibility
- Reported variance should be fair
- Should be an incentive to deal with cause of variance
- Variances should be reported in a timely manner

Participation in budgeting

Bottom-up budgeting

- Time consuming
- May not promote goal congruence
- Morale and motivation is improved
- Based on information from employees most familiar with the department

Top-down budgeting

- The acceptance of organisational goals and objectives could be limited
- Lower-level management initiative may be stifled
- Strategic plans are likely to be incorporated into planned activities
- They use senior management's awareness of total resource availability

Standard costing in the modern environment

Just-in-time (JIT)

- Production is managed on the principle that items should not be produced until they are required to meet sales orders
- Idle time should therefore be expected

Total quality management (TQM)

- Get it right first time
- Continuous improvement
- Involve all employees
- Design for quality

The modern business environment

- Lower labour cost, higher overhead (than traditional manufacturing)
- Rapidly changing environment/products
- Customised products
- Focus on quality
- JIT philosophy

Knowledge diagnostic

1. Using variance analysis

Variance analysis is used to analyse and evaluate past performance. It is also used for control purposes: significant variances may indicate that an aspect of performance is out of control and that measures should be taken to improve performance in the future.

Used correctly, a budgetary control and variance reporting system can **motivate** managers and employees to improve performance, but it may also produce undesirable **negative reactions**.

2. Setting the difficulty level for a budget

The level of difficulty in a standard cost may range from very challenging to fairly undemanding: standard costs may be **ideal**, or may establish either a **target** or a **currently attainable** level of performance.

3. Participative budgeting

A budget can be set from the **top down (imposed** budget) or from the **bottom up (participatory** budget).

4. Standard costing in the modern business environment

Standard costing and variance analysis may sometimes be inappropriate in a production environment based on just-in-time (JIT) methods or a total quality management (TQM) approach. The **role of standards and variances** in the rapidly changing modern business environment is open to question.

Further study guidance

Question practice

Now try the following from the Further question practice bank [available in the digital edition of the Workbook]:

Number	Level	Marks	Approximate time
Section A Q52	Examination	2	4 mins
Section A Q53	Examination	2	4 mins
Section A Q54	Examination	2	4 mins

Further reading

N/A

Activity answers

Activity 1: TQM

The correct answer is:

(a) only

Standard costing systems are not compatible with a TQM approach to operations, as with standard costing the aim is to achieve a standard cost, whereas with TQM the overriding philosophy is 'continuous improvement'. This means that reaching the standard would not be sufficient in a TQM environment. TQM is not exclusively used in a rapidly changing environment; it can also be applied to improve performance in a stable industry.

19

Performance measurement

Learning objectives

On completion of this chapter, you should be able to:

	Syllabus reference no.
Describe, calculate and interpret financial performance indicators (FPIs) for profitability, liquidity and risk in both manufacturing and service businesses. Suggest methods to improve these measures.	E1 (a)
Describe, calculate and interpret non-financial performance indicators (NFPIs) and suggest methods to improve the performance indicated.	E1 (b)
Analyse past performance and suggest ways for improving financial and non-financial performance.	E1 (c)
Explain the causes and problems created by short-termism and financial manipulation of results and suggest methods to encourage a long-term view.	E1 (d)
Explain and interpret the balanced scorecard, and the Building Block model proposed by Fitzgerald and Moon.	E1 (e)
Discuss the difficulties of target setting in qualitative areas.	E1 (f)
Performance analysis in not for profit organisations and the public sector	E3
Describe, calculate and interpret non-financial performance indicators (NFPIs) and suggest methods to improve the performance indicated.	E3(e)
Discuss the difficulties of target setting in qualitative areas.	E3 (f)

	Syllabus reference no.
Analyse past performance and suggest ways for improving financial and non-financial performance.	E3 (g)
Explain the causes and problems created by short-termism and financial manipulation of results and suggest methods to encourage a long-term view.	E3 (h)

Exam context

This chapter begins by introducing the term **performance measurement** and then describes various performance measures that are used by organisations (other than variances).

It is important that the performance of an organisation is monitored; this is most commonly done by calculating a number of ratios.

The chapter concludes by considering alternative views of performance measurement, such as the **balanced scorecard** and **building blocks**, which offer a contrast to the more **traditional** approaches to performance measurement.

You must be able to explain as well as calculate performance indicators and apply your analysis to the organisation in the question. The organisations may be profit seeking or non-profit seeking.

Chapter overview

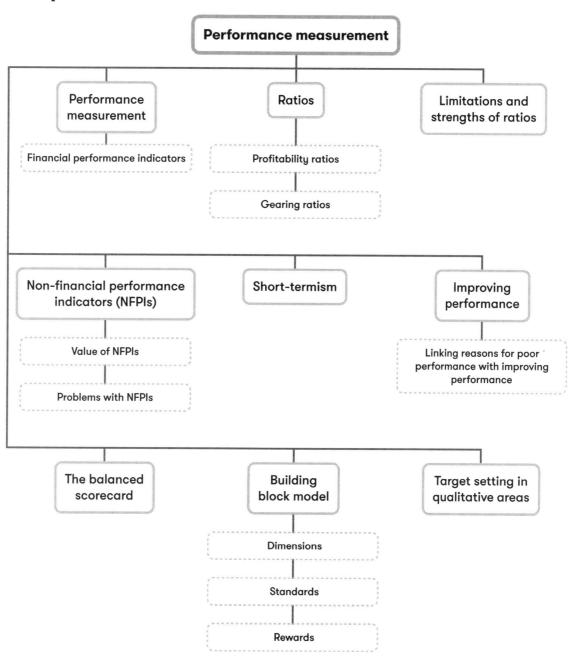

1 Performance measurement

Performance measurement is a **vital part** of the **planning and control process.**

Performance measurement aims to establish how well something or somebody is doing in relation to a plan.

Performance measures may be divided into two types:

- Financial performance indicators
- Non-financial performance indicators

1.1 Financial performance indicators

Analysis and interpretation of a company's accounts will give an indication of the company's performance.

The aims would be to:

- Assess the company's performance and financial position (in comparison with other companies in the same industry)
- Try to assess the potential future performance or to identify weakness

1.1.1 Company performance assessment

This would usually involve:

(a) Ratio analysis

(b) Review of the accounts to highlight issues not disclosed by ratio analysis (eg contingent liabilities)

(c) Review of the benefits/wealth from the point of view of the other stakeholders

(d) Analysis of other financial and non-financial information from external sources

1.1.2 Areas for analysis

(a) Profitability – how well a company performs, given its asset base

(b) Liquidity – short-term financial position

(c) Gearing – measure of risk

These areas can all be assessed using ratios but when presented with a set of accounts, you should start by looking at obvious trends or changes in figures (you will normally be given figures with some sort of comparative data).

Details of these ratios are provided in Section 2 of this chapter. You must ensure that you learn these; however, the focus for PM is application.

1.1.3 Basis for comparison

(a) Over time

(b) With other companies

(c) With industry averages

(d) With other performance measures

Exam focus point

You need to be prepared for 20-mark Section C questions that provide you with data and ask you to discuss 'the organisation's financial and non-financial performance'. You will need to calculate ratios and discuss what they mean, relating your answer to the scenario.

2 Ratios

2.1 Profitability ratios

Formula to learn

Return on capital employed (ROCE) = (profit before interest and tax / capital employed) × 100%
Capital employed = total assets less current liabilities

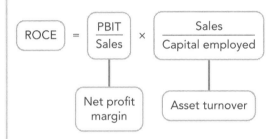

ROCE states profit as a percentage of capital employed and shows how well the business utilises the funds invested in it.

There are three comparisons that can be made:

(a) The change in ROCE from year to year

(b) Comparison to other similar businesses

(c) Comparison to the market borrowing rate

Note. ROCE should be increasing. If it is static or reducing, it is important to determine whether this is due to a reduced profit margin or asset turnover. If both profit margin and asset turnover are deteriorating, the company has a profitability problem.

To improve a ratio, the company would need to investigate each element of the calculation to see whether increasing or reducing the numbers would improve the result. For example, to improve ROCE a company could look at the elements which make up the profit figure and look at ways to increase sales revenue or reduce costs. Alternatively, they could look to improve the capital employed figure by selling unused assets.

Net profit margin

$$\frac{\text{Net profit}}{\text{Sales}} \times 100\%$$

A high profit margin indicates that either sales prices are high or total costs are being kept well under control.

This ratio could be improved by increasing the selling price (as long as sales volumes were not compromised) or looking at ways to reduce costs.

Gross profit margin

$$\frac{(\text{Sales} - \text{cost of sales})}{\text{Sales}} \times 100\%$$

A high gross profit margin also indicates that either sales prices are high or production costs are being kept well under control.

Again, this ratio could be improved by increasing the selling price (as long as sales volumes were not compromised) or looking at ways to reduce cost of sales.

Asset turnover

The ratio of sales turnover to the amount of capital employed

$$\frac{\text{Sales}}{\text{(Total assets} - \text{current liabilities)}}$$

This shows the turnover that is generated from each $1 worth of assets employed.

This ratio could be improved by increasing sales or reducing total assets or increasing current liabilities.

2.1.1 Liquidity

A company can be profitable but at the same time get into cash flow problems. Liquidity ratios (**current** and **quick**) and **working capital turnover ratios** give some idea of a company's liquidity and ability to generate cash from its business operations.

> **Liquidity: Liquidity** is the amount of cash a company can obtain quickly to settle its debts (and possibly to meet other unforeseen demands for cash payments too).

The **current ratio** is the standard test of liquidity, calculated by dividing the most liquid assets in the business (receivables, inventories and cash) by the business's payables.

$$\text{Current ratio} = \frac{\text{Current assets}}{\text{Current liabilities}}$$

A ratio comfortably in excess of one should be expected, but what is 'comfortable' varies between different types of business.

The current ratio can be amended by excluding the inventory from the current assets. This gives the quick ratio or acid test.

> **Formula to learn**
>
> $$\text{Quick ratio} = \frac{\text{Current assets} - \text{inventories}}{\text{Current liabilities}}$$

For businesses with a **fast inventory turnover**, a quick ratio can be **less than one** without suggesting that the company is in cash flow difficulties.

Do not forget the other side of the coin. The current ratio and the quick ratio can be bigger than they should be. A company that has large volumes of inventories and receivables might be **overinvesting in working capital**, and so tying up more funds in the business than it needs to. This would suggest **poor management of receivables or inventories** by the company.

By calculating the following ratios, we can see how long a company holds inventory for, the length of time it takes them to pay their suppliers, and the length of time it takes them to receive cash from their customers:

1	Receivables period	$\dfrac{\text{Average receivables}}{\text{Credit sales}}$	× 365	=	days
2	Inventory period	$\dfrac{\text{Average finished goods}}{\text{Cost of sales}}$	× 365	=	days

3	Payables period	$\dfrac{\text{Average payables}}{\text{Credit purchases}}$	× 365	=	days

Note. If average data is not available year-end values should be used.

The receivables period is a rough measure of the average length of time it takes for a company's accounts receivable to pay what they owe.

A lengthening inventory turnover period indicates:

(a) A **slowdown** in **trading**; or

(b) A **build-up** in **inventory levels**, perhaps suggesting that the investment in inventories is becoming excessive.

2.2 Gearing ratios

Formula to learn

$$\text{Gearing ratio} = \frac{\text{Long - term debt}}{\text{Long - term debt} + \text{equity (shareholders' funds)}}$$

Gearing measures the **financial risk** of a company.

Business risk refers to the variability in earnings which is due to the business activities of the organisation. This can result from the organisation's products, customers, suppliers or cost structure.

Operating gearing is a ratio which is calculated to quantify **business risk**. It looks specifically at the operating cost structure of the organisation.

Formula to learn

$$\text{Operating gearing} = \frac{\text{Contribution}}{\text{Profit before interest and tax (PBIT)}}$$

If operating gearing is high this indicates that a large proportion of the organisation's operating costs are fixed. Fixed costs make profit more volatile as PBIT becomes more vulnerable to downturns in business volume.

Activity 1: Financial performance

Preston Financial Services is an accounting practice specialising in providing accounting and taxation work for dentists and doctors. The clients are mainly wealthy, self-employed and have an average age of 52.

The business was founded by and is wholly owned by Richard Preston, a dominant and aggressive sole-practitioner. He feels that promotion of new products to his clients would be likely to upset the conservative nature of his dentists and doctors and, as a result, the business has been managed with similar products year on year.

You have been provided with financial information relating to the practice.

Financial information

	Current year	Previous year
Turnover ($'000)	945	900
Net profit ($'000)	187	180
Average cash balances ($'000)	21	20
Average trade receivables days (industry average 30 days)	18 days	22 days
Inflation rate (%)	3	3

Required

Using the financial information above only, comment on the financial performance of the business (briefly consider growth, profitability, liquidity and credit management).

Solution

1

---

3 Limitations and strengths of ratios

Limitations:

(a) Not useful on their own – need to be compared to yardstick

(b) Must be carefully defined

(c) Inflation needs to be adjusted for – often forgotten

(d) Different basis of calculating between companies

(e) Based on historical costs – but is this an accurate reflection of future?

Strengths:

(a) Easier to understand than absolute measures

(b) Easier to look at changes over time

(c) Puts performance into context

(d) Can be used as targets

(e) Summarise results

3.1 Other problems with financial performance indicators

(a) Focus only on variables which can be expressed in monetary terms **ignoring other important variables which cannot be expressed in monetary terms**

(b) Focus on **past**

(c) **Do not convey the full picture** of a company's performance in a modern business environment, eg quality, customer satisfaction

(d) Focus on the **short-term**

4 Non-financial performance indicators (NFPIs)

Non-financial performance indicators (NFPIs) are measures of performance based on non-financial information which operating departments use to monitor and control their activities.

Examples of NFPIs are summarised in the following table:

Area Assessed	Performance measures
Service Quality	Number of complaints Proportion of repeat bookings On-time deliveries Customer waiting time
Personnel	Staff turnover Days lost through absenteeism Days lost through accidents/sickness Training time per employee

Different industries will place a different weighting on each area depending on those most critical to their success.

Essential reading

See Chapter 19 Section 1 of the Essential reading for more detail on NFPIs.

The Essential reading is available as an Appendix of the digital edition of the Workbook.

4.1 Value of NFPIs

(a) **Information** can be **provided quickly** for managers (eg per shift, daily or hourly) unlike traditional financial performance reports.

(b) **Anything can be measured**/compared if it is meaningful to do so.

(c) **Easy to calculate** and easier for non-financial managers to **understand** and use effectively

(d) **Less likely to be manipulated** than traditional profit related measures

(e) Can be **quantitative or qualitative**

(f) Provide information about key areas such as **quality, customer satisfaction** etc

(g) Better **indicator of future prospects** than financial indicators which focus on the short term

4.2 Problems with NFPIs

(a) Too many measures can lead to **information overload** for managers, providing information which is not truly useful.

(b) May lead managers to **pursue detailed operational goals** at the expense of overall corporate strategy

(c) Need to be **linked with financial measures**

(d) Need to be developed and refined over time to ensure remain relevant

Exam focus point

Note that many NFPIs can be used in not-for-profit and public sector organisations, too.

5 Short-termism

> **Short-termism:** **Short-termism** is when there is a bias towards short-term rather than long-term performance.

If a manager's performance is measured on a short-term basis or a company is under pressure to report positive growth, short-termism may occur.

Activity 2: Short-termism

The following are all decisions a manager could make:

(a) Postpone repairs/maintenance expenditure until the following year

(b) Reduce R&D expenditure

(c) Postpone recruitment of new staff

(d) Train staff to complete work faster

Required

Which of the above decisions are consequences of a bonus based on short-term profits?

○ (a) and (b)

○ (a) and (c)

○ (a), (b) and (c)

○ All of the above

Solution

Activity 3: Encouraging a long-term view

Required

Which of the following could be used to encourage managers to take decisions in the long-term interests of the company?

(a) Link bonus to share price

(b) Link bonus to profit

(c) Award bonus in shares rather than cash

○ (a) and (b)

○ (a) and (c)

○ (b) and (c)

○ (a) only

Solution

Essential reading

See Chapter 19 Section 2 of the Essential reading for more detail on methods to encourage a long-term view.

The Essential reading is available as an Appendix of the digital edition of the Workbook.

---

6 Improving performance

PER alert

One of the competencies needed to fulfil performance objective 14 of the PER is to advise on appropriate ways to maintain and improve performance. You can apply the knowledge you obtain from this section of the text to help to demonstrate this competence.

When performance is measured, the objectives should be to:

(a) Identify aspects of performance that may be a cause for concern

(b) Explain differences between actual performance and the plan or expectation, or deteriorating performance over time

(c) Consider ways of taking control measures to improve performance

In an exam question on performance measurement, it is highly likely that you will be required to do all three of these things in your answer.

Essential reading

See Chapter 19 Section 3 of the Essential reading for more detail on objectives (a) and (b).

The Essential reading is available as an Appendix of the digital edition of the Workbook.

6.1 Linking reasons for poor performance with improving performance

Having identified reasons for poor performance, whether financial or non-financial, the final step is to consider and implement methods of improving performance. **Methods of improving performance should be linked to the possible reasons for the poor performance.**

The aim of corrective measures should be to tackle the problems that are the cause of the poor performance.

Illustrative control measures are shown in the following table:

Aspect of performance	Possible reasons	Possible measures to improve performance
Increase in rejection rates for faulty products	Using relatively inexperienced staff to do the work Using cheaper materials (to save money)	Hire more experienced staff Provide training Switch back to better-quality materials
Increase in time between taking a customer order and delivering the product to the customer	Administrative delays in processing customer orders	Review procedures and remove any unnecessary administrative tasks such as duplication of paperwork
Increase in frequency of machine breakdowns	Reduction on amount of routine maintenance work	Increase routine maintenance of machines
Customer dissatisfaction with online sales service	Poor website design	Redesign the website. Hire web design specialists if necessary
Longer average time to answer customer calls in a call centre	Reduction in number of call centre staff	Employ more staff
Declining labour productivity	Failure to train staff Increase in complexity of the work Use of inexperienced staff	Hire more experienced staff Provide training Give the most complex tasks to specialist staff

Some structured approaches to performance measurement have been developed, which combine measurements of financial and non-financial performance. Two of these are described in the next sections.

Activity 4: Improving performance (ACCA 6/08 amended)

Bridgewater Co provides training courses for many of the mainstream software packages on the market.

The business has many divisions within Waterland, the one country in which it operates. The senior managers of Bridgewater Co have very clear objectives for the divisions and these are communicated to divisional managers on appointment and subsequently in quarterly and annual reviews. These are:

• Each quarter, sales should grow and annual sales should exceed budget

• Trainer (lecture staff) costs should not exceed $180 per teaching day

• Room hire costs should not exceed $90 per teaching day

• Each division should meet its budget for profit per quarter and annually

It is known that managers will be promoted based on their ability to meet these targets. A member of the senior management is to retire after Quarter 2 of the current financial year, which has just begun. The divisional managers anticipate that one of them may be promoted at the beginning of Quarter 3 if their performance is good enough.

The current quarterly forecasts, along with the original budgeted profit for the Northwest division, are as follows:

	Q1 $'000	Q2 $'000	Q3 $'000	Q4 $'000	Q5 $'000
Sales	40.0	36.0	50.0	60.0	186.0
Less:					
Trainers	8.0	7.2	10.0	12.0	37.2
Room hire	4.0	3.6	5.0	6.0	18.6
Staff training	1.0	1.0	1.0	1.0	4.0
Other costs	3.0	1.7	6.0	7.0	17.7
Forecast new profit	24.0	22.5	28.0	34.0	108.5
Original budgeted profit	25.0	26.0	27.0	28.0	106.0
Annual sales budget					180.0
Teaching days	40	36	50	60	

The manager of the Northwest division has been considering a few steps to improve the performance of his division.

Voucher scheme

As a sales promotion, vouchers will be sold for $125 each, a substantial discount on normal prices. These vouchers will entitle the holder to attend four training sessions on software of their choice. They can attend when they want to but are advised that one training session per quarter is sensible. The manager is confident that if the promotion took place immediately, he could sell 80 vouchers and that customers would follow the advice given to attend one session per quarter. All voucher holders would attend planned existing courses and all will be new customers.

Software upgrade

A new important software programme has recently been launched for which there could be a market for training courses. Demonstration programs can be bought for $1,800 in Quarter 1. Staff training would be needed, costing $500 in each of Quarters 1 and 2 but in Quarters 3 and 4 extra courses could be offered selling this training.

Assuming similar class sizes and the usual sales prices, extra sales revenue amounting to 20% of normal sales are expected (measured before the voucher promotion above). The manager is keen to run these courses at the same tutorial and room standards as he normally provides. Software expenditure is written off in the income statement as incurred.

Delaying payments to trainers

The manager is considering delaying payment to the trainers. He intends to delay payment on 50% of all invoices received from the trainers in the first two quarters, paying them one month later than is usual.

The revised forecast would be:

Revised forecasts

	Q1 $'000	Q2 $'000	Q3 $'000	Q4 $'000	Total $'000
Existing sales	40.0	36.0	50.0	60.0	186.0
Voucher sales ($125 × 80/4)	2.5	2.5	2.5	2.5	10.0
Software training			10.0	12.0	22.0
	42.5	38.5	62.5	74.5	218.0
Less:					
Existing trainer costs	8.0	7.2	10.0	12.0	37.2
Additional training costs ($200 × teaching days)			2.0	2.4	4.4
Room hire	4.0	3.6	5.0	6.0	18.6
Additional room hire ($100 × teaching days)			1.0	1.2	2.2
Staff training	1.0	1.0	1.0	1.0	4.0
Additional staff training	0.5	0.5			1
Other costs	3.0	1.7	6.0	7.0	17.7
Software	1.8				1.8
Forecast net profit	24.2	24.5	37.5	44.9	131.1
Original budget profit	25.0	26.0	27.0	28.0	106.0

Required
Comment on whether each of the proposed steps by the manager will improve the manager's chances of promotion.

Solution
1

7 The balanced scorecard

A popular approach in current management thinking to performance measurement (for service **and** non-service organisations) is the use of a 'balanced scorecard', consisting of a variety of indicators, both financial and non-financial. It is commonly used in not for profit organisations and the public sector.

The balanced scorecard focuses on **four different perspectives** and aims to establish goals for each together with measures which can be used to evaluate whether these goals have been achieved.

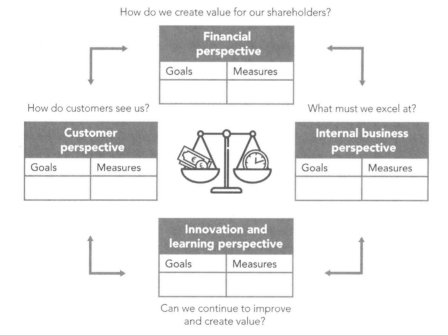

Features:

(a) Traditional measures are mainly inward looking and narrow in focus with over emphasis on financial measures and short-term goals.

(b) The balanced scorecard focuses on both internal and external factors and links performance measures to key elements of a company's strategy.

(c) It requires a balanced consideration of both financial and non-financial measures and goals to prevent improvements being made in one area at the expense of another.

(d) It attempts to identify the needs and concerns of customers. This information can then be used to identify new products and markets. Comparison with competitors can be made in order to establish best practice.

Activity 5: Balanced scorecard

The following statements have been made about the use of the balanced scorecard:

(a) Percentage of customers ordering a dessert could be used as a measure of customer satisfaction for a restaurant.

(b) Percentage of revenue from meals sold from the specials board could be used as a measure of innovation for a restaurant.

Required

Which of the above statements is/are true?

- ○ (a) only
- ○ (b) only
- ○ Neither (a) nor (b)
- ○ Both (a) and (b)

Solution

Activity 6: Analysing performance

1 Preston Financial Services is an accounting practice. The business specialises in providing accounting and taxation work for dentists and doctors. The clients are mainly wealthy, self-employed and have an average age of 52.

The business was founded by and is wholly owned by Richard Preston, a dominant and aggressive sole practitioner. He feels that promotion of new products to his clients would be likely to upset the conservative nature of his dentists and doctors and, as a result, the business has been managed with similar products year on year.

You have been provided with financial information relating to the practice.

Financial information

	Current year	Previous year
Turnover ($'000)	945	900
Net profit ($'000)	187	180
Average cash balances ($'000)	21	20
Average trade receivables days (industry average 30 days)	18 days	22 days
Inflation rate (%)	3	3

You have also been provided with non-financial information which is based on the balanced scorecard format.

Balanced scorecard (extract)

Internal business processes

	Current year	Previous year
Error rates in jobs done	16%	10%
Average job completion time	7 weeks	10 weeks

Customer knowledge

	Current year	Previous year
Number of customers	1,220	1,500
Average fee levels ($)	775	600
Market share	14%	20%

Learning and growth

	Current year	Previous year
Percentage of revenue from non-core work	4%	5%
Industry average of the proportion of revenue from non-core work in accounting practices	30%	25%
Employee retention rate	60%	80%

Notes

(a) Error rates measure the number of jobs with mistakes made by staff as a proportion of the number of clients serviced.

(b) Core work is defined as accountancy and taxation. Non-core work is defined primarily as pension advice and business consultancy. Non-core work traditionally has a high margin.

Required

Using the data given in the balanced scorecard, extract comment on the performance of the business. Include comments on internal business processes, customer knowledge and learning/growth, separately, and provide a concluding comment on the overall performance of the business.

Solution

1

8 Building block model

Performance measurement in service businesses has sometimes been perceived as more difficult than in manufacturing businesses.

Fitzgerald and Moon (1996) suggest that a performance management system in a service organisation can be analysed as a combination of three building blocks.

- Dimensions of performance
- Standards
- Rewards

> **Dimensions of performance**
> Profit
> Competitiveness
> Quality
> Resource utilisation
> Flexibility
> Innovation

> **Standards**
> Ownership
> Achievability
> Equity

> **Rewards**
> Clarity
> Motivation
> Controllability

This framework is also known as the **results** and **determinants** framework.

PER alert

One of the competencies needed to fulfil performance objective 14 of the PER is to use review and reward systems to monitor and assess performance. You can apply the knowledge you obtain from this section of the text to help to demonstrate this competence.

8.1 Dimensions

Performance of the organisation is viewed over six dimensions, the first two listed on the diagram; Profit and Competitiveness are the results of the other four determinants:

(a) **Quality** – being reliability, courtesy, competence and availability

(b) **Flexibility** – the ability to deliver at the right time, response to customer requirements and changes in demand

(c) **Resourceutilisation** – best use of inputs to create outputs. This is usually measured in terms of productivity

(d) **Innovation** – ability to develop new products or services, move into new markets and continuous improvement

8.2 Standards

The second part of Fitzgerald and Moon's framework for performance measurement concerns setting the standards or targets of performance, once the measures for the dimensions of performance have been selected.

There are three aspects to setting standards of performance:

- Individuals need to feel that they 'own' the standards and targets for which they will be made responsible.
- Individuals also need to feel that the targets or standards are realistic and achievable.
- The standards and targets should be seen as 'fair' and equitable for all the managers in the organisation.

8.3 Rewards

The third aspect of Fitzgerald and Moon's performance measurement framework is rewards. This refers to the structure of the rewards system, and how individuals will be rewarded for the successful achievement of performance targets.

There are three aspects to consider in a reward system:

- The system of setting targets and rewarding individuals for achieving the targets should be clear. Clarity will improve motivation to achieve the targets.
- Achievement of performance targets should be suitably rewarded.
- Individuals should be made responsible only for aspects of performance that they are in a position to control.

Essential reading

See Chapter 19 Section 5 of the Essential reading for more detail on Fitzgerald and Moon's building blocks.

The Essential reading is available as an Appendix of the digital edition of the Workbook.

Activity 7: Performance measures

The following statements have been made about performance measurements:

(a) Non-financial performance measures are important because they can provide a good indication of future financial prospects.

(b) A problem with using multiple measures of performance is that the organisation may lose sight of its overall aim.

Required
Which of the above statements is/are true?

- ○ (a) only
- ○ (b) only
- ○ Neither (a) nor (b)
- ○ Both (a) and (b)

Solution

9 Target setting in qualitative areas

The balanced scorecard and Fitzgerald and Moon's Building Block model are based on the assumption that performance targets can be set and measured for non-financial aspects of performance. This **presumes** that all **key non-financial aspects** of performance **can be measured** and quantified.

In practice, this is not necessarily the case. There are several problems with qualitative non-financial performance targets.

(a) **Difficulties selecting a suitable performance measure**

For example, an important objective for an organisation may be winning and retaining customer loyalty. But how is a reliable target for customer loyalty decided?

- Opinion research by a market research firm and setting a 'target score for loyalty'?
- The percentage of customers who make a repeat order within x months?

Similarly, a performance objective may be to deliver a high standard of service to a customer, but how is service quality defined? Having defined service quality, how is it measured?

(b) **Qualitative data is not quantified**

At best, qualitative measures are converted into quantitative measures using a subjective scoring system. When performance is not quantified, it is difficult to target and monitor.

(c) **Lack of information system**

An organisation may have a well-established system for measuring quantitative data, especially in the areas of accounting and sales statistics. It is much **less likely** to have a reliable and comprehensive **system for collecting data** about **qualitative** aspects of performance.

Chapter summary

Performance measurement

Performance measurement

Financial performance indicators

- Ratio analysis
- Profitability
- Liquidity
- Gearing

Ratios

Profitability ratios

- ROCE = (PBIT/Capital employed) × 100%
- Net profit margin = (Net profit/ Sales) × 100%
- Gross profit margin = [(Sales – cost of sales)/ sales] × 100%
- Asset turnover = (Sales/total assets – current liabilities)
- Liquidity ratios
  - Current ratio = current assets/current liabilities
  - Quick ratio = current assets - inventories/current liabilities
- Working capital ratios
  - Receivables period = (Average receivables/credit sales) x 365 days
  - Inventory period = (Average finished goods/cost of sales) x 365 days
  - Payables period = (Average payables/credit purchases) x 365 days

Gearing ratios

- Gearing ratio = Long-term debt/(Long term debt + equity)
- Operating gearing ratio = Contribution/ PBIT

Limitations and strengths of ratios

- Not useful on their own – need to be compared to yardstick
- Focus on past
- Focus on the short term
- Ignore important variables which cannot be expressed in monetary terms
- Easier to understand than absolute measures
- Easier to look at changes over time
- Can be used as targets

Non-financial performance indicators (NFPIs)

Value of NFPIs
- Can measure anything
- Quantitative and qualitative
- Gather information on key areas eg quality, customers, employees
- Good indicator of future prospects

Problems with NFPIs
- Can provide too much information
- Can forget overall goal

Short-termism

Focus on short term goals at the expense of long term goals

Improving performance

- Identify aspects of performance that may be a cause for concern
- Explain differences between actual performance and the plan or expectation, or deteriorating performance over time
- Consider ways of taking control measures to improve performance

Linking reasons for poor performance with improving performance

Methods of improving performance should be linked to the possible reasons for the poor performance

The balanced scorecard

- Enables focus on both internal and external factors and on key elements of business strategy
- Four dimensions are:
  – Customer
  – Internal business
  – Financial
  – Innovation and learning

Building block model

Dimensions
- Profit
- Competitiveness
- Quality
- Resource utilisation
- Flexibility
- Innovation

Standards
- Ownership
- Achievability
- Equity

Rewards
- Clarity
- Motivation
- Controllability

Target setting in qualitative areas

- Problems with qualitative non-financial performance targets:
  – Difficulties selecting a suitable performance measure
  – Qualitative data is not quantified
  – Lack of information system

Knowledge diagnostic

1. Performance measurement

Performance of a business can be evaluated by financial indicators.

Financial indicators focus on the **past** and are **short-term** measures; as such, non-financial indicators also need to be used. A balance is needed between both.

2. Limitations and strengths of ratios

Whilst ratios are very helpful as a target and a means of assessing performance, they should not be used on their own. They only focus on the past and monetary measures and are very often short term.

3. Non-financial performance indicators

These measures when used in conjunction with financial measures enable the whole picture to be seen. They can be **quantitative** or **qualitative**. Anything that is important to the business can be measured and these ratios are not easily manipulated.

4. The balanced scorecard

Tools such as the balanced scorecard help to evaluate a business by looking at all key areas using a variety of financial and non-financial indicators.

The four key areas are:

- Customer
- Financial
- Internal
- Innovation and learning

5. Building block model

Fitzgerald and Moon's **building blocks** for **dimensions, standards** and **rewards** attempt to overcome the problems associated with performance measurement of service businesses.

Further study guidance

Question practice

Now try the following from the Further question practice bank [available in the digital edition of the Workbook]:

Number	Level	Marks	Approximate time
Section A Q55	Examination	2	4 mins
Section A Q56	Examination	2	4 mins
Section A Q57	Examination	2	4 mins

Further reading

There are two technical articles available on ACCA's website, called *Tackling performance evaluation questions* and *Building blocks of performance management*.

You are strongly advised to read these articles in full as part of your preparation for the PM exam.

Activity answers

Activity 1: Financial performance

1 The correct answer is:

Turnover has increased by 5%, which is higher than the 3% rate of inflation, indicating that the business has grown in real terms.

Net profits have risen by 3.9% (($187 − $180)/$180 × 100%) and net profits of $187,000 for a sole practitioner look very healthy.

Net profit margin has however fallen from 20% ($180/$900 × 100%) to 19.8% ($187/$945 × 100%). This suggests either that costs have risen disproportionately or that the profit margin on fees charged has declined, perhaps due to increased competition.

Average cash balances have increased by 5% (($21 − $20)/$20 × 100%) indicating that liquidity has improved and the business has a healthy cash balance.

Average trade receivables days have fallen by four days indicating that the business has become more efficient at collecting amounts owing from customers. The industry average is 30 days so the working capital management must be particularly effective. However, Richard Preston is apparently dominant and aggressive and the methods used to collect debts may upset customers and lose business.

In conclusion, the business is healthy and successful with just some minor concerns over margins and low growth.

Activity 2: Short-termism

The correct answer is:

(a), (b) and (c)

Postponing repair/maintenance expenditure until the following year, not recruiting new staff and cutting back on R&D will all increase short-term profits, but potentially have a detrimental long-term effect. Investing in staff training will actually reduce profits in the short term; the benefits would usually take time to filter through to profits

Activity 3: Encouraging a long-term view

The correct answer is:

(a) and (c)

Linking bonuses to share price and awarding bonuses in shares should ensure that employees are committed to increasing the wealth of shareholders, rather than just maximising short-term profits.

Activity 4: Improving performance (ACCA 6/08 amended)

1 The correct answer is:

Voucher scheme

The voucher scheme looks like a good idea as the manager is confident that the take-up would be good and customers would follow his advice to attend one session per quarter. This will **increase revenue** without incurring additional costs as customers would attend existing planned courses. However, some additional unforeseen costs may still be incurred.

The additional revenue and profit will help, but targets for Quarters 1 and 2 will still not be met so the voucher scheme will not necessarily improve the manager's promotion prospects.

There is always the danger with offering a discount that **existing customers** will be disgruntled, particularly if they have already paid a higher price for a course that is now being offered at a discount. The vouchers are however only being offered to **new** customers so the manager should be able to offer this promotion without upsetting existing customers.

Software upgrade

It is essential that a software training company uses the **latest software technology** on its courses. The investment in software and staff training is therefore a **necessity** and cannot be avoided.

The courses will generate **extra revenue** but not until Quarters 3 and 4. This software upgrade will therefore further damage the achievement of targets in Quarters 1 and 2, as costs will rise but the extra revenue will be too late for the promotion assessment.

It is to be hoped that the senior managers will recognise the essential long-term planning being undertaken.

Delaying payments to trainers

This is not a good idea. None of the performance targets will be affected, as the plan will not affect costs or profits. The only positive impact will be on **cash flow**. The worrying aspect is the negative impact it may have on **relationships with trainers**. Software training is a competitive market and good trainers will be in demand by a number of training providers. If the company is to offer quality training, it must have the best trainers and this is not the way to retain them.

In conclusion, if all the proposals were taken together, they will **not improve** the manager's chance of promotion as any benefits will accrue after Quarter 2.

Activity 5: Balanced scorecard

The correct answer is:

Both (a) and (b)

Both of these performance measures would be suitable for a restaurant and it should be possible to get the information.

Activity 6: Analysing performance

1 **The correct answer is:**

Internal business processes

Error rates in jobs done have increased from 10% to 16%, possibly as a result of the reduction in the average job completion time. This is unacceptable as accuracy is a primary concern for clients of an accounting practice. Such errors could cause clients to have problems with the tax authorities, banks etc and the clients may well sue Mr Preston for negligence.

Customer knowledge

The number of customers has fallen dramatically by 18.7% ((1,500 − 1,220)/1,500 × 100%) and this is a serious cause for concern. Existing clients are obviously not happy with the service that has been provided and the repeat work that an accountancy practice relies on has suffered.

Average fees have increased dramatically by 29% ((775 − 600)/600 × 100%) and this could explain why clients have been lost. It does also explain the increase in the turnover figure.

Market share has fallen from 20% to 14% so competitors are offering a better service and taking clients from Preston Financial Services.

Learning and growth

The percentage of revenue from non-core work is considerably lower than the industry average and has fallen from 5% to 4% compared to a growth in the industry average from 25% to 30%. It would appear that clients are wanting a wider range of services from their accountants which Mr Preston is failing to provide.

The employee retention rate has fallen indicating that staff have become more dissatisfied and have left the business. Clients of accountancy practices like to have continuity of service and may resent having to deal with different people each year, especially as information is often private and confidential. Staff may be leaving more frequently as they have been put under pressure to complete jobs more quickly or because they want to develop their knowledge and experience in non-core work.

Conclusion

The non-financial information indicates that there are fundamental problems with the business which need to be addressed. Future prospects for growth do not look good unless Mr Preston responds to changes in his business environment. In particular, he needs to improve the quality of the work being done and offer a wider range of services to clients.

Activity 7: Performance measures

The correct answer is:

Both (a) and (b)

Although it is useful to consider a range of performance measures, the organisation must ensure that it does not become too focused on achieving one objective. For example, customer satisfaction is clearly important, but if achieving top results in feedback surveys means that the company cannot operate profitably, this is not going to be good news in the long run.

20

Divisional performance and transfer pricing

Learning objectives

On competition of this chapter, you should be able to:

	Syllabus reference no.
Explain and illustrate the basis for setting a transfer price using variable cost, full cost and the principles behind allowing for intermediate markets.	E2 (a)
Explain how transfer prices can distort the performance assessment of divisions and decisions made.	E2 (b)
Explain the meaning of, and calculate, return on investment (ROI) and residual income (RI), and discuss their shortcomings.	E2 (c)
Compare divisional performance and recognise the problems of doing so.	E2 (d)

Exam context

This chapter looks at **divisional performance** and **transfer pricing** which is a system of charging other divisions of your organisation when you provide them with your division's goods or services.

In a **divisionalised organisation** structure of any kind, if one division does work that is used by another division, transfer pricing may be required. Do not be misled by the term 'price': there is not necessarily any suggestion of **profit** as there usually is with an external selling price. But as we shall see, transfer pricing is particularly appropriate where divisions are designated as **profit centres**.

You may be required to calculate transfer prices in this exam. You must be able to explain how and why they are used and the problems they can create. You must also be able to calculate return on investment (ROI) and residual income (RI) and compare performance of divisions.

Chapter overview

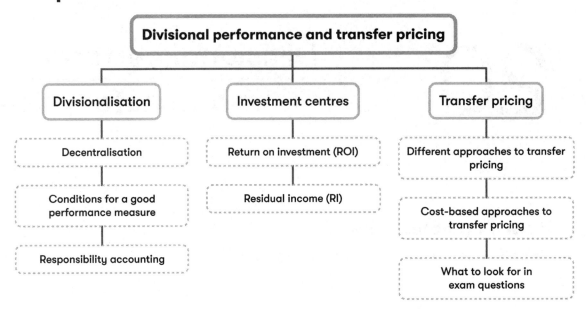

1 Divisionalisation

Divisionalisation is a term for the separation of an **organisation into divisions**. Each divisional manager is responsible for the performance of the division. A division may be a cost centre (responsible for its costs only), a profit centre (responsible for revenues and costs) or an investment centre or Strategic Business Unit (responsible for costs, revenues and assets).

1.1 Decentralisation

Generally, a company with several divisions will be a **decentralised organisation**. In such organisations, divisional managers tend be responsible for making their own decisions concerning the operation of the division.

Advantages of decentralisation can include:

(a) Decisions made more quickly

(b) Increased motivation of management

(c) Increased quality of decisions due to local knowledge

(d) Reduced head office bureaucracy

(e) Better training for all levels of management

Disadvantages of decentralisation include:

(a) Potential for dysfunctional decision making, ie not in the interests of the whole organisation

(b) Duplication amongst divisions leading to greater cost

(c) Senior management loss of control

Appropriate performance **evaluation methods** are therefore needed in order to counteract the possible disadvantages.

1.2 Conditions for a good performance measure

A good performance measure should:

(a) Provide incentive to the divisional manager to make decisions which are in the best interests of the overall company (**goal congruence**)

(b) Only include factors for which the manager (division) can be held **accountable**

(c) Recognise the **long-term** objectives as well as short-term objectives of the organisation

1.3 Responsibility accounting

Responsibility accounting is used to measure performance of decentralised units.

Responsibility structure	Manager's area of responsibility	Typical financial performance measure
Cost centre	Decisions over costs	Standard costing variances
Revenue centre	Revenues only	Revenues
Profit centre	Decisions over costs and revenues	Controllable profit
Investment centre	Decisions over costs, revenues, and assets	Return on investment and residual income

So far, we have seen many of the performance measures dealing with the first three of these responsibility centres.

Activity 1: Investment centres

The following are some of the areas which require control within a division:

(a) Generation of revenues

(b) Investment in non-current assets

(c) Apportioned head office costs

(d) Salary costs

Required

Which of the above does the manager have control of in an investment centre?

○ All of the above

○ (a) and (b)

○ (b) and (d)

○ (a), (b) and (d)

Solution

---

2 Investment centres

Within an investment centre, as well as being responsible for profits, managers also have responsibility over investments and assets. To measure their performance purely on say profit would be focusing only on part of the picture. To overcome this, we use two methods that measure the assets and the profit they generate.

The performance of an investment centre is usually monitored using either or both **ROI** and **RI**.

2.1 Return on investment (ROI)

Return on investment (ROI): ROI shows how much profit has been made in relation to the amount of capital invested and is calculated as (profit/capital employed) × 100%.

Formula to learn

ROI = (divisional profit (PBIT) / divisional investment) × 100

or

(Divisional controllable PBIT / divisional net controllable assets) × 100

Profit should be before interest and tax (PBIT). It may also be helpful in measuring performance to calculate ROI based on controllable profit.

For the investment, use opening book value of total assets less current liabilities. Alternatively, an average book value may be used.

ROI enables performance in different divisions to be compared.

Similarly, new investments can also be appraised using ROI.

Decision rule

Only projects which **increase the existing ROI** should be undertaken.

2.1.1 Problems with ROI

- **Dysfunctional behaviour** – only projects which increase ROI will be accepted; this could be at the expense of growth in corporate profits
- The ratio will be distorted by the **age of the assets**
- Profit can be **manipulated**

2.1.2 Manipulating the ROI

If a manager's bonus depends on ROI being met, the manager may feel pressured into manipulating the measure. The **asset base** of the ratio can be **altered** by increasing/decreasing payables and receivables (by speeding up or delaying payments and receipts).

Exam focus point

You must learn the problems with using ROI. A Section C question could contain a scenario in which ROI is being used and abused. You would need to use the scenario to demonstrate each problem.

Essential reading

See Chapter 20 Section 1 of the Essential reading for more detail on ROI and new investments.

The Essential reading is available as an Appendix of the digital edition of the Workbook.

Exam focus point

The June 2018 examining team report highlighted a question on performance management that caused problems for students in the exam. The question related to decisions made by a manager which could lead to a bonus without benefiting the organisation. The examining team said, 'Holding on to heavily depreciated assets gives a low figure for 'capital employed' which, in turn, gives a higher figure for ROI which could lead to bonuses for divisional managers. However, there are likely to be higher running costs for an old machine, making the organisation less profitable than it might be. Low depreciation charges may also hide this, but cash flow would be affected'. As such, make sure you understand the relationship between ROI, investments and bonuses.

2.2 Residual income

Residual income: Residual income is a measure of the centre's profits after deducting a notional or imputed interest cost.

Formula to learn

Traditionally the main alternative to ROI, RI provides a hurdle figure for profit based on the company's minimum required percentage return from a division.

	$
PBIT (or controllable profit)	X
Less 'imputed interest' (= divisional investment × cost of capital)	(X)
Residual income	X

The result is an absolute figure.

2.2.1 Advantages of residual income

The advantages of using RI

(a) Residual income will **increase** when investments earning above the cost of capital are undertaken and investments earning below the cost of capital are eliminated.

(b) Residual income is **more flexible** since a different cost of capital can be applied to investments with **different risk** characteristics.

The **weakness** of RI is that it **does not facilitate comparisons** between investment centres, **nor does it relate the size of a centre's income to the size of the investment**. If a company has two identical divisions but one is four years older than the other, the older division will have suffered more depreciation and will therefore have a lower capital employed. RI will favour the older division because the imputed interest (capital employed multiplied by cost of capital) for the older division will be smaller.

Essential reading

See Chapter 20 Section 2 of the Essential reading for more detail on RI versus ROI.

The Essential reading is available as an Appendix of the digital edition of the Workbook.

Activity 2: Measuring performance

Brenda and Eddie have two franchises in different parts of town and want to monitor the performance of the two managers who have full control over investments.

Forecast results for the year are:

	Vittorio's	Dugaldo's
	$	$
Profits	90,000	135,000
Investment	500,000	750,000

Required

Which of the following statements would explain why profit or ROI would be more equitable for comparing Vittorio's and Dugaldo's forecast performance?

O Profit because this relates to shareholder wealth

O Profit because maximising profit is the overriding objective of all companies

O ROI because it takes into consideration the fact that Dugaldo has more investment than Vittorio

O ROI because it is based on prior results which are historical information

Solution

Activity 3: ROI and RI

Brenda and Eddie have two franchises in different parts of town and want to monitor the performance of the two managers who have full control over investments.

Forecast results for the year are:

	Vittorio's $	Dugaldo's $
Profits	90,000	135,000
Investment	500,000	750,000

Vittorio is considering investing in a labour-saving piece of equipment which will cost $8,000. This will generate an increase in net profit of $1,200 each year for 10 years, after which time the equipment is expected to have no resale value. Vittorio uses straight-line depreciation.

Dugaldo has been offered a replacement oven for one of his existing ones. The existing one is written down in the books to an NBV of $2,000 and is very inefficient. Total costs are $25,000, including maintenance and depreciation.

The replacement will cost $75,000, will have no downtime and negligible maintenance costs in its early years. Depreciation will be 20% p.a. straight-line.

Each oven is estimated to generate $60,000 per year before these costs are considered.

The directors demand a minimum return on capital employed of 12%.

1 **Required**
   What is the current ROI of each division?
   ○ Vittorio 18% and Dugaldo 8%
   ○ Vittorio 18% and Dugaldo 18%
   ○ Vittorio 15% and Dugaldo 8%
   ○ Vittorio 15% and Dugaldo 18%

2 **Required**
   What is the ROI of the new labour-saving equipment Vittorio is considering?
   ○ 18%
   ○ 17.95%
   ○ 15.00%
   ○ 5.00%

3   **Required**

What decision would the manager and the company reach regarding the new equipment?

○   Manager: Accept and Company: Reject

○   Manager: Accept and Company: Accept

○   Manager: Reject and Company: Accept

○   Manager: Reject and Company: Reject

4   **Required**

What is the ROI of the new oven?

○   1750%

○   60%

○   18%

○   15%

5   **Required**

What decision would the manager and the company reach regarding the new oven?

○   Manager: Accept and Company: Reject

○   Manager: Accept and Company: Accept

○   Manager: Reject and Company: Accept

○   Manager: Reject and Company: Reject

6   **Required**

What is the RI of each investment?

○   Vittorio $240 and Dugaldo $1,000

○   Vittorio $960 and Dugaldo $9,000

○   Vittorio $240 and Dugaldo $9,000

○   Vittorio $960 and Dugaldo $1,000

Solution

1

2

3

4

5

6

3 Transfer pricing

Within a decentralised organisation, there may be a division which makes units that are then transferred to another division. It will usually be necessary to charge the receiving division for the goods that it has received in order for **performance to be measured equitably**. The price charged is called a transfer price and it can be calculated in several different ways.

> **Transfer price:** A **transfer price** is the price at which goods or services are transferred from one department to another, or from one member of a group to another.

The transfer pricing policy will have a significant impact on responsibility accounting and performance measurement.

It is vital that the transfer price is carefully selected to ensure all parties act in the best interest of the company. The overriding question should be:

'Whether the transfer is in the company's best interest'

If so, the price charged should ensure that the transfer satisfies the company, the supplying division and the receiving division.

The goals of a transfer pricing system are:

(a) Goal congruence

(b) Equitable performance measurement

(c) Retained divisional autonomy

(d) Motivated divisional managers

(e) Optimum resource allocation

The diagram below shows how two divisions of a company could make decisions that are not in the best interests of the whole company. For example, the Supply division may want to sell their products to external customers as they are willing to pay a higher price than the internal transfer price. The Receive division may be able to source the products cheaper from an external supplier. Overall, these decisions may have negative impacts (both financial and non-financial) on the company as a whole, so a transfer price must be set at a level which satisfies both divisions.

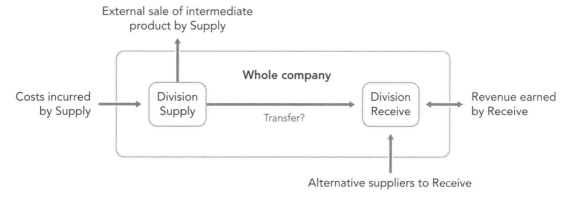

Essential reading

See Chapter 20 Section 3 of the Essential reading for more detail on the problems with transfer pricing.

The Essential reading is available as an Appendix of the digital edition of the Workbook.

3.1 Different approaches to transfer pricing

Method	Impact on selling division	Impact on buying division	Impact on company
Market based	• Earns same profit as external sales • Equitable performance management	• Happy to accept transfer (cannot buy cheaper elsewhere) • Equitable performance management	Goal congruent behaviour should arise
Full cost	No incentive to transfer unless spare capacity	Happy to accept (if less than market price)	May lead to dysfunctional behaviour
Variable cost	No incentive to transfer	Happy to accept	May lead to dysfunctional behaviour
Full cost plus %	Covers all costs and makes a contribution to profit so happy to sell	May not accept as price could be higher than market price	May lead to dysfunctional behaviour
Variable cost plus %	May not cover all fixed costs	Will accept if lower than market price	May lead to dysfunctional behaviour
Head office intervention	Lack of autonomy so demotivating	Lack of autonomy so demotivating	Goal congruent behaviour should arise

3.2 Cost-based approaches to transfer pricing

Problems arise with the use of **cost-based** transfer prices because one party or the other is liable to perceive them as unfair.

Cost-based approaches to transfer pricing are often used in practice, because in practice the following conditions are common:

(a) There is **no external market** for the product that is being transferred.

(b) Alternatively, although there is an external market, it is an **imperfect** one because the market price is affected by factors such as the amount the company setting the transfer price supplies to it, or because there is only a limited external demand.

In either case, there will not be a suitable market price on which to base the transfer price.

3.2.1 Transfer prices based on full cost

Under this approach, the **full cost** (including fixed overheads absorbed) incurred by the supplying division in making the 'intermediate' product is charged to the receiving division. The obvious drawback to this is that the division supplying the product **makes no profit** on its work so is not motivated to supply internally. In addition, there are a number of alternative ways in which fixed costs can be accounted for. If a **full cost-plus** approach is used, a **profit margin** is also included in this transfer price. The supplying division will therefore gain some profit at the expense of the buying division.

3.2.2 Example: Transfer prices based on full cost

Suppose a company has two profit centres: A and B. A can only sell half its maximum output of 800 units externally because of limited demand. It transfers the other half of its output to B which also faces limited demand. Costs and revenues in an accounting period are as follows:

	A	B	Total
	$	$	$
External sales	8,000	24,000	32,000
Costs of production in the division	13,000	10,000	23,000
Profit			9,000

Division A's costs include fixed production overheads of $4,800 and fixed selling and administration costs of $1,000.

There are no opening or closing inventories. It does not matter, for this illustration, whether marginal costing or absorption costing is used.

If the transfer price is at full cost, A in our example would have 'sales' to B of $6,000 (($13,000 – $1,000) x 50%). Selling and administration costs are not included, as these are not incurred on the internal transfers. This would be a cost to B, as follows:

	A	A	B	B	Company as a whole
	$	$	$	$	$
Open market sales		8,000		24,000	32,000
Transfer sales		6,000		–	
Total sales, inc transfers		14,000		24,000	
Transfer costs			6,000		
Own costs	13,000		10,000		23,000
Total costs, inc transfers		13,000		16,000	–
Profit		1,000		8,000	9,000

The **transfer sales of A are self-cancelling with the transfer costs of B** so that total profits **are unaffected by the transfer items**. The transfer price simply spreads the total profit of $9,000 between A and B.

By setting the transfer price at cost, Division A makes no profit on the products they have made, and the manager of Division A would much prefer to sell output on the open market to earn a profit, rather than transfer to B, regardless of whether or not this would be in the best interests of the company as a whole. Division A needs a profit on its transfers to be motivated to supply B; therefore, transfer pricing at cost is inconsistent with the use of a profit centre accounting system.

> **KEY TERM**
>
> **Intermediate product:** An **intermediate product** is one used as a component in another product; for example, car headlights or food additives.

3.2.3 Transfer price at variable cost

A variable cost approach entails charging the variable cost (which we assume to be the same as the marginal cost) that has been incurred by the supplying division to the receiving division.

The problem is that with a transfer price at marginal cost, the **supplying division does not cover its fixed costs**.

Activity 4: Transfer pricing approaches

The Fruity Bakers specialise in making delicious cakes. Their trademark fruit cake is made in Division A (the supplying division) and sold to external customers for them to decorate, or it can be enjoyed plain. It is also transferred to Division B (the receiving division) where it is iced and decorated to be sold as a luxury wedding cake. Fruity Bakers are currently trying to decide what the optimum price to sell the cakes from Division A to B should be in order to motivate the managers of both divisions. The following data shows the costs incurred by Division A to make a fruit cake and by Division B to ice and decorate the wedding cake:

		$/unit
Division A	Variable costs	20.00
	Fixed overhead	8.00
		28.00
Division B	Variable costs	40.00
	Fixed overhead	5.00
		45.00

- Plain fruit cakes can be sold and purchased externally for $30.
- Wedding cakes can be sold for $100.

1 Required

Should the company make the fruit cakes internally or buy them in?

2 Required

What non-financial factors should also be taken into consideration?

3 Required

What would be the implication of using the following transfer pricing policies?

(a) Full cost plus 10%

(b) Variable cost plus 55%

(c) Variable cost only

(d) The external market price

Solution

1

2

3

An opportunity cost based approach is the optimum approach to setting transfer prices.

Minimum transfer price	Maximum transfer price	
Variable cost	Lower of:	External market price or Divisional new revenue
+		
Opportunity cost		

Where the supplying division has **spare capacity**, the opportunity cost of transferring units internally is nil as there is no external market for the additional units.

Where the supplying division is at **full capacity**, the opportunity cost will be the **lost contribution** from the other sales.

Opportunity cost based approaches should always result in **goal congruent** behaviour with both buyer and seller happy to transfer when it is in the group's best interest to do so.

Activity 5: Spare and full capacity

1 It has now been identified that Division A also makes excellent sponge cakes. These are sold externally only. The bakers can make either 100 fruit cakes per month or 800 sponge cakes per month or any combination of the two. The following information is available:

	Fruit cake $/Unit	Sponge cake $/Unit
Selling price	30	10
Variable costs	(20)	(6)
Fixed overheads	(8)	(2)
Profit	2	2
Labour hours per cake	2	0.25

Required

Using the above information, provide advice on the determination of an appropriate transfer price and provide a reasoned recommendation of a policy. The Fruity Bakers should adopt for the transfer of fruit cakes from Division A to Division B in the following conditions:

(a) When Division A has spare capacity and limited external demand for sponge cakes

(b) When Division A is operating at full capacity with unsatisfied external demand for sponge cakes

Solution

1

Illustration 1: Minimum and maximum transfer prices

Division X produces three products: A, B and C. Each product has an external market, but B can also be transferred to Division Y.

After incurring extra costs of $60, Division Y then sells the unit for $300.

The maximum quantity that might be required for transfer is 150 units of B.

Information on the products is as follows:

	A	B	C
External market price per unit	$150	$200	$140
Variable production cost per unit	$86	$95	$83
Labour hours required per unit	4	6	3
Maximum external sales, in units	2,000	1,250	2,400

In the current period, labour hours in division X are limited to 20,000, and this is insufficient to satisfy maximum external demand.

Therefore, using limiting factor analysis, the optimal production plan has been calculated as:

	A	B	C
Contribution per unit	$64	$105	$57
Labour hours required	4	6	3
∴ Contribution per hour	$16	$17.50	$19
Ranking	3rd	2nd	1st

∴ Optimal Production Plan

Product	Units	Hours/unit	Hours
C	2,400	3	7,200
B	1,250	6	7,500
A (balance)	1,325	4	5,300
			20,000

Required

Given that Division X is operating at full capacity, what are the minimum and maximum transfer prices that could be used for Product B?

O   Minimum $191 - Maximum $200

O   Minimum $105 - Maximum $200

O   Minimum $191 - Maximum $210

O   Minimum $105 - Maximum $210

Solution

The correct answer is:

Minimum $191 - Maximum $200

If labour is diverted for the transfer, hours will come from Product A which is earning contribution of $16 per hour.

Minimum transfer price:

	$
Variable unit cost of Product B	95
Opportunity cost of Product A 6 hrs × $16	96
	191

Maximum transfer price:

Maximum transfer price:	$
Lower of : external market price	200
: divisional net revenue	240
	$200

3.3 What to look for in exam questions

Checklist of things to look out for in exam questions:

- Impact on both divisions and the company as a whole
- Capacity issues
- Opportunity costs
- Remember the current situation does not always result in goal congruent behaviour!

Chapter summary

Divisional performance and transfer pricing

Divisionalisation

Decentralisation
- Decisions taken more quickly
- Increased motivation of management
- Increased quality of decisions due to local knowledge
- Potential for dysfunctional decision making
- Duplication amongst divisions leading to greater cost

Conditions for a good performance measure
- Must produce goal congruence
- Only include factors for which manager can be held accountable
- Recognise long-term objectives as well as short-term

Responsibility accounting
- Cost centre
- Revenue centre
- Profit centre
- Investment centre (ROI and RI)

Investment centres

Return on investment (ROI)
- ROI = divisional profit (PBIT)/ divisional investment
- Only projects which increase the existing ROI should be undertaken
- Problems with ROI
  - Dysfunctional behaviour
  - The ratio will be distorted by the age of the assets
  - Profit can be manipulated

Residual income (RI)
- RI = divisional profit (PBIT) - imputed interest
- Imputed interest = divisional investment × cost of capital
- Projects with a positive residual income should be undertaken
- Problems with RI
  - The ratio will be distorted by the age of the assets
  - Profit can be manipulated
  - Gives an absolute number

Transfer pricing

Different approaches to transfer pricing
- Market based
  - Selling division gets same profit on internal and external sales
  - Buying division pays a commercial price (possibly less savings in selling and distribution)
  - Equitable performance measurement for both divisions
- Opportunity cost
  - Minimum acceptable to seller: Marginal cost + opportunity cost
  - Maximum payable by buyer: External market price
- Cost based

Cost-based approaches to transfer pricing
- Full cost plus
  - Covers all costs
  - Seller encouraged to make transfer
  - Buyer may wish to buy externally
- Variable cost plus
  - Selling division does not cover all costs
  - Buyer encouraged to make transfer

What to look for in exam questions
- Impact on both divisions and the company as a whole
- Capacity issues
- Opportunity costs
- Remember the current situation does not always result in goal congruent behaviour

Knowledge diagnostic

1. Divisionalisation

A good performance measure should be one that drives **goal congruence**, measures managers only on those items that they can **control** and recognises **long-term** as well as short-term objectives.

2. Investment centres

Performance measures need to reflect not just profit but also the investment made to generate that profit.

ROI is the most commonly used measure within a decentralised business but can result in dysfunctional behaviour.

3. Transfer pricing

Within a decentralised business it may be necessary to set transfer prices when goods are transferred between divisions. Transfer prices can be set on the basis of cost, market price or opportunity cost.

Cost based transfer prices are most likely to result in dysfunctional behaviour.

Further study guidance

Question practice

Now try the following from the Further question practice bank [available in the digital edition of the Workbook]:

Number	Level	Marks	Approximate time
Section A Q58	Examination	2	4 mins
Section A Q59	Examination	2	4 mins
Section C Q6	Examination	20	36 mins

Further reading

There are two technical articles available on ACCA's website, called *Transfer pricing* and *Decentralisation and the need for performance measurement*.

You are strongly advised to read these articles in full as part of your preparation for the PM exam.

Activity answers

Activity 1: Investment centres

The correct answer is:

(a), (b) and (d)

The manager of an investment centre will have control over all the income and expenditure and investment decisions within that division; they will not however be able to control expenses incurred centrally.

Activity 2: Measuring performance

The correct answer is:

ROI because it takes into consideration the fact that Dugaldo has more investment than Vittorio

ROI would be more equitable as it is a relative measure, and takes into consideration the differing sizes of the alternative investments.

Activity 3: ROI and RI

1   **The correct answer is:**

Vittorio 18% and Dugaldo 18%

Vittorio: Current ROI = 90,000 / 500,000 = 18%

Dugaldo: Current ROI = 135,000 / 750,000 = 18%

2   **The correct answer is:**

ROI of new equipment = 1,200 / 8,000 = 15%

3   **The correct answer is:**

Manager: Reject and Company: Accept

The return of the labour-saving equipment is less than current (18%) so the manager would turn it down.

However, 15% is better than the company's minimum required return of 12% so the company would want to accept it.

This is an example of dysfunctional decision-making caused by the chosen performance measure.

4   **The correct answer is:**

60%

ROI of replacement oven = (60,000 - 15,000) / 75,000 = 60%

5   **The correct answer is:**

Manager: Reject and Company: Accept

ROI of current oven = (60,000 - 25,000) / 2,000 = 1750%

Replacement is not as good as current so Dugaldo's manager would reject it.

Since 60% > 12%, the company would want to accept the replacement oven. Again, this is another example of dysfunctional decision-making.

6   **The correct answer is:**

Vittorio $240 and Dugaldo $1,000

Vittorio:

		$
Cost saving (profit) of proposal	=	1,200
Imputed interest = 12% × 8,000	=	(960)
Residual income	(Positive so accept)	240

Dugaldo:

Profit from proposal = (60,000 − 15,000) =		45,000
Existing profit = (60,000 − 25,000) =		35,000
Incremental profit		10,000
Imputed interest = 12% × 75,000		(9,000)
Incremental RI	(Positive so accept)	1,000

Activity 4: Transfer pricing approaches

1 **The correct answer is:**

Cost to buy in $30.

Variable cost to make internally $20.

Therefore, it is $10 cheaper for the company to make the fruit cakes internally.

2 **The correct answer is:**

Non-financial factors:

- Quality/taste/appearance of bought cakes
- Unsatisfied customer demand due to capacity constraints

3 **The correct answer is:**

	Transfer price	Division A (selling)	Division B (receiving)	Result
(i)	Full cost plus 10% – $30.80	Happy to supply as covers all costs and makes contribution to profit	Would prefer to buy externally as can be purchased for $30.	Dysfunctional behaviour may arise
(ii)	Variable cost plus 55% – $31	Happy to supply as covers all costs and makes contribution to profit	Would prefer to buy externally as can be purchased for $30.	Dysfunctional behaviour may arise
(iii)	Variable cost only – $20	No incentive to transfer	Happy to buy as cannot source cheaper	Dysfunctional behaviour may arise
(iv)	External market price – $30	Happy to supply	Happy to buy	Cheaper to transfer internally than buy externally (part (a)). There may even be savings from transferring internally.

Activity 5: Spare and full capacity

1 **The correct answer is:**

(a) Spare capacity = no opportunity cost

The minimum transfer price is variable cost + lost contribution $20 + $0 and the maximum transfer price is $30.

(b)

	Fruit cake	Sponge cake
Contribution $	10	4
Hours	2	0.25

Contribution/hr $	5	16
Rank	2	1

Variable cost + lost contribution

$20 + (2 × $16) = $52

The company can buy fruit cakes in for $30 or make them internally at a cost of $52. Thus, the optimal policy is to buy the fruit cakes externally for $30 from the external market and use the capacity in Division A to make sponge cakes to sell externally.

Skills checkpoint 5

Performance management questions

Chapter overview

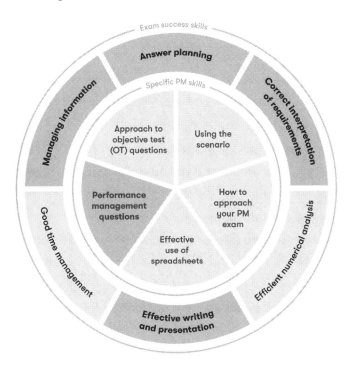

Introduction

The exam name is Performance Management. It therefore makes sense that applying the concepts of performance management to a business is likely to feature in a scenario-based (Section C) question. Sometimes the requirements in these questions can seem vague, for example: 'appraise the performance of the company'. In the performance management questions, you need to ensure that you apply your answer to the scenario (Skill 2). Like the other syllabus scenario-based questions, you must relate your answer to the scenario, and we recommend using the PEA approach. This involves making a **p**oint, P, **e**xplaining why it is relevant, E, **a**nd applying it to the scenario, A. It is important to spend time digesting the requirement and planning your answer before you start your writing.

When you are assessing the financial performance, you must ensure that you do more than calculate ratios.

Performance management questions

A step-by-step technique for ensuring that your performance management questions are answered in a way that makes reference to the scenario and the relevant theory is outlined below. Each step will be explained in more detail in the following sections and illustrated by answering a requirement from a past exam question.

> **STEP 1:**
> Allow some of your allotted time for analysing the scenario and the requirements.
> Don't rush into starting to write your answer.

> **STEP 2:**
> Prepare an answer plan using key words from the requirements as headings (eg a
> bullet-pointed list). You can then use these headings in your answer.

> **STEP 3:**
> As you write your answer, use the PEA approach. Firstly, make your point, secondly
> explain what you mean and why it is relevant and finally apply it to the scenario.
> Start each explanation in a new paragraph.

Exam success skills

The following illustration is based on an extract from a past exam question, about a hairdressing salon, called 'Oliver's Salon'. This extract was worth 17 marks.

For this question, we will also focus on the following **exam success skills:**

- **Managing information.** It is easy for the amount of information contained in scenario-based questions to feel overwhelming. To manage this, focus on the requirement first – noting the key exam verbs to ensure you answer the question properly. Then read the rest of the question, noting important and relevant information from the scenario.

- **Correct interpretation of requirements.** Parts (b) and (c) are looking for an assessment of the performance of the company, from both financial and non-financial perspectives.

- **Answer planning.** Everyone will have a preferred style for an answer plan. For example, it may be a mind map, bullet-pointed lists, or simply making notes. Choose the approach that you feel most comfortable with or, if you are not sure, try out different approaches for different questions until you have found your preferred style.

- **Effective writing and presentation.** It is often helpful to use key words from the requirement as headings in your answer. You may also wish to use sub-headings in your answer. You could use a separate sub-heading for each paragraph from the scenario that contains an issue for discussion. Underline or embolden your headings and sub-headings, and use full sentences, ensuring your style is professional.

Skill activity

STEP 1 Allow some of your allotted time for analysing the scenario and requirements; don't rush into starting to write your answer.

Start by analysing the requirements so that you know what you are looking for when you read the scenario.

(a) **Assess the financial performance of the salon using the data above. (11 marks)**

(b) **Analyse and comment on the non-financial performance of Oliver's business, under the headings of quality and resource utilisation. (6 marks)**

The first key action verb is 'assess'. This is defined by the ACCA as: 'Judge the worth, importance, evaluate or estimate the nature, quality, ability, extent or significance'. This means that you must determine the strengths, weaknesses, importance, significance and ability to contribute.

These requirements are worth 17 marks and at 1.8 minutes a mark, they should take 30.6 minutes.

Part (b) appears vague, but these requirements are common in PM exams, so you need to be prepared for such requirements and a have a plan about how to approach them.

Oliver's salon (17 marks)

Oliver is the owner and manager of Oliver's Salon which is a quality hairdresser that experiences high levels of competition. The salon traditionally provided a range of hair services to female clients only, including cuts, colouring and straightening.

A year ago, at the start of his 20X9 financial year, Oliver decided to expand his operations to include the hairdressing needs of male clients. Male hairdressing prices are lower, the work simpler (mainly haircuts only) and so the time taken per male client is much less.

The prices for the female clients were not increased during the whole of 20X8 and 20X9 and the mix of services provided for female clients in the two years was the same.

The latest financial results are as follows:

	20X8 $	20X8 $	20X9 $	20X9 $
Sales		200,000		238,500
Less cost of sales:				
Hairdressing staff costs	65,000		91,000	
Hair products – female	29,000		27,000	
Hair products – male	–		8,000	
		94,000		126,000
Gross profit		106,000		112,500
Less expenses:				
Rent	10,000		10,000	
Administration salaries	9,000		9,500	
Electricity	7,000		8,000	
Advertising	2,000		5,000	
Total expenses		28,000		32,500
Profit		78,000		80,000

Oliver is disappointed with his financial results. He thinks the salon is much busier than a year ago and was expecting more profit. He has noted the following extra information.

Some female clients complained about the change in atmosphere following the introduction of male services, which created tension in the salon.

Two new staff were recruited at the start of 20X9. The first was a junior hairdresser to support the specialist hairdressers for the female clients. She was appointed on a salary of $9,000 per annum. The second new staff member was a specialist hairdresser for the male clients. There were no increases in pay for existing staff at the start of 20X9 after a big rise at the start of 20X8 which was designed to cover two years' worth of increases.

Oliver introduced some non-financial measures of success two years ago.

	20X8	20X9
Number of complaints	12	46
Number of male client visits	0	3,425
Number of female client visits	8,000	6,800
Number of specialist hairdressers for female clients	4	5
Number of specialist hairdressers for male clients	0	1

STEP 2 Now you should be ready to prepare an answer plan using key words from the requirements as headings. This could take the form of a bullet-pointed list.

Complete your answer plan by working through each paragraph of the scenario identifying specific points that are relevant to the requirement to make sure you generate enough points to score a pass mark (ACCA marking guides typically allocate 1–2 marks per relevant well-explained point).

Completed answer plan

Having worked through each paragraph, an answer plan can now be completed. A possible answer plan is shown here.

Part (b)	Ideas
Assess financial performance. Use the information in the financial results to form the structure of the answer. You will need to make a judgment as to which are most significant and therefore require the most detail.	Financial results: **Sales:** Growth % Male vs female revenue stream **Gross margin** Margin vs prior year Reason Male vs female revenue stream **Rent:** No change **Advertising spend:** % change Impact **Staff costs:** % change compared to sales growth **Electricity:** % change Reasons **Net profit:** % increase compared to increase in sales Comment

Part (c)	Ideas
Analyse and comment on non-financial performance measures	Quality*: Complaints – number and per visit Suggest reasons for changes **Resource utilisation:** Salon Staff Relate to complaints

* These headings were given in the requirement - make sure you use them in your answer.

STEP 3 As you write your answer, use the PEA approach. Firstly, make your point, secondly explain what you mean and why it is relevant and finally apply it to the scenario. Start each explanation in a new paragraph. Ensure that you do more than just calculate ratios to assess performance.

Required

Suggested solution

(a) Financial measures[7]

Financial performance

Sales growth

Sales have grown[8] by 19.25% (($238,500 – $200,000)/$200,000 × 100%) from 20X8 to 20X9. This is

[7] Use the headings in the financial information to give your answer structure.

[8] Make the point - Sales have grown.

particularly impressive as Oliver's Salon experiences high levels of competition.

This[9] growth has come from the new **male hairdressing** part of the business, as female sales have fallen by 15% (($200,000 − $170,000)/$200,000 × 100%). There was **no price increase** during this time, so this fall is due to fewer female client visits.

[9] Apply back to information from scenario that supports the point.

Gross profit

The gross profit margin in 20X8 was 53% ($106,000/$200,000 × 100%) and in 20X9 had **fallen** to 47.2% ($112,500/$238,500 × 100%). This is predominantly due to a 40% increase (($91,000 − $65,000)/$65,000 × 100%) in **staff costs** as a result of the recruitment of two new staff.

The new specialist hairdresser for male clients is on a salary of $17,000 ($91,000 − $65,000 − $9,000) whereas the female hairdressers were paid an average of $16,250 ($65,000/4) in 20X8.

However[10], it is the **female client** business which has been responsible for the drop in gross profit margin.

[10] Numbers can be used to support answer, but will not be sufficient to score enough marks to pass.

	20X8 Female $	20X9 Female $	20X9 Male $
Sales	200,000	170,000	68,500
Less cost of sales:			
Hairdressing staff	(65,000)	(74,000)	(17,000)
Hair products – female	(29,000)	(27,000)	
Hair products – male			(8,000)
Gross profit	106,000	69,000	43,500
Gross profit margin	106/200 × 100% = 53%	69/170 × 100% = 40.6%	43.5/68.5 × 100% = 63.5%

The gross profit margin from male clients is higher than for female clients.

Rent

This has not changed so is a **fixed cost** at the moment[11].

[11] Can still earn marks for obvious statements if explain what it means/why it is important.

Administration salaries

These have increased by only 5.6% (($9,500 − $9,000)/$9,000 × 100%) which is impressive given the expansion in the business.

This has increased by 14.3% (($8,000 − $7,000)/$7,000 × 100%. More clients would involve more electricity, so it is a semi-variable cost. There may also have been a general increase in electricity prices, which would be beyond the control of Oliver.

Advertising

This has increased by 150% (($5,000 − $2,000)/$2,000 × 100%) which could be expected at the launch of a new service. Provided the advertising has generated new clients, it should not be a cause for concern.

Net profit

Net profit has only increased by 2.6% (($80,000 − $78,000/$78,000 × 100%) which is disappointing compared to a 19.25% increase in sales.

(b) Non-financial performance

Quality

has increased significantly by 283% ((46 − 12)/12 × 100%). This is not just due to the increase in client numbers.

Complaints per customer visit have increased from 0.15% (12/8,000 × 100%) to 0.44%. This is a cause for concern in a service business, especially as many customers will not actually complain but will just not come back.

The complaints could be from the new male clients who are not happy with the new hairdresser, or they could be from female clients who do not like having men in the salon. More information is needed and action to be taken to reduce the complaints.

Resource utilisation

The resources[14] in Oliver's Salon are the **salon** itself and the **staff.** The salon is being utilised more as a result of the increase in clients from 8,000 in 20X8 to 10,225 (6,800 + 3,425) in 20X9. This is a 27.8% ((10,225 − 8,000)/8,000 × 100%) increase. This increase in

[14] Consider what the resources are and how changes in sales would affect them.

utilisation has not however resulted in a proportionate increase in profit.

The **female specialist hairdressers** served 2,000 (8,000/4) clients per specialist in 20X8 and this fell to 1,360 (6,800/5) in 20X9, following the recruitment of two new staff. Oliver may be prepared to accept this reduction in resource utilisation in order to boost service levels and reduce complaints.

This contrasts with the higher figure of 3,425 clients per **male specialist** in 20X9. The time taken per male client is much less, so this should be expected.

Exam success skills diagnostic

Every time you complete a question, use the diagnostic below to assess how effectively you demonstrated the exam success skills in answering the question. The table has been completed below for the Oliver's Salon activity to give you an idea of how to complete the diagnostic.

Exam success skills	Your reflections/observations
Managing information	Did you identify the relevant financial information to include in your assessment of the financial performance of Oliver's Salon in part (b)?
Correct interpretation of requirements	Did you identify that part (b) was about **financial** performance only?
	Did you identify that part (c) was about **non-financial** performance only and should consider both **quality** and **resource utilisation**?
Answer planning	Did you draw up an answer plan using your preferred approach (eg mind map, bullet-pointed list)?
	Did your plan help to create a structure for your answer?
Effective writing and presentation	Did you use headings (key words from requirements)?
	Did you use full sentences?
	And most importantly – did you explain why your points related to the scenario?
Most important action points to apply to your next question	

The exam is called Performance Measurement and it is therefore likely that you will have to assess the performance of an organisation. Although you cannot prepare for every organisation, you can equip yourself with the skills to attempt performance management questions, by using the information given in the question to guide the structure of your answer. A key skill is then applying this back to the given scenario. You will not be able to pass these questions by just calculating ratios from a list. It is therefore essential that you try to create a practical answer that is relevant to the scenario, and/or addresses the issues identified in the scenario, instead of simply calculating rote-learned ratios.

As you move into practising questions as part of your final revision, you will need to practise taking in information from a scenario quickly (using active reading), accurately understanding the requirements, and creating an answer plan and a final answer that addresses the requirements in the context of the scenario.

Performance management question preparation is like preparing for your driving test. You cannot practise on every road, but you can equip yourself with the skills to deal with any road layout you face in your test through lots of practice.

21

Further aspects of performance management

Learning objectives

On competition of this chapter, you should be able to:

	Syllabus reference no.
Comment on the problems of having non-quantifiable objectives in performance management.	E3 (a)
Comment on the problems of having multiple objectives in this sector.	E3 (b)
Explain how performance could be measured in this sector.	E3 (c)
Outline value for money (VFM) as a public sector objective.	E3 (d)
Describe, calculate and interpret non-financial performance indicators (NFPIs) and suggest methods to improve the performance indicated.	E3 (e)
Discuss the difficulties of target setting in qualitative areas.	E3 (f)
Analyse past performance and suggest ways for improving financial and non-financial performance	E3 (g)
Explain the causes and problems created by short-termism and financial manipulation of results and suggest methods to encourage a long-term view.	E3 (h)
Explain the need to allow for external considerations in performance management, including stakeholders, market conditions and allowance for competitors.	E4 (a)
Suggest ways in which external considerations could be allowed for in performance management.	E4 (b)
Interpret performance in the light of external considerations.	E4 (c)

Exam context

This final chapter on performance measurement looks at performance analysis in not for profit organisations and the public sector. The problems of having non-quantifiable and multiple objectives are discussed. We then go on to consider how external considerations are allowed for in performance measurement.

Scenarios in your exam may relate to not for profit organisations and the public sector and you need to understand their particular needs and issues. Always apply your answers to the specific organisation.

Chapter overview

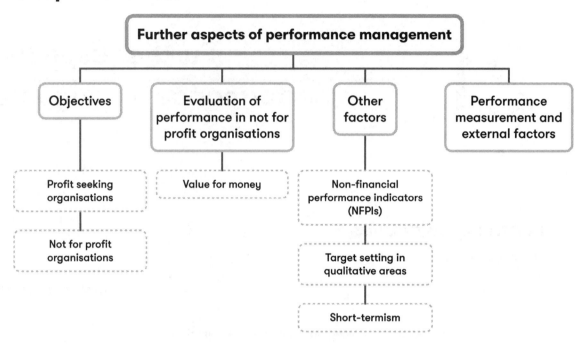

1 Objectives

1.1 Profit seeking organisations

Primary objective

- Maximise the wealth of owners (shareholders) of the business - (equity)

Secondary objectives might be

- Ensure survival
- Provide a quality product/service (customer satisfaction)
- Be a good corporate citizen (health and safety/environment)
- Create wealth/benefits for management/employees
- Secure competitive advantage and grow market share

The objective of profit or wealth maximisation is thus modified to meet the needs of different interest groups (stakeholders).

1.2 Not for profit organisations (NFPOs)

A major problem with many not for profit organisations (NFPOs), particularly government bodies, is that it is extremely **difficult to define their objectives** at all. In addition, they tend to have **multiple objectives,** so that even if they could all be clearly identified it is impossible to say which is the **overriding** objective.

Public sector organisations

Primary objective might be:

- Provision of a quality product/service within a value for money framework

Secondary objectives might be:

- Be a good corporate citizen (health and safety/environment)
- Adopt an ethical social stance in decision-making
- Create wealth/benefit for management/employees
- Earn sufficient profits to provide for future capital investment and perhaps provide a surplus for the exchequer

Other NFPOs

Primary objective might be:

- Provision of a social or community service for the wellbeing of society

Secondary objectives might be:

- Be a good corporate citizen (health and safety/environment)
- Adopt an ethical social stance in decision-making
- Increase wealth/benefit for management/employees

Activity 1: Objectives

1 Required

What objectives might the following NFPOs have?

(a) An army

(b) A local council

(c) A charity

(d) A political party

(e) A college

Solution

1

More general objectives for NFPOs include:

- Surplus maximisation (equivalent to profit maximisation)
- Revenue maximisation (as for a commercial business)
- Usage maximisation (as in leisure centre swimming pool usage)
- Usage targeting (matching the capacity available)
- Full/partial cost recovery (minimising subsidy)
- Budget maximisation (maximising what is offered)
- Producer satisfaction maximisation (satisfying the wants of staff and volunteers)
- Client satisfaction maximisation (the police generating the support of the public)

1.2.1 Non-quantifiable objectives

It is difficult to judge whether **non-quantifiable objectives** have been met. For example, assessing whether a charity has improved the situation of those benefiting from its activities is difficult to research.

Essential reading

See Chapter 21 Section 1 of the Essential reading for more detail on the problems with performance measurement of NFPOs.

The Essential reading is available as an Appendix of the digital edition of the Workbook.

2 Evaluation of performance in not for profit organisations

NFPOs and public sector organisations will **not have wealth maximisation** as a primary objective. However, they will still have strategic objectives (albeit non-financial) and stakeholders (clients, members etc), who will wish to measure their performance.

Activity 2: Suitable performance measures

Required

Which THREE of the following would be suitable performance measures for ensuring that a hospital is achieving its objectives?

- ○ Incidents of abuse against staff
- ○ Death rates
- ○ Re-admission rates
- ○ Use of agency staff
- ○ Number of cases of flu reported

Solution

2.1 Value for money

One of the ways that performance can be measured in public sector organisations is to prove that they operate economically, efficiently and effectively and achieve **value for money** as part of the continuing process of good management.

> **Value for money (VFM): Value for money (VFM)** means providing a service in a way which is economical, efficient and effective.

- **Economy** (spending money frugally)
- **Efficiency** (getting out as much as possible for what goes in)
- **Effectiveness** (getting done, by means of the above, what was supposed to be done)

These are sometimes referred to as the 3Es. More formal definitions are as follows:

> **Economy: Economy** is attaining the appropriate quantity and quality of inputs at the lowest cost.
>
> **Efficiency: Efficiency** is the relationship between inputs and outputs.
>
> **Effectiveness: Effectiveness** is the relationship between an organisation's outputs and its objectives.

Illustration 1: Value for money

1 Imagine a bottle of washing up liquid for cleaning dishes. We'll call it Angeldishes. The advertising says Angeldishes is good 'value for money' because it washes twice as many plates as any other washing up liquid. Bottle for bottle it may be more expensive, but plate for plate it is cheaper. Not only this, but Angeldishes gets plates 'squeaky' clean. To summarise, Angeldishes gives us VFM because it exhibits the following characteristics:

- **Economy** (more clean plates per $ spent)
- **Efficiency** (more clean plates per squirt)
- **Effectiveness** (plates as clean as they should be)

Solution

1 The correct answer is:

Activity 3: Effectiveness

Required
Which TWO of the following performance measures would be appropriate for measuring effectiveness for a public sector higher education college?

O Teaching hours per student

O Sourcing lecturers of appropriate quality at an acceptable cost

O Percentage of graduates employed within 12 months of the course ending

O Percentage of students achieving target pass rates

Solution

Essential reading

See Chapter 21 Section 2 of the Essential reading for more detail on the 3Es.

The Essential reading is available as an Appendix of the digital edition of the Workbook.

3 Other factors

3.1 Non-financial performance indicators (NFPIs)

In Chapter 19 Section 4, we covered NFPIs and their value. These aspects can be applied to the public sector also. As with profit-seeking businesses, NFPOs can measure quality, efficiency, delivery, reliability, customer satisfaction and innovation. VFM and the 3Es include performance measures which are non-financial.

> ### Exam focus point
>
> Performance management questions regularly appear as a constructed response question in the exam. Therefore, you must be comfortable discussing this area and applying your knowledge to the scenario in the question. You may be given numbers relating to financial or non-financial indicators and you must be able to talk about them. The examining team have said that subtracting one number from another is not enough to earn a calculation mark. For example, if the number of complaints received one year was 50 and the next year was 60, it would not be sufficient to simply say that there were 10 more complaints in the second year. You must state the percentage increase in complaints in order to earn marks, which is this case would be a 20% increase ([(60-50)/50] × 100) (ACCA, 2017).

3.2 Target setting in qualitative areas

In Chapter 19 Section 9 we discussed the difficulties of measuring non-financial aspects of performance. The same problems arise for not for profit and public sector organisations. Problems include:

- Selecting a suitable measure for performance,
- Having data which by its very nature is not quantified
- A lack of system for collecting data about qualitative areas

3.3 Short-termism and manipulation

In Chapter 19 Section 5 we discussed how organisations often make a trade-off between short-term and long-term objectives. This applies to not for profit and public sector organisations too.

4 Performance measurement and external factors

When devising performance measures for any organisation, consideration needs to be given to three key external factors:

- Stakeholders
- Economic environment
- Competition

> **Stakeholders: Stakeholders** are groups of people or individuals who have a legitimate interest in the activities of an organisation. They include customers, employees, the community, shareholders, suppliers and lenders.

Stakeholders can be broken down into three key groups:

- **Internal**   – such as employees
- **Connected**   – shareholders, customers, suppliers
- **External**   – community and the Government

There will often be a conflict between the stakeholder objectives. For example, shareholders want larger returns whereas employees want pay rises. Performance measures need to be considered carefully. A suitable measure in this case might be performance related pay.

Essential reading

See Chapter 21 Section 3 of the Essential reading for more detail on stakeholders, the economic environment and competition.

The Essential reading is available as an Appendix of the digital edition of the Workbook.

Chapter summary

```
┌─────────────────────────────────────────────────────┐
│      Further aspects of performance management        │
└─────────────────────────────────────────────────────┘
```

Objectives

Profit seeking organisations

Maximise shareholder wealth

Not for profit organisations

- Difficult to define objectives
- Tend to have multiple objectives
- Difficult to judge whether non-quantifiable objectives have been met

Evaluation of performance in not for profit organisations

Value for money

- Providing a service in a way which is economical, efficient and effective
- Economy (spending money frugally)
- Efficiency (getting out as much as possible for what goes in)
- Effectiveness (getting done, by means of the above, what was supposed to be done)

Other factors

Non-financial performance indicators (NFPIs)

Quality, efficiency, delivery, reliability, customer satisfaction, innovation

Target setting in qualitative areas

- Problems include:
  - Difficulty selecting a suitable measure for performance
  - Having data which by its very nature is not quantified
  - A lack of system for collecting data about qualitative areas

Short-termism

A bias towards short-term rather than long-term performance

Performance measurement and external factors

- Stakeholders
- Economic environment
- Competition

Knowledge diagnostic

1. Objectives

Performance measurement in public sector or not for profit (NFP) organisations can be difficult as they often have **multiple objectives** and these are often hard to quantify and measure

2. Value for money

There are a range of problems in measuring the performance of NFP organisations.

Performance is judged in terms of inputs and outputs, hence the **value for money criteria** of **economy, efficiency** and **effectiveness.**

3. Other factors

NFPIs can usefully be applied to **employees** and product/service **quality.**

Short-termism is when there is a bias towards short-term rather than long-term performance. It is often due to the fact that managers' performance is measured on short-term results.

4. External considerations

Performance management needs to allow for **external considerations** including stakeholders, market conditions and allowance for competitors.

Further study guidance

Question practice

Now try the following from the Further question practice bank (available in the digital edition of the Workbook):

Number	Level	Marks	Approximate time
Section A Q60	Examination	2	4 mins
Section A Q61	Examination	2	4 mins
Section A Q62	Examination	2	4 mins
Section C Q7	Examination	20	36 mins

Further reading

There is a two-part technical article available on ACCA's website, called *Not for profit organisations*.

You are strongly advised to read these articles in full as part of your preparation for the PM exam.

Activity answers

Activity 1: Objectives

1 The correct answer is:

Here are some suggestions:

(a) To defend a country

(b) To provide services for local people (such as the elderly)

(c) To help others/protect the environment

(d) To gain power/enact legislation

(e) To provide education

Activity 2: Suitable performance measures

The correct answers are:

- Death rates
- Re-admission rates
- Use of agency staff

Whilst a hospital management team would be concerned about abuse against staff it is not directly linked to its primary objective. The primary objective will be centred around improving health and life expectancy as efficiently as possible; therefore the other measures would be appropriate. The numbers of cases of flu reported is not within the hospital's control and would therefore not be an appropriate performance measure.

Activity 3: Effectiveness

The correct answers are:

- Percentage of graduates employed within 12 months of the course ending
- Percentage of students achieving target pass rates

Securing appropriate staff who represent good value for money would be an economy measure, whilst teaching hours per student would be an efficiency measure. Pass rates are only part of the story regarding effectiveness as employability following the course will also be important to students and potential students.

Appendix 1: Exam formulae

Demand curve

P = a -bQ

b = Change in price / Change in quantity

a = price when Q = 0

MR = a - 2bQ

Learning curve

$Y = ax^b$

Where   Y   = the cumulative average time per unit to produce X units

        a   = the time taken for the first unit of output

        x   = the cumulative number of units

        b   = the index of learning (log LR/log 2)

        LR   = the learning rate as a decimal

Index

Y

Yield variance, 343

Bibliography

Anthony, R. N. (1965) *Planning and control systems: A framework for analysis*, 1st edition. Boston, Division of Research, Harvard Business School.

Bennett, P. and James, P. (2000) *The green bottom line: environmental accounting for management: current practice and future trends*, 2nd edition. Sheffield, Greenleaf Publishing Limited.

Big data: are we making a big mistake? *Financial Times (2014)*. [Online] https://www.ft.com/content/21a6e7d8-b479-11e3-a09a-00144feabdc0 [Accessed 25 September 2019].

Cooper, R. (1990a) Cost classifications in unit-based and activity-based manufacturing cost systems, Journal of Cost Management, Fall, 4-14

DHL, (December 2013). *Big Data in Logistics: A DHL perspective on how to move beyond the hype.* [Online] Available from: http://www.dhl.com/content/dam/downloads/g0/about_us/innovation/CSI_Studie_BIG_DATA.pdf [Accessed 13 September 2019]

Drury, C. (2005) *Management and cost accounting*, 6th edition. London, Thomson Learning.

Drury, C., Braund, S., Osborne, P. and Tayles, M. (1993) A survey of management accounting practices in UK manufacturing companies, ACCA Research Paper, Chartered Association of Certified Accountants

Fitzgerald, L. and Moon, P. (1996) *Performance measurement in service industries: Making it work.* 1st edition. Chartered Institute of Management Accountants.

Goldratt, E.M. and Cox, J. (1992) *The Goal.* 2nd edition. London, Gower Publishing Ltd.

Gray, R.H. and Bebbington, J. (2001) *Accounting for the environment*, 2nd edition. London, SAGE publications Ltd.

Hope, J. and Fraser, R. (2003) *Beyond Budgeting*, 1st edition. Harvard Business School Publishing Corporation.

Kotler, P. and Armstrong, G. (2010) *Principles of Marketing.* 13th edition. London, Pearson Education Ltd

McKinsey & Company (2011). *Big data: The next frontier for innovation, competition, and productivity.* [Online] Available from: http://www.mckinsey.com/business-functions/business-technology/our-insights/big-data-the-next-frontier-for-innovation [Accessed 13 September 2019]

United States Environmental Protection Agency (1995) *An introduction to environmental accounting as a business management tool* [Online]. Available from: https://archive.epa.gov/parchive/web/pdf/busmgt.pdf [Accessed 25 September 2019].

Review form – ACCA Performance Management (PM)

Name: _____

Address: _____

_____

_____

How have you used this Workbook?
(Tick one box only)

☐ Home study (book only)

☐ On a course: college _____

☐ With 'correspondence' package

☐ Other _____

Why did you decide to purchase this Workbook?
(Tick one box only)

☐ Have used other BPP products in the past

☐ Recommendation by friend/colleague

☐ Recommendation by a lecturer at college

☐ Saw advertising

☐ Other _____

During the past six months do you recall seeing/ receiving either of the following?
(Tick as many boxes as are relevant)

☐ Our advertisement in *Student Accountant*

☐ Our advertisement in *Pass*

☐ Our advertisement in *PQ*

☐ Our brochure with a letter through the post

☐ Our website www.bpp.com

Which (if any) aspects of our advertising do you find useful?
(Tick as many boxes as are relevant)

☐ Prices and publication dates of new editions

☐ Information on product content

☐ Facility to order books off-the-page

☐ None of the above

Which BPP products have you used?

☑ Workbook   ☐ Kit   ☐ Other

Your ratings, comments and suggestions would be appreciated on the following areas.

	Very useful	Useful	Not useful	
Passing your exam advice	☐	☐	☐	
Skills Checkpoints	☐	☐	☐	
Activities	☐	☐	☐	
Essential Reading	☐	☐	☐	

	Excellent	Good	Adequate	Poor
Overall opinion of this Workbook	☐	☐	☐	☐

	Yes	No
Do you intend to continue using BPP Products?	☐	☐

The BPP author of this edition can be e-mailed at: learningmedia@bpp.com

Review form (continued)

Tell us what you think – please note any further comments and suggestions/errors below.